945.091

MUSSOLINI MEMOIRS
1942–1943

Benito Mussolini was the Italian Fascist leader in Italy before and during the war until his country's capitulation. He was then imprisoned, rescued by his ally, Hitler, and finally executed by partisans at the end of the war.

Raymond Klibansky is Frothingham Professor at McGill University, Montreal, and Emeritus Professor of Wolfson College, Oxford. At the end of the war, it was Professor Klibansky who gathered the numerous first-hand accounts of Mussolini's last months that make up the appendices.

ALSO BY RAYMOND KLIBANSKY

New Letters of David Hume
Contemporary Philosophy
Philebus and Epinomis
Continuity of the Platonic Tradition During the Middle Ages
Philosophy and Science in the Middle Ages

THE MUSSOLINI MEMOIRS 1942-1943

with Documents Relating to the Period

Edited by
Raymond Klibansky

Introduced by
Cecil Sprigge

Translated by
Frances Lobb

PHOENIX
PRESS

5 UPPER SAINT MARTIN'S LANE
LONDON
WC2H 9EA

A PHOENIX PRESS PAPERBACK

First published in Great Britain
by Weidenfeld & Nicolson in 1949
This paperback edition published in 2000
by Phoenix Press,
a division of The Orion Publishing Group Ltd,
Orion House, 5 Upper St Martin's Lane,
London WC2H 9EA

A CIP catalogue record for this book
is available from the British Library.

Printed and bound in Great Britain by
Clays Ltd, St Ives plc

ISBN 1 84212 025 5

CONTENTS

MUSSOLINI'S MEMOIRS

EYEWITNESSES

APPENDICES

by Raymond Klibansky

MUSSOLINI'S MEMOIRS

1942–1943

FOREWORD

by Raymond Klibansky

MUSSOLINI'S ACCOUNT OF THE fateful events from Alamein and Algiers to his downfall and subsequent rescue serves as the basis for his presentation of Italian and European history since the foundation of Fascism.

The aim of Mussolini's book is threefold: propaganda, apologia, and vendetta. His tacit propaganda for the new Puppet State (founded with German aid after his liberation, and whose grandiloquent title of Italian Social Republic he does not once mention) consists in the discrediting of the Monarchy and High Command and in an attempt to exploit the strong anti-Monarchist sentiment then prevailing. Thus he angles for the sympathies of the Left Wing, of whose feeling of frustration under the Badoglio régime he is fully aware.

His crafty propaganda, however, is overshadowed by his dominant intention—to provide an apologia for the signal failure of his policy and leadership ; an apologia, above all, for having caused his country to enter a war which resulted in defeat and disaster.

Thirdly, the process of exculpating himself involves the shifting of all blame on to others ; and in apportioning the guilt he gives free rein to his desire for vengeance against those who were the immediate cause of his downfall. The fate of those on whom he could lay hands is known ; the book represents his literary vendetta against those beyond his reach.

In such a book, no one will look for historical accuracy.

Now, there are many ways of perverting history, from the purposeful substitution of the wrong for the right to the suppression of relevant evidence, shift of emphasis from primary to secondary causes and subsequent creation of a false perspective. All these are found in this book.

To unravel the tissue of facts, half-truths and cunning lies would need an elaborate commentary. This could obviously be written only after Fascist and Badoglio Italy's archives have become accessible to the historian. We have therefore confined ourselves to setting right some outstanding questions of fact; to indicating the principal sources from which even now the author's distortions of events such as the encounter with Hitler at Feltre, the meeting of the Fascist Grand Council and the Armistice negotiations could be rectified; to commenting in some detail on the cause and effect of an action by which Mussolini decisively influenced the course of the war; and to including three narratives which act both as corollary and corrective to parts of his story.

The first of these is *What Mussolini Told Me*, by Rear-Admiral Maugeri, then Chief of Italian Naval Intelligence, who escorted Mussolini to the islands where he was first imprisoned. Maugeri was the first man of importance whom Mussolini met after his arrest, the first to whom he could speak on equal terms. The Admiral arrived at the psychological moment when Mussolini's urge to justify himself after the shock of his downfall was particularly strong, but before he had had time to build up a consistent defence. Maugeri's critical judgment adds to the value of his account.

The second narrative, *With Mussolini at the Campo Imperatore*, by the managers of the hotel on the Gran Sasso, deals with simpler and more domestic matters. It also throws a sidelight on Mussolini's escape, and will enable the reader to judge the efficiency of the measures devised by the Badoglio Government to guard its captive.

The third is Cardinal Archbishop Schuster's account of his last meeting with Mussolini which he has graciously put at the editor's disposal. The prominent part played by the Cardinal in the negotiations resulting in the withdrawal of the Germans from Milan gives the document an added interest. His aim was to prevent further devastation to the Lombard plain, and the issue between Fascism and its opponents mattered little to him. His portrait of Mussolini a few days before his death can therefore not be suspected of anti-Fascist bias.

Mussolini was the first of the principal actors in the drama of the Second World War to publish his memoirs. The book is thus an historical document, illustrating the character of the man who for twenty-one years was the evil genius of his country. Designed to be an apologia for his life and work, it is in fact a self-revelation, laying bare the personality of the writer and providing abundant material for the study of the pathology of dictators.

Of the four main aspects under which the author appears, the two first are the most familiar: the opportunist, bound by no scruple, ready to shift his ground to seize any advantage; and the actor seeing himself for the last time in his favourite role of Napoleon. More truly, he presents himself as the cynic who, friendless himself, is a friend to none, least of all to his people, for whom he shows only distaste and contempt; mistrusting his most intimate henchmen, of whose sayings and doings, as of those of "200,000 citizens, great and small," he keeps elaborate files.

Lastly—and this trait is most apparent in the talks with Maugeri—he emerges as the gambler who feels himself favoured by Fortune, up to the black day when she abandons him, never to return. The 28th of June, 1942, is considered as this fatal day, the turning-point of both the war and his own career—the day when Rommel's march on Alexandria and Cairo, designed as the death-blow to the British Empire, was stemmed by General Auchinleck's men,[1] and the tide of battle began to recede from the Egyptian plain.

Obsessed by this feeling of the turn of fate, he tried to play on the superstition of his fellow dictator, to make him cut his losses, conclude peace with Russia and concentrate on the Mediterranean to achieve a decision there. But in this move, too—the only one which, he foresaw, could avert disaster—he failed, and an undertone of bitter disillusionment is clearly heard in the pages of his book. When he composed his memoirs, the brilliance with which, in former times, he had been able to exploit any weakness among his opponents, had gone. The spell which he had cast for so long on the crowds at home, and even on some eminent

[1] Actually, General Auchinleck's counter-attacks became effective only at the beginning of July. On June 29th, the Italians claimed the capture of Mersa Matruh, and advanced as far as the El Alamein defences. Mussolini may have made a slip, but this is unlikely in a date so important to him. Perhaps he had hoped that the 28th would see a decisive break-through; and when this failed, he realised that, in spite of individual advances, the initiative was lost.

statesmen and journalists abroad, was broken. He feels it, and writes without true belief in himself.

Apart from the vivid light which Mussolini's memoirs and conversations throw on his person, students of the events which led to the Second World War will find many points of interest in them. To mention only a few: Mussolini's acknowledgment of the existence of a systematic plan for aggression against Abyssinia at a time when the world was assured of Italy's peaceful intentions; his admission of Italy's participation in the Spanish Civil War—if proof were needed; and the full text (given in our Commentary) of a meeting to decide on the war against Greece, showing that the plan was hatched long before a manufactured provocation gave the signal for attack.

Finally, the book merits attention as an involuntary tribute to the prowess of British arms. The African campaign is acknowledged in its decisive impact on the war; and Mr. Churchill's strategy in the Mediterranean, "having for its primary object the recovery of the command of that vital sea, but also having for its object the exposure of the under-belly of the Axis to heavy attack," is thus vindicated from an unexpected quarter. It is made clear, by implication and by actual statement, that the outcome of the campaign was determined by the Royal Navy forcing and, finally, "dominating absolutely" the Sicilian Straits; by the Royal Air Force, whose superiority is described as "shattering"; and by the Eighth Army chasing Rommel from Alamein to final defeat at Cape Bon.

The Book's History

The first copy to reach this country was smuggled out of Northern Italy when the Germans were still holding the "Gothic Line." It was a small green booklet, published on August 9th, 1944, as a Supplement to the Milan *Corriere della Sera*. It contained a series of articles which had appeared there between June 25th and July 18th of the same year, with a new preface.

The name of the author, first revealed at the conclusion of the series, was now prominently displayed. Even without this acknowledgment, there could be no doubt as to the identity of the writer. While the evidence of style and narrative will be convincing to most, if not conclusive to all, the quotations from German authors and allusions to comparatively little known incidents in Prussian history in the Napoleonic age, bear the unmistakable imprint of Mussolini's specialized, life-long interest in the time of his hero.[1]

The Supplement to the *Corriere* based on the galley proofs of the newspaper articles was soon exhausted. A new edition appeared, in handsome book form and under Mussolini's name in bold characters, published by the Milan firm of Mondadori in November 1944. It was soon followed by a reprint in December of the same year.[2]

The first edition of the work had shown many signs of haste and carelessness. The Mondadori book corrects a few of these errors though leaving many more untouched. Its principal interest lies in the additional subject matter it contains:

(*a*) Two new chapters, *The Messe Case* (Chapter II), and the last chapter, *Calvary and Resurrection*, added to round off the whole.

(*b*) The text of the three motions presented at the meeting of the Fascist Grand Council on the eve of Mussolini's fall, inserted after Chapter VII.

(*c*) *Documentary Notes* containing memoranda, mainly from Badoglio, concerning the Supreme Command of the Armed Forces in time of war. (After Chapter VII in this translation.)

(*d*) A facsimile reproduction of the first page of the *Corriere della Sera* of September 29th, 1938, vaunting the English-speaking world's acclamation of the decisive part played by the Duce at Munich, under the headings *Mussolini's intervention in answer to Chamberlain's appeal*, and *Memorable sitting at the House of Commons. Overwhelming demonstrations in honour of the Duce of Fascist Italy.*

[1] While the present book was in the Press, the Italian news agency ANSA announced, on 24.11.1945, that the Police at Como had discovered, among a batch of Mussolini's papers, "the manuscript of his book *History of a Year* as well as other historical essays."

[2] Benito MUSSOLINI, *Storia di un anno. Il tempo del bastone e della carota.*

(*e*) Facsimiles of letters from Grandi and from Marshal Badoglio to Mussolini. They are translated in this book at the end of Mussolini's account.

While thus considerably enlarged, the edition in book form makes little attempt to fit the new material into the structure of the whole. The lack of co-ordination sometimes leads to surprising results. The full text of evidence given in the documentary notes shows up Mussolini's version in the body of the book as purposely garbled, and destroys his case. It may be that a secretary acting on Mussolini's instructions to enhance the reliability of the book by adding documentary material, included these texts without noticing (or caring to notice) the harm he was doing.

Not only the Fascist Social Republic was interested in the book. An authorized Spanish version based on the original supplement appeared, lavishly produced, in Madrid. Exhaustive reviews and commendations were published in the Franco Press. It soon ran into many editions, of which the present writer used the sixth, dated March 1st, 1945.[1] According to Transocean (the National Socialist Overseas News Service) of March 16th, 1945, a German edition was also made. Swiss reports stated that Mussolini had written a German Preface especially intended for Germans. No copy has yet reached this country[2]; nor has a rumoured Czech edition. Newspapers in liberated Italy—*e.g.*, the Rome *Risorgimento Liberale* and the Naples *Gazzetta del Mezzogiorno* —published some extracts from the original. A few pieces in German appeared in the Swiss Press.

The present translation was made from the first Italian edition. When, after the liberation of Milan, a copy of the second edition became available, the text was carefully compared, all additions inserted and major discrepancies noted. The chapter headings of the first edition, omitted in the Mondadori book, were retained, although their arrangement, careless to the point of senselessness, had often to be altered.

[1] Benito MUSSOLINI, *Historia de un año*. Colección Temas Actuales. Ed. y Publ. Españolas, Madrid.

[2] The Editor has since received a copy of this rare book, found by Miss Christina Drake, of the British Embassy, Rome, who kindly put it at his disposal. It is entitled Benito MUSSOLINI, *Geschichte eines Jahres. Enthüllungen über die tragischen Ereignisse zwischen dem 25. Juli und dem 8. September, 1943*. Transl. by H. Ellwanger and S. Wiesel, Mondadori, Milan, 1945. In the Preface, dated "H.Q., November 8th, 1944; in the XXIIIrd year of the Fascist Era", Mussolini, with the adaptability of the true journalist, uses Hitler's terminology for the benefit of his German public.

Mussolini's book is written throughout in the third person. While this may be partly accounted for by its origins in anonymous newspaper articles, the fact that the form of indirect presentation was kept even after the author's name appeared on the title page, can be explained by a design to enhance the objectivity of the narrative. It would have been absurd to retain this affectation of Julius Cæsar's historical style in the translation ; and the first person has therefore been substituted throughout.

The title of the first edition, *The Time of the Stick and the Carrot*, kept in the second as sub-title, alludes to a remark said to have been made by Mr. Churchill at a Press Conference in Washington, held jointly with President Roosevelt, on May 26th, 1943. Its text is given by the *Christian Science Monitor* of the following day:

> *Most specific of all the declarations was the grim counsel to Italy by Mr. Churchill, who carried the brunt of the questions, that it cast off the wicked rulers who had got it into its present terrible plight and throw itself on the justice of the Allies. If it did so, Mr. Churchill indicated, no cruel or inhuman penalties would be exacted. There will be, he said firmly, a place for Italy in the new Europe. Speaking of what was to be done about Italy, he sandwiched a neat metaphor, "of this you may be sure, we shall continue to operate on the donkey at both ends with the stick and the carrot."*

Fascist propagandists were quick to fasten on this remark, severing it from its context.

Lastly, the book cannot be judged without remembering the circumstances in which it was written. From internal evidence, the first edition can be proved to have been written in late spring and, in parts (as appears, for instance, from the reference to Prince Doria-Pamphili's co-operation with the Allies in Rome) in early summer, 1944 ; the date of the original newspaper publication may well have been advanced under the impact of the liberation of Rome. The second, enlarged edition, was composed in the autumn of the same year.

While he was writing, the whole of North Italian economy had been harnessed to the German war effort. Entire Italian provinces had been brought under German rule. Workers were being deported to Germany, and patriots were being tortured in the ill-famed Milan prison of San Vittore. For the maintenance even of his shadowy power, Mussolini had to rely on

German force, being himself in his villa at Lake Garda guarded and watched by German SS. All his references to Germany, therefore, are to be read in the light of this situation. How far they represent his real opinion may be gauged from his talks with Maugeri.

He knew that Germany must lose, but he could not now escape from her stranglehold. And so he lived on, watching his doom draw nearer, until, at last, savagely and ingloriously, it overtook him.

ORIEL COLLEGE, OXFORD.

The comments were written while Mussolini was still alive, and were concluded shortly after his death. In the meantime, several new sources have come to light; they confirm the thesis put forward in these pages that it was his deep resentment against Hitler, latent for many years, which determined Mussolini's conduct in a decisive moment of the war.

In the few years since his execution many legends have emerged embroidering Mussolini's memory; and the belief is growing, not only among some of his compatriots, that had he only kept his ambitions within bounds and stopped at a certain stage, he would have gone down in history as the greatest benefactor to his country. Such a view betrays singular blindness to the character of the man and the logic of his development from the violent Socialist agitator to the autocrat thriving on that mixture of incomprehension, pusillanimity and connivance with which he was met by the governments of the Western world.

Shortly after Mussolini's rise to power, Lord Curzon used to dismiss him as "that absurd man"; to which the American Ambassador to Italy, R. W. Child, retorted by calling the Duce "the greatest figure of his sphere and time". Only a little earlier, Mussolini had proclaimed in one of his published essays: "Be it known once and for all that Fascism has walked and, if need be, will calmly walk again over the decaying corpse of the goddess of Freedom".

Not long before his death, in a conversation with a village priest, Mussolini, giving a new twist to a Ciceronian tag, delivered himself of a last epigram. Surveying the recent past, he summed up: "*Historia magistra vitae*—but she has bad pupils!" Should the myth growing up round his name prove him right ?

AUGUST 1949

Acknowledgments

The editor is much indebted to Miss Penelope Babington Tremayne for the preparation of the index. He also wishes to thank Miss Christina Drake and Miss E. Jamison for their kind help in revising the notes.

INTRODUCTION

by Cecil Sprigge

The History of a Year

MUSSOLINI's "resignation" from the leadership of the Italian State, baldly announced by the Italian radio stations late on Sunday evening, July 25th, 1943, resulted from the activity of three distinguishable internal enemies: (1) Mussolini's own rebellious Fascist subordinates; (2) the Savoy dynasty and its generals, resolved to unlink themselves from a disastrous association; (3) Italian political anti-Fascism, which had for twenty years been vigilant for the moment of revenge and rehabilitation. To these forces of internal hostility against Mussolini, so different in character and in consistency of purpose, a chance for action had been opened up in that torrid July by the external defeat of Fascist Italy, then nearing its climax in the Sicilian campaign.

By the time that Mussolini published the following pages he had been able, or obliged, in one of history's ironic rebounds, to wreak bloody vengeance upon the first internal enemy, that is upon many of those Fascist chieftains who, after sharing his glamour and potency for a quarter of a century, had turned against him when external defeat stared Fascism in the face. His own son-in-law, Galeazzo Ciano, and his oldest friend among the high army personnel of Italy, Emilio de Bono, had topped the list of executions of "traitors" ordered by the High Court of resurrected Fascism at Verona.

But not all of the "traitors" had fallen to Mussolini's vengeance and Hitler's demand for examples. Dino Grandi, most conspicuous of all, had escaped to neutral Portugal. Federzoni and Bottai had found shelter, ecclesiastical or otherwise. Mussolini, in the retrospective and dispirited *Mein Kampf* which is here offered to the British reader, scarcely pauses over those figures in the ranks of the first internal enemy against whom he had instructed the Verona Court to pronounce the death sentence. Ciano is passed by with colourless references, likewise de Bono, but a whole chapter is directed against Grandi, "the Count of Mordano," chosen as a personification of that "treason" of his own creatures against himself which is one of the leading themes of Mussolini's book. In a *Life of Jesus* read by Mussolini and left by him at his first place of imprisonment at Ponza, passages relating to the betrayal of the Saviour have been found underscored with the marginal comment in Mussolini's hand: *Just so.* It is one of the main consolations of Mussolini in adversity to compare his lot with that of the greatest figures of humanity.

It was at the Grand Fascist Council, officially the supreme organ of the Fascist State, though it had for long been inactive, that on the night of July 24th insurrection against Mussolini first came to a head, and exploited by the King and his circle with a suddenness and completeness which astounded, bewildered and frustrated Grandi and his associates, precipitated the collapse of Fascism itself within twenty-four hours.

The account of the meeting given by Mussolini does not greatly differ, as far as it goes, from others emanating from the circles of Grandi and Bottai[1]. The Council, flouting Mussolini, adhered in its majority to a resolution proposed by Grandi, implying that Mussolini had failed in his conduct of the war and should be relieved of his supreme powers. Since this resolution immediately provided the King with an occasion for extorting Mussolini's resignation, at this stage of the story Mussolini turns his accusations against the group of persons constituting collectively his second internal enemy—the monarch, the high generals Badoglio, Ambrosio, Roatta, the royal princes.

Mussolini argues that the monarchy had long desired to be quit of him, and had actually sabotaged the war in order that Mussolini's régime might collapse under military defeat. However, he reports that the King had enthusiastically supported the declaration of war against Britain and France. Both contentions are necessary for Mussolini's purpose: he must shift the blame for Fascist Italy's military breakdown upon princes and generals who, he alleges, chose to lose the war in order to discredit

[1] It is the omissions which matter.

himself, and he must show their subsequent passage to the allied camp, and the King's declaration of war against Germany, in the most luridly treasonable light.

Dino Grandi, in Mussolini's pages, is not only the ringleader of the Fascist rebels, but also their go-between with internal enemy number two, with the monarchy and the generals. In the second Italian edition, samples of Grandi's personal correspondence with Mussolini are reproduced in facsimile. The letters are heavy with fawning and adulation. One, written from Grandi in his London Embassy in Spring 1939, gloats over the discomfiture of Britain and plainly heralds a future Fascist aggression against Greece. The letter is aptly chosen to damn Grandi as a diplomatic crook in the eyes of any future Allied Tribunal. The story of Grandi's solicitation of heraldic honours is told with gusto, as elsewhere Mussolini tells that of Marshal Pietro Badoglio's lobbying for Ethiopian dukedoms and Italian marquisates for his offspring.

If in any of these pages Mussolini writes more in sorrow than in rancour, it is in his analysis of the case of Marshal Giovanni Messe, whom, in the later winter of 1943, the Allies released from imprisonment to collaborate in the Brindisi administration of Badoglio. Mussolini laments Messe as his own military favourite, supported and cherished by Fascism in an honourable military career up to the moment of his defeat in Tunisia. . . . *Et tu Brute* !

Badoglio is treated with irony and without sentiment. Mussolini depicts the Marshal as corroded by the appetite for honours and wealth, pompously insistent on his status. He exhumes from the enormous dossier of personal documents which was one of Mussolini's instruments of authority a twenty-year-old warning that Badoglio, if given high military position, would use it to hoist himself into political power. He does not omit still earlier accusations that Badoglio was the real culprit for the Caporetto disaster of 1917.

In the series of events described by Mussolini in this narrative or patchwork of narratives, there followed within twenty-four hours of the fateful Grand Council, Mussolini's visit to the King, the King's staggering notification that the government had been transferred into the hands of Badoglio, and the abduction of the fallen Dictator in an ambulance waggon "to safeguard his person against public hostility." The King and Badoglio are shown engaged in a mean intrigue to gain Mussolini's acquiescence in his own "safeguarding" by promises of honourable retirement, while preparing instead to deliver him over to the Allies. King and Marshal meanwhile plot to disintegrate and bewilder the Fascist masses by the feint of continuing the war on the German side, and to deceive the Germans —which was absurdly naïve and impossible—by protestations of faith to the Alliance. It is Mussolini's argument that internal enemy number two, the clan of royalty and the generals, were from the beginning sold to the Allies by their desire for the destruction of Fascism, and that their behaviour to himself was fully premeditated and unmitigated treachery. Yet, on other pages, Mussolini produces evidence telling against this version. History, when full records are available, will judge whether, at the moment of Mussolini's arrest, King and Marshal were not toying with the design of a nominally non-Fascist but in effect quasi-Fascist Government and of a diplomatic action calculated to get Italy out of the war, like Pétain's France, without the need of hostilities against the former Ally. Of such a fantasy a genuine intention to consign Mussolini to honourable retirement could well have been a feature.

Though originally entitled "History of One Year" the main narrative starts really with July, 1943, and terminates with Mussolini's release by German aviators in the following September from the Appenine peak to which Badoglio finally shifted his important and dangerous captive. Incidentally, the work also discusses many aspects of the war and its antecedents.

Mussolini's enemy number three, the forces of Italian political anti-Fascism, is hardly mentioned in this story. In the picture left by Mussolini the personages are: the Duce, sole authentic incarnation of the Fascist nation (for little praise goes to the few who stuck by him after July, and the gratitude expressed to the Germans is conventional, even faintly critical); secondly, the Fascist traitors; thirdly, the Court and Army clique, with the invading Allies far in the background. The forces of political anti-Fascism which instantaneously upon the news of Mussolini's "resignation" came into the open, rendering vain and ludicrous any attempt to install a semi-Fascist régime by collusion between King, Badoglio, and Grandi, or to redirect Italian policy on any lines short of a complete alignment at the side of the Allies, figure in Mussolini's narrative only as the "mob" which rushed to destroy busts and portraits of his person, a mob "unworthy to be called a people," though the noise of their agitation, he confesses, reached even to his Appenine confinement.

Of the last chapter of Fascism, the Gestapo-propped Fascist Social Republic, not too shadowy to maintain its own sadistic activities in North Italy until April 25th, 1945, Mussolini has nothing here to relate. It was the shabby equivalent, for him, of Napoleon's Hundred Days. So small was his faith in German and Fascist recovery even as long ago as the penning of these articles in the spring of 1944, that he complacently publishes a prophecy of ultimate rehabilitation for himself, *à la Napoléon*, by the slow workings of developing historical judgment.

Character of the Book

The book is a collection of articles published in the middle of 1944 in the North Italian Fascist Press. In his twenty years of authentic power Mussolini's origins in the paternal blacksmithy and in the building yard gave good material for adulators. Detached observers knew that his spiritual home was in the profession of journalism. Articles professedly anonymous, but designed to be recognised as Mussolini's own, appeared frequently, during the dictatorship, in the Italian Press. The study of press cuttings, Italian and foreign, was an important part of the Duce's routine in peace-time and war-time.

In his spectral existence as "Duce" of the Fascist Social Republic between September, 1943, and April, 1945, Mussolini was at liberty to give even more time to his journalistic pen. He had been "in" on the melodrama of his own overthrow, incarceration, and rescue. Mussolini the journalist in some of these articles merely exploits his own inside knowledge. Recounted in the third person (for these articles, too, were originally pretended to be anonymous) personal experiences are worked up with "atmosphere", as when we are told that the City of Rome on July 24th ". . . . . *turned pale. - Cities too have their countenances, on which are reflected the motions of the mind. - Rome felt that some grave matter was in the air.*" Here writes the journalist who is also an autobiographer keen to establish that, in his case as in that of Caesar, the heavens themselves, viewed sensitively from a Rome automobile, bore visible witness to the eclipse of a great man. Journalistic technique repeatedly obtrudes itself. A Swedish press cutting is dragged forth to testify that at Pantelleria Italian soldiers might have been expected to fight stubbornly for their fatherland. A *Times* clipping serves similarly in regard to the battle of Sicily.

This brief introduction cannot pass detailed judgment upon the accuracy of Mussolini's journalism. Mussolini had at his disposal a vast collection of records including much that is not yet available from other sources.

To probe one portion of the narrative—the account of the clandestine visit of General Maxwell Taylor to Rome on the eve of the publication of the Armistice on September 8th, 1943, omits the vital circumstance that the General was sent to arrange an Allied airborne landing near Rome, and that plans were suddenly changed when General Carboni refused to guarantee the airport against German attacks. The omission is deliberate, since it heightens the impression of futility on the part of the Royal Government—unless it be supposed that Mussolini remained for months ignorant of facts known to tens of thousands of people.

The journalist had also been an elementary schoolmaster, and a quotation from the Greek philosopher Thales will surprise no one who is familiar with Mussolini's prose. "Forgive my learned references" was a catchphrase dear to humorists at Mussolini's expense. On Ponza island, Mussolini tells us, he spent his leisure translating the elaborately erudite poetry of Carducci into German. No specimen is offered.

But Mussolini the man had long indulged in comparison of his journalistic self with the politico-military genius Napoleon Bonaparte. For at least twenty years a photograph of the Duce with hand in breast and forelock falling across furrowed brow between piercing eyes had been in circulation among devotees. In his Sardinian notebook the comparison with Napoleon is made explicit. Mussolini, fresh from his overthrow, stakes a claim to enter into the permanent memories of Italy on the same footing as that gained by Napoleon Bonaparte in France. There are indications—and the fact may explain why Mussolini cannot claim to have been a good journalist—that like his favourite author Nietzsche he found points of similarity also between his career (as founder of Fascism) and that of the Founder of Christianity.

The End of Mussolini

After writing these articles, Mussolini eked out some nine months of pseudo-sovereignty in the territory of the "Fascist Social Republic" occupied by the Germans. The degree of authority exercised by him has still to be properly assessed. In his private secretariat at Salò, Lake Garda, a visitor found a vast collection of photographs of himself, some ephemeral literature, with personal annotations, and stacks of letters begging the Duce's aid or pardon.

Early in 1945 Mussolini moved his quarters to the Prefecture in Milan, where he lived under the shelter of a small die-hard Fascist Army encamped (towards the end) in the large adjoining gardens. German SS were also in constant attendance. His hopes by then were perhaps reduced to that of arranging a getaway for himself with his latest and fondest mistress, Clara Petacci, and with the abundant gold and jewels laid by for the last emergency.

On April 24th Mussolini made approaches to an old Socialist acquaintance with an astonishing proposal. He requested to know whether the Socialist Party (in hiding) would consider forming with the "Fascist Republican Party" a united front against the monarchy. It was at the moment when with the fall of Bologna, Allied troops were bounding forward to bring about, in unison with the partisans of the Socialist and other parties, the liberation of the North and its integration in the nominally monarchical Italian State. Had Mussolini like so many propagandists fallen victim to his own propaganda? The offer was made to the Socialists and the Action Party, neither of them at the moment represented in the Bonomi Government, by contrast with the Communists who had not stickled at serving nominally under Prince Umberto of Savoy. Did Mussolini believe in a serious rift in the Left front of Liberated Italy, such that one of the dissentient groups would have accepted the collaboration of the last lurid Blackshirts from whose society all conventionally respectable people had long since withdrawn in horror?

The following day, April 25th, Mussolini realistically approached Cardinal Ildefonso Schuster, Metropolitan of Milan, with a view to negotiating for the surrender of the Fascist Army to the North Italian Committee of National Liberation, still in hiding but ready at a signal to launch the final insurrection for freedom. The Cardinal's conversation with Mussolini on this occasion is given in the last of the outside contributions to this book. The surrender was never negotiated. The same night Mussolini fled from Milan. Only his riddled corpse, with that of Clara Petacci, returned three days later to be hung head downwards above a frenzied mob of demonstrators in the public square which had been his own followers' execution ground for Italian patriots. The corpses of his principal followers lay bleeding in a muddled heap below.

REUTER'S OFFICE
MILAN
MAY 1945

CHAPTER I

FROM EL ALAMEIN TO THE MARETH LINE

THOSE WHO HAVE WRITTEN of the Italian disaster in the summer of 1943 have so far completely overlooked one fact; namely, that the prime origin of the disaster was French and goes back to one date—November 8th, 1942.

It was the so-called "dissident", Gaullist France, the France of the Jews, Freemasons and Bolsheviks, that opened the door of the Mediterranean to America. In that November dawn a decisive episode in the conspiracy against Italy was enacted. While the English kept in the offing from fear of wounding any still existing French susceptibilities, the American convoy reached the port of Algiers[1] and disembarked the first formations of troops and armoured cars, not merely unopposed but triumphantly received by their accomplices. De Gaulle's betrayal of France was only the prelude to Badoglio's betrayal of Italy; two links in the same chain.

It was clear from the first moment that the landing of an American army in the Mediterranean constituted an event of major strategic significance, destined to modify if not reverse the balance of power in a sector which Italy had always considered of the greatest importance, if not actually decisive. The great pincer movement traceable in the summer of 1942 when the Germans were climbing the first slopes of the Caucasus and Rommel's Italo-German armies were knocking at the door of Alexandria—this movement was now stultified and rendered inachievable. Instead, there might be discerned the

[1] In fact, the Algiers landing was effected by a mixed force of British and American troops. The author, in playing down, here and elsewhere, the British contribution, is deliberately misleading.

no less great Allied strategic manœuvre which, starting from Algeria and Egypt, was to end by squeezing the Italo-German forces in Libya into a position from which there was no way out. The Axis took immediate counter-measures and occupied the whole of France as well as Corsica and Tunisia.

The Eve of the Algiers Landing

Only on one condition could these measures have modified the fundamental strategic situation created by the Allied landing ; namely, if the flow of troops and supplies to the Axis had been on a scale enabling them not only to resist but to attack, particularly in the initial period, when the American forces had not yet reached the size they subsequently attained. But in order to attack we should have needed an air superiority which did not exist[1], and as to supplies, these were hindered on a growing and almost prohibitive scale by the English naval and air forces which had command even of the shortest crossing, i.e., the Sicilian Channel, which might well be called the graveyard of the Italian mercantile marine.[2]

Viewed schematically the situation was as follows : a steadily growing inflow of Allied forces ; and steadily growing difficulties for the Axis. On October 23rd, on the eve of the Algiers landing, Montgomery attacked and broke through our positions at El Alamein ; and the enemy forces in east and west began their march towards each other.

[1] At the time, Mussolini's propagandists strove hard to maintain the opposite, e.g., Gayda, his star journalist, claimed in "*Giornale d' Italia,*" November 16th, 1942, that Italian and German forces had passed immediately to the attack and had already achieved notable successes. Rome Radio enlarged on this (November 24th, 1942) : "As usual, the British are in a position of inferiority in the Eastern Mediterranean" ; adding on the same day : "The Axis air offensive is therefore very efficient." On January 3rd, 1943, the official Stefani Agency stated that in the air Axis forces continued to show distinct superiority over the enemy in Tunisia.

[2] A startling admission, if compared with official statements of the time which led Italians to believe the opposite, *e.g.*, Senator Admiral Romeo Bernotti, broadcasting over Rome Radio on November 15th, 1942, said : "The failure of the Mediterranean enterprise will not leave the situation unaltered because the consequences of the attrition which the enemy naval forces will suffer, will have repercussions of the greatest importance on the general progress of the war." A few days later, Stefani (November 25th, 1942) devoted a long despatch to the activity of Italian aircraft and submarines off the coast of French North Africa : "Their activity and their success hit the enemy in the vital sector of sea transport, preventing him from receiving by sea the supplies indispensable for the continuation of operations."

In Italy the moral repercussions of the American landing in Algiers were immediate and profound. Every enemy of Fascism promptly reared his head ; the first of the traitors, minor figures even though some were National Councillors, emerged from the shadows. The country began to feel the strain. As long as only the English were in the Mediterranean, Italy, with Germany's help, could hold firm and resist, though at cost of ever greater sacrifices ; but the appearance of America disturbed the weaker spirits and increased by many millions the already numerous band of listeners to enemy radio, while the Anglo-American landing in Algiers furnished those traitors who had not yet dared declare themselves, with an "alibi" for their future conduct. Only one measure could have reversed the situation—the taking of the original enemy positions in North Africa in the rear ; but this, although envisaged, was not attempted.

The sixteen days from October 23rd to November 8th were of incalculable historical importance as succeeding events have shown. From that moment the strategic initiative passed to the Allies.

The attack on the El Alamein front revealed the crushing land and, above all, air superiority of the English. Rommel's previous thrust, which had made a promising start on August 28th, was brought to a standstill three days later owing to lack of fuel which, like the convoys, had been sent to the bottom.

Once this attempt had failed, it would have been wiser not to hold the El Alamein-El Quattara line any longer, but to withdraw the non-motorized Italian troops on to the Sollum-Halfaya line. When I left Derna in July I had given written orders to Marshal Bastico and General Barbasetti to reorganise this line and to garrison it with all available forces drawn from men resting at the base lines which were always full. Instead of this, the Italo-German command decided to remain where they were, fortify the line they had reached, and there await the anticipated enemy attack. A retreat of the Italian non-motorised units in September could have taken place almost unimpeded, and once the Italian units had reached the Sollum-Halfaya line the same movement could have been effected by the completely motorised German units.

The Sollum-Halfaya Line

By this we should have placed some three hundred-odd miles of desert between our lines and the enemy's, compelling him to move his imposing supply depots ; this would have taken time and would have enabled still more reinforcements to be sent to the Italo-German forces on the Sollum-Halfaya line, already strong enough in itself.[1]

The battle which broke out on October 23rd at once assumed a character of extreme violence and decisiveness. During the first few days there were the inevitable fluctuations, but the enemy's air and artillery superiority at once began to tip the scales. The infantry—especially Italian, who had no defence system worth the name—were subjected to murderous artillery fire and ceaseless bombardments for days on end. Nevertheless, they resisted, some of them—such as the "Folgore"—heroically.

Then the enemy tanks—here, too, the Americans had appeared with their armoured formations[2]—made a break through and turned the positions held by the Italian infantry. Many divisions fought gallantly, as even the enemy admitted. Then began a withdrawal which could not be effected by the Italian infantry who were poorly supplied with motor transport, much of which, besides, had been immobilized by enemy fire. There was a great haul of prisoners, and these were not spared a last tragic march across the desert towards the infamous and notorious prison 'cages.' One of the greatest retreats in history was carried out by Rommel's armoured columns which, though harried by the enemy on land and from the air, succeeded in disengaging themselves although they could not rest at any of the halts planned. The names, dear to Italians, of Sidi-el-Barrani, Sollum, Tobruk, Derna and Benghasi, appeared once more in our war communiqués, for the last time. Owing to lack of material, no delaying action could be organised on the El Agheila-Marada line, the door of Tripolitania.[3] The retreat continued as far as Homs in the hope that the Sirte desert would

[1] For Mussolini's real opinion of Rommel and the German campaign in Africa, see below, p. 219.

[2] No American troops took part in the battle of El Alamein, although American material was used (cp. above, page 1, n. 1).

[3] Mussolini forgets this "lack of material" when, a few lines farther on, he says, "During a retreat of over 1,250 miles very little material was lost."

slow up enemy pressure, which, however, it did not. Thus the battle for Tripoli was never fought.

From then on, all available forces were despatched towards Tunisia to the Mareth line which, owing to the lie of the land, lent itself to prolonged resistance. Many men and much material reached that line. During a retreat of over 1,250 miles very little material was lost, as may be seen from a very detailed report sent to Rome by General Giglioli, who was Quartermaster-General for Libya.

The Operations in Tunisia

The two arms of the enemy pincers had thus, in the short space of three months, drawn extraordinarily close together. It was now clear that after the battle of Tunisia was over, the battle of Sicily would begin. General Messe was sent to command operations in Tunisia ; he who later betrayed his country. His task was a peculiarly difficult one. He had given an excellent account of himself as commander in Albania, where he had succeeded in blocking the Greek thrust in its most dangerous direction, that of Valona ; and later as commander of the CSIR,[1] the Italian Expeditionary Corps in Russia, where the troops under his command fought very well. He was replaced when the CSIR became the ARMIR,[2] the Italian Army in Russia, that is to say, when the original Army Corps was transformed into an Army of ten divisions whose names may be noted here: The *Julia*, the *Tridentina*, the *Cuneense*, the *Ravenna*, the *Cosseria*, the *Sforzesca*, the *Celere*, the *Pasubio*, the *Torino*, and the *Vicenza*. This replacement was a mistake due to the usual jealousy, to Messe's reputation as a staunch Fascist, and above all to a sacrosanct worship of the Army List with its relative positions of seniority. Messe's successor was General Gariboldi who had not so far distinguished himself particularly, not, at least, in the recent wars in Ethiopia and Libya.

Recalled to Rome, Messe accepted the task though realising its arduous nature ; and he left by air for Tunis. Once at his post, he spent the first few weeks in getting the troops into shape both materially and morally ; they were, naturally, exhausted, either by their interminable retreat or by their long stay in

[1] CSIR: abbreviation for "*C*orpo *S*pedizione *I*taliano in *R*ussia".

[2] ARMIR: abbreviation for "*ARM*ata *I*taliana in *R*ussia".

African territory, a stay which for thousands of soldiers could be reckoned in terms of years. The fate of Tunisia was bound up with supplies. No fewer than three hundred thousand men were concentrated in a small space. The problem of organisation and supplies assumed disquieting dimensions.[1] Naval losses were increasingly heavy. In April alone 120,000 tons of Italian shipping went to the bottom and a further 50,000 tons was damaged. While the enemy troops were more than well supplied, the Italo-German forces were threatened with mortal anæmia.[2]

When the first efforts of the German thrust were spent, having achieved nothing except an extension of the bridgehead, the English went over to the attack along the Mareth line.

The Battle of the Mareth Line and the Messe Report

In Rome the date of the attack was discussed, and it was thought that Montgomery would delay it in order to profit by the full moon as had been the case at El Alamein. Instead, the English general launched the attack on a pitch dark night. To prevent the artillery mowing down the infantry ahead of them, each soldier wore a white cloth on his back. The Mareth line was strong for some fifteen miles—from the sea to about half its length. The rest was weaker and the last sector almost non-existent; moreover, it was entrusted to the Saharan formations which had reached these positions after a highly exhausting march across the most remote desert trails. These formations, besides, had little artillery and lacked the necessary preparation for meeting the shock of mobile and armoured columns. The Italian troops entrenched on the Mareth line and protected by a broad anti-tank ditch resisted bravely and counter-attacked.

[1] Mussolini's chief propagandist, Alessandro Pavolini, "Minister for Popular Culture," told a different story, when broadcasting on January 23rd, 1943; "On the credit side we must place the concentration of Axis forces in a homogeneous space, well provided with internal communications, hospitable from the point of view of inhabitants, food and climate, and the utilisation at last of a short line of communication from Sicily to Bizerta, where the air protection of the fighters and the naval and anti-submarine protections have reached an obvious grade of efficiency."

[2] The opposite was conveyed by Mussolini's propagandists. Thus the Air Force paper, *Le Vie dell'Aria* (quoted by the German Transocean Agency, February 1st, 1943), stated that it was completely safe to supply the forces in Tunisia, and contrasted the advantages of short, well-protected lines of supply, such as those of the Axis, with the disadvantages of the long supply lines of the Allied forces.

Montgomery did not succeed in breaking through. Let us say frankly, too, because it is true, that in that sector the English were beaten. Then the enemy switched his attack over to the weakest side, on the extreme right of Messe's position, and there, profiting by an extensive use of armour, he had no difficulty in overcoming the Libyan forces and outflanking them. This forced General Messe to retreat some sixty-odd miles on a line running roughly halfway between the Mareth line and Tunis. Meanwhile, the Germans to the north-west were being hard-pressed by the Americans—here, also, with infinitely greater resources. Thus the circle contracted to the point of making further resistance impossible.

History has already revealed how the last scenes of the drama were enacted. While the rhythm of events in Tunisia took on the accelerating tempo of a finale, at Rome the spotlight was focussed on the Messe affair. This was chiefly on account of his long, detailed and interesting report of the battle of the Mareth line, in which some people thought he praised the Staff and men of the British Eighth Army too highly[1]. It was agreed, however, that such praise reflected honour also on the Italians in so far as it showed that our soldiers had been fighting against first-class and not second-class troops.

Today, in the light of Messe's peculiarly disgraceful betrayal, we may ask whether all this were not calculated and deliberate, with an eye to capture, which Messe could not exclude from the realms of possibility. It is likewise certain that, thanks to his report, Messe at once enjoyed a good press in England, and there is also photographic evidence that on his arrival by air just outside London a group of generals received him not as a prisoner—and an Italian into the bargain—but as an honoured guest.[2]

[1] Marshal (then General) Messe's report on the battle of the Mareth line was published on April 14th, 1945. The version broadcast by the Italian Home Service stated: "The report admits that the British 8th Army is the most modern and renowned force in all the theatres of this World War and that the infantry which Great Britain is sending to the Middle East are of the highest quality, in physique, training and morale. Their armament and equipment are in the forefront compared to those of any infantry in the world. Furthermore, the British artillery, as well as the armoured units, have very large resources at their disposal. The Commanders and the Staffs are very strictly selected. The co-operation between the R.A.F. and the ground forces could be taken as a model by anyone."

[2] Mussolini purposely misinterprets the facts. Marshal Messe arrived in England by air on May 17th, 1943. The press of the 18th published pictures of his arrival in which he appeared in company with British officers;

Then there was the question of Messe's captivity. Two theories were advanced; the first held that Messe should return to his country and take over the command of the troops stationed in Sicily, which was considered a base for Tunisia; the other, on the contrary, affirmed that in accordance with the regular tradition of the Italian army a commander should share the fate of his men as the Duke of Aosta had done. I held this latter view. It was decided that General Messe should receive some recognition which might also console him for his capture, and he was promoted Marshal of Italy. The King did not particularly favour this solution, simply because he did not want a marshal as well as a prince to be numbered among the human booty which fell to the enemy.

Owing to the enemy's complete sea and air command of the Sicilian Channel only very few soldiers and officers escaped capture. A few boatloads of intrepid navigators left the shores of Cape Bon and succeeded in reaching the western coast of Sicily.

Pantelleria, a counter-Malta

With the Tunisian page closed the chapter of Pantelleria opened; an attack on the most distant point of metropolitan territory loomed imminent, the first territory within the borders of our home country.

Pantelleria was known to Italians as an island for deportation or banishment. Seen on the map, it looked like an almost insignificant dot. So it was until the day when, flying over it, I discovered Pantelleria to be a big enough island to become a counter-Malta, capable of blockading the Sicilian Channel in its narrowest sector.[1]

The English were not so far wrong when, after conquering it, they christened it Mussolini Island.

But the decision to transform Pantelleria into an aero-naval

their rank was not given, nor were their names stated. On June 9th, Mr. Arthur Henderson, Financial Secretary to the War Office, stated in the House of Commons that General von Arnim and Field-Marshal Messe were being treated strictly in accordance with the Geneva Convention.

[1] The assertions made by Mussolini in this and the following paragraphs are in flat contradiction with what he had published in the press, when it was necessary to minimise the loss of the island. *Regime Fascista* (June 17th, 1943) declared that "no one had ever thought of making it a real air and naval base," and added, "it is absurd to compare Pantelleria with Malta."

base met with much opposition, and the first objections were naturally made by the professional experts. They told me there was no need to fortify Pantelleria in order to blockade the Channel. To which I replied : "How do you blockade a street best, by planting yourself in the middle of it or by standing at one side ? Even if Pantelleria gains us only a few minutes, might not this advantage in time become a determining factor of success ?"

The objections raised by the experts, General Valle among them, were overcome, and work was begun at full speed. Some thousands of workmen were sent out there. In the course of a year or two we had to improve the harbour basin so as to make it suitable for ships and other craft of medium tonnage, construct an airfield and a two-storey underground aerodrome, install anti-aircraft and shore batteries, concentrate ample reserves of supplies and munitions, improve the network of communications and mine the short stretches of coast where the possibility of a landing existed. This programme was tackled with admirable energy. The garrison was steadily reinforced. A year later, on August 18th, 1938, I flew to Pantelleria, landed on the airfield there (though it was not yet quite completed), inspected the gigantic underground hangars—the first of their kind in the world—and was able to announce that at least fifty per cent. of the programme was as good as realised.

The English watched the creation of this Italian aero-naval base in the middle of the Mediterranean with increasing and spiteful interest. Work did not stop when war broke out. The flow of arms and 'planes, men and supplies continued ; when the enemy General Spaatz launched an aero-naval attack against Pantelleria towards the middle of May, the island contained forty batteries, several squadrons of fighter 'planes and a garrison of about twelve thousand men. The commander of the base was Admiral Pavesi ; the land forces were under General Mattei.

CHAPTER II

THE MESSE CASE[1]

IF YOU LOOK closely at the man who was promoted Marshal of Italy after the unlucky Tunisian campaign, his is not really a traitor's face. That is to say, he has not the pointed or triangular chin, the pale complexion, the shifty glance or the hot hands; none, that is, of the bodily characteristics which go with the typical traitor in all literature. Messe is rather below the average in height, his face is broad and open—he has a clear eye which looks you straight in the face and his speech is blunt ; on seeing him you would conclude that here was a gentleman, that is, a man sincere and loyal. On the contrary, Marshall Messe is really one of the most typical and loathsome traitors of all those whom Badoglio cherished and protected, and for me he represented one of my most disagreeable surprises.

Messe's military past may be considered brilliant. In the first World War he held various commands, even of shock troops towards the end, and as an "*ardito*" (Commando) he was known and respected among ex-servicemen.

From the Fascist political point of view he was generally considered one of the safest of all the generals who were more or less complacent recipients of the Party ticket.

In November, 1940, the situation which had arisen on the Græco-Albanian front demanded vigorous generalship. Messe came to my mind. He was entrusted with the defence of the Valona sector ; to be precise, with the task of blocking any enemy thrust in the Shushicë Valley. Messe accomplished his

[1] This chapter was added in the Second Italian Edition, regardless of the awkward break it makes in the narrative of the Mediterranean campaign.

task admirably, and in March, during my visit to Albania, I gave him ample recognition of the fact.

On arriving at Valona on December 1st, 1940, he telegraphed my Private Secretary as follows :

Please inform the Duce that his exact instructions are very much present in my mind and that his flattering confidence, which fills me with pride, will not be misplaced. The Duce's will, which is also ours, will be master of events.

General MESSE.

Once the Albanian chapter was closed, preparations began for an expeditionary corps to Russia. This included three very sound and courageous divisions, the *Torino*, the *Pasubio* and the *Celere*, plus Blackshirt formations. The abbreviation CSIR stood for *Corpo Spedizione Italiano in Russia* (Italian Expeditionary Corps in Russia). CSIR's engagements were brilliant. On September 30th, 1941, I telegraphed Messe as follows :

After mention in the German communiqué, I want my own congratulations to reach you on the brilliant operation concluded which has given its name to an Italian victory stop Convey the above to officers and men stop I am sure that you will do ever better and will hit the enemy ever harder.

This was the conquest of Stalino, an important mining and industrial centre in the Ukraine. On October 1st following, Messe replied as follows :

The victorious troops of the CSIR received your praise with pride and exultation and showed their great joy by shouting after the fleeing enemy that name which for us is a symbol of victory— "Duce!"

MESSE.

The months of October and November were really terrible for the CSIR troops. The whole vast Ukrainian plain was transformed into a sea of mud. Problems of administration seemed insuperable. Nothing functioned any more. Supplies, munitions and reinforcements reached the front as and when they could. I sent Colonel Gandin to the spot, who gave a startling account when he returned to Rome of the difficulties which the CSIR had encountered and had still to encounter. When I had heard the report, I sent Messe the following telegram, dated December 4th, 1941 :

Colonel Gandin has given me details of the difficulties faced by the CSIR and the superhuman endurance of your troops stop Two months of being bogged in primitive or non-existent Soviet roadways must have created formidable obstacles in the supply domain which only generalship like yours and men like the troops of the CSIR could have overcome stop Though far away we have felt these difficulties due to circumstances stop Gandin tells me that the situation has now improved stop Convey my congratulations to the officers and men of the CSIR also for the difficulties faced with Roman calm and Fascist fortitude stop I send you, my dear Messe, my warmest regards.

The next day, the 5th, Messe replied as follows :

Your high recognition of what the CSIR has done in the first five months of campaign in Russia, during which it has tirelessly marched and fought with never a break, fully rewards us for all the difficulties which the troops have always faced with manly fortitude, iron will and a great spirit of self-sacrifice. The terrible Ukrainian mud has never halted us, much less the enemy, though always more numerous and very heavily armed. I assure you, Duce, that the bitter Russian winter will not halt us either. The enemy will always be heavily and forcefully engaged wherever he appears, just as is happening precisely at this time, in which he is showing particular eagerness to try and oppose our inexorable advance. We have always taken a realistic view of this most bitter and fierce war, and for that reason we have been able to face it with a full knowledge of our strength and with a completely calm mind. You may be sure, Duce, that the CSIR, which feels you so near to it and which follows what you are doing for its greater reinforcement with a profoundly grateful heart, will bring the task which it has pleased you to entrust to it to a worthy conclusion.

At Christmastime, 1941, using forces and weapons far superior to the effective strength and material of the Italian divisions, the Russians launched a violent attack. They counted on taking the Italians by surprise, morally, at least. They thought they would find them in a moment of depression and homesickness owing to the recurrence of the great feast of the Nativity, which the men of sunny Italy had to spend far from their family and country. But the Bolsheviks' calculations were shown to be false. In a bloody battle, lasting a week, the Italian troops defeated the Bolshevik forces and put them to flight.[1] On December 28th I telegraphed as follows:

Once more I send you my congratulations and my satisfaction at the fresh hard blow which the magnificent troops of the CSIR have inflicted on the Bolsheviks. The nation is proud of you. Let everyone know this.

General Messe telegraphed as follows on the 29th:

The victorious troops of the CSIR have received your high praise and your flattering and encouraging satisfaction with exultant pride, and they join with me in repeating to you our firm determination to remain decisively in the struggle until all Bolshevik resistance has been broken.

In Spring, 1942, further and greater participation in the Russian campaign was thought necessary.[2] No longer three, but now ten divisions were to take part. The glorious CSIR became part of the ARMIR—that is, the *Armata Italiana in Russia* (Italian Army in Russia); in doing so, it became the 35th Army Corps. As already stated, this did not please Messe or the troops under his command either. He obeyed with bad grace. Although some said the contrary, Father Salza, a brave Chaplain wounded in the war, who had always been with the CSIR, re-established the truth of the matter as follows on May 8th, 1942:

Duce,

I have heard from both soldiers and civilians that His Excellency Messe had said that he was very pleased at being promoted to fourth place among the generals of the 8th Army (ARMIR)*; some even say that he asked for this himself. Permit me to tell*

[1] To judge by the press of the time the battle was neither so important nor so decisive a victory for the Italians as Mussolini makes out. There is little mention of it in general accounts of the fighting and even the official Stefani version is forced to admit that Marshal Timoshenko's forces "succeeded in achieving some infiltrations," before they were "compelled to retire several kilometres."

[2] Hitler and Mussolini met in Salzburg on April 29th–30th, 1942. A few days later neutral correspondents in Berlin announced that more Italian troops were to be sent to the Eastern Front and regarded this as one of the first results of the meeting.

you, Duce, that the matter is quite otherwise. Messe is ambitious. I can tell you that he has a real passion for serving you and devoting his whole life to you, as he has always done. But that does not prevent him thinking of this change as a sort of depth-charge which lessens his prestige considerably in the eyes of our allies, of the nation and of his glorious troops. The ignorance in which he has been kept till now as to the new situation has deeply mortified him. For that reason he would prefer to be transferred, always provided you are agreeable. This is the simple truth, which you may hear better from his own mouth. Forgive me for presuming to pass on this information ; I have only one aim—your glory, Italy's glory and the glory of God.

Outwardly, however, nothing transpired of Messe's resentment. On May 9th, almost as he was leaving, he issued the following Order of the Day :

Officers, Warrant Officers, N.C.O.s, Soldiers and Blackshirts !

On the threshold of the dry season which brings us nearer to the recommencement of the march eastwards, in our tenth month on Russian soil, the Italian Expeditionary Corps ends its first cycle of operations in this extremely difficult campaign. My thoughts turn to our Fallen with compassion and gratitude. To you and to your units of the Army, Militia and Air Force, to all the Commands, Divisions and Departments which I have had and still have under my command in a marvellous unison of ardent strength, invincible arms and active faith, I send you with a proud heart my warm and grateful greetings as Commander.

In this greeting vibrates the warm recognition of the great and memorable tasks which you have accomplished and which, adding fresh lustre to the flags, standards, banners and ensigns with which the country has entrusted you, have enriched the military history of Italy with pages which will shine in letters of gold in the annals of the Nation.

Soldiers of the CSIR!

Once again I see your brave and compact ranks crossing the Roumanian border, marching along the rutted tracks of Bessarabia, advancing at the price of unequalled fatigue and of untold difficulties through the boundless extent of the fertile Ukraine which, tomorrow, will be the granary of the conquerors and which denied you, scorched as you were by the blazing summer, even the comfort of water.

No obstacle stopped you. Hard on the heels of the retreating enemy, you received your baptism of fire on the Bug and, impatient to add to our race's ancient titles of honour and valour, in direct comparison with allies of high military prestige, you leaped forward to the Dnieper, you forced the river-crossing, you hurled yourselves upon the enemy divisions who were barring your passage, and in seven days of bitter fighting, while our Air Force intrepidly dominated the sky over the battlefield, you set the seal on the first phase of the struggle with the victory of Petrikovka.

Following up the pursuit, you crossed the river Woltchia, you overthrew the stubborn enemy rearguard and, advancing under the freezing and driving rain while the supply columns were bogged in the flooded tracks, you penetrated hundreds of miles into a territory ambushed by partisans, and victoriously reached the heart of the Donetz basin.

Later, braving the bitter inclemency of a premature winter, blinded by blizzards and racked with cold, you attacked the enemy who awaited you, grim, determined and entrenched in strong defensive positions, you wrested his fortified strongholds from him one after another, and with proud determination you established yourselves on the line previously planned for the winter halt.

Neither the barbarous violence with which the Bolsheviks reacted, nor the weight of numbers with which they hoped to overcome you, nor the adversity and exceptional rigour of the cold which equalled Arctic temperatures, nor privations and sufferings of the highest physical and moral degree, could weaken your ranks which at all times inviolably held the position taken from the enemy.

My Brave Men !

Your Commander, who has led you in this titanic task, who has shared with you the vicissitudes of so many supreme trials, lived with you through the anxieties and troubles of the eve of battle and the joy of your successes, who has been a witness of your faithful courage, your humble, constant and silent self-sacrifice, the manly will with which you have overcome an expert, stubborn and savage enemy and very great difficulties—your Commander says to you that "Well done !" which is due to brave men and which shows that you have well earned the title of valiant.

Army Corps Commander,
General G. MESSE.
May 9th, 1942—*XX.*[1]
Russian Front.

[1] The Roman number indicates the year of the Fascist Era, reckoned from the March on Rome (28.10.1922). This chronology was instituted by Mussolini's circular of 25.10.1926. Its use in all official documents, in addition to the civil calendar, was made compulsory from 29.10.1927.

Towards the end of the same month he returned to Italy, where I received him. A communiqué which appeared in the papers on June 3rd, 1942, announced this as follows:

The Duce has received General Giovanni Messe, Commander of the CSIR, who is now in Italy for a short period of leave. General Messe gave the Duce a full report on the course of the Italian troops' operations on the Eastern front and the victorious engagements carried out by all branches of the Expeditionary Corps. The Duce expressed his complete satisfaction to General Messe. During the winter period particularly, which was the hardest of the campaign, General Messe and his officers and men showed themselves possessed of a high degree of courage and physical endurance, in standing up to very great difficulties. General Messe gave the Duce a copy of eighteen separate mentions of the CSIR in communiqués from the German Command, and many Orders of the Day in which German Army Group Commanders amply acknowledged the valour and fighting spirit of the Italian troops.

This bulletin was designed, among other things, to smooth away the resentment which the transformation of the CSIR had caused in the mind not only of the Commander. The latter, on sending three copies of the first number of *Dovunque* (an Expeditionary Corps weekly printed with what could be found in an ex-Red printing-press in Stalino by Ukrainian workmen), declared to my Private Secretary that "the high honour of participating in the struggle in arms against the chief enemy of the Fascist Revolution has not eluded the Italian fighting men."

The first number contained a photograph of *The Duce in Russia, conversing with General Messe.*

His leave over, he returned to Russia as Commander of the 35th Army Corps, and it was not long before the quarrel with Gariboldi broke out. On August 31st, XX (1942), General Messe addressed a letter to me which was brought to Italy by Major Vecchini, whom Messe recommended in the accompanying letter. Here is the text:

Duce,

When your Chief Private Secretary, in June last, informed me that you would give me an audience, he also told me that I might apply directly to Your Excellency through the Secretariat, if need arose. Moreover, during the audience itself you did me the honour of telling me that I could always express my thoughts to you with absolute frankness. When the appointment of Commander of the 8th Army had been made, in the person of H.E. General Gariboldi, I returned to Russia, as was your explicit wish and my duty as a soldier, and because, too, it was thought that my presence out there might give the new Commander all the benefit of a very long experience, both with regard to the enemy and the country, and in relations with our German allies.

At this point I must in all loyalty point out to you that this last essential condition has not been realised, in so far that the new Commander has not asked anything more of me than he could have asked of any of the other Army Corps Commanders freshly arrived from Italy.

To this I must add that the sentimental reasons for my attachment to the old CSIR are now also lacking, because, owing to operational demands, only the " Pasubio," of the old divisions that composed it, still remains with me. But even this last relic of the Expeditionary Corps is to be shorn of its oldest elements, so that nothing of the old CSIR will remain save its glorious name and memory.

This being the case, allow me, Duce, to put forward for your careful consideration, that the time has come for my repatriation immediately on the conclusion of the battle now in progress, which chiefly concerns my sector, so that you may employ me wherever it best pleases you, but where I may continue to give all that is in my power and in my indomitable enthusiasm. You know that I have but one ambition : to serve as a soldier Fascist Italy and yourself, its great leader.

Since I returned to Russia I have had the honour of leading my troops in the victorious battle of Krassny-Lutsk, mentioned in the German communiqué. For twelve days these same troops, deployed on the Don in contact with the German 6th Army, have been fighting heroically and bloodily to bar the way against the Bolshevik hordes which, to the tune of three divisions of twenty-seven battalions, have hurled themselves savagely on the sector held by only one of our divisions, of six battalions, seriously threatening the supply lines of the 6th Army itself, extending towards Stalingrad. But they have not broken through ! And they shall not ! The extremely fierce battle is still in progress, but it will end inevitably with a new and splendid Italian achievement. The sacrifices made at this time have been great. Soldiers and Blackshirts have touched the highest peak of heroism and devotion to duty. This fresh proof of courage and tenacity afforded by our troops will greatly strengthen the links between the two great allies and will increase our national prestige. Allow me, Duce, to express my most faithful attachment and sincere devotion.

General GIOVANNI MESSE.

At the New Year, the Fuehrer awarded Messe the Knight's Cross of the Iron Cross, in recognition of his merits. This high decoration was brought him personally by Army Commander General von Kleist. Towards the end of the year, in November, Messe was promoted Army General.

After the letter quoted above, Messe was recalled to Italy. He busied himself first of all in bringing out a report on the first year of the Eastern campaign, and he requested that there should appear on the frontispiece in my own hand the words I had spoken in my speech of December 2nd, 1942, to the Chamber of Fasci and Corporations: "It must be admitted," I had said, "that only an army like the German one and only the Italian CSIR, today become the ARMIR, could have overcome the trials of a winter without parallel for a hundred and forty years."

For Messe the Russian chapter was henceforth definitely closed, and the Tunisian chapter opened. On April 5th, 1943—XXI—Messe replied as follows to the congratulations I had sent him after the battle of the Mareth:

Duce,

Your high praise of the way in which the 1st Army acquitted itself in the battle of the Mareth and El Hamma, has been made known to the Italian and German divisions, who have learned of it with lively satisfaction. All, from Commanders to rank and file, join with me in thanking you. On arriving here, Father Salza repeated the flattering words which you had expressed in respect of me and my work. I am deeply grateful to you. You, Duce, know by experience that in fulfilling the tasks with which you have entrusted me in the past, I have always employed all my energy and all my capacity. You may be sure that this has been the case again, is still the case and will be the case in Tunisia. A propos of this I take the liberty of sending you a short report on the latest battle. Thus you will be able to judge whether and how the task assigned me as Commander of the 1st Army has so far been carried out. Other and sterner trials await us. The Army has been considerably reduced and time, and perhaps also the means, are lacking, to make good the heavy losses suffered. Everywhere, all are firmly resolved to fight to the last. My respectful and warm regards,

General MESSE.

As already stated, the report was printed and gave rise to the discussions mentioned.

When the report had been published, I sent a letter in my own hand to Messe on April 14th, 1943, couched in these terms :

Dear Messe,

Your report on the first victorious battle on the Mareth line is so vivid, thrilling and exhaustive that I have decided to make it known to the Italian people by having it printed. I have introduced merely a few alterations for comprehensible motives. By this, and not only by this, I intend to give full recognition to your work as Commander and to the courage shown by your soldiers. Between the end of March and today the situation has changed, that is, has become more difficult. I wish to tell you that I count on you to protract resistance to the uttermost and thus upset the enemy plans, at least with regard to their time-table, which aim at a landing on the mainland, after a landing on the islands. Once again: we are doing and will continue to do the impossible *to supply you with what you need. My hearty good wishes and regards, as ever,*

MUSSOLINI.

After the battle of the Mareth line, the second delaying battle in Tunisia took place, the battle of the so-called Shotts, a sort of salt marshes. Of this battle, too, Messe sent me a report accompanied by this note :

Duce,

I take the liberty of sending you, after the preceding report on the Mareth-El Hamma battle, the report of the battle of the Shotts, and the beginning of the difficult retreat on to the Enfidaville line.

The report relates with perfect frankness the course of the bloody and violent struggle undergone and the extremely grave circumstances in which there occurred the disengagement of the large forces on the Shotts line and their retreat; also our very heavy losses, in virtue, chiefly, of the enemy superiority in the matter of armour and of artillery and, more particularly, in the air, where they had complete and unopposed mastery. But I can say that once again officers and men fought desperately and by their sacrifices did honour to our country's flag. My humble regards,

General MESSE.

Finally, Tunisia was defended in a third fierce battle, à propos of which Messe reported as follows on April 22nd, 1943:

Duce,

Thank you very much for the letter you were good enough to send me and for the high praise accorded to the 1st Army. I see that, according to your wish, the report on the battle of the Mareth line has been made known to the Italian people through publication in all our newspapers. All the fighting men of the Army are grateful to you for that particular form of recognition for the work carried out by them in this really most bitter struggle in Tunisia. For my own part, I am glad of having once again earned your and the nation's confidence. As you know, the 1st Army is at this moment fighting its third and fiercest battle. The English 8th Army launched its great attack on the night of the 20th, hurling against our positions the mass of its infantry supported by an imposing amount of artillery, and equipped with ammunition and many tanks. Today is the third day of the battle, and the enemy, though enormously superior in men and material, has so far been effectively contained, and has made very little progress and at bloody cost. You know the state of the 1st Army, which has been fighting for 36 days. I am perfectly aware that the responsible authorities, on your initiative, are doing all they can to help us. But I am also aware of the very grave difficulties of transport, owing to which very little, in point of fact, reaches us. The troops are physically very tired, and seriously diminished in numbers. The men fighting are, almost all of them, the same who retreated from Libya. But all my energy and all the energy of the various Commanders is being directed to helping and supporting these fine and heroic soldiers of ours, who are really working miracles. There has not been a single point at which the enemy has set foot inside our positions without our launching a fierce and violent counter-attack. For your satisfaction and for our country's pride, I should like to tell you that the proofs of courage, dash and endurance afforded by our troops at this time surpass those during the battle of the Mareth line. And I should like to tell you one thing more—that our troops at this time, compared with our allies (always first-class soldiers) have shown the greater willingness and dash. Owing to the very serious exhaustion of the troops, the inadequacy of artillery and ammunition and the almost complete lack of armoured vehicles, compared with the enemy's crushing superiority in material, the situation is growing steadily graver. Our air force—and our ally's as well—may be called non-existent, compared with the really overwhelming and intensively active enemy air force. In spite of all, you may be sure that the order to resist to the last will be faithfully carried out. I send you the third report which deals with the retreat and the deployment on the new Enfidaville line.

Your humble and devoted servant,

General MESSE.

Then came the epilogue, and captivity.

On re-reading these documents it is really difficult to believe that such a man could have agreed to be set free by the English[1] ; one is very loath to believe that the leader of the CSIR should today find himself in the same camp as the Russians and the Balkan Bolshevik partisans, abjuring one of the most significant pages in his life as a soldier, an Italian and a Fascist—for such he always, and publicly, professed himself. One is very loath to believe that, by making himself a party thereto, he should have accepted the infamous unconditional surrender and should have subscribed to the rule forbidding the wearing of decorations gained on the Eastern Front. General Messe has not the slightest justification for his conduct, unless it is a question of personal spite, which would lead one to have a very poor opinion of his patriotism and loyalty as a man. By his conduct he has insulted the living—and, above all, the fallen—in the war against Bolshevism ; those dead whom, without a trace of shame, he betrayed and abandoned on the Russian steppes, in the numberless graves unmarked by even a cross.

[1] Marshal Messe was released from captivity in November, 1943. He returned to Italy and, on November 22nd, took up the post of Chief of General Staff of the Italian Armed Forces under Marshal Badoglio. Replaced April 17th, 1945.

CHAPTER III

FROM PANTELLERIA TO SICILY

TOWARDS THE BEGINNING OF JUNE the air offensive became intense every day and by day and night, often accompanied by naval bombardments. G.H.Q. of the armed forces mentioned enemy raids in communiqués Nos. 1102, 1103, 1104, 1105, 1106, 1107, 1108 and 1109. Communiqué No. 1109 announced that *the garrison of Pantelleria has been facing the ceaseless enemy air attacks with unflinching courage, and yesterday destroyed six aeroplanes.* Communiqué No. 1110, referring to the activity on June 8th, particularly struck the Italians and moved them deeply. It announced that *the garrison of the island of Pantelleria, which throughout yesterday, June 8th, underwent ceaseless enemy bombardment, has not replied to the enemy's demand to surrender.* And it added that during the air attacks fifteen enemy 'planes had been brought down. This communiqué caused a surge of pride in the heart of everyone.

Communiqué No. 1111 announced fresh enemy raids on Pantelleria and the bringing down of eleven more enemy 'planes. Communiqué No. 1112 announced that *throughout yesterday, June 10th, and last night, heavy enemy bomber and fighter formations followed one another uninterruptedly over Pantelleria, whose garrison, though battered by the onslaught of some thousand enemy machines, has proudly left unanswered a fresh demand to surrender.*

On the same day the Italo-German fighters had brought down twenty-two enemy 'planes. This second rejection of the demand to surrender radioed by General Spaatz filled many Italian hearts with enthusiasm. Now at last ! The neutral and even the enemy press underlined the fact. Foreign opinion in general was that

Italian soldiers had not fought brilliantly until now because they were far from their country ; but now that it was a question of the "sacred soil" of Italy, the Italian soldiers (so said a Swedish paper) would "astonish the world."

The Commander's Volte-Face

What was happening at Pantelleria seemed to justify the foreign observer. But the congratulations sent out from Rome and addressed to the Commander of the base of Pantelleria crossed with another telegram from the Commander himself in which he declared the impossibility of further resistance, chiefly owing to lack of water.

A meeting was called with Admiral Riccardi and Generals Ambrosio and Fougier. The surrender occurred exactly on the anniversary of Italy's entry into the war. Admiral Pavesi's telegram had been addressed to me. To order him to resist to the last seemed to be a useless gesture which had already been tried out on former occasions to no purpose, as at Klisura in Albania, and elsewhere. Pavesi's telegram painted the situation as absolutely untenable ; to resist further would mean nothing but a useless blood bath. But then what was the point of rejecting the demands to surrender made twenty-four and forty-eight hours earlier ? Did Admiral Pavesi by any chance think that General Spaatz, touched by the rejection and lost in admiration at it, would stop the raids ?

Was it therefore only a question of a *beau geste* destined to remain nothing but a *beau geste* ? A gesture more theatrical than military ? At length with much heartburning the telegram anxiously awaited by Pavesi was sent off: *Radiotelegraph Malta that owing to lack of water you are ceasing all resistance.* A large white flag was hung out over the port and on some of the buildings on the island : fire ceased. The English disembarked peacefully. A few soldiers who had not realised what had happened let off a shot or two which wounded two enemy soldiers. That was all !

The landing at Pantelleria which, according to an English paper, would have been impossible with any other garrison, cost the English the blood of two slightly wounded soldiers ![1] And

[1] At the time, Rome Radio was made to tell a different story. On June 14th, 1943, it said : "By concentrating all his overwhelming air force against the small islands of the Sicilian Channel, the enemy was able to break the heroic

what did the defence of the first island of home territory cost the Italians?

The Chief of Staff, when directly questioned, based his information on such scanty and indirect documentation as there was (Admiral Pavesi had always been somewhat sparing of information) and sent me a report giving the following figures: in one month 56 dead and 116 wounded, almost all of them Blackshirts in the anti-aircraft defences. The civil population and troops barricaded in the underground hangars had suffered only insignificant losses. The entire garrison of some 12,000 men was taken prisoner almost intact. Some weeks later Admiral Jachino put in a very detailed report reducing the total losses suffered by the garrison of Pantelleria in one month of aerial attack to thirty-five fallen.[1] The hangars, dug out of the rock, had nullified the effects of the enemy bombs. The 2,000 tons of bombs certainly did fall on the island, but on rock, not on men.

Later it was learned—from enemy evidence—that there had not even been a shortage of water; in any case, French-made sea-water distillers of medium capacity were on their way.

The Surrender of the Island

Communiqué No. 1113 announcing the fall of the island burst on the Italians like a shock of cold water. It was followed by a war report which, passing from Pantelleria to Lampedusa, exalted "the heroic little garrison which was resisting with heroic determination," while in fact they had already hoisted the white flag. Admiral Pavesi had lied; today we may say that he had betrayed us[2]. Not even the underground hangars were demolished, and the airfield was left almost intact.

resistance of its defenders, helped by the exhaustion of water supplies. But to occupy it, he had to suffer losses in ships and troops, which proved the difficulties of an attempted landing in areas where air operations would not be enough to achieve results."

[1] The *Giornale d'Italia,* June 13th, 1943, had described the surrender of the island thus: "The garrison resisted for over six weeks, proudly refusing all demands for surrender and facing the enemy, in spite of daily increasing casualties and superhuman sacrifices, with the proud and manly fighting qualities of heroes." Now that Mussolini intends to emphasise Pavesi's "treachery," it is to his advantage to reveal the true facts.

[2] In May, 1944, Admiral Pavesi was condemned to death *in absentia* by the Republican Fascist Special Tribunal, for surrendering the island without putting up the resistance which "the code of duty and honour necessitated."

It was a pity the execution squad did not reach the first of the treacherous admirals who a few months later were to bring the most shameful treachery to a fine art, by handing over the entire fleet to the enemy.

The Drama of Sicily

With the fall of Pantelleria the curtain went up on the drama of Sicily.

Even before war was declared, measures of a military character had been taken to reinforce the island's defences. As soon as hostilities had commenced, I sent Marshal Emilio De Bono (who was in command of the southern armies) on a tour of inspection in Sicily. On June 25th, 1940, Marshal De Bono sent Marshal Graziani, at that time Chief of Army Staff, a shrewd and detailed report containing "the principal observations made concerning the disposition and efficiency of troops ; coastal guard and defence ; anti-aircraft defence."

With regard to the efficiency of the troops Marshal De Bono wrote: "Morale is high and a fighting spirit universal. The effective in manpower has almost reached the prescribed percentage. The same cannot so far be said of livestock and mechanised transport." Marshal De Bono's report continued with observations and criticisms, and indicated various deficiencies, mainly owing to the advanced age of the soldiers in the coastal divisions ; parts of equipment either lacking or incomplete ; the conscripts' scant familiarity with modern automatic weapons ; and the unpreparedness of certain formations. A propos of this De Bono cited the case of two second-lieutenants who, without having been recalled or had any training since they had been demobilised as second-lieutenants after the 1915-18 war, were now in command of a battalion.

On July 7th following, the Deputy Chief of Staff, General Roatta, informed Marshal De Bono of "steps being taken following your visit to Sicily, namely, the existing twenty-four coastal battalions have been dissolved and re-formed with elements ten years younger." The military situation in Sicily had been notably improved by the "Piemonte" infantry division being placed at the disposition of the local command, the XIIth Army Corps. And Roatta concluded : "Reinforcements of material and the necessary machine-guns for coastal defence will be despatched in the greatest possible number."

General Ambrosio's Diary

The Sicilian command was held first by General Ambrosio, then by General Rosi, later by General Roatta and finally, from June 1st, 1943, by General Guzzoni.

During the first three years of war much was done to strengthen the island's defences. General Ambrosio, in the haste of his flight, forgot his diary. It is not a document of exceptional value ; it deals mainly with administrative matters. On May 6th, 1942, Ambrosio refers to a conversation he had with the Prince of Piedmont, who declared on returning from a visit to Sicily that "the coastal divisions are in excellent order and it is only necessary to number the battalions in the usual manner ; the soldiers on the island carry themselves well and salute. Many roads are in the worst possible condition ; there is confusion in the public services at Palermo and a poor postal service which is especially complained of by the soldiers of the Pachino garrison."

General Ambrosio's diary has this note on October 17th : "Must hold one's tongue. Spies on the Staff. Instances : movements of high-ups, and Scuero's visit to me. Political situation obscure. Duce ill." Still quoting from General Ambrosio's diary we find on November 10th, 1942, 5 p.m.: "Went to the Duce's with Cavallero and Rosi to review Sicilian defences and necessary material for Rosi."

The First Hint of the Coup d'Etat

The diary continues, November 11th, 12 noon, as follows : "At the Duce's to complete review of defence of Sicily. The Duce tells me that on December 1st the class born in the second four months of 1923 must be called up so as to provide forty thousand men immediately for Sicily ; those born at the end of 1923 to be called up on January 15th, 1943." On November 16th : "The Duce is in great pain owing to his illness." It is perhaps in connection with that, that we read the following symptomatic note on December 4th : "Bonomi's visit—Badoglio's proposition—H.M.'s abdication—The Prince—Weapons—Cavallero." This was the first hint of the *coup d'état.*

Despite my illness I devoted myself almost exclusively to the military preparations for Sicily. On January 10th, 1943, we read: "At the Duce's with Cavallero and Rosi. The latter said, 'The King was satisfied with his tour of Sicily. The divisions showed up well; the best is the *Livorno*, followed by the *Assietta* and the *Napoli*. The coastal divisions are good, too, and so is the progress and disposition of the defence works, but the road system still needs improving.' "

As the result of what Rosi said, I wanted only thirty per cent. of the Sicilians called up in the 1924 class to be drafted to Sicilian regiments, the remaining strength to be made up of recruits from the mainland. To my mind the defence of Sicily ought to be the job of every Italian; just as in the 1915-18 war Sicilians fought to defend our land frontier on the Alps, so now mainlanders should take part in the defence of our country's sea frontier.

Once Tunisia had fallen, the threat to our larger islands appeared imminent. Because of this I sent General Ambrosio on a tour of inspection in Sardinia. He remained there for four days and on May 8th, 1943, he sent me a report of which certain essential portions are worth reproducing. After a preamble of a geographical nature concerning the characteristics of the probable landing zones, General Ambrosio expressed himself as follows concerning the defence works:

"In general a certain divergence of basic aims is to be observed in the various sectors of the defence system, a divergence due to the different directives sent out one after another during the last few years from the Centre. This depended on the progress made in theories of coastal defence methods as compared with the gradual evolution of methods of attack together with that of new inventions.

"And since for obvious reasons we could not destroy what had been carried out in the recent past and begin all over again with new criteria, we have adapted the old to the new, modifying it wherever possible.

"Thus the second line of defence (hedgehogs for containing the enemy) is constructed far more solidly than the army formations, which are considerably weaker, and that despite the modern technique with which it is proposed to break up any attempted landing on the beach or possibly even sooner, i.e., while still at sea.

"In order to make both of them, especially the front line, stronger, guns and more guns are needed, shore batteries, anti-landing guns and anti-tank guns, not only to halt the first resistance, but above all to defeat on the coast itself any craft attempting to approach the beaches and any soldier setting foot on the ground.

"It is all the more necessary to halt the attack on the beaches before they have dug themselves in on land since, having little armour, we could not overcome a modernly equipped enemy once he had succeeded in landing and was pushing on towards the interior."

The Defence of Sardinia and the Position in Sicily

"The defence system, despite its original defects, is almost complete as regards fortifications and armaments and provides a good framework for resistance. A further reinforcement of automatic weapons and artillery is being made, which will serve to increase its strength. Everywhere, people are working with speed and enthusiasm. A healthy spirit reigns, the commanders are equal to the honourable task assigned them, the soldiers are disciplined, ready to fight, ready to face anything.

"During my visit to Sardinia I was once more obliged to ask myself whether the theory that the enemy would try to seize the island was a tenable one or not.

"A landing in Sardinia would not be an easy matter ; the stretches of coast which lend themselves to such a landing are few and narrow ; the hinterland is difficult ; we could bring aero-naval opposition heavily to bear on the convoys and decimate them ; supplies would suffer the same fate ; and our land defences are not to be underestimated.

"The enemy might reckon with a high percentage of losses, but he would at least want to be sure of success. Not only would this assurance be lacking, and thus the risks great, but the severe losses which he must in any case suffer should at least be compensated by the importance of the objective.

"Now Sardinia is not an object of capital importance in the strategic picture of the Mediterranean.

"Unless the Anglo-Americans intend to invade Italy, in which case, acting consecutively, i.e., without a break, they might even conquer Sardinia to make it a springboard for invasion, I do not see an adequate proportion between the aim of the operation and its difficulty.

"I do not believe in an invasion of the mainland because it would be a long affair and would not decide the final result of the war ; Italy, even if reduced to the Po Valley, would not give in ; our adversaries must know this by now."

As may be seen, the attitude of the Chief of Staff, General Ambrosio, at the beginning of May, 1943, did not envisage, even as the wildest possibility, an unconditional surrender, such as occurred four months later.

The report on Sardinia concluded thus: "All things considered, I believe that the chances of an attack on Sardinia are remote, and in any case I think them much slighter than the chances of an attempt to invade Sicily whose strategic position in the Mediterranean presents a far greater obstacle to our enemies. The conquest of Sicily need not presuppose a further operation against the mainland, but could be an end in itself, because it would give the enemy safety of movement and would lessen the engagements of his naval forces and the losses of his mercantile marine ; that is to say, it is in itself an objective of real and pre-eminent importance, worth pursuing with all energy and at any cost."

At the beginning of June, General Guzzoni assumed command of the troops in Sicily. The first appreciation he made of the situation was contained in a telegram which pointed out many deficiencies, including those of a morale nature. A more detailed report was asked for, which arrived by courier a few days later. Despite three years of preparation the position was considered difficult.[1] Amongst other things, a most unfortunate manifesto issued by his predecessor, General Roatta, had justly wounded the patriotic susceptibilities of the Sicilians. The state of the island was wretched in the extreme. Cities razed to the ground, people starving and wandering homeless about the countryside, and an almost total disorganization of civil life.[2]

[1] As long ago as August 20th, 1937, Mussolini himself said in a speech at Palermo: "You have watched the military, naval and aerial defences of the island growing under your very eyes. To think of an invasion would be supreme folly. No one, not even one soldier, will land here."

[2] The account of the preparations for the defence of Sicily shows how Mussolini shifts his ground in accordance with what he wants to put across at a given moment.

(*i*) He gives a detailed description of defensive measures ordered by him in Sicily between 1940 and 1943. Their net result is summed up in the telegram from Guzzoni, "which pointed out many deficiencies, including those of a morale nature." Here Mussolini wishes to lay the blame on his commanders, implying that they had failed to carry out his orders.

(*ii*) A few pages farther on, Chapter IV, page 35, he describes the forces in Sicily on the eve of the Allied landing and concludes : "There was, in short, enough to make a landing difficult and, at the very least, to prolong resistance to the invader across the island's complicated and mountainous road system."

To prove his first point, he has to show that the defence of Sicily was ill-prepared ; to prove his second, he has to show that the defenders had adequate means.

CHAPTER IV

THE LANDING IN SICILY

On June 12th, after the surrender of Pantelleria and a heavy bombardment of La Spezia which caused severe damage to our warships, General Ambrosio sent me a note in which he informed me of the new dispositions taken for the defence of the mainland, namely, the divisions *Ravenna* and *Cosseria, Sassari, Granatieri, Pasubio,* and *Mantova* for the western coast, together with five reserve divisions, the *Piacenza, Ariete, Piave, 16th German Armoured,* and the *Panzer-Grenadiere.* The despatch was also envisaged of the 1st Armoured Division *M* (Blackshirt) which had been a sort of incubus to the General Staff and the Crown ever since the day of its establishment in the Bracciano district.[1] General Ambrosio's directive, based on the experience gained at Pantelleria and Lampedusa, was as follows:

"(1) Prompt intervention of our air force which should immediately consider the difficulties it is likely to encounter and the means of avoiding them;

"(2) base our plan for resistance on *defence in depth* (so as to minimize, as far as possible, the danger of air attacks to our men and material) and on the *intervention of reinforcements,* so as to defeat the enemy as soon as disembarked and while still in difficulties;

"(3) enable the divisions to act on their own initiative when, as will certainly occur, they are cut off;

"(4) take prompt measures with regard to supplies for maintaining any divisions which may be isolated;

[1] The district round Lake Bracciano, about 25–30 miles north-west of Rome.

"(5) stiffen the morale of the troops so that all of them realise that the sacred soil of our country must be defended yard by yard to the death."

Very fine words, but only words, because in reality neither senior nor junior officers had ever given a thought to the morale of the troops; and consequent on the perturbation caused by the staggeringly unexpected surrender of Pantelleria, there was born in high circles an attitude of mind tending towards capitulation.[1] There was a fresh chorus of defeatism. Enemy propaganda—always greatly listened to—declared that an attack on Sicily was not only certain but imminent. During the whole of June the enemy air force subjected towns of all sizes in Sicily to a methodical bombardment, increasing the confusion and disorganisation of the food situation due to the interruption of the ferry and the destruction of the island's railways.

I Convene the Chiefs of Staff

On the afternoon of June 14th, in defiance of doctor's orders, I convened the Chief of General Staff, the three Chiefs of Staff of the armed forces, and the Minister for War Production at the Villa Torlonia.

I read the assembly a "note on the strategic situation in Italy in the middle of June," containing the following:

"(1) It seems almost superfluous to begin by stating as a preliminary that politics do not enter into the matter at all. Capitulation would be the end of Italy not only as a great Power, but as a Power at all, since the first consequence of capitulation—apart from the other easily foreseen ones of a territorial and colonial nature—would be total and permanent disarmament on land, sea and in the air, as well as the destruction of all industries directly or indirectly concerned with war.

"(2) In the present phase of the war there is no possibility

[1] Mussolini's defence is based on the "treachery" of his military and naval commanders and on defeatism in the Army. Commenting on the invasion of Sicily, Rome Radio was made to say, July 11th, 1943: "Eisenhower cannot enjoy the experience of the previous landing in French North Africa. Here the people are waiting for him only to contest his landing. There are neither traitor generals nor compliant admirals, much less a people who believe in the fairy tale of liberation. In Italy there is a people determined to fight, to defend their own land, compact around their King and Duce, linked by one sole ideal."

of the Italian armed forces taking the initiative. They are restricted purely and simply to defence.

"The Army cannot take the initiative. For one thing, the terrain is lacking. Only if the enemy should land on any piece of home territory could they counter-attack and throw him back into the sea.

"The Navy's initiative is limited to whatever our small craft and submarine fleet can do against enemy shipping. For some months now the results have been modest. Our battleships are now a deadweight exposed to growing dangers.

"The Air Force's capacity of initiative, too, is now limited to sporadic attacks on enemy shipping. We lack a large bomber force and the fighters to protect it. From now on even the Air Force has only defensive possibilities.

"Conclusions: the only thing we can do is defend our home territory. But to this defence we must pledge ourselves to the last drop of blood.

The Enemy's Plans and Procedure

"Enemy tactics—in order to assist the war of nerves—consist in giving the press and radio free rein in any hypothesis concerning the Second Front, even the most absurd and fantastic.

"But under cover of this noisy though harmless babble the enemy's political and strategic conduct of the war is obeying the laws of geography and the rule of the maximum result with minimum effort. Thus the attack on the Italian islands in the central Mediterranean was fatally obvious—because it was logical. Thus, too, we may anticipate a further action against the other Italian islands in the Mediterranean, Sicily, Sardinia and Rhodes. All this cannot yet be called an invasion of Europe, but it would be the necessary prelude to it. And this may perhaps fill the bill for 1943.

"It has been said that artillery conquers terrain and infantry holds it. This needs altering to: 'Flying artillery conquers terrain, infantry holds it.' There is the classic case of Pantelleria, the first in history. It was the Air Force which conquered Pantelleria. The question arises whether similar methods would obtain a similar result in a larger island, such as Sicily. I would not rule that out. The enemy will begin by a systematic attack on the airfields, with consequent destruction of machines on the ground, destruction of plants and disorganisation of services. With the airfields neutralised, the enemy—from now on virtually unhindered—would go over to the attack on the land defence systems so as to wear them down and make a landing possible. Our land defence can be considered efficient only if protected by our Air Force.

Directive for War Production

"This being the case, our war production must henceforward concentrate *exclusively* on the production of means of defence, and since the most dangerous offensive is that from the air—in so far as its development may facilitate that of the other attacks, such as invasion—it is necessary to increase our efforts to produce:

"(*a*) the greatest possible number of fighter planes,

"(*b*) the greatest possible number of A.A. and anti-tank guns, together with an imposing quantity of ammunition, and

"(*c*) the greatest possible number of mines and other means of passive defence.

"The actual production of lorries may be limited to the strict minimum. We no longer need enormous quantities of lorries as in the first phase of the war, when the length of the supply lines in Africa was astronomical. Given the present situation, there is also no point in occupying thousands of workmen and a corresponding amount of raw material in building bombers which at best would only yield us a few specimens in the second half of next year at the earliest.

"But since the danger is imminent and this new directive for war production cannot be realised in a day but requires a certain period of time, it will be necessary for Germany to supply us with what we need for the aerial defence of metropolitan territory, namely, aeroplanes and guns.

"There is an Italian proverb that he who defends himself is lost. A passive defence would certainly result in that conclusion. An active defence can, on the contrary, wear out the enemy forces and convince him of the futility of his efforts. Today the essential part of active defence falls to the lot of the Air Force. On the day the enemy finds himself the unopposed master of the sky, all liberties will be permitted him."

On June 12th, I sent this note to the King. *It is clear*, so my letter ended, *that the failure of the plans for invasion, especially in the first phases of the landing, would alter the course of the war.*

The Conception of Active Defence

As to the activities of the Air Force, in October, 1942, I convened a meeting of the military chiefs at the Palazzo Venezia in order to promote a further strengthening of the Air Force, particularly of fighter 'planes. With regard to active defence, in June, 1942 (General Ambrosio refers to it in his diary), I had given orders to :

(1) Intensify the construction of Jachino automatic gun-sights.
(2) Bring the number of modern pieces of artillery (90-53 and 75-46) up to 3,000 and lighter pieces up to 4,000.
(3) Bring the number of high-powered searchlights up to 1,000.
(4) Draft the necessary personnel to the A.A. defences.
(5) Give the maximum impetus to the training of personnel.
(6) Ensure co-operation between A.A. artillery and day and night fighters.

At the end of June a thousand omens went to show that the landing in Sicily would take place in the first half of July.

On July 1st, there were present in Sicily : 230,000 soldiers of the Army and the Fascist Militia (including 10,000 officers) incorporated in six coastal divisions and four mobile divisions (the *Napoli, Livorno, Assietta* and *Aosta*), three German divisions, one armoured, plus the air and naval forces. All told, no less than 300,000 men, along a fairly deep system of strong points. There were no fewer than 1,500 pieces of artillery of all calibres and thousands of machine-guns. There was, in short, enough to make a landing difficult and, at the very least, to prolong resistance to the invader across the island's complicated and mountainous road system.[1]

The prelude to the landing took its usual form : a series of heavy bombardments which the war communiqués announced regularly, together with the losses—which were enormous—among the civil population. From July 1st–10th the enemy losses in 'planes were also considerable ; no fewer than 312 machines were shot down by the Axis fighters and A.A. artillery. Allied losses in ships were also heavy.

The attack began on the night of July 9th-10th. It was a

[1] See above, p. 29, n. 2.

Saturday. That morning I had gone to inspect the armoured division *M* in the Bracciano district, which had just completed some very successful manœuvres. Communiqué No. 1141 announced the landing in these terms: *Last night the enemy launched an attack on Sicily supported by strong naval and air forces and by the dropping of parachutists. Our combined armed forces are strongly opposing the enemy attempt. Battles are in progress along the south-east coastal strip.*

The nation held its breath at this first announcement. Various rumours were circulating in Rome on Sunday, July 11th, but basically optimistic ones. Excessively optimistic even, such as to make one suspect the presence of defeatist propaganda.

The following communiqué, No. 1142, issued in the course of the Sunday, said nothing substantially different. *A bitter battle is raging along the south-east coastal strip of Sicily, where Italian and German troops are closely engaged with the enemy landing forces and are successfully containing the pressure.* That communiqué aroused a little uncertainty; the word " contain" had an ugly ring already known from experience.

On Monday, the 12th, at 1 p.m. all Rome and all the nation hung over the wireless with keen ears and eager hearts. Crowds gathered round the loud-speakers. Late that Sunday evening it had been announced that Augusta had been retaken and that, following a counter-attack by the *Napoli* and *Goering* divisions, an enemy smoke screen in the Bay of Gela gave grounds for thinking that he might be re-embarking his men and material. Communiqué No. 1143 seemed to confirm these reports. It said: *In Sicily the struggle continued bitterly and without pause throughout yesterday, during which the enemy tried vainly to extend the slight depth of the coastal strip occupied.*

The Italian and German troops after counter-attacking decisively have defeated enemy units at several points, compelling them in one sector to withdraw.

The fighting spirit of the Italian and German divisions is extremely high; the behaviour of the civil population in the island, like that of the dashing Sicilian soldiers who form a large part of our units, is beyond all praise.

The 206*th Coastal Division, commanded by General d'Havet, deserves special mention for its magnificent defence of the sectors entrusted to it.*

An Over-Optimistic Communiqué

Before that communiqué was issued a discussion had taken place at the Palazzo Venezia between myself and General Ambrosio, other officers also being present. I wanted to modify its tone. I thought that what it said was too binding. The Augusta affair was obscure. Telegraphic communications from Guzzoni were scant, telephone messages confused and somewhat noncommittal. General Ambrosio insisted, saying that the reports from Guzzoni and his Chief of Staff, Faldella, justified the form and content of the communiqué. Needless to say, communiqué No. 1143 aroused a wave of enthusiasm all over Italy. Everyone considered it a prelude to victory.

The nation's enthusiasm was considerably damped after the issue of the later communiqué, No. 1145, which said: *The enemy, who is continually reinforcing his offensive with new contingents, has succeeded in conquering the coastal strip from Licata to Augusta, and is pushing on to the mountainous region of south-east Sicily, and approaching the plain of Catania. Along the whole front Italian and German troops are engaged in hard fighting.*

This communiqué was received first with stupefaction and then with intense bitterness. Not only did enthusiasm crumble, but mistrust spread far and wide. The divergence between the two communiqués was too great. The nervous system of the Italian people—though stronger than is generally believed—had been subjected to too severe a strain. Nevertheless, people were still inclined to hope. But the later communiqué, No. 1147, which, barely five days after the landing, already spoke of battles in the plain of Catania, gave the impression that from now on the game was irrevocably jeopardised. The conquest of all Sicily was already regarded as a foregone conclusion. The disillusion was great.[1]

Extremely harsh strictures began to come in from abroad. The capture of Augusta and Syracuse almost without a shot fired, the rapid march on Palermo and Catania, the very slight resistance offered at the time of landing—there was something mysterious about it all.

[1] The author omits to mention his own boastful "water-line" speech to the Party directorate (June 24th, made public on July 5th), which more than any communiqué had been designed to lull apprehension: "As soon as the enemy attempts to land, he must be blocked at the line which sailors call the foreshore, the sand line where the water comes to an end and the land begins.

If by any chance they should make penetration, the reserve forces which are there must hurl themselves against the landing forces, destroying them to the very last man, so that it may be said that they did occupy a piece of our country, but only by remaining there forever in a horizontal position, and not in a vertical one." Mussolini himself admits that this was not understood as hortatory, but as an assurance that the landing would not succeed. (See below, p. 238.)

CHAPTER V

THE INVASION AND THE CRISIS

WITH THE DISRUPTION OF ALMOST all communications, and the shifting of the Commands, it was not easy to weigh up the situation. Nevertheless, certain factors emerged, and this explains the note which I sent the Chief of General Staff on July 14th.

The Note of July 14th

The note said:

"At four days' remove from the enemy landing in Sicily I consider the situation exceedingly delicate and disquieting, though not yet wholly jeopardised. We must make a short analysis of the situation and decide what must and should be done. The situation is critical:

"(*a*) because after the landing, penetration in depth took place with enormous rapidity:

"(*b*) because the enemy possesses a crushing air superiority:

"(*c*) because he possesses trained and special service troops (parachutists and air-borne troops):

"(*d*) because he has almost unopposed command of the sea:

"(*e*) because his Staff are showing decision and elasticity in their conduct of the campaign.

"Before deciding what to do it is absolutely necessary to know what has happened so as to evaluate men and material accordingly. This is absolutely essential. All the reports from the enemy (who tells the truth when he is winning) as well as the official communiqués of our ally, impose a re-examination of what has occurred in these first few days.

"1. Did the coastal divisions resist long enough, that is, the minimum of which they were thought capable ?

"2. Did the second line, containing the so-called strong-points, offer any resistance or was it overrun too quickly ?

"3. We must find out what happened at Syracuse, where the enemy found the port installations intact, and at Augusta, where no resistance worth the name was offered and where there was the mendacious announcement of the recapture of a base which had never been occupied by the enemy.

"4. Were the movements of the three divisions, *Goering*, *Livorno* and *Napoli*, carried out with the necessary direction and with the no less necessary co-ordination ? What happened to the *Napoli* and the *Livorno* ?

"5. Granted that the logical direction of the attack will be towards the Straits, has any defence been prepared there ?

"6. Granted that 'penetration' has now taken place, do there exist the means and the will to build up at least a Sicilian 'front' to the north towards the Tyrrhenian Sea, such as was formerly contemplated and sketched out ?

"7. Have the two remaining divisions, the *Assietta* and the *Aosta*, still a task to perform in the west and are they equal to it ?

"8. Has anything been done or is it about to be done to check the military chaos now being added to the civil chaos occasioned by the bombardments of the whole island ?

"9. The irregularity and poverty of communications has given rise to false news which has created a profound depression in the country.

"In conclusion, we can still keep the situation under control, provided we have a plan and the will and capacity to apply it, as well as the necessary resources.

"Briefly, the plan can only be this :

"(*a*) resist on land at all costs :

"(*b*) hold up enemy supplies by the extensive use of our sea and air forces."

The First Rumours of Betrayal

In the meantime, while the Tyrrhenian line (eastwards from Termini Imerese, to protect Messina and the Straits) was being prepared, the first rumours of betrayal began to circulate. Colonel Schmalz, a German brigade commander, sent the German Supreme Command the following telegram (a copy of which

General Rintelen sent me on the evening of July 12th) which does something to explain the mystery of Augusta:

Up to today no enemy attack has been launched against Augusta. The English have never been in there. Notwithstanding this, the Italian garrison has blown up its guns and ammunition and set fire to a large fuel dump. The A.A. gunners in Augusta and Priolo have thrown all their ammunition into the sea and blown up their guns.

By the afternoon of the 11th not an Italian officer or soldier was to be found in the neighbourhood of Schmalz's brigade.

In the course of the morning many officers had already abandoned their troops and taken motor transport to Catania or elsewhere. Many soldiers either isolated or in small groups are roaming about the country; some have thrown away their arms and uniforms and are wearing civilian clothes.

In view of the rumours concerning the surrender of Augusta, which were circulating not only in Rome, Naval Headquarters sent me on July 15th a memorandum (No. 28) in which, referring to a speech made at a meeting of hierarchs, notice was given of an investigation which would take some time to carry out, owing to present events. After various remarks on the efficiency of the base, Naval Headquarters ended nevertheless by admitting that there was no doubt the destruction and evacuation of the fortifications to the north of the fortress had been premature, and that the evacuation had been carried out in a disorderly manner.

The note given me by General Rintelen did not remain unanswered. On July 18th I sent a cable to the Führer in which, basing my information on elements which had now reached Rome, I modified the view expressed in Rintelen's note and said, among other things: *In Italy, the enemy has opened the second front on which England and America will concentrate their enormous offensive potentiality, in order not only to conquer Italy but also to open the way to the Balkans at a moment when Germany is heavily committed on the Russian front.*[1]

Meanwhile the first eye-witness accounts of events began to reach Rome. Here are a few extracts from a report written by a high official of the Ministry of Popular Culture who had been

[1] The account of the surrender of Augusta is full of omissions and misinterpretation of facts:

(*i*) In referring to his reply to Colonel Schmalz's telegram, Mussolini manifestly leaves out the passages bearing on Augusta.

sent on a mission to Sicily and had remained there from the 5th to the 15th of July. After stressing the utter chaos occasioned by the incessant bombardments, he said :

"Despite the somewhat agitated state of mind of the Sicilians with regard to the internal situation, with regard to the war, up to July 10th, their feeling was one of resignation to the burden of the constant enemy air activity (with outbursts of revulsion and hatred for American barbarity) and of firm faith concerning the outcome of the war.

"Confronted with the possibility of enemy invasion, one may say that there was not a single Sicilian who did not express the certainty that any attempt of the sort would be foiled in a very short time and that all Italy would unite in helping Sicily and crushing the enemy offensive on our country's soil. At Palermo, news of the invasion was learned on the first morning, at first through proclamations by the military authorities and then through edicts stuck on the walls or published in the papers. One can say in all conscience that in general the population remained calm, absolutely confident that the attempt would be foiled at once. What on the contrary began to cause a certain unrest was the application of martial law."

The State of Emergency

"No practical measures had been taken in advance to ensure the continuation of civil life by means of essential services. The city of Palermo was left practically without bread as the bakers could not get to the city, being held up at the evacuation centres. Every remaining means of transport was blocked wherever it was. Later on, in view of the many inconveniences, the military authorities arranged with the civil authorities for special passes to be issued for travel between town and countryside.

"On the third day it was finally decided to call off the state of emergency from 5 a.m. to 5 p.m. But meanwhile the chaos born of it created a feeling of complete confusion. Up to the

(*ii*) The memorandum from Italian Naval H.Q., his second source, was compiled to enable him to answer criticism at an interview granted to high Fascist officials on July 16th, 1943 (see Chapter VI, page 49, n. 1). Here, by quoting only one sentence, he makes the document serve the opposite purpose to that for which it was intended.

(*iii*) He ignores the official account of the whole affair which he himself caused to be published in the Press of July 24th, in the form of a spirited defence of Admiral Leonardi and his garrison.

12th, people remained calm in face of the new situation, but the holding up of all news, due to lack of any means of telegraphic or telephonic communication, began to make itself felt. Palermo was virtually isolated—no news except for the communiqué. But everyone still eagerly awaited the sudden announcement that the enemy attempt had been frustrated. Instead, the communiqué continued to speak of the enemy being 'contained.' The morale of the population began to go down.[1] Even the officers began to show signs of doubt. Sick of waiting for the communiqué, people began to seek out the news broadcast by the B.B.C. and by Algiers Radio, and gobble it up."

After relating the various stages of his journey from Palermo to Messina, having learned that Enna had already been evacuated, the high official's account continues as follows :

"On the morning we arrived at Messina, the port was still in flames and the city half destroyed. We found people at the end of their tether. I had a feeling of sudden and unexpected disaster. In the Prefecture and the offices of the Commissariat as well as in the upper quarter of the town (so far preserved from enemy action) people were talking of the betrayal of Augusta. Everyone was overcome with alarm and misgivings, even the soldiers. Meanwhile the aerial bombardment began again, overtaking us just as we were on our way to Punta del Faro to try and get more accurate news from the Germans. Halfway there, in open country, we saw at least four terrific raids on Messina, Villa San Giovanni and Reggio. One might say that we saw what was left of Messina destroyed under our very eyes. The fire of the A.A. guns was terrific, but their aim was inaccurate. We saw a few aircraft hit. At the sight of bands of soldiers (and, more especially, airmen and sailors, in rags, who were straggling in disorderly fashion towards the German ferries, we decided to cross the Straits, it being impossible either to go on or to turn back. The spectacle at Scilla and Bagnara railway stations was even more lamentable. Crowds of civilians and hordes of soldiers were storming the passenger trains and ferries. Sailors, airmen and soldiers, some from Augusta, some from Catania, some from Riposto and some from Messina, apparently driven by hunger and fatigue, jostled each other, shouted and swore.

[1] Mussolini, in his own account, takes care to make his readers forget that the morale of the people was the specific concern of the Party ; that at his orders an intensive propaganda campaign to raise morale had started in the weeks preceding the invasion ; and that the campaign had utterly failed.

There was an atmosphere of defeat. Whether at Messina or on the Calabrian coast, even the officers, who ignored the soldiers' cursing, did not seem of a very different frame of mind."

Inadequacy of the Staff

Thus far the high official of the Ministry of Popular Culture. Here is another eye-witness account by the editor of a Palermo daily paper:

"Despite two years of preparation, the Enna Command which occupied the central and highest point of the island was not equipped to withstand even an ordinary air-raid. The Enna Command left the city immediately after its first and only air-raid. Such a fact, together with its wanderings about the triangle of the Peloritani mountains, must have created a confusion the effects of which on the unity of our troops and the organisation of war services have certainly been deleterious.

"In the same region we had a feeling of military disaster because there were plain signs of the formations crumpling up, that is, of marines and airmen straggling towards Messina to re-embark and get back to the mainland. The case of Augusta which would not put up a defence, the case of certain divisions which melted quietly away without fighting, had their *raison d'être* in the inadequate organisation of the different Commands. The conduct of the *Bersaglieri* and the Gela coastal division was well spoken of. On the other hand, the case of the air and naval formations which dissolved instantly at the mere sight of the enemy forces had a devastating effect."

A third account of Augusta was given by a Party Inspector sent to Sicily, who said à propos of certain salvage operations:

"It is a fact, first, that the base of Augusta was blown up twenty-four hours before the first Englishman came in sight of the fortress, and second, that before the arrival of the English at Augusta the scattered sailors and airmen of this fortress had already arrived at Messina."

Here is another account, this time by the Chief of Police at Catania, who telephoned: "One can see long trails of scattered and famished Italian soldiers approaching the country round Etna, spreading panic and terror everywhere. The population fears an outbreak of dangerous brigandage."

Perfunctory and Half-hearted Resistance

The world press seemed surprised by the scant opposition offered the enemy landing. Bearing in mind that this is an enemy source, here is what *The Times* wrote in one of its leaders :

"The Axis armies in Sicily continue to crumble away under the Allied blows. Before the invasion it was natural to expect that the Italian troops, who had fought, if anything, with increasing stubbornness as the Tunisian campaign went against them, would redouble their determination when it came to defending the soil of their native land. That has not been the experience.[1] Perhaps the Italian troops[1] see little point in fighting to preserve their country for domination by Germans, perhaps the long-standing unpopularity of Fascism in Sicily has had its effect, not only on the population but also on the minds of the garrison destined to defend the island[2] as well as of the people ; at any rate, the resistance of a great part of the defending force has from the first been perfunctory and half-hearted. Especially on the extreme left of the Allied advance the Americans have reported a general readiness to surrender ; they have collected thousands of prisoners with very little fighting, and such difficulties as they have encountered in the later stages of their advance have been rather due to the ruggedness of the country than to any resistance by the enemy. In the sector where[3] the invaders have struck deep into the heart of the island, a more resolute attempt has been made to bar their way, since they were approaching the important rail and road junctions of Enna, the node of the communications of all the southern part of Sicily. On the 21st,[4] however, this important key city was evacuated by the Italians, and immediately occupied by the Canadians and Americans ; they have pushed on over the mountain ridge, which forms the backbone of the island, and now have only forty miles, though over difficult country, to traverse before reaching the northern shore.

"Some of the defeated Italian troops in these western and central sectors are complacently waiting to be rounded up into the allied prison camps."

[1] The original adds "in Sicily."

[2] The original omits "destined to defend the island."

[3] "In the sector where"; the original has "further to the east where."

[4] "On the 21st"; the original has " Yesterday."

Only a week later the game in Sicily was as good as over. Among many contradictory opinions, there was one which was unanimously held by both officers and men, civilians and soldiers, namely, that everywhere, and particularly in the plain of Catania, the Germans had fought with great valour.

CHAPTER VI

FROM THE FELTRE MEETING TO THE NIGHT OF THE GRAND COUNCIL

THE MILITARY CRISIS COULD NOT but be accompanied by a political crisis compromising the Régime both in its head and in its whole system. History—above all, modern history—has shown that a régime never falls for internal reasons. Moral questions, economic distress, party struggles never place a régime in jeopardy. These are questions which never embrace the whole population, but only limited sections of it.

A régime, whatever régime it may be, falls only under the weight of defeat. The Second Empire crumbled after Sedan; the empires of the Hapsburgs, the Hohenzollerns and the Romanoffs fell after the defeat of the 1915–18 war; the democratic Third Republic waned in 1940 after the Pétain armistice. The Italian monarchy and its accomplices had therefore but one aim—to bring about the ruin of Fascism through defeat in war.

The King Behind the Plot

The King was behind this plot because he had reason to believe that a victory won or snatched from defeat by Fascism would make him more insignificant than ever. For twenty years he had been awaiting a good opportunity. He was waiting until a certain national frame of mind had been reached, a popular and universal emotion which at a given moment would flare up at a word.

With the advent of Scorza, the Party planned to take the situation in hand again.[1] They made a good beginning. The

[1] Scorza's appointment was accompanied by ruthless measures of suppression and a wave of arrests of potential enemies of the régime, as well as

directive was to "call forth" the Royal House from the non-committal and ambiguous shade in which it had been lurking, and to gain for the Party the support of the Church. All this was bound up with a comb-out of the ranks, certain reforms of a social nature, and the regular rotation of men in political and military offices—a work which should have been undertaken during a period of relative tranquillity, whereas the events of war were constantly interrupting it.[1]

Prior to the attack on Sicily, the Party Secretary had arranged a series of regional rallies at which the most important members of the Party were to have spoken. It is well known that Grandi refused to speak and resisted all appeals to do so.[2] Scorza wanted to punish him for this "refusal of obedience," but he later agreed that it was not worth the trouble of bringing up the "Grandi case" at this time. Grandi's defection was symptomatic. Nevertheless, after a radio speech made by Scorza on the evening of July 18th, Grandi sent him from Bologna a telegram of congratulations on the speech in which he detected, as he said, "the impassioned accents of the great men of the Risorgimento." Grandi had shown equal enthusiasm after a speech made by Scorza at the Adriano Theatre on May 5th. Grandi, in the regulation black Saharan uniform,[3] was among the hierarchs who accompanied Scorza to the Palazzo Venezia from the balcony of which I was to speak (for the last time!) to the people of Rome.

Grandi's Attitude

Grandi seemed moved and cried out: "What a speech! The very spirit of our dawn! We feel as if we had been reborn."

by a purge of the National Directorate of the Fascist Party. It was a last attempt to cope with the crisis which had been developing since the time when an early victorious end of the war began to appear out of the question.

[1] Mussolini conceals that the address presented to him by Scorza on behalf of the Party Directorate on June 14th, calling for drastic social and economic reforms which should have been put in practice years before, implied a strong criticism of his own conduct of affairs and was, in fact, generally interpreted as such.

[2] These meetings were to be held from 12th–18th July in the principal cities, with the object of arousing patriotic fervour and a spirit of national unity. Each was to be presided over by some leading Fascist. Grandi, who had been chosen with twelve other speakers, replied that he considered the plan ill-advised.

[3] This was the Fascist full-dress black uniform.

A large crowd filled the square to listen to the few words I pronounced ; but the warmth of their demonstrations was very much below that of former times ; it was—if one may say so—a rather worried enthusiasm. After the attack on Sicily had started there was no longer any question of organising the regional rallies which had been planned. In any case, one would have had to await the outcome of military operations at least in their first phase. Nevertheless, the twelve speakers had been convened to Rome ; they had met several times in the Piazza Colonna in the offices of the Party Secretary, who at one point asked me to receive them. This meeting took place about 8 p.m. on July 16th.[1] Together with the Party Secretary, Farinacci, De Bono, Giuriati, Teruzzi, Bottai, Acerbo and De Cicco were present. I did not welcome this meeting much, as I did not care for meetings not prepared in advance with a regular agenda.

The following spoke : De Bono, who asked for details of the course of operations in Sicily ; Farinacci, who pressed insistently for a convocation of the Grand Council as almost an absolute necessity to enable everyone to make himself heard ; Bottai, who stressed the same subject, "not"—he said—"in order to evade our separate responsibilities but to assume them in full" ; Giuriati, who made a harangue of a constitutional nature which he amplified in a long letter the next day ; Scorza, who stressed the necessity of changing the men in command and replacing them with some of his own candidates (who later on showed a basely treacherous spirit) ; all of them, or nearly all, insisted on the necessity of convening the Grand Council, if only to enable me to inform the members of the highest assembly in the Régime of certain facts which could not be given to the general public.

At the end of this discussion which, not having been prepared, revealed nothing but a sceptical frame of mind all round, I announced that I would convene the Grand Council in the second half of the month.

Once my decision was known, political tension increased in

[1] The high Party officials who were to have presided at the regional rallies met instead in Rome at the Palazzo Wedekind, in order to impress on Scorza the need of obtaining from Mussolini a true picture of the grave war situation. Scorza's request for an interview came under the immediate impact of the news of the loss of Augusta and the gloomy communiqués Nos. 1144 and 1145, published in the papers of July 14th and 15th. The explanatory *pro memoria* No. 28 supplied by Naval Headquarters on the 15th (see Chapter V, page 42) was intended for use by Mussolini in replying to criticism by the Party hierarchs.

political and Fascist circles. Some have mocked at the existence of such circles. But they do exist. They are those hundreds (or, in the capital, those thousands) of persons who live in the shadow of government activity. Each of them forms the centre of a constellation. The general frame of mind of these constellations represents at certain moments the frame of mind of the whole town and hence, in little, that of the nation. The coming and going of the hierarchs in the Piazza Colonna was incessant. Everyone was asking himself the question: "What will the Grand Council decide on—peace or war?" For by now a spirit of weariness, a spirit of capitulation, was making headway among the weaker souls, and the steadily worse news from Sicily only increased that spirit.

In the late afternoon of Sunday the 18th, I left by air for Riccione,[1] where I listened to a speech by Scorza, excellent in content but not corroborated by his tone of voice. On the morning of the 19th I left by air for Treviso, where I arrived at 8.30 a.m. At 9 a.m. Field-Marshal Keitel arrived and, a few minutes later, the Führer.

The Feltre Meeting

The meeting was as usual cordial,[2] but the entourage—the attitude of the higher air force officers and of the troops—was chilly. As the Führer had to return to Germany the same afternoon the time had to be used to the best advantage. The talk could have taken place at Treviso itself in the local Headquarters of the airport or in the Prefecture, instead of at Feltre (a three-hour journey there and back). But by now the regular routine of the ceremonial had been fixed and no power on earth could have altered it.[3]

The Führer, myself and our staffs did an hour's journey by train. After another hour by car we reached the Villa Gaggià. There was a most beautiful, cool, shady park; and a labyrinthine building which some people found almost uncanny. It

[1] Seat of one of Mussolini's country villas, some ten miles south of Rimini.

[2] Even the official communiqués omit the usual reference to cordiality. Many reports speak of Mussolini's discomfiture.

[3] The shortness of Hitler's stay was obviously unexpected by Mussolini; preparations to meet near Feltre at the Villa Gaggià, two hours' journey from the airport at Treviso, pointed to the usual conference of at least two days. But Hitler had come with his mind made up ready to dictate his terms. Mussolini saves his face by throwing the blame for the now awkward arrangements on the department in charge of the ceremonial.

was like a crossword puzzle frozen into a house. After a few moments' rest the talk began ; the Führer, myself, Under-Secretary Bastianini, the ambassadors von Mackensen and Alfieri, the Italian Chief of General Staff Ambrosio, Marshal Keitel, General Rintelen, General Warlimont, Colonel Montezemolo and others less important were present. It was 11 a.m. when the Führer began to speak. He began his speech with a clear and systematic résumé of the raw material situation and the necessity for defending the territories where they were to be found. He went on to speak of the air force, its employment and its present and future possibilities. Passing to the battle now being fought in Sicily he promised the despatch of fresh reinforcements, particularly artillery and troops.[1]

The Führer had been speaking for half an hour when an official entered the room. He was pale and agitated. He begged pardon for interrupting. He came up to me and said : "At this moment Rome is undergoing a violent enemy air bombardment."[2] This news, which I myself conveyed aloud to the Führer and bystanders, made a deep and painful impression. During the rest of the Führer's résumé, news of the attack on Rome continued to come in. Then a talk took place between myself and Hitler in which I stressed the necessity of sending further aid to Italy. This talk continued on the return journey in the car and train. On parting from Hitler I said to him : "Ours is a common cause, Führer ! "

The Bombardment of Rome

It was 5 p.m. when the Führer's aeroplane took off from the Treviso airfield. Half an hour later my machine took off, direct for Rome. Even before we passed over Mount Soracte, Rome seemed to the crew of my aeroplane to be enveloped in a huge black cloud. It was the smoke rising from hundreds of waggons on fire in the Littorio railway station. The workshops of the

[1] In this way, Mussolini glosses over Hitler's refusal to send what was most required, viz., aircraft and tanks. Nor does he mention the number of troops promised or the conditions on which their despatch was made dependent. That the help granted was unsatisfactory is evident from Mussolini's own account in the next paragraph. See also his statement to Maugeri, below, p. 218.

[2] The daylight raid on Rome began between 11 a.m. and noon on July 19th and continued for two and a half hours, the objectives being the airport of Littorio, north-west of Rome, and the marshalling yards of San Lorenzo, on the north-eastern edge of the city.

airport were destroyed. The airfield, pitted with bomb craters, was unusable. Flying over Rome from Littorio to Centocelle, one received the distinct impression that the attack had been heavy and the damage enormous.

A few high officials awaited me at the airport. Getting into my car I drove towards the Villa Torlonia. Meanwhile in the streets a multitude of men, women and children, in cars, on bicycles or on foot, and with all sorts of domestic 'impedimenta,' was making its way towards the suburbs and the countryside; a multitude—or rather a torrent.

One more illusion had vanished in smoke, namely, that Rome, the Holy City, would never be raided. That the best anti-aircraft artillery was the Vatican itself, that Myron Taylor had brought the Pope a guarantee to that effect from the American President, and other things of that nature—hopes, desires—all of that had been wiped out by a brutal bombardment which had lasted nearly three hours, had caused thousands of victims and destroyed whole quarters of the city.

When the King went to visit the damaged areas he was not stoned, as people have said, but the crowd remained silent and hostile at his passing.

The next day I went to visit the Littorio station and airport as also the University and (in the same afternoon) the airports of Ciampino, and I was received everywhere with demonstrations of sympathy.

The Last Talk with the King

On the Wednesday morning I went to the King to report on the Feltre talks.

As I told an intimate friend, I found the King frowning and nervous. "A tense situation," he said. "It can't go on much longer. Sicily has gone west now. The Germans will double-cross us. The discipline of the troops has broken down. The airmen at Ciampino fled as far as Velletri[1] during the attack. They call it 'dispersing.' I followed the attack the other day from the Villa Ada over which the waves of planes passed. I don't think there were 400 aircraft as they said. There were half that number. The 'Holy City' legend is over. We must tell the Germans our dilemma . . ."

[1] A distance of about 10 miles.

That was the gist of the talk. It was the last. The last of a long series. From November 1922, I had gone regularly twice a week to the Quirinal, on Mondays and Thursdays. I went there at 10.30 in civilian clothes and a bowler. Besides these bi-weekly talks many others took place for various reasons—almost every day during the summer military manœuvres. I never went to San Rossore. I was once his guest at the Villa Ada in Rome to attend after dinner at the showing of a film of the King's voyage in Somaliland. I once went to Sant' Anna di Valdieri and once to Racconigi for a wedding, and finally to report on the negotiations which led to the Reconciliation with the Vatican.

The King was once my guest at Rocca delle Caminate after the conquest of the Empire. Our relations were always cordial but never friendly. There was always something between us which prevented our reaching a relationship of real confidence. During the various wars, the King was only a passenger and vacillated perpetually. He was less so in the 1940 war, when he not only raised no objections of any sort but considered the war against France and Great Britain a necessary decision. As the war went on, this attitude changed.

Preparations for the Grand Council Meeting

On Wednesday at noon, the hour of the usual report, the Party Secretary Scorza presented me with a motion which Grandi and others proposed to present to the Grand Council. I read the document (a pretty long one of more than three pages) and handed it back to Scorza declaring that the document was inadmissible and contemptible. Scorza put it back in his briefcase and did not insist further. It was on that occasion that Scorza made me a rather ambiguous speech in which he spoke of a "shocker" or rather "super-shocker" which might be in store, a speech to which I did not attribute great importance. In the afternoon I received Grandi, who gave me a volume containing the minutes of the meetings in London of the Committee of Non-Intervention in the Spanish Civil War. Grandi touched on various points but said nothing of what was to come.

The following day[1]—Thursday—Scorza once more stressed the

[1] In the first edition, this paragraph is preceded by a new sub-heading, "The Evening of July 24th." It has been omitted as the end of the chapter deals, in fact, with events from July 22nd to the afternoon of July 24th.

possibility of a "shocker," or rather a "super-shocker," but as he gave no further details I had the impression that it was merely a matter of one of the usual outcries over the changes in the Command and the Government.

There was much coming and going in the Piazza Colonna on Thursday and Friday. At a certain point, Grandi put forward the idea of postponing the Grand Council—a clever move to look like an alibi. Scorza telephoned to know if this were a possibility. I replied that it was now absolutely essential to reach a general clarification of the position. The date had been fixed. The invitations had been issued. Of all the constitutional organs the convening of which was envisaged that week, the Chamber or the Senate, the Grand Council was the most suitable for reviewing the problems of war in the light of recent events such as the invasion of national soil.

The nervous tension became more and more acute. On the afternoon of Saturday, July 24th, Rome turned pale. Cities as well as men have a face, and the emotions of the soul are reflected on that face. Rome felt that something serious was in the air. The cars which brought the members of the Grand Council were not parked in the square but jammed into the courtyard. Even the musketeers were relieved of their usual office of guarding the Palazzo during this meeting[1]. They had discharged this task excellently over a number of years.

[1] This is said to have been a precautionary measure ordered by Albini to prevent any move by Mussolini to arrest the members of the Council by the musketeers who were his personal bodyguard and wholly devoted. Albini had further filled the Palazzo Venezia with armed police in case of an attack by the Fascist Militia.

CHAPTER VII

THE GRAND COUNCIL MEETS

I INTENDED THE MEETING to be a confidential one in which everyone would have the chance of asking for explanations and receiving them ; a sort of secret committee. In expectation of a long discussion, the Grand Council was convened for 5 p.m. instead of the usual hour of 10 p.m.

All the members of the Grand Council were in black Saharan uniform. The session started promptly at five o'clock. I asked Scorza to call the roll of those present. No one was missing. Then I began my résumé, a pile of documents on the table before me. The essential points of my discourse, which were taken down by one of the listeners, were as follows :[1]

"The war," I said, "has reached an extremely critical stage. What seemed impossible (and indeed was thought by some to be an absurd hypothesis), even after the entry of the United States into the Mediterranean, has come to pass—the invasion of our home territory. From this point of view, one may say that the real war began with the loss of Pantelleria. The peripheral war on the African coast was intended to avert or frustrate such an eventuality. In a situation like this, all official or unofficial trends of opinion openly or clandestinely hostile to the Régime make common cause against us, and they have already provoked symptoms of demoralisation even among the ranks of Fascism, particularly among the 'vested interests,' that is, among those who see their own personal positions threatened. At this moment," I said, "I am certainly the most intensely disliked or, rather, loathed man in Italy, which is only natural on

[1] For Mussolini's garbled version of the proceedings at the Grand Council meeting see below, p. 61.

the part of the ignorant, suffering, victimised, under-nourished masses subjected to the terrible physical and moral burden of the 'Liberator' raids and to the suggestions of enemy propaganda. Political and military circles aim their sharpest criticisms at those who bear the responsibility for the military conduct of the war. Let it be said once and for all that I did not in the least desire the delegation of Command of the Armed Forces in the Field given to me by the King on June 10th. That initiative belongs to Marshal Badoglio."

The Command of the Armed Forces in the Field

"Here is one of his letters, dated May 3rd, 1940, protocol No. 5372.

SUBJECT: ORGANISATION OF THE COMMAND.

To the Duce of Fascism, Head of the Government.

In my letter dated April 15*th last, No.* 5318, *I had the honour of calling your attention to the absolute necessity of arriving at an organisation of the Command which would assign the tasks and respective responsibilities of the various military hierarchies. At a meeting held in your office on that same day, the* 15*th, you, Duce, told me verbally that sometime during the week this very important question would be settled. As I have so far heard nothing further on this subject, I take the liberty, Duce, of giving you my exact views on the matter in greater detail.*

"Of the French and German solutions of the problem, Badoglio preferred the latter, which had been applied during the 1915–18 war, that is:—Commander-in-Chief (purely nominal) the King; Chief of General Staff, the actual commander of the Army.

"Badoglio's letter continued thus:

After the war we were the first to recognise the need of a single direction of the armed forces. The office of Chief of General Staff was therefore created, but his duties definitely applied only to times of peace and not in the event of war. Now it is indispensable for us to arrive at this organization and immediately to determine—since the present situation does not admit of delay—the respective competences and consequent responsibilities.

Badoglio's "Boundless" Devotion to Me

"Badoglio preferred the German solution of the problem because with his confirmation as Chief of General Staff his functions would remain 'of prime importance.' And he concluded: *I thought it my strict duty to put forward these considerations with all frankness, as I have always done with you, Duce. It was certainly no feeling of pride which actuated me, only a justifiable regard for the name which, by so much work and so many sacrifices, I have acquired during the Great War, in Libya and in the Ethiopian campaign. If I have any pride, it is in having always served you faithfully and with boundless devotion, Duce.*

"On June 4th, that is, six days before the declaration of war, Badoglio issued the following circular (No. 5569) to all Chiefs of Staff, Colonial Governors and the Minister for Foreign Affairs.

SUBJECT: CONSTITUTION AND FUNCTION OF THE SUPREME COMMAND OF THE ARMED FORCES IN THE EVENT OF WAR.

Some clarification and definition is necessary with regard to the constitution and function of the Supreme Command of the Armed Forces in the event of war.

1. *Supreme Commander in war and of all the Armed Forces*[1] *wherever stationed, the Duce, in the name of H.M. the King.*
2. *The Duce exercises this command through the Chief of General Staff who has his own general staff. The main functions of the Chief of General Staff are:*
   (a) *To keep the Duce informed of the general picture of the military situation of the armed forces and of their possibilities of action in relation to the enemy's position. In consequence, to receive orders and general directives for the conduct of operations;*
   (b) *to inform the Chiefs of Staff of the various Services of consequent orders and directives for the development of the said operations in the strategic field;*
   (c) *to follow the course of operations, intervening should the necessity arise, particularly to ensure co-ordination and the timely employment of each Service.*

"After defining the tasks of each Chief of Staff, the circular ended as follows:

The organisation of the Supreme Command of the Italian Armed

[1] The translation follows Mussolini's text as found in both editions: "Supreme Commander *in war* (*di guerra*) and of all the Armed Forces." In fact the document, as reproduced in the Documentary Notes attached to the second edition, has "Supreme Commander of the Armed Forces, *individually* (*di ognuna*) and collectively." (See below, page 75.)

Forces, differing from any other, rests upon these principles[1]*:* (a) *a single and totalitarian conception of the command personally exercised by the Duce, by delegation of the King;* (b) *strategic conduct of the war and co-ordination of action between the various Services and between the various sectors of the operations, exercised according to and on the orders of the Duce, by the Chief of General Staff;* (c) *exercise of command over the various Services stationed at home or overseas, carried out by the Chief of Staff or the commanders-in-chief of the Services;* (d) *absolute devotion and obedience to the Duce and absolute unity of thought and action on the part of everyone, in keeping with Fascist style and tradition.*

"This is how things stand. I have never technically directed military operations. It was not my job. Only once—in Cavallero's absence—did I take the place of the technical Chiefs of Staff, and that was on the occasion of the air and sea battle on June 15th, 1942, which took place in the waters of Pantelleria. That decisive victory was due to me, as was acknowledged at an important review of the officers of the 7th Naval Division in Naples by the Chief of Naval Staff himself, Admiral of the Fleet Riccardi, before I decorated the officers and crews who had specially distinguished themselves in that battle, during which Great Britain 'for the first time felt the teeth of the Roman Wolf sink into her flesh.'[2]

"When I fell ill in October, 1942, I contemplated giving up my military command, but I did not do so because it seemed to me unseemly to abandon the ship in the midst of a tempest. I postponed doing so until after a 'sunny day,' which has not so far appeared. I think there is nothing further to be said on the question of the command.

Germany's Aid

"In some circles Germany's aid has been called into question. Well, we must admit in all fairness that Germany has met us generously and substantially. On purpose for this meeting I

[1] The text of this document as published in the second edition reads: "The organisation of the Supreme Command . . . rests, in other words (*in altri termini*), upon these principles." (See below, page 77.)

[2] Compare with these fanciful claims the British account of this action contained in a joint announcement by the Admiralty and Air Ministry (*The Times*, June 17th, 1942): "The Royal Navy and the Merchant

had asked the competent Ministry for a list of Germany's effective contribution of the principal raw materials in 1940, 1941, 1942 and the first six months of 1943. The total was imposing: coal, 40,000,000 tons; metals, 2,500,000 tons; synthetic rubber, 22,000 tons; aviation spirit, 220,000 tons; petrol, 421,000 tons. It is unnecessary to quote the minor contributions of vital metals such as nickel.

"After the heavy bombardments had begun on Milan, Genoa, and Turin (October, 1942) the Führer was asked to contribute to anti-aircraft defence. The request was granted. According to data submitted by General Balocco, Secretary of the Supreme Commission of Defence, German pieces of artillery numbered no fewer than 1,500 on April 1st, 1943. That therefore gives the lie to the thesis of the defeatists, according to which the Germans had not given Italy the necessary help.[1]

"Another point of the capitulationists is that 'the people's heart is not in the war.' Now the people's heart is never in any war. Not even in those of the Risorgimento, as can be proved by unimpeachable documents. We need not disturb those great shades; let us remember more recent events. Was the people's heart in the 1915–18 war, by any chance? Not in the least. The people were dragged into the war by a minority which succeeded in winning over three cities—Milan, Genoa and Rome—and some minor towns such as Parma. Three men launched the movement—Corridoni, d'Annunzio and myself. Even then there was no sort of 'sacred unity.'

"The country was divided into neutralists and interventionists, and this division continued even after Caporetto. Was the people's heart in a war which produced 535,000 deserters in the country? The 'people's heart' seems to have been far less in

Navy, with the co-operation of the R.A.F. and the United States Army Air Corps, have delivered supplies to the garrisons in Malta and Tobruk. The operations have been carried through in the face of very heavy attacks by superior enemy naval forces and air forces, and were not completed without loss. Fantastic enemy claims to have sunk cruisers and to have damaged a battleship and an aircraft carrier are without foundation. Loss and damage have also been inflicted upon the enemy by H.M. ships, naval aircraft, the R.A.F., and the United States Army Air Corps. One 10,000-ton 8-in. gun cruiser of the Trento class has been sunk and at least two destroyers have been sunk, and heavy losses have been imposed upon the enemy air forces."

[1] While dwelling on Germany's help in the past, Mussolini says nothing of his reply to the questions which mattered most to his audience: What help could Italy expect now and in the immediate future as a result of the Feltre meeting? On what conditions was such help made dependent?

that than in the present one. The truth is that no war is ever 'popular' when it starts, and it is easy to see why; it becomes popular if it goes well, and if it goes badly it becomes extremely unpopular. Even the war for the conquest of Abyssinia became popular only after the victory of Mai Ceu.[1] There is therefore no need to be overcome by these psychological fluctuations, even if, as in the present stage of the war, they are profound. The masses are disciplined, and that is the essential thing."

I continued as follows:

"War is always a party war, a war of the party which desired it; it is always one man's war, the war of the man who declared it; if today this is called Mussolini's war, in 1859 it could have been called Cavour's war. This is the moment to tighten the reins and to assume the necessary responsibility. I shall have no difficulty in replacing men, in turning the screw, in bringing forces to bear not yet engaged, in the name of our country whose territorial integrity is today being violated. In 1917, some provinces of the Veneto were lost but no one spoke of 'surrender.' Then, they spoke of moving the Government to Sicily: today, if we must, we shall move it to the Po Valley.

Gentlemen, Beware!

"Now Grandi's motion calls upon the Crown: his is an appeal not so much to the Government as to the King. Well, there are two alternatives. The King might make the following speech to me: 'Dear Mussolini, things haven't gone exactly well lately, but a difficult phase of the war may be followed by a better one; you have begun, carry on.' The King might also, which is more likely, say this instead: 'So, gentlemen of the Régime, now that you are in it up to your necks, you remember that a certain Statute exists: that in that Statute there is a certain

[1] The engagement of Mai Ceu, March 31st, 1936, was the last offensive action undertaken by the Emperor of Abyssinia and resulted in an Italian success. Checked and thrown back, the Emperor's armies were counter-attacked on April 2nd and finally scattered on April 4th. In the account of Mussolini's speech given in *Italia Nuova*, the Rome Monarchist paper, on July 9th, 1944, he says something quite different. "Even the Ethiopian campaign which seemed inspired by popular fury, had its period of defeatism after the ambush of Dembeguinà." The action at Dembeguinà took place between December 15th–17th, 1935, and resulted in an Abyssinian victory, the Italians being forced to retire with many losses.

Article 5[1]: that as well as that Statute, there is a King: well, I myself, accused of having broken the Statute of the Realm for twenty years, I shall step into the limelight and shall accept your invitation, but since I consider you responsible for the situation, I shall profit by your strategem and liquidate you at one blow.'

"Reactionary and anti-Fascist circles, the elements devoted to the Anglo-Saxons, will press for the latter. Gentlemen," I concluded, "beware! Grandi's motion may place the very existence of the Régime in jeopardy."

These were the essential points in my speech as the listener took them down. The discussion was then opened. Marshal De Bono began, and defended the army against the accusations levelled at it of 'sabotaging' the war.

The *quadrumvir*[2] De Vecchi did not agree with De Bono's view. A few days earlier he had suddenly moved heaven and earth to get a military command, and had obtained one of a coastal division between Civitavecchia and Orbetello. De Vecchi affirmed that many officers, generals and others, were tired, defeatist or worse, and exercised a deleterious influence on the morale of the troops.

Grandi's Attack

Then Grandi rose to speak. His speech was a violent philippic: the speech of a man who was at last giving vent to a long-cherished rancour. He bitterly criticised the activity of the Party, particularly during Starace's administration (of which he had been an enthusiastic supporter) and also declared himself disappointed in Scorza, though he had made a promising beginning. "My

[1] The *Statuto del Regno* or Constitution of the Kingdom, originally of Sardinia and later of Italy, was promulgated on March 4th, 1848, by King Charles Albert and forms the fundamental constitutional law of Italy. The important Article 5 runs as follows: "To the King alone appertains Executive Power. He is the Supreme Head of the State; he commands all the Armed Forces on land and sea; he declares war, makes treaties of peace and alliance, of commerce and others, announcing them to the Chambers of Parliament so soon as the interests and safety of the State permit, together with the relevant information. Treaties which involve a financial burden or modifications in the territory of the State shall not take effect until they have received the assent of the Chambers."

[2] Designation of the four Fascist chiefs (De Vecchi, De Bono, Balbo, Bianchi) who led the 'March on Rome' on October 28th, 1922, while Mussolini was waiting in Milan.

motion,"[1] he said, "would tend towards the creation of a 'national home front' which has not existed so far, and which has not existed because the Crown in Italy has held aloof in an attitude of prudent reserve. It is high time for the King to emerge from obscurity and assume his responsibilities. After Caporetto he took up position and launched an appeal to the nation. Today he is silent. Either he assumes his share of historical responsibility, in which case he has the right to remain Head of the State, or else he does not, in which case he will show how much the dynasty is worth."

The purport of this dilemma—previously agreed upon with Court circles—was evident. Grandi's speech aroused a feeling of uneasiness in the members of the Grand Council. Count Ciano followed him, recapitulating the diplomatic history of the war in order to show that Italy had not caused the war but had done the impossible to avoid it. He ended by declaring himself in agreement with Grandi's motion.

Grandi's criticisms, inspired by the blackest defeatism, were answered by General Galbiati, who, as a soldier and old Blackshirt, made a lyrical rather than a political speech. Roberto Farinacci explained his motion and asked the Grand Council to summon General Ambrosio to report. The proposal was not followed up.

Then the President of the Senate, Suardo, spoke. He remarked that he was not quite clear about Grandi's motion, especially after the speech in which it had been explained ; and he declared that if no more light was thrown upon it he would abstain from voting.

The Minister of Justice, De Marsico, asked and received permission to speak, and let off one of his usual dialectical firework displays on the constitutionalism or not of Grandi's motion. Bottai made a speech fervently supporting Grandi's suggestions, while Biggini spoke against Grandi.

At midnight Scorza proposed adjourning the session till the next day, but Grandi leaped to his feet, shouting, "No ! I am against the proposal. We have started this business and we must finish it this very night ! " I was of the same opinion. I adjourned the sitting for a quarter of an hour, however, and

[1] Mussolini never explains and only lets it be inferred that there were three motions on the Table : Grandi's, Farinacci's and Scorza's. Nevertheless, in the second edition of his book he publishes all three *in extenso*. (See below, pp. 65-67.)

retired to my study to read the latest telegrams which had arrived during the evening from the battle areas.

When the session reopened, the following spoke: Bignardi, who touched on the morale of the rural community; Frattari, on the same subject; Federzoni, who mentioned the problem of wars which did not have the " people's heart in them "; and Bastianini, who took up the same subject, hotly criticising the propaganda issued during the war by the appropriate Ministry, and, after deploring the fact that instructions had been given designed to weaken the memory of the Piave victory[1], had a squabble with the Minister Polverelli, the only moment when voices were raised above normal.

The Vote: " You Have Caused the Crisis of the Régime "

Bottai spoke again, still more excitedly, followed by Cianetti. The Party Secretary, Scorza, then began to speak, explaining his motion which was not unlike Grandi's. Scorza defended the Party against Grandi's accusations, attacked the Staffs, and ended by affirming that the Party, purged of its dross, would represent the core of a united national front. After Scorza's motion had been read, Count Ciano rose to say that any mention of the Vatican would not be welcomed on the other side of the Bronze Door.[2]

The discussion, lasting nearly ten hours, took place in an exceedingly tense atmosphere but without the smallest incident of a personal nature.

All that was said in that connection—about free fights or revolver threats—belongs to the realm of shocker stories. The discussion was orderly and civilized. It never got out of hand. In fact, every time the speakers flattered me, I interrupted them and asked them not to labour the point.

The position of each member of the Grand Council could be discerned even before the voting: there was a group of traitors

[1] The Ministry of Popular Culture had forbidden the newspapers to whip up enthusiasm by recalling Italian resistance during the Risorgimento, or on the Piave during the First World War (the enemy in those days being Austria). The text of an explicit order to this effect, issued on July 10th, is found in Claudio Matteini, *Ordini alla Stampa*, Rome 1945, p. 251. This provoked resentment among some Fascists such as Grandi.

[2] The Bronze Door, *Portone di Bronzo* (at the end of the colonnade on the right-hand side of the Piazza di San Pietro) is the chief entrance to the Vatican Palace. Count Ciano at the time was Italian Ambassador to the Holy See.

who had already negotiated with the Crown, a group of accomplices, and a group of uninformed who probably did not realise the seriousness of the vote. But they voted just the same !

The Party Secretary read Grandi's motion and called the names of those present. Nineteen replied Yes—seven replied No.[1] Two abstained, Suardo and Farinacci, who voted for his own motion.

I rose and said: "You have provoked a crisis of the Régime. The Session is closed."

The Party Secretary was going to give the "Salute to the Duce" when I checked him with a gesture, saying, "No, you are excused."

They all went away in silence. It was 2.40 a.m. on July 25th. I retired to my study where I was shortly afterwards joined by the group of members of the Grand Council who had voted against Grandi's motion. It was 3 a.m. when I left the Palazzo Venezia. Scorza accompanied me as far as the Villa Torlonia.[2] The streets were deserted, but in the air, already almost light as dawn was breaking, there seemed to be a feeling of that inevitability which the wheel of Fate gives when it is once in motion, Fate, of which men are often the unconscious tools.

During that night, which will be remembered as the "Night of the Grand Council," the discussion had lasted ten hours—one of the longest sessions ever recorded in political annals. Almost everyone spoke, some several times. That the crisis would have come to a head without the session, the discussion and the relative resolution, is highly probable, but history takes no account of hypothetical events which do not come to pass. What did come to pass, came to pass after the session of the Grand Council. The cup may have been full, but it was the proverbial last drop that made it run over.

[1] For the distribution of the votes see below, p. 285.

[2] Villa Torlonia: Mussolini's sumptuous private residence in the Via Nomentana.

APPENDIX OF DOCUMENTS TO CHAPTER VII

I. THE TEXT OF THE THREE MOTIONS

Grandi's Motion

The Grand Council, meeting at this time of great hazard, turns its thoughts first of all to the heroic warriors of every Service who, shoulder to shoulder with the proud people of Sicily, in whom the unanimous faith of the Italian people shines at its brightest, are renewing the noble traditions of hardy valour and undaunted spirit of self-sacrifice of our glorious Armed Forces.

Having examined the internal and international situation and the political and military conduct of the war:

IT PROCLAIMS the duty of all Italians to defend at all costs the unity, independence and liberty of the motherland, the fruits of the sacrifice and labour of four generations, from the Risorgimento down to today, and the life and future of the Italian people.

IT AFFIRMS the necessity for the moral and material unity of all Italians in this grave and decisive hour for the destiny of our country.

IT DECLARES that for this purpose the immediate restoration is necessary of all State functions, allotting to the King, the Grand Council, the Government, Parliament and the Corporations the tasks and responsibilities laid down by our statutory and constitutional laws.

IT INVITES the Head of the Government to request His Majesty the King—towards whom the heart of all the nation turns with faith and confidence—that he may be pleased, for the honour and salvation of the nation, to assume, together with the effective command of the Armed Forces on land, sea and in the air, according to Article 5 of the Statute of the Realm, that supreme initiative of decision which our institutions attribute to him and which, in all our national history, has always been the glorious heritage of our august dynasty of Savoy.

GRANDI.

Farinacci's Motion

The Grand Council of Fascism, having learned the internal and international situation and the political and military conduct of the war on the Axis fronts:

SALUTES proudly and gratefully the heroic Italian Armed Forces and those of our Ally, united in toil and sacrifice in the defence of European civilisation; the people of invaded Sicily, today closer than ever to the heart of our other peoples; the working masses in industry and agriculture who by their labours are strengthening the nation in arms; and the Blackshirts and Fascists in all Italy who are marching in the ranks with immutable loyalty to the Régime.

IT AFFIRMS the sacred duty of all Italians to defend the sacred soil of the motherland to the last, standing fast in the observance of the alliances concluded.

IT DECLARES that the urgent necessity for this purpose is the complete restoration of all State functions, allotting to the King, the Grand Council, the Government, Parliament, the Party and the Corporations the tasks and responsibilities laid down by our Constitution and legislation.

IT INVITES the Head of the Government to request His Majesty the King, towards whom the heart of the whole nation turns with faith and confidence, to be pleased to assume effective command of all the Armed Forces and thus to show the entire world that the whole population is fighting, united under his orders, for the salvation and dignity of Italy.

FARINACCI.

Scorza's Motion

The Fascist Grand Council, convened while the enemy—emboldened by success and rendered arrogant by his riches—is trampling down the soil of Sicily and menacing the Peninsula from the sea and from the air:

AFFIRMS solemnly the vital and incontrovertable necessity of resistance at all costs.

Assured that all organisations and citizens, in the full and conscious responsibility of the hour, will know how to do their duty up to the supreme sacrifice, IT INVOKES all the spiritual and material resources of the nation for the defence of the unity, independence and liberty of the motherland.

Rising to its feet, the Grand Council of Fascism:

SALUTES the cities razed to the ground by enemy fury, and their people, who find in Rome—mother of Catholicism, cradle and repository of the highest civilisations—the most worthy expression of their resolution and discipline.

ITS THOUGHTS TURN with proud emotion to the memory of the Fallen and of their families who are transforming their sorrow into the will to resist and fight.

IT SALUTES in His Majesty the King and in the dynasty of Savoy the symbol and strength of the nation's continuity and the expression of the courage of all our Armed Forces which, together with the valiant German soldiers, are defending the motherland on land, sea and in the air.

IT ASSOCIATES ITSELF reverently with the Pontiff's grief at the destruction of so many famous monuments dedicated for centuries to the cult of Religion and Art.

The Grand Council of Fascism is convinced that the new situation created by the events of the war must be faced by new methods and means.

IT PROCLAIMS, therefore, the urgent necessity of putting these reforms and innovations into effect, in the Government, in the Supreme Command and in the country's internal life, which, through the full functioning of the constitutional organs of the Régime, may bring victory to the united effort of the Italian people.

SCORZA.

II. THE COMMAND OF THE ARMED FORCES IN THE FIELD[1]

The Command of the Armed Forces in the Field was entrusted to me on Badoglio's initiative

In this chapter, in reporting some of the statements I made at the meeting of the Grand Council on July 24th, I wrote: "Let it be said, once and for all, that I did not in the least solicit the

[1] This Appendix of Documents appears for the first time in the second edition. It is inserted in the wrong place after Chapter XIX, which, although it deals with Badoglio, has no mention of the Supreme Command. Mussolini is obviously referring to Chapter VII, *The Grand Council Meets*, where the documents are already quoted in part. In the present translation they have therefore been inserted at the end of this chapter.

mandate of Command of the Armed Forces in the Field, handed over to me by the King on June 10th. The initiative for that belongs to Marshal Badoglio." We are now in a position to publish five "secret" documents which unimpeachably confirm my categoric statement.[1]

1.

Ministry of War,
Cabinet.

Rome,

19th April, 1940—XVIII.

MEMORANDUM FOR THE DUCE

SUPREME COMMAND OF THE ARMED FORCES

Since, present conditions apart, the organisation of the Supreme Command is the indispensable preliminary to the organisation of the High Command of each of the Armed Forces, I put before you, Duce, the following considerations and suggestions:

The organisation consists in the definition of:

functions;
dependence and relationships;
structure.

Functions:

Granted the view that the conduct of the war in all fields (political, economic and military) is concentrated in the hands of the Duce, the Supreme Command is the organ for the employment of the Armed Forces.

This, because it decides the aims, combines them in objectives, assigns these latter to the various Armed Forces, and co-ordinates the operations of the Armed Forces against the objectives themselves.

[1] Mussolini does not mention that, in an address to the Senate on March 30th, 1938, he had explicitly stated: "In Fascist Italy the problem of the unified command, which torments other nations, has been solved. The political and strategic directives for the conduct of the war are laid down by the Head of the Government. Their execution is entrusted to the Chief of the General Staff and the various subordinate bodies. . . . In Italy, at the order of the King, the war will be conducted—as was the case in Africa—by one man alone, by him who speaks to you, should Destiny once more ordain this weighty task to him." (*Scritti e discorsi*, Vol. XI, p. 241, Milan, 1938.)

Dependence and Relationships :

As it is necessary that, at the top, all the authorities should culminate in a *single head*, so it is correspondingly necessary that in the hierarchic scale the executive tasks should be divided according to the unavoidable requirements of work and specialisation, though always remaining in close contact.

The war resolves itself into two fundamental activities :

organisational (which prepares the means),
operational (which employs them),

activities which, in time of peace, are entrusted respectively to the Minister (Under-Secretary) and the Chief of General Staff (study of and preparation for operations).

It appears that such an allocation may continue also in time of war, with the advantage of continuity ; the more so as it is not within the power of the Minister, occupied by organisational work of gigantic dimensions and enormous pressure, to look after the conduct of operations, which, in its turn, requires a knowledge which can be acquired only by long practice and kept up by continual application.

Structure :

I would therefore envisage :

directly below you,

the Chief of General Staff, with the task of issuing, under your orders, directives of an operational character to the various High Commands ;

in a descending scale :

the Ministers (Under-Secretaries), with functions concerning the organisational part, and the Chiefs of Staff, responsible for the conduct of operations ;

Headquarters of the Supreme Command and of the High Commands : Rome.

Subject to your approval, Duce, your sanction on the question would be opportune, so that one might lay down the organisation of the High Commands of each of the Armed Forces, an organisation which, in view of the present situation, I consider particularly urgent.

2. *Chief of General Staff's Office.*
Rome,
3rd May, 1940—XVIII.

No. 5372

SUBJECT: ORGANISATION OF THE COMMAND.

TO THE DUCE OF FASCISM, HEAD OF THE GOVERNMENT, ROME.[1]

In my letter dated April 15th last, No. 5318, I had the honour of calling your attention to the absolute necessity of arriving at an organisation of the Command which would assign the tasks and respective responsibilities of the various military hierarchies.

At a meeting held in your office on that same day, the 15th, you, Duce, told me verbally that sometime during the week this very important question would be settled. As I have so far heard nothing further on this subject, I take the liberty, Duce, of giving you my exact views on the matter in greater detail.

In the comprehensive picture of the present belligerents, two distinct solutions of the question of the Command are to be observed.

1. *The German Solution.*

The Führer has personally assumed command of all the Armed Forces. To exercise that function he has at his disposition a General Staff, with General Keitel at the head.

Each of the Armed Forces has a Commander on its own account,

General Brauchitsch, for the Army,
Admiral Raeder, for the Navy,
Marshal Goering, for the Air Force.

The Führer has the direction, that is, the strategic responsibility; the respective commanders of the Armed Forces have complete and absolute authority over their respective Services, and consequent responsibility for the operations which they direct in obedience to the strategic directives emanating from the Führer.

In that organisation, General Keitel has the normal functions of any Chief of Staff; that is, collection of all manner of intelligence, drafting of orders and possible technical consultation.

[1] Part of this document has been published from the original, taken from Mussolini's *Archivio Segreto*, in *L'Italia Libera*, Rome, March 23rd, 1945. The text is the same as that given by Mussolini.

2. *The French Solution.*

General Gamelin, with the title of Chief of General Staff for National Defence and Commander-in-Chief of the land forces, has, with regard to the whole of the Armed Forces, the power to give strategic directives to the Admiral commanding the naval forces and to the general commanding the Air Force ; and he has, further, direct command of the land forces.

In developing his strategic intentions, however, General Gamelin has first of all to come to an agreement with a War Committee composed of members of the Government.

Although it is to be supposed that, so long as he is kept in office, his strategic intentions prevail over, or coincide with, those of the members of the Committee, it is obvious that his powers are less wide or less free than those exercised by the Führer.

In *our* military organisation in force during the whole of the Great War there were :

Commander-in-Chief (purely nominal) : H.M. the King ;
Chief of Army Staff : the acting commander of the Army and the Air Force ;
Chief of Naval Staff : Commander of the Fleet and the Fleet Air Arm.

After the war we were the first to recognise the need of a single direction of the Armed Forces. The office of Chief of General Staff was therefore created, but his duties definitely applied only to times of peace and not in the event of war. Now it is indispensable for us to arrive at this organisation and to determine immediately—since the present situation does not admit of delay—the respective competences and consequent responsibilities.

If, Duce, you decide on the German type of solution, then we come to the nomination of the Commanders of the respective Armed Forces and, also, of the Chief of General Staff.

I repeat, of the Chief of General Staff also, because I could not accept General Keitel's position, obviously a general of good grounding but without any previous war experience which might have brought him to the fore.

In the present German situation, he plays a somewhat secondary rôle or, at least, one not of the first importance.

But a commander of Badoglio's stature (to use the expression which you were good enough to employ with regard to me) cannot be assigned a task which, though important, is not of the first rank.

I thought it my strict duty to put forward these considerations with all frankness, as I have always done with you, Duce. It was certainly no feeling of pride which actuated me, only a justifiable regard for the name which, by so much work and so many sacrifices, I have acquired during the Great War, in Libya and in the Ethiopian campaign. If I have any pride, it is in having always served you faithfully and with boundless devotion, Duce.

Marshal of Italy,
Chief of General Staff,
signed BADOGLIO.

3.

Ministry of War,
Cabinet.

Rome,
May 10th, 1940—XVIII.

MEMORANDUM TO THE DUCE.

ORGANISATION OF THE SUPREME COMMAND AND OF THE HIGH COMMANDS IN GERMANY, ENGLAND AND FRANCE.

In order to throw more light on the problem of the Supreme Command and of the High Commands, I summarise for you the solutions adopted in this respect by Germany, England and France.

Germany.

The Führer, as Supreme Commander, outlines directives, examines the plans put forward by the various Armed Forces and decides on operations.

The Supreme Command of the Armed Forces is the consultative organ of the Führer ; it does not make plans but is a *possible* channel to ensure co-operation between the Armed Forces, a co-operation which is normally carried out direct.

The Supreme Commands of the Army, Navy and Air Force put into operation the plans approved by the Führer.

England.

The supreme direction and conduct of the war in all fields devolves on the *War Cabinet,* from which derive :

The Standing Committee for Military Co-ordination (Ministers of the three Services and Chief of General Staff), which gives advice on the conduct of the war ;

Committee of Chiefs of Staff which deals with questions connected with the military aspects of the war.

Two sets of high officials exist:
organisational (Ministers),
operational (Chiefs of Staff).

France.

The supreme conduct of operations devolves on the *War Committee* upon which is dependent the Commander-in-Chief, who co-ordinates the action of all the Armed Forces.

In France also two sets of officials exist, organisational and operational.

What has been said fully supports the solution approved by you, Duce, and may be summarised as follows:

Yourself Supreme Commander, assisted on the operational side by the Chief of General Staff;

Two sets of officials:
organisational (Ministers);
operational (Chiefs of Staff);
closely dovetailed and collaborating.

4. (*Confidential Minute of which no copy exists at the War Ministry.*)

Ministry of War,
Cabinet.
(*Office for Laws and Decrees*).
Rome,
May 10th, 1941—XIX.

CONDUCT OF THE WAR.

Article 5 of the Statute of the Realm lays down that " to the King alone belongs executive power; it is he who is the Supreme Head of the State; *he commands all forces* on land and sea; he declares war," etc., etc.

In virtue of this statutory ruling, H.M. The King was the *Supreme Commander* of the Armed Forces during the war of 1915–18.

In his decree of May 23rd, 1915, H.M. the King laid it down that from that day onwards " his orders concerning the operations of the Army and the Fleet and of their various branches were communicated, *by his order*, to the Army and the Navy by the Chief of Army and Naval Staff respectively, who put them into effect as far as concerned land and sea operations, informing the respective Ministers of War and of Marine, of any dispositions that might interest them."

At the beginning of the present war, H.M. The King-Emperor addressed the following proclamation, dated June 11th, 1940, XVIII, from the zone of operations, to the fighting men on land, sea, and in the air.

"*Fighting Men on land, sea, and in the air!*

"As Supreme Head of all the Forces on land, sea, and in the air, in accordance with my own feelings and the tradition of my House, I once more, as twenty-five years ago, come among you.

"I entrust the command of the troops in action on all fronts to the Head of the Government, Duce of Fascism, First Marshal of the Empire.

"My first thought goes out to you, while, sharing with me the deep attachment and complete devotion to our immortal country, you are preparing, together with our ally Germany, to face fresh and difficult trials with an invincible faith in overcoming them.

"*Fighting Men on land, sea, and in the air!*

"United with you as never before, I am sure that your courage and the patriotism of the Italian people will once more find means to ensure the victory of our glorious forces.

Zone of Operations.

June 11th, 1940—XVIII.
VICTOR EMMANUEL."
(*Stefani agency.*)

The said proclamation, which is one of the means of making known the Head of the State's wishes, constitutes the sole act by which H.M. the King-Emperor assigned the command of the troops in action on all fronts to the Head of the Government, Duce of Fascism, First Marshal of the Empire.

On the basis of the above Acts, the situation which emerges is as follows:

The King, by virtue of the statutory ruling aforesaid, confirmed in the first part of his proclamation, where he says that "*As Supreme Head of all Forces on land, sea and in the air*" he comes among his soldiers once more as he did twenty-five years ago—the King is the supreme commander of all the Armed Forces.

The Duce is *commander of the troops in action on all fronts,* and this qualification was adopted by the Duce himself in the first proclamation he issued to the troops and in all headings of proclamations sent out on the basis of War regulations.

5. *H.E. the Chief of General Staff's Office.*
Rome,
June 4th, 1940—XVIII.

Ref. No. 5569.

To

H.E. Marshal of Italy, Rodolfo Graziani, Chief of Army Staff, Rome.

H.E. Admiral of the Fleet, Domenico Cavagnari, Chief of Naval Staff, Rome.

H.E. General-Designate of the Air Arm, Francesco Pricolo, Chief of Air Staff, Rome.

For information :

H.E. Cavaliere Galeazzo Ciano, Minister for Foreign Affairs, Rome.

H.E. Army-Corps General Attilio Teruzzi, Minister for Italian Africa, Rome.

H.E. Army-Corps General Ubaldo Soddu, Under-Secretary of State for War, Rome.

H.E. Lieut.-General Achille Starace, Chief of Blackshirt Militia Staff, Rome.

H.R.H. Prince Amedeo Savoia-Aosta, Viceroy of Ethiopia. Addis Ababa.

H.E. Air Marshal Italo Balbo, C.-in-C. Armed Forces in N. Africa, Tripoli.

H.E. Cesare Maria De Vecchi di Val Cismon, C.-in-C. Armed Forces in Italian Islands in the Aegean, Rhodes.

SUBJECT : CONSTITUTION AND FUNCTIONING OF THE SUPREME COMMAND OF THE ARMED FORCES IN THE EVENT OF WAR.

Some clarification and definition is necessary with regard to the constitution and function of the Supreme Command of the Armed Forces in the event of war.

(1) Supreme Commander of the Armed Forces, individually and collectively, wherever they may be, is, by delegation of His Majesty the King, the Duce.

(2) The Duce exercises this command through the Chief of the General Staff who has his own general staff.

(3) The main functions of the Chief of General Staff are:

(*a*) To keep the Duce informed of the general picture of the military situation of the Armed Forces and of their possibilities of action in relation to the enemy's position. In consequence, to receive orders and general directives for the conduct of operations;

(*b*) to inform the Chiefs of Staff of the various Services of consequent orders and directives for the development of the said operations in the strategic field;

(*c*) to follow the course of operations, intervening should the necessity arise, particularly to ensure co-ordination and the timely employment of each Service.

(4) On the basis of orders, which they will receive from the Duce as C.-in-C. or from the Chief of General Staff:

(*a*) The Chiefs of Staff of the Armed Forces—Army, Navy and Air Force—will exercise effective and complete command over their respective Armed Forces stationed in the motherland (Italian peninsula, islands, Albania). Such command, however, must not be understood as a function of their rank as High Commanders, as was formerly agreed, but as a function of their rank as Chiefs of Staff; by order therefore and in the name of the Duce, C.-in-C. of all the Armed Forces.

(*b*) The High Commands of the Armed Forces stationed in overseas territory (Italian N. Africa, Italian E. Africa, Aegean possessions) will exercise effective and complete command over the forces placed at their disposition, as effective Commanders of such forces, and therefore with full authority, initiative and responsibility, directly providing for co-ordination of action.

(5) The General Staff—the organ of the Chief of General Staff—in order to fulfil the tasks required of it in respect of what has been said in item 3 above, does not possess—nor is the establishment thereof envisaged—its own complete organisation, but will make use of those already functioning on the Staffs of the various Armed Forces and other bodies: Supreme Defence Commission, General Commissariat for War Production, etc.

There will be needed, however:

(*a*) constant close liaison between the Chief of General Staff and the Chiefs of Staff of the various Armed Forces.

I will make it my business to obtain this by frequent meetings and exchanges of ideas;

(*b*) uninterrupted passing on of news of every sort by the Staffs of the Armed Forces to the General Staff. This will be obtained by establishing the closest liaison between the Staffs and the other bodies, and by the regular or occasional transmission of news as will be laid down by degrees.

(6) The organisation of the Supreme Command of the Italian Armed Forces being different from any other, rests, in other words, upon these principles:

(*a*) a single and totalitarian conception of the command personally exercised by the Duce, by delegation of His Majesty the King;

(*b*) strategic conduct of the war and co-ordination of action between the various Services and between the various sectors of the operations, exercised according to, and on the orders of the Duce, by the Chief of General Staff;

(*c*) exercise of command over the various Services stationed at home or overseas, carried out by the Chief of Staff or the commanders-in-chief of the Services;

(*d*) absolute devotion and obedience to the Duce and absolute unity of thought and action on the part of everyone, in keeping with the Fascist style and tradition.

The present arrangements will, as far as necessary, be sanctioned by appropriate legal provisions.

Marshal of Italy,
Chief of General Staff.
signed BADOGLIO.

Divisional-General Seconded.
countersigned QUIRINO ARMELLINI.

CHAPTER VIII

FROM THE VILLA SAVOIA TO PONZA

On the morning of Sunday, 25th, I went to my office as I had done now for nearly twenty-one years, and arrived there about nine o'clock. In the early hours of the morning fantastic rumours had been circulated about the session of the Grand Council, but the city itself—flooded with summer sunlight—looked tranquil enough. Scorza did not appear but telephoned to say that " the night had brought wisdom, and some were beginning to have qualms." " Too late," I answered. Indeed, a little later, Cianetti's famous letter arrived, in which he bitterly repented of having voted for Grandi's motion, the gravity of which he had not realised, resigned from the Ministry of Corporations and asked to be recalled immediately to his regiment in his capacity of captain in the Alpine artillery. It was that letter—to which I made no reply—which later saved the writer's life.[1]

Sunday Morning

Grandi had vanished completely since the early hours of the morning and was searched for in vain.[2] The Command of the

[1] Those members of the Fascist Grand Council who voted against Mussolini on July 25th, 1943, were tried, on a charge of high treason, by a Special Tribunal set up for the purpose at Verona by the Fascist Republican Government. Of the six members present at the trial, Ciano, De Bono, Gottardi, Marinelli and Pareschi were sentenced to death, and shot the following day, January 11th, 1944. In view of "extenuating circumstances," i.e., the letter he wrote to Mussolini, Cianetti's life was spared. He was sentenced to thirty years' imprisonment and deprived of holding any public office.

[2] According to other accounts (*Gazzetta Ticinese*, Lugano, September 9th, 1943, reproduced in *Come cadde Mussolini*, Bari, 1944 ; and "Comandante

Fascist Militia also announced that there was no fresh news. General Galbiati was invited to the Palazzo Venezia at one o'clock.

About eleven the Under-Secretary for the Interior, Albini, brought me the usual morning post containing news of the last twenty-four hours. The most important and regrettable item was the news of the first heavy raid on Bologna. Having gone through the reports I asked Albini: "Why did you vote for Grandi's motion last night? You are a guest, not a member of the Grand Council."[1] Little Albini seemed embarrassed by the question, blushed, and burst into profuse excuses on these lines: "I may have made a mistake, but no one could possibly doubt my absolute devotion to you, a devotion not merely of today but of all time." And as he left the room, his livid face revealed him as a self-confessed traitor. (He was to beg in vain for a place under Badoglio, dancing constant attendance on him and proposing himself for all manner of menial offices.) A little later I told my private secretary to telephone General Puntoni[2] to know what time in the afternoon the King would be prepared to receive me, adding that I would come to the interview in civilian dress. General Puntoni replied that the King would receive me at the Villa Ada at five o'clock.[3] The Party Secretary gave signs of life again with this communication:

Here is the letter I propose sending the members of the Grand Council:

"*The Duce asks me to inform you that having convened the Grand Council according to the Law of December 9th,* 1928, *in order to consult it upon the present political situation, he has taken*

X dello Stato Maggiore," *La caduta del Fascismo*, Rome, 1944), Grandi had gone to the Villa Savoia with Federzoni to report to the King what had happened at the Grand Council.

[1] Albini was only Under-Secretary, not Minister for the Interior, and therefore could not be an *ex-officio* member of the Grand Council. But since, in this case, the Minister was Mussolini himself (who already had a seat as President of the Council) Albini was appointed as one of those members who could be nominated for a period of three years by decree of the Head of the Government.

[2] Mussolini here wishes it to appear that he had sought an interview with the King on his own initiative; in fact, the King had commanded him to come.

[3] Villa Ada was the former name of Villa Savoia, the King's private residence in the Via Salaria, on the outskirts of Rome.

note of the various motions presented and of your statements."[1]

It seemed from this communication (which was never actually sent out—it would have been useless to send it) that Scorza anticipated a normal development of the situation.

About 1 p.m. the Japanese ambassador, Hidaka, accompanied by Under-Secretary Bastianini, arrived at the Palazzo Venezia. I gave him an account of the Feltre meeting. The talk lasted about an hour.[2]

I Visit the Tiburtino Quarter

At two o'clock, accompanied by General Galbiati, I went to visit the Tiburtino quarter, which had suffered particularly heavily in the terror raid of July 19th. I was at once surrounded by a crowd of the victims, who cheered me. At three o'clock I returned to the Villa Torlonia.

At 4.50 my private secretary arrived at the Villa Torlonia and came with me to the Villa Ada. I was absolutely calm. I took with me a book containing the Grand Council Act, Cianetti's letter, and other papers from which it emerged that the Grand Council's resolution was not binding on anyone, in view of the consultative function of the organ itself. I thought the King would withdraw his delegation of authority of June 10th, 1940, concerning the Command of the Armed Forces, a command which I had for some time past been thinking of relinquishing. I entered the Villa Ada, therefore, with a mind completely free from any forebodings, in a state which, looking back on it, might really be called utterly unsuspecting.

Punctually at 5 p.m. the car entered the main gates on the Via Salaria which had been thrown open. Everywhere within there

[1] The law of December 9th, 1928, laid down the Constitution and Powers of the Grand Council of Fascism as the supreme co-ordinating organ of the Fascist State. Article I states that, in addition to specific questions outlined in its constitution, it must also advise on subjects of political, economic, social and national interest, on which it is consulted by the Head of the Government. Article II provides that the Council be summoned by the Head of the Government who prepares the agenda to be put before it.

[2] According to P. Monelli, *Roma* 1943, page 180, Mussolini in his conversation with Hidaka, urged the necessity for Germany and Italy to conclude peace with Russia and begged the good offices of the Tokyo Government, "in accordance with the Tripartite Pact," for bringing pressure upon Moscow to take the initiative in opening negotiations. His preoccupation with getting rid of the Eastern Front in order to facilitate German assistance to Italy appears in many accounts of his conversations during this period. It is suppressed in his own version.

were reinforcements of Carabinieri, but that did not seem out of the ordinary. The King, in Marshal's uniform, stood in the doorway of the villa. Two officers were stationed in the hall inside. When we had entered the drawing-room, the King, in a state of abnormal agitation, and with his features distorted, said, clipping his words:

"My dear Duce, it's no longer any good. Italy has gone to bits. Army morale is at rock bottom. The soldiers don't want to fight any more. The Alpine regiments are singing a song which says they don't want to make war on Mussolini's account any longer." (The King repeated the verses of the song in Piedmontese dialect.) "The Grand Council's vote is terrific—nineteen votes for Grandi's motion and among them four holders of the Order of the Annunciation.[1] You can certainly be under no illusion as to Italy's feelings with regard to yourself. At this moment you are the most hated man in Italy. You can no longer count on more than one friend. You have one friend left you, and I am he. That is why I tell you that you need have no fears for your personal safety, for which I will ensure protection. I have been thinking the man for the job now is Marshal Badoglio. He will start by forming a government of experts for purely administrative purposes and for the continuation of the war. In six months' time we shall see. All Rome already knows about the Grand Gouncil's resolution, and they are all expecting a change"

I replied: "You are taking an extremely grave decision. A crisis at the moment would mean making the people think that peace was in sight, once the man who declared war had been dismissed. The blow to the Army's morale would be serious. If the soldiers—Alpini or not—don't want to make war for Mussolini any more, that doesn't matter, so long as they are prepared to do it for you. The crisis would be considered a triumph for the Churchill-Stalin set-up, especially for the latter, who would see the retirement of an antagonist who has fought against him for twenty years. I realise the people's hatred. I had no difficulty in recognising it last night in the midst of the Grand Council. One can't govern for such a long time and impose so many sacrifices without provoking resentments more or less temporary or permanent. In any case, I wish good luck to the man who takes the situation in hand."

[1] i.e., Grandi, Federzoni, Ciano, De Bono.

It was exactly 5.20 p.m. when the King accompanied me to the door. His face was livid and he looked smaller than ever, almost dwarfish. He shook my hand and went in again. I descended the few steps and went towards my car.

My Arrest

Suddenly a Carabinieri captain stopped me and said: "His Majesty has charged me with the protection of your person."

I was continuing towards my car when the captain said to me, pointing to a motor-ambulance standing nearby: "No. We must get in there."

I got into the ambulance, together with my secretary, De Cesare. A lieutenant, three Carabinieri and two police agents in plain clothes got in as well as the captain and placed themselves by the door armed with machine-guns. When the door was closed the ambulance drove off at top speed. I still thought that all this was being done, as the King had said, in order to protect my person.

After a half-hour's run the ambulance stopped at a Carabinieri barracks.[1] The windows of the lodge were closed but I could see that it was surrounded by sentries with fixed bayonets, while an officer stood guard permanently in the next room. I stayed there about an hour and thence, still in the ambulance, was taken to the barracks of a Carabinieri cadet school.[2] It was 7 p.m. The deputy-commander of the school seemed moved when he saw me arrive and said a few conventional words of sympathy. Then I was accompanied to the room used as an office by Colonel Tabellini, the officer commanding the training-school, while an officer stood on guard in the small room adjoining.

During the evening a few Carabinieri officers came to see me, among them Chirico, Bonitatibus and Santillo, with whom I spoke on general matters. They said that it was entirely a question of protecting me and that this very delicate task had been entrusted specially to their Corps. I did not touch a morsel.

[1] According to the account given in the Rome Liberal paper, *Risorgimento Liberale*, July 25th, 1944 (reproduced in Comandante X, "*La caduta del Fascismo,*" Rome, 1944, pp. 15–17), this was the barracks of the "Podgora" division at Via Corsini No. 16, in Trastevere. Mussolini spent a short time in the buildings of the officers' club.

[2] This barracks occupied part of the vast Caserna Vittorio Emanuele II, looking on to Via Legnano, on the west bank of the Tiber.

I asked to go out, and an officer accompanied me along the corridor. I noticed then that at least three Carabinieri were mounting guard at the door of the office, which was on the second floor. And it was then, as I sat thinking in my room, that for the first time a doubt began to trouble my mind—was this protection or captivity?

That certain circles were plotting against my life was known also to the police, who, however (particularly under Chierici's truly wretched administration) had maintained that these were only fleeting aspirations with nothing practical about them—everything could be boiled down to an expression of understandable discontent. It is worth mentioning, in parenthesis, that Chierici's nomination as Chief of Police was especially sponsored by Albini.

But, I asked myself, what menace to my life can exist in a barracks where there are as many as 2,000 Carabinieri cadets? How could the conspirators get at me? How could the 'fury of the populace' get at me either?

About 11 p.m. I put out the light, the light next door remaining on, where an officer mounted permanent guard, not even answering the ring of the telephone bell.

A Message from Badoglio

At 1 a.m. on the 26th Lieut.-Col. Chirico came into my room and said: "General Ferone has just arrived with a message for you from Marshal Badoglio."

I rose and went into the next room. I had known General Ferone in Albania.[1] He was now wearing a strangely smug expression.

Marshal Badoglio's letter, in a green envelope headed "War Office," was addressed in the Marshal's own hand to *Cavaliere Sig. Benito Mussolini* and said:

To H.E. the Cavaliere Benito Mussolini.

The undersigned Head of the Government wishes to inform Your Excellency that what has been done in your regard has been done solely in your personal interest, detailed information having reached us from several quarters of a serious plot against your person. He much regrets this, and wishes to inform you that he

[1] Major-General Ernesto Ferone was at the time seconded for special duties at the War Ministry. (See also below, p. 217.)

is prepared to give orders for your safe accompanying, with all proper respect, to whatever place you may choose.

The Head of the Government,
Marshal of Italy,
BADOGLIO.

That letter, of a perfidy unique in history, was designed to convince me that the King's word concerning my personal safety would be respected and that the crisis would be dealt with within the framework of the Régime—i.e., of Fascism; for Badoglio had too often explicitly and solemnly declared his allegiance to the Party, of which he was a regular member, together with all the members of his family, his wife included; he had all too often held high office under the Régime; he had discharged too important political and military missions; he had accepted too many honours and too much cash; anything was possible rather than that he should have prepared this betrayal and intrigued for it for months, perhaps from the time of his dismissal from the office of Chief of General Staff. He had also agreed to serve the Régime on the National Council of Research—where, as a matter of fact, he did not do a thing except turn up in the morning to read the papers.

From the moment I entered the training-school barracks I had no more news of the world at large. I was merely told that the King had made a proclamation and Badoglio another, declaring that they would carry on the war; that the city was calm and that people now thought peace was near.

Having read Badoglio's missive, I dictated the following points to General Ferone, who wrote them on a piece of paper in his own hand.

July 26*th*, 1943. 1 *a.m.*

1. *I wish to thank Marshal Badoglio for the attention he is according my person.*

2. *The only residence at my disposal is Rocca delle Caminate, whither I am prepared to go at any moment.*[1]

3. *I wish to assure Marshal Badoglio, if only in remembrance of the work we have done together in the past, that not only will I raise no difficulties of any sort but I will co-operate in every possible way.*

[1] Rocça delle Caminate, where Mussolini owned a country house, is a village in the commune of Meldola, eight miles from Forlì in his native Romagna.

4. *I am glad of the decision to continue the war together with our allies, as the honour and interests of the country require at this time, and I express my earnest hope that success will crown the grave task which Marshal Badoglio is assuming by order and in the name of His Majesty the King, whose loyal servant I have been for twenty-one years and shall continue to be. Long live Italy* !

This indirect communication was the only one sent to Badoglio. I never sent a word or a sign to the King. By this reply which Badoglio never dared publish, contenting himself with giving a mangled oral version of it to his circle, I showed that I genuinely believed that Badoglio, though modifying the Government, would not change the general policy dictated by the war.

When General Ferone had left, I retired, and lay awake till the early hours of the morning.

The "Private Residence" Farce

During the whole of Monday there continued what might be called the "private residence" farce. Several times during the day they came to say that the residence at Rocca delle Caminate was the best from the point of view of my 'personal safety,' that the General of the Bologna Carabinieri had already inspected it and confirmed that Rocca lent itself excellently to "security" and that they were only awaiting the word to arrange the mode of departure, possibly by air. So the day went by, with no further news. The only thing they said was that all was quiet at the Villa Torlonia—which was untrue.

In the evening Major Bonitatibus arranged a camp bed in Colonel Tabellini's room as usual. The whole morning of Tuesday, 27th, as well, there continued the farce of an "imminent departure" which never took place. There was, however, an increased vigilance about the place. At 7 p.m. a platoon of Carabinieri and one of metropolitan police entered the barrack square, at the far end of which the famous words "Believe, Obey, Fight" were written on the wall in huge letters. They took up position near a group of lorries. Towards 8 p.m. a few motor-cars arrived with a group of officers.

At a given moment an officer, striding into the middle of the square, shouted: "All inside ! Close the windows !" to the cadets who had crowded on to the parapets, attracted by the unusual arrival of so many vehicles.

Night had already fallen when an officer came into the room and said to me: "The order has come to leave."

I went downstairs, accompanied by a group of officers to whom, on reaching the ground floor, I said goodbye. I was about to step into the car when a general introduced himself with these words: "I am Brigadier General Pòlito, Chief of Military Police of the Supreme Command."

I asked no questions, convinced that the goal of this nocturnal journey was Rocca delle Caminate. The blinds were lowered but not the windows; through a slit I became aware that the vehicle was passing the Santo Spirito Hospital.[1] We were, therefore, going not towards the Via Flaminia but the Via Appia. At the innumerable road-blocks the Carabinieri, warned in advance by a despatch-rider, contented themselves with slowing down our machine slightly. When we reached the main road to Albano I asked: "Where are we going?"

"Southwards."

"Not to Rocca delle Caminate?"

"Another order came."

"And who are you? I used to know a Police Inspector called Pòlito."

"I am he."

"How did you become a general?"

"They gave me equivalent rank in the Army."

Police Inspector Pòlito was well known to me. During the years of the Régime he had carried out some brilliant operations such as the capture of Cesare Rossi at Campione[2] and the liquidation of the Pintor gang in Sardinia. While on the journey, Pòlito related many extremely interesting and hitherto unpublished details of these operations. Beyond Cisterna the machine slowed down. Talk ceased. Pòlito, who had been smoking continuously, lowered the glass partition, called to Colonel Pelaghi of the Carabinieri, and asked where we were.

"Near Gaeta," he replied.

[1] Santo Spirito Hospital: on the west bank of the Tiber, a little further downstream than Castel S. Angelo, on the direct route south from the barracks.

[2] Cesare Rossi was one of Mussolini's most intimate collaborators during the early days of Fascism. He took part in the March on Rome and was later made head of the Fascist Press Bureau. Implicated in the murder of the Socialist Deputy Matteotti in 1924, he took his revenge on Mussolini by compiling a memorandum on the case which he sent to the King and a few anti-Fascists. He escaped to France where he published many virulent

"Is Gaeta to be my new residence?" I asked. "Where Mazzini was banished to, by any chance?[1] They do me too much honour."

"It has not yet been decided," returned Pòlito.

When we reached Gaeta, which was deserted, a man came towards us waving a torch. The car stopped and a naval officer said: "To the Ciano Wharf."

On the Island of Ponza

There Admiral Maugeri was waiting and accompanied me to the corvette *Persephone.*[2] A little later we weighed anchor. Dawn was already breaking. I went down to the cabin together with the officers escorting me. In daylight the corvette dropped anchor in sight of the island of Ventotene, and Inspector Pòlito went ashore to see if the island was suitable for accommodating me. A little later he returned, and said it was out of the question. There was a German garrison on the island. The corvette then proceeded to the island of Ponza and anchored in the roadstead there at 1 p.m. on July 28th. Pòlito approached me and, pointing out a greenish-coloured house half hidden by big, laid-up

articles and reviews attacking the Fascist leaders. In August 1928, while staying at Lugano, he was lured to the Italian enclave of Campione by Fascist agents posing as tourists and there arrested by the Italian police. The incident led to an exchange of notes between the Swiss and Italian Governments, since Switzerland considered that her territory had been violated.

Rossi himself was tried in Rome by the Special Tribunal for the Defence of the State and condemned to 30 years' imprisonment on a charge of high treason. Though after ten years Mussolini granted him an amnesty, he was not set at liberty, but confined at Ponza (among other places). He was discovered and arrested by the Allies after their landing on the Sorrento peninsula. Later released, he was re-arrested at Naples by the Italian Purge Commission in July, 1944, and imprisoned in Rome to await trial for his part in the Matteotti murder. Found guilty of Fascist crimes during the period of the March on Rome, he was sentenced to four years and two months' imprisonment, June 8th, 1945, but a petition for reprieve was granted, June 15th, 1945. However, he was not released, being held for the second Matteotti trial. Acquitted for lack of evidence, April 4th, 1947.

[1] In mid-August, 1870, Mazzini was on his way to Sicily to make the last of his attempts against the Government which, however, was informed of his movements by a spy. As he disembarked at Palermo he was arrested, put on board a battleship and taken to the fortress of Gaeta. He was there when Rome was united to the Kingdom of Italy in October, 1870, and was released as a result of the amnesty proclaimed on that occasion.

[2] From this point Mussolini's account may be checked by the narrative of Admiral Maugeri. (See below, p. 211.)

fishing boats, said: "That is your temporary home." Meanwhile, through some unexplained impulse, all the windows and balconies were suddenly filled with men and women armed with binoculars who were watching the boat as it came inshore. In a flash the whole island knew of our arrival.

Towards evening a few local people came to welcome me. The fishermen of Terracina sent me a gift. On the whole there was nothing in the islanders' attitude to remind one of the "fury of the populace"; but with the arrival of more police agents vigilance was increased and all contact with the outside world was prevented.

At Ponza I realised the miserable conspiracy which had got rid of me, and I was convinced that all this would lead to capitulation and to my being handed over to the enemy.

The days were long at Ponza. Fresh officers came, Lieut.-Col. Meoli and 2nd Lieut. Elio di Lorenzo, as well as Sergeant-major Antichi. The garrison was reinforced, in view also of the presence there of Italian deportees and Balkan internees. I was twice permitted to bathe, at a specially arranged and well-guarded spot. No newspapers. Only one telegram—though an eloquent one—from Goering![1]

I spent my time at Ponza in complete solitude, translating Carducci's *Odi barbare* into German and reading Giuseppe Ricciotti's *Life of Jesus*[2] which I later left behind as a gift to the parish priest.

Ponza certainly cannot be compared with Ischia, let alone with Capri. Nevertheless, it has its own rustic beauty and its own history, even of the prison. An expert in such matters told me that ever since ancient times famous people had been banished there—Nero's mother Agrippina, Augustus's daughter Julia and, to make up for these, a saint—Flavia Domitilla and, in 538 A.D., a pope, St. Sylvester the Martyr[3]; then, skipping a few centuries, moderns such as the Grand Master of the Freemasons, Torrigiani,[4] General Bencivenga,[5] the Civil Engineer Bordiga,[6] and finally—the last of the series and very recent indeed—Ras Imeru with his inevitable Abyssinian Dedjaz.[7]

[1] The text of this telegram is given below, in Chapter XV, p. 132.

[2] For Mussolini's characteristic notes to this book, see below, p. 229.

[3] Nero's grandmother (not mother) was sent to Ventotene, not Ponza, as was Augustus's daughter, Julia. The Pope mentioned is not Sylvester (A.D. 335) but Silverius, who died A.D. 537 (not 538).

[4] Marchese Domizio Torrigiani (1877–1932). Banished in 1925 when Freemasonry was suppressed by the Fascists.

[5] General Roberto Bencivenga, born 1878. Deputy for Campania in 1924 and President of the Italian Press Association until its dissolution by the Fascist Government. Arrested in 1927 and sentenced to banishment. Released after the fall of Fascism, in August 1943 ; a leader of the underground Resistance Movement in Rome during the German occupation. After liberation, representative of the Italian Armed Forces in Rome, till July, 1944.

[6] One of the leading Socialist extremists in the years after the First World War, he left the Socialist Party at the Congress of Leghorn, 1921, to become one of the founders of the Italian Communist Party. Attacked by the Fascists, he was also opposed by the leaders of Russian Communism. See Lenin's essay, "Extremism as Infantile Disease of Communism."

[7] Ras Imeru, a cousin of the Emperor of Abyssinia, fought throughout the Abyssinian campaign and was captured only in May, 1936. Transported to Italy, he was held as a hostage, until his release was secured by the Allied forces in November, 1943, when he was sent back to Abyssinia. Dedjaz, an Amharic word denoting chieftain and leader of a district (in Italian Army parlance considered the equivalent to a Colonel), who might well act as aide-de-camp to a Ras.

CHAPTER IX

FROM PONZA TO LA MADDALENA AND THE GRAN SASSO

IT WAS 1 a.m. on August 8th when Sergeant-major Antichi rushed into my room shouting: "There is imminent danger! We must leave!"

Sure enough, since the early hours of the evening, almost uninterrupted light-signalling from the hill opposite had been noticed, from which one might have guessed there was something new in the air.

I collected my few things and, accompanied by my armed escort, went down to the beach where a barge was waiting. The superstructure of a warship showed clearly in the distance at the entry to the roadstead. I went on board and saw Admiral Maugeri again, as on the Persephone. As usual, I went down to the Admiral's cabin, followed by Meoli, Di Lorenzo and Antichi. The vessel was the Panther, formerly French. Towards dawn we weighed anchor. The crew were all on deck. Those not on watch slept. Towards eight o'clock a very high sea got up, but the Panther rode it extremely well. There were also two alerts owing to the passage of enemy planes, but nothing came of them.

I exchanged a few words with the second-in-command, an officer from La Spezia, from whom I learned that Badoglio had dissolved the Party.

The Meeting with Admiral Brivonesi

Only after a voyage of four hours did I learn that the goal of our journey was La Maddalena. A little later the coastline of Sardinia could be discerned through the mist. About 2 p.m. I disembarked and was handed over to Admiral Bruno Brivonesi, commanding the naval base. This admiral (who had married an Englishwoman) had been the subject of an enquiry owing to the destruction of an entire convoy of as many as seven merchant ships plus three warships—an extremely important convoy escorted by a good twelve warships, two of them 'ten-thousand tonners' and sunk with all hands in a few minutes' battle against four English light cruisers which did not suffer the slightest damage.[1] The enquiry—conducted by the naval authorities with evident negligence—merely resulted in disciplinary measures within the Service being taken against the admiral, who was directly responsible for the loss of ten ships and several hundred men.[2] He was deprived of his command and, after some time, was given a shore command at La Maddalena.

My meeting with him was not, and could not be, very cordial. The house destined for my use was situated outside the town, on a height surrounded by a park thickly studded with pine trees. The villa had been built by an Englishman called Webber who, strangely enough, of all the places in the world where he could have settled, chose just the most stark and lonely island of all those to the north of Sardinia. The Secret Service ? Possibly.

My stay at La Maddalena was fairly long and the solitude still more rigorous. Not a single civilian remained on the island. It had already been evacuated after the May raid which had caused tremendous damage to the base and had sunk two naval units of medium tonnage. That had been a mysterious raid, with an exact knowledge of the targets. One could still see the hulks of the big ships which had been sunk. From the balcony of the house the view stretched beyond the harbour towards the smooth peaks of the Gallura mountains, which reminded one a little of the Dolomites. I was allowed to write. I seem to have made daily notes of a philosophical, literary and political character, but I have not been able to lay my hands on

[1] This action took place in the Central Mediterranean on November 8th, 1941. The British Admiralty communiqué, November 9th, 1941, stated that ten (not seven) merchant ships were destroyed, one destroyer sunk and at least one other seriously damaged, no casualties or damage being suffered by the British ships. The Italian communiqué No. 526, November 10th, 1941, admitted the attack, stating that "the ships" (no figures given) "which were hit, later sank. Of the Italian escorting destroyers which returned the attack with torpedoes, two were sunk." It claimed torpedo hits on a British cruiser and destroyer, and the loss of three British planes.

[2] But see Mussolini's statement below, p. 213 : "I am convinced he could not have done more."

this diary of a sort.[1] Vigilance was strengthened at La Maddalena. A full hundred men, Carabinieri and police agents, watched Webber's house by day and night, a house which I left only once, for a short walk in the wood, accompanied by the Sergeant.

General Basso's Fears

The scorching days went monotonously by without the slightest news of the world outside. Not until August 20th was I, as a prisoner, allowed to receive the war communiqué from base headquarters. The banishment was almost complete, but it still did not seem sufficient to Army Corps General Antonio Basso, Commander-in-Chief of the armed forces in Sardinia, who wrote the following to the Minister Secretary of State, General Sorice, on August 11th :

I have learned of the recent stay of a high personage at La Maddalena, in a villa overlooking the harbour.

I would draw your attention to the fact that in these waters there are numerous German naval units (and very few of our own) used for the sea traffic to Corsica and for the defence of the German supply base at Palau.

In view of this, the possibility of inconveniences arising cannot be overlooked.

I think it would be more convenient if this personage were transferred either elsewhere or, if he has perforce to keep to the islands, to one of the mountainous districts in the interior of Sardinia, where surveillance could be more thorough and rigorous.

On the margin of this paper there is the following note in red pencil :

A brainwave. B.

The only surprise was a gift from the Führer, a splendid complete edition of Nietzsche's works in twenty-four volumes with a signed dedication. A real marvel of German book-production.

[1] However, below (Chapter XIV, p. 129) Mussolini says : "In a sort of diary I kept at La Maddalena and which may one day see the light, I wrote . . ." and proceeds to give considerable extracts.

The Führer's Gift

The gift was accompanied by a letter from Marshal Kesselring which said:

Duce,

By order of the Führer I send you, through the kind offices of His Excellency Marshal Badoglio, a present from the Führer for your birthday.

The Führer will consider himself happy if this great work of German literature gives you a little pleasure, Duce, and if you will consider it as an expression of the Führer's personal attachment to you.

I add my own personal respects.

FIELD-MARSHAL KESSELRING.
G.H.Q. *August 7th,* 1943.

I had time to read the first four volumes containing Nietzsche's early poems—which were very beautiful—and his first philological works on the Latin and Greek languages, which the German thinker knew as well as his mother-tongue.

Another surprise was the unexpected appearance one evening about eight o'clock of a German machine coming from Corsica, which flew very low over the house—perhaps about 180 feet up, so that I could see the pilot's face and wave to him. I thought that this flight would lead to my leaving La Maddalena. Sure enough, on the evening of August 27th, Captain Faiola, who had replaced Meoli on the 14th, announced: "We leave tomorrow morning!"

A Red Cross plane had been moored in the harbour for several hours, almost opposite Webber's house.

Towards the Gran Sasso

At 4 a.m. on the 28th I was called and went down to the harbour. I got into the machine which took off with something of an effort as it was overladen and needed a lot of room before it could leave the water. After an hour and a half the machine alighted at Vigna di Valle on Lake Bracciano. There a Carabinieri Major and a Police Inspector, Gueli, were waiting with the usual motor-ambulance, which took us along the Via Cassia towards Rome but, on reaching the by-pass, bore left and went towards the Via Flaminia. On reaching it, beyond the iron bridge over the Tiber, it became clear that we were making for the main Sabine road. This was a route well known to me, as it was I who 'discovered' the Terminillo which later became the 'Mountain of Rome.'

Having passed Rieti and Cittaducale, the voyage was interrupted on the outskirts of L'Aquila by an air raid warning. Everyone got out of the motor-ambulance. A squadron of enemy machines was flying so high that they could scarcely be seen. But what happened during the alert gave one the distinct impression that the Army was in a fair way to breaking up. Groups of soldiers in their shirtsleeves fled in all directions shouting, and the crowd followed their example. So did the officers. A lamentable spectacle ! When the alert was over, the car went on again, but a little beyond L'Aquila we halted because of slight engine trouble.

After lowering the windows of the ambulance a man approached me and said : "I am a Fascist from Bologna. They have swept everything away. But it won't last. People are disgusted with the new government because it has not brought peace."

After Assergi the column reached the starting-point of the funicular railway to the Gran Sasso. A small villa housed myself and my guards, Captain Faiola and Police Inspector Gueli of Trieste. An even stricter watch was enjoined. I was allowed to read the Official Gazette, including the back numbers.

One day I asked Gueli : "Have you any idea why I am here ?"

Inspector Gueli replied : "You are considered an ordinary detainee."

"And what is your job here ?"

"It is always the same one—to keep guard so you don't try to get away, and above all to see that no one tries either to set you free or to harm you."

"*They Have Killed Muti*"

During the few days at Villetta—that was the name of the house—nothing special occurred.

I could listen to the wireless. No papers arrived there ; nor did books. A transmitting and receiving station had been set up in the square. One morning a police official came up to me and said : "Engines coming from the Brenner have got your picture on them. The coaches are full of inscriptions of your name. Something big is being prepared. At Rome confusion has reached its peak. It will not be surprising if the ministers all bolt without warning. Startling rumours are in circulation as to the German attitude in the event of a betrayal by Badoglio."

Another morning a police agent from the Trieste inspectorate, who was taking six Alsatians for a walk, found means of approaching me and saying: "Duce, I am a Fascist from the Trevisan March. Do you know what they did in Rome yesterday? They killed Muti. The Carabinieri did it. We must get ready to avenge him." And he moved off.

It was in this fashion that I learned of Muti's brutal assassination.[1] Gueli later confirmed this news to me.

A few days passed, and then off we went again—on the last stage of the journey—to the Refuge Inn, on the Gran Sasso, 7,600 feet high; the highest prison in the world, as I said to my guard one day.

You get there by a funicular, which spans a difference of level of some 3,600 feet by means of two arches. The funicular and the inn were both built during the twenty years of Fascism.

On the Gran Sasso there ended my first month of captivity, that tragic August of 1943.

[1] Ettore Muti, Secretary of the Fascist Party from October 31st, 1939, till October 29th, 1940. After his dismissal from the post of Party Secretary little was heard of him until his mysterious death after his arrest in August, 1943. The official account issued by the Badoglio Government stated that rifle shots were fired from a wood on Muti and his escort of Carabinieri; Muti attempted to escape in the ensuing confusion but was killed when fired on by the Carabinieri. Other reports, however, suggested that he was killed by Carabinieri while he was conspiring against the Badoglio régime.

CHAPTER X

THE DYNASTY'S FIRST CRY OF ALARM

BEFORE STARTING TO RELATE the events of September 1st-15th, the *coup d'ètat* must be reviewed. One cannot but admit that, prepared long and minutely as it was, it revealed a really perfect technique. If the Italian generals had acted with the same spirit during the war they would have won it rapidly and triumphantly.

At 5.30 p.m., as soon as I had been captured, all telephone communications were cut except those of Badoglio's exchange which, for several days now, had been linked with the offices of the traitor marshal. This fact did not pass unobserved. Already by 7 p.m. an increased excitement could be discerned in the city. At 10.30 p.m. the radio issued the first bulletin, immediately followed by others. As if at a prearranged signal, the first popular demonstration broke out. Surprise increased the liveliness of the demonstrations themselves. Of whom was this mass of demonstrators composed? A fruitless question, perhaps. Not wishing to call it 'the people,' one might call it 'the mob.' Thousands of people were acclaiming the King and the Marshal. The Fascists were more surprised than anyone. The local headquarters were shut down. There was no time to man them. The anti-Fascist nature of the movement was clear from the very first announcement. The Fascists were stunned, almost as if confronted with a sudden vision. They were witnessing a complete volte-face. In half an hour a nation had changed its whole way of thinking, its whole feelings, its whole history.

The Technique of the Coup d'Etat

The form and content of the bulletins issued increased the confusion in the public's mind. They led one to suppose that it was on the whole a constitutional crisis, a normal transfer of authority. Some Fascists could not make head or tail of the matter.

The laying down of a 'smokescreen' in the guise of confusion worked marvellously. The people believed in the imminence of peace, called for it and thought they were nearing it since I, who wished to carry on the war (the only one who did !) was no longer there. A few, on the contrary, were under the illusion that it would mean a more energetic prosecution of the war, and a more or less Fascist government, but without the Duce. Was not Marshal Badoglio among the regular members of the Fascist Party ?

This might—note the conditional—explain the immediate telegraphic and written allegiance to the Marshal declared by many Fascist personalities.

If, on the evening of July 25th, any uncertainty as to the nature of the *coup d'état* still existed, every doubt must have vanished by the following morning.

That was the morning when the mob rushed about the streets, organised and protected by the Carabinieri, who had put the *coup d'état* into effect locally. The crowd destroyed the headquarters of all the Fascist organisations, pulled down the Lictor symbol, assaulted people, and, with a stupid and brutal iconoclasm wiped out everything which might remind them of Mussolini or Fascism.

While thousands of portraits and busts of myself were hurled out of the window, pictures of Victor of Savoy and Pietro Badoglio were hung out everywhere.

The People's Sudden Volte-Face

What is one to think of a nation which makes such an exhibition of itself, with such a sudden and, one might add, hysterical change of attitude ? Some of those who hastened to telegraph Badoglio justified themselves by the uncertainty aroused by the first communiqués, in which it was announced that "the war will continue," and that there were to be no recriminations, and which also hinted at national unity and the 'military' character of the Government.

And yet, a few minutes' reflection on the tenor of the communiqués would have been enough to raise a doubt at least as to the real truth of the matter—a truth which could mean only one thing: "Capture of the Duce and preparations for capitulation." Did it not seem odd to them that the announcement of my dismissal was not accompanied by any word of appreciation or recognition of my work? I don't mean by this the usual autographed letters which the King sends his generals on certain fixed occasions; but a man who had served for twenty-one years in peace and war and who, after the conquest of Abyssinia, was awarded the highest military decoration—did such a man not merit a single word, a word such as one would not even refuse a mediocre servant?

And if there was nothing in the communiqué, why was I not permitted to say farewell to the troops or somehow to make myself heard by the nation? Why did they not even mention the transfer of my powers to the new Head of the Government? Why this sudden silence? Why this complete disappearance?

The most fantastic rumours circulated at that time and there was one, mainly spread in Crown circles, according to which I was the King's guest in an unspecified villa, and which said that in a few days, when popular ferment had subsided, I should be able to go peacefully about again. This work of confusion—which succeeded admirably—was already over by the early hours of the morning of the 26th, when the mob gave itself up to the crazy excesses complacently recorded by the press.

The Month of 'Liberty'

From the morning of the 26th no Fascist could entertain the slightest doubt as to the character, scope and intentions of the Badoglio government; it was a government which aimed purely and simply at destroying everything in the sphere of ideas, institutions or anything else created in the twenty years of Fascism. And men lent themselves to this miserable business who, until 10.29 p.m. on July 25th, had declared themselves Fascists, though their membership went back to different dates—some of them to the very beginning. Meanwhile, the order was to ignore my existence—the silence of the tomb must surround my name. I was a corpse whose death they hesitated to announce. Thus began the month of August, 1943, the month of infamy, of betrayal and of capitulation.

Nothing connected with Fascism was respected—not even the

dead! The executors of Badoglio's policy (and they brought a ghoulish zest to their task such as few could have imagined) were the officers and men of that Corps[1] which I had so much praised and protected, and which had risen to the imposing total of 156,000 in the first six months of 1943.

It was the month of 'liberty'—a liberty with a curfew and a state of siege, a liberty consisting simply in the defamation of everything connected with Fascism. No one was spared. There was not a Party official who was not supposed at very least to have hidden a pile of gold and hoards of stolen victuals in his cellars. The English hailed my fall as the greatest political victory of the whole war, and in August they carried out air bombardments of exceptional violence in order to 'soften up' the nation's moral resistance and make them ripe for a surrender which was already being mentioned.

The material and moral disorder had now reached such proportions as to cause a certain uneasiness in Crown circles.

A Memorandum from the King

Among the many papers which the fugitives of September 8th did not succeed in concealing as they had planned near the Swiss frontier, was a significant one headed as follows in Badoglio's handwriting:

Memorandum which H.M. the King told me he had composed and which he gave me in audience on August 16th, 1943.

BADOGLIO.

Here is the actual text of the memorandum:[2]

The present Government must conserve and maintain in all its activities its character of a "Military Government" as declared in the proclamation of July 25th and as clearly emerges from its very constitution—Head of the Government: Marshal Badoglio; the ministers: all technical experts.

The tackling of political problems must be shelved till a future period and the formation of a new government, and must take place in a very different atmosphere, one more tranquil for the country's fate.

[1] i.e., the Carabinieri.

[2] It is difficult to decide whether this document is authentic or not. The Rome liberal (i.e., Conservative) paper, *Risorgimento Liberale*, August 26th, 1944, publishing it in an extract from Mussolini's book, is inclined to believe in its authenticity since "it corresponds exactly with Victor Emmanuel's intentions." (Authenticity since confirmed by Badoglio.)

The promise given by the King in his proclamation and countersigned by Marshal Badoglio must be kept: "No recriminations will be allowed."

The elimination on principle of all ex-members of the Fascist party from all public activity must therefore definitely cease.

All Italians, once their good faith is known, must have an equal duty and an equal right to serve their King and country.

A revision of single posts must be carefully undertaken so as to dismiss the unworthy and punish the guilty.

No open organisation of any party should be permitted or tolerated. Nor should they make themselves known in publications and pamphlets, whether Labour Democrats, the Republican Party or any other. There are many papers in circulation the authorship of which is easily discernible and which "the existing laws punish severely."

All tolerance is weakness, all weakness a lack of loyalty to the country.

The Commissions set up in excessive number by the Ministries have been unfavourably received by the sounder part of the country; all, at home or abroad, may be led to believe that every branch of public administration is definitely corrupt. Everyone will expect the laws and institutions to be overset at every change in the government.

If the original scheme is persisted in we shall end up with the absurdity of implicitly judging and condemning the work of the King himself.

The bulk of ex-members of the Fascist Party, who were honest and are now suddenly eliminated from all activity through no special fault of their own, will be easily led to transfer their own organisation and technique to the extremist parties and thus add to the future difficulties of any legal government.

The majority of these, seeing themselves abandoned by the King, persecuted by the Government, misjudged and insulted by the exiguous minority of the old parties (which for twenty years had supinely accepted any compromise and let their own political tendencies become assimilated), this majority will in a short time reappear in the squares in defence of the bourgeoisie against Communism, but this time they will lean decidedly to the Left and away from the monarchy.

The time is a difficult one. The Government will find it easier if all Italians, free from fear of constantly fresh repression, viewed and judged with a single though severe judgment, can again take up normal life which, for all honest people without exception, began on July 25th as the King solemnly promised.

The Monarchy's Regrets and Fears

Here ends the royal memorandum, the significance of which is evident. What the Marshal, to whom the note was handed personally, replied is not known. It is clear that already by the middle of that unlucky August, Victor of Savoy began to have fears for his future. He had started the avalanche and now—seeing its accelerating motion—attempted to slow it up. Too late ! He seemed to be regretting the liquidation of a régime in the ranks of which he had found sincere and numerous champions, but now the die had been cast. Even if Badoglio had wished to do so, he could no longer have freed himself from the parties who had assisted him in the *coup d'état*, whose prisoner he now was and with whom he was to perfect the manœuvre leading to the capitulation of September.

The royal document of August 16th is an attempt—a fruitless one—to absolve himself from his responsibilities and to leave a door of escape open ; the hint at a revival of Communism is eloquent. Did Victor of Savoy perhaps sense the approach of something or someone later to be revealed as Palmiro Togliatti ?

It was a pious illusion to think that the mighty torrent which had burst its bounds could return to the river-bed of more or less legality, under a government of officials.

The Marshal passed the memorandum along to the files, where it was later found. That document might well be called "The Dynasty's First Cry of Alarm."

CHAPTER XI

TOWARDS CAPITULATION

IN THE SECOND HALF of August, having taken down the flags from the windows where they had remained for over a fortnight as if to celebrate the most triumphant victory, having exhausted the pæans on liberty regained, having seen the terrible raids and the wild disorder of food supplies, it became necessary to 'distract' public opinion ; and so the fortnight of the 'scandals' began.

"*Illicit Enrichment*"

It began with 'illicit enrichment.'[1] All the higher Party officials had been thieves, all of them profiteers. Not one honest man among them, even if you searched for him with the proverbial lantern of Diogenes. They even got as far as fixing at 120 milliards the total of money which the Party officials had stolen from the Italian nation.

By the restitution of that really astronomical sum to the Treasury they hoped to make good the budget deficit. All this would seem almost incredible if it had not actually appeared in print. The cellars and attics of the houses belonging to Fascists were full of all sorts of food. That was one of the most singular examples of 'mass psychosis'—the piles of gold and the sides of bacon.

[1] On August 4th, 1943, the Badoglio Cabinet instituted a "Special Commission" "to inquire into the rapid growth of the personal and real property of persons who held public office or exercised political activity between October 28th, 1922 (March on Rome) and July 24th, 1943," and to consider the transfer of such property to the State. On September 2nd, 1943, the Commission stated that the long list of officials who had accumulated illicit wealth included many Fascist Ministers, Under-Secretaries, Ambassadors, and high Party chiefs. The investigations had been particularly fruitful in the case of Ciano and his wife, Edda.

All this was designed to arouse the lowest instincts of the mob. One of the families particularly singled out by the notorious Commission presided over by the traitor Casati, was that of Ciano.

It was an indirect manœuvre aimed at myself—of whom many people may often have been thinking, although, in accordance with the instructions issued by the Badoglio censorship, no one dared utter my name.

As to the fortune belonging to Count Galeazzo Ciano's family, it was mentioned in terms of milliards. The letter which Count Ciano addressed to Marshal Badoglio on August 23rd, 1943, is a political rather than a private document.

Here is the actual text:

Rome,
23rd August, 1943.

Illustrious Marshal,

I read with great bitterness an article in the Corriere della Sera *which outraged the memory of my father. I scorn to descend to polemics with anonymous journalists who rake mud in order to fling it in the face of the dead, but I hold it my duty instead to inform Your Excellency (pending the findings of the Commission in this matter) of the exact total of the whole inheritance left me and my late sister by my father.*

At his death he was in possession of the following estate:

1. *Three-quarters of the printing and publishing firm of the newspaper* Il Telegrafo *of Leghorn.*
2. *Four buildings in Rome to the value of about five million lire at the time of his death.*
3. *Industrial holdings as follows: "Società Romana di elettricità,"* 1,400 *shares; Terni,* 500 *shares; Montecatini,* 2,000 *shares; Valdagno,* 1,000 *shares; Metallurgica*[1], 1,000 *shares; "Navigazione generale,"* 300 *shares; Ilva,* 500 *shares; Anic,* 1,000 *shares; Monte Amiata,* 1,000 *shares; I.M.I,* 100 *shares; "Consorzio Credito Opere Pubbliche,"* 24 *shares; Treasury Bonds,* 1 *million; cash, Lire* 355,089*; current postal account, Lire* 32,975.

Proof of this information is in my hands and is of course completely at Your Excellency's disposal.

I am sure that these figures, far removed from the astronomical flights of fancy of anonymous calumniators, will be estimated by

[1] The words "Metallurgica, 1,000 shares" are omitted in the second edition.

Your Excellency's impartial mind not as the dishonourable booty of a profiteer, but rather as the just reward of an extremely active life. And it is for this reason, Your Excellency, that I turn only to Marshal Badoglio, in order that the memory and honour of a soldier of Italy may be protected. GALEAZZO CIANO.

The Handing Over of my Person one of the Terms of Surrender

Churchill's speech of September 22nd proves that already by the last ten days of August the principal clauses at least of the unconditional surrender had been fixed at Lisbon. Among them was one proposing the handing over of my person to the enemy. That is without precedent in the history of mankind! During the troubled days of September after my liberation on the Gran Sasso, the journals did not publish the full verbatim text of Churchill's speech. Though now rather late in the day, it is worth publishing it, in order to complete the evidence. At the House of Commons on September 22nd[1], while speaking of events in Italy, Churchill said:[2]

"Unconditional surrender of course comprises everything, but not only was a special provision for the surrender of war criminals included in the longer terms, but a particular stipulation was made for the surrender of Signor Mussolini.[3] It was not, however, possible to arrange for him to be delivered specially and separately before the Armistice and our great landing took place, for this would certainly have disclosed the intentions of the Italian Government to the enemy, who were intermingled with them at every point and who had them completely[4] in their power.

[1] It was in fact on September 21st.

[2] The Italian differs somewhat from the original. Only those variations which are of interest are given in footnotes.

[3] The 'Longer Terms' (as distinct from the 'Short Terms,' i.e., the Armistice of Cassibile, Sicily, of September 3rd) are the 'Additional Conditions,' known as the 'Instrument of Surrender of Italy,' signed at Malta on September 29th by Marshal Badoglio and General Eisenhower. Section 29 stipulates: "Benito Mussolini, his chief Fascist associates and all persons suspected of having committed war crimes or analogous offences whose names appear on lists to be communicated by the United Nations will forthwith be apprehended and surrendered into the hands of the United Nations. Any instructions given by the United Nations for this purpose will be complied with."

[4] "... *completely* in their power ..."; Mr. Churchill said, "... *so largely* in their power ..."

"So the Italian position had to be that although an internal revolution had taken place in Italy, they were still the allies of Germany and were carrying on common cause with them. This was a very difficult position to maintain day after day with the pistol of the Gestapo pointing at the nape of so many necks.

"We had every reason to believe that Mussolini was being kept under a strong guard at a secure place, and certainly it was very much to the interests of the Badoglio Government to make certain[1] that he did not escape.

"Mussolini has himself been reported to have declared that he believed that he was being delivered to the Allies. This was certainly the intention and is what would have taken place but for circumstances unhappily[2] beyond our control. The measures which the Badoglio Government took were carefully conceived and were the best they could do to hold Mussolini, but they did not provide against so heavy a parachute descent as the Germans made at the particular point where he was confined. It may be noticed that they sent him some books[3] of Nietzsche and some other works to console or diversify his confinement,[4] and they no doubt were thus pretty well acquainted where he was and the conditions under which he was confined. But the stroke was one of great daring and conducted with a heavy force.

"It certainly shows there are many possibilities of this kind open in modern war. I do not think there was any slackness or breach of faith on the part of the Badoglio Government, and they had one card up their sleeve.

"The Carabinieri guards had orders to shoot Mussolini if there was any attempt to rescue him, but they failed in their duty, having regard to the superior[5] German force who descended upon them from the air and who undoubtedly would have held them responsible for the prisoner's health and safety. So much for that."

[1] ". . . to *make certain* that he did not escape"; Mr. Churchill said, ". . . to *see* that he did not escape——"

[2] ". . . circumstances *unhappily* beyond our control"; Mr. Churchill said, ". . . circumstances *entirely* beyond our control."

[3] ". . . *they* sent him some books"; Mr. Churchill said, ". . . *Hitler* sent him some books."

[4] ". . . to console or diversify his confinement"; Mr. Churchill added, "The Italians could hardly have refused this civility and the Germans. . . ."

[5] ". . . having regard to the *superior* German force". Mr. Churchill said, ". . . *considerable* German force."

Those were the words transmitted by Reuter at 7 p.m. on September 22nd, 1943.

That Marshal Badoglio had, as Churchill said, "carefully" conceived the measures taken to ensure my captivity and my eventual handing over to the enemy, is proved by this letter in the Marshal's own handwriting to the Chief of Police, Senise:

Excellency,

This morning I have informed the Commander-in-Chief of the Carabinieri, His Excellency Cerica, as follows:

"*The Inspector-General of Public Security, Saverio Polito, is responsible for the custody of the former Head of the Government, Benito Mussolini.*

"*He alone is personally responsible to the Government for ensuring that the aforesaid Mussolini does not escape or is not removed from prison by anyone whatsoever.*

"*General Polito will ask the High Command of the Carabinieri and the Chief of Police for all the personnel he requires, giving the names of those he desires.*

"*All his demands are to be met. Inspector Polito will keep me frequently informed.*"

BADOGLIO.

Rome,
16*th* *August*, 1943.

The 'Scandal' Campaign

Having decided on my being handed over to the English and laid down the terms of it, they had to build up a scandal about me, and to cover me with ridicule and abuse, so that the nation, already forgetful of me, would consider my handing over to the enemy as the handing over of a man now not only politically but also physically and morally spent.

Suddenly, the floodgates of gossip were thrown open, and the five per cent. of truth was embroidered with wild fancies of all sorts which, however, did not fail to excite the curiosity of the mob. No one was in a position to cast the first stone—none of the great or lesser men of the past, none of the present, least of all Marshal Badoglio; but the blow was struck. It was necessary to make an end of me, first of all by a silence of the grave, and then by ridicule.[1] The affair lasted two days—but that was enough. There was no lack of those who deplored these tactics and spoke of a "boomerang," but this was to delude oneself. The stroke was successful. It is the Jesuits, those great scholars of the human heart, who are credited with originating the well-known maxim: "Keep on slandering, some of the mud will stick."

And there is no doubt that some did stick.

Capitulation is Imminent

At the end of August, capitulation was in the air. The enormous crime which will weigh heavily for centuries on the country's history was about to be committed; they were in process, that is, of transforming Italian soil into a bloody battlefield for enemy armies.

Only a fool could have thought that things would turn out otherwise—only a fool, who had neglected to read the telegraphed and telephoned bulletins which were sent to Rome every morning by the frontier officials and contained precise details of the despatch to Italy of German men and materials. These bulletins were left on the table by the fugitives of September 8th. Ever since the morning of July 26th, news and details had been coming in from the Brenner, the Tarvisio and the Ventimiglia passes, of movements of German divisions. Every day hundreds of vehicles—lorries, armoured cars and troop formations. Right from the beginning, Germany had grasped that the Badoglio Government had only one programme—to surrender, and then to take up arms against their ally. It is true that on July 28th Marshal Badoglio had had the effrontery to send the following telegram to the Führer—but words deceive no one:

Führer,

After taking the oath to His Majesty the King Emperor, the Council of Ministers presided over by myself took up office yesterday. As already declared in my proclamation issued to the Italian people and officially communicated to your ambassador, we shall carry on the war in the spirit of our alliance. I wish to confirm

[1] After a month's complete silence on Mussolini, the Rome papers of August 29th came out with sensational articles on the Dictator's private life, illustrating his relations with the Petacci sisters.

this to you and to ask you to give audience to General Marras who is coming to your headquarters on a special mission from me. I am glad of this opportunity, Führer, of expressing my kindest regards.

signed,
BADOGLIO.

By the second half of August the now overt signs of the King's and Badoglio's policy could no longer escape the notice of German observers either in Rome or Lisbon. All of it could be summed up in one word: Capitulation.[1]

Withdrawal of Large Formations Stationed Abroad

One of the most suspect symptoms was the request to the German Supreme Command to authorise the withdrawal of many of the large Italian formations stationed outside the country. Territory conquered with blood would have to be abandoned, but they wanted the divisions within reach, so as to take their ally in the rear, once the fronts had changed over. A telegram signed Guariglia and bearing the date August 10th, rings false. The text is:

To the Royal Embassy, Berlin.

Please contact German Foreign Office immediately and inform them of the following:

"*As was said at the Tarvisio meeting*[2] *on the 6th inst., the Italian Supreme Command has decided to recall the whole of the 4th Army stationed in metropolitan France, and an Army Corps of three divisions from the troops now stationed in Slovene-Croat territory.*

The reasons prompting the present decision are various and have already been explained at Tarvisio.

First of all, the Supreme Command feels the necessity of reinforcing the defence of home territory. Apart from this, it seems

[1] The paragraph "By the second half of August . . . Capitulation" is omitted in the second edition.

[2] On August 10th, 1943, it was stated in Berlin that conversations were proceeding with Italy, but no official announcement was made either in Germany or Italy about the meeting of the two Foreign Ministers. According to the *Neue Zürcher Zeitung* (quoted in the British Press, August 18th, 1943), they had met on August 6th at *Treviso*. Mussolini's reading *Tarvisio*, here and below, is correct, as appears from other sources.

to us opportune that our own units should complete the formations of the German divisions in Italy, whose task appears to be limited to the defence of a few sectors, whereas it is obvious that on our part we must provide for the defence of our whole national territory. As I myself pointed out explicitly to Herr von Ribbentrop, reasons of a political and moral nature make it necessary for the nation to feel that the defence of its territory is not being entrusted only to the troops of our ally, but also, and mainly, to Italian soldiers.

You will take the opportunity of drawing attention to these and any other points which may seem more appropriate to you, to make the German Foreign Office realise the necessity of this decision.

We realise that the evacuation of these forces will involve problems and questions of a political nature, as von Ribbentrop himself said, but we earnestly hope that everything can be settled in a manner satisfactory to both parties.

To this end, therefore, the necessary contacts must immediately be made by the competent authorities concerned, both political and military.

GUARIGLIA.

CHAPTER XII

SEPTEMBER ON THE GRAN SASSO

IN MY SPEECH TO the Grand Council I had declared that, à propos of a 'popular' or 'unpopular' war, I did not wish to waken the "great shades of the past," that is, I did not wish to go back to the nineteenth century in order to discover which wars were more popular and which less, in the cycle of the Risorgimento.

Here is the part of my speech which was then condensed into a few words.

A Popular or Unpopular War

I began by recalling the 1915–18 war which was declared in an atmosphere of nothing less than civil war, in a struggle between neutralists and interventionists with no quarter given—a civil war which continued until Caporetto, had a ten months' truce during our recovery on the Piave, and started again immediately afterwards, the minute the sham peace of Versailles had been signed. Was the 1915–18 war 'popular'? It was called the Milanese war, and many soldiers in the ranks had to conceal the fact that they came from the Lombard capital in order to escape the wrath and insults of their comrades.

Let the volunteers of those days speak—if there are any left, as it is to be hoped there are! The 'volunteers' were harassed in all manner of ways. "Are you a volunteer?" they said. "Then show how *voluntarily* you do everything!" Not even the Irredentists who enthusiastically enrolled themselves in the Italian ranks found the atmosphere in the least comradely. Men like Battisti[1] and Sauro[2] met with so much bitterness that only their boundless love for Italy enabled them to overcome it.

Groups of volunteers leaped from the trenches in October 1915 in a fury of heroism which contained also an element of disgust and exasperation at the hostile, rebellious surroundings in which they found themselves. The regular Army never had the slightest sympathy for the volunteers. The Army was considered as the domain of the Royal House. Its task was chiefly to defend existing institutions and, also, to make war, in which case the majority of officers considered it not as the long-desired and crowning glory of a mission but as a regrettable nuisance which everyone wished to avoid.

Already by October, 1915, the flower of the Italian volunteers, from Corridoni to Deffenu, had been mown down in the trenches on the first heights of the Carso beyond the Isonzo. There were probably no volunteers left in the Italian army when, after Battisti's martyrdom on August 14th, 1916, General Cadorna decided to issue a circular of two printed pages in which he said that 'volunteers' were not to be made objects of derision but were to be respected by officers and men.

The 1915–18 war was not 'popular' with the aristocracy or in Court circles, still less among the clerical and would-be political sets. It was to the accompaniment of violent popular agitation ; of the famous manifesto "*War or a Republic*" which I wrote on the spur of the moment after a meeting of the leaders of the Milanese interventionists held in the Via Palermo ; and of d'Annunzio's gigantic demonstrations in Rome, that the three hundred deputies of the Giolitti caucus buried themselves in the depths of their constituencies and a declaration of war was brought about through the 'Malthusian' instinct.

It is a law of history that when there are two contrary currents of opinion in a nation, one wanting war and the other peace, the latter party is invariably defeated even when, as always happens, it represents, numerically speaking, the majority. The reason for this is obvious. Those who call themselves "interventionists"

[1] Cesare Battisti, born 1875 at Trento ; at the age of 20 entered politics as an Irredentist and Socialist. Enthusiastic supporter of Italy's intervention in the Great War ; joined the Alpini on May 29th, 1915 ; in July, 1916, he was captured by the Austrians and executed for high treason.

[2] Nazario Sauro, born 1880 at Capodistria, was among the first refugees from Austrian territory to undertake interventionist propaganda when the Great War broke out. Volunteered for the Italian Navy, May, 1915. Fell into Austrian hands and was executed for high treason in August, 1916.

are young and ardent, they make up a dynamic minority as against the static majority.

Were the wars of the Risorgimento 'popular,' by any chance?

The history of the Risorgimento has still to be written; a synthesis has still to be made of its history as manipulated by the monarchists (who held a mortgage on the Risorgimento) and the republican version. Judgment must be passed on the contribution made by the people and that made by the Crown—that made by revolution and that made by diplomacy. Among the oleographs which were inflicted on us in childhood was one formerly very widely diffused, representing the four 'makers' of the Risorgimento: Victor Emmanuel, in immensely long pantaloons with spurs sticking out beneath them, and the large moustachios which made him look like a countryman dressed up; Cavour, with spectacles diplomatically concealing his expression, while with his short beard framing his face, he looked a little like a distinguished elderly gentleman; these two represented the Royal House and diplomacy. Then came Garibaldi, the epitome of strength and humanity, the generous volunteer for every great adventure, in love with Italy with all the ardour personified by his Red Shirts, ingenuous and "rowdy" as he called himself, using an original and unrhetorical adjective, a true champion of the ancient Liguro-Italian race. Fourth and last came Mazzini, of the same race, born by the same sea, preoccupied, thoughtful, hard as granite, fanatical, with a sublime, though for long impracticable Republican orthodoxy. It was these two latter who made the wars of the Risorgimento possible, even if not popular.

The public had not then access to the sources which we now possess; we may therefore recall the attitude of the Piedmont Parliament with regard to the wars which, in the twenty odd years between 1848 and 1870, brought the House of Savoy to Rome.

The War of the Risorgimento

The war of 1848 seems to have been fairly popular. But even from the beginning, certain deputies did not fail to make criticisms and reservations, especially Brofferio[1] who, as early as May 29th, in the course of a discussion on the speech in reply to the Crown, touched on the subject—always a painful one in Italy—of the generals' conduct of the war. In a later sitting, the deputies

[1] Angelo Brofferio, born 1802, fought for constitutional reforms. As deputy in the Piedmont Parliament, he became famous in 1848–9 for his vehement Republicanism.

Moffa di Lisio[1] and Grossi continued their criticisms, which naturally became extremely lively as often as military operations took a not exactly brilliant course. In these criticisms the inactivity of the generals was denounced over and over again, which Cesare Balbo,[2] President of the Council, found somewhat embarrassing.

Agitation rose to the pitch of causing a crisis in the Government, even though in the middle of a war, and in a difficult phase of it at that. The new Cabinet, presided over by Casati[3], proclaimed at the sitting of July 27th that "the war goes on" (as Badoglio did on July 26th), but now events were leading to an armistice which was considered a betrayal.

Brofferio cried: "If you persist in a peace which would be fatal to us, we shall answer you with cannons and not with protocols, and the representatives of the people will declare war on you yourselves, a ceaseless, stubborn, tireless war."

Casati could not carry on, and Gioberti[4] appeared on the scene, but he in his turn could not control the passions that had been unleashed, and he dissolved the Chamber. Three cabinets in nine months! Vincenzo Gioberti took the helm again in March, 1849, in a completely negative atmosphere, and lasted a little over a week. Charles Albert abdicated,[5] thus setting an example which his descendant, in infinitely graver circumstances, has so far taken good care not to imitate!

[1] Guglielmo Moffa Gribaldi di Lisio, born 1791, deputy, then Minister for War in the Casati Ministry which replaced that of Cesare Balbo in 1848, at the time of the defeat at Custozza.

[2] Cesare Balbo, born 1789, in Turin; appointed President of the first constitutional Ministry by Charles Albert on March 13th, 1848; after three months he resigned (July 25th, 1848) as a result of the unsuccessful conduct of the War of Independence.

[3] Count Gabrio Casati, born 1798 in Milan, played a leading part in the Milan insurrection of 1848. He was in favour of the union of Lombardy with Piedmont. Succeeded Cesare Balbo as President of the new ministry on the eve of the defeat at Custozza. On August 7th, he went with Gioberti to ask the King to continue the war, but Charles Albert entrusted Revel with the negotiation of an Armistice.

[4] Vincenzo Gioberti, the philosopher, on his return from fifteen years' exile, became a member of Casati's Government from August 4th-18th, 1848; from December 16th, 1848, to February 10th, 1849, he was President of the Council.

[5] On March 12th, 1849, Charles Albert denounced the Vigevano Armistice (which had been signed on August 9th, 1848), but he was decisively beaten at Novara on March 23rd, 1849, and abdicated in favour of his son on the same evening.

The Intervention in the Crimea

Still less popular was the Crimean war, or rather, Piedmont's intervention in the war which had broken out between Russia and Turkey. The ratification of the Treaty of Alliance between Piedmont and the Great Powers (France and England)—a real masterpiece of Cavour's policy—was brought before the Chamber on February 3rd, 1855, and met with lively opposition as much from the Right as the Left.[1]

Brofferio, among other things, accused Cavour of not having a clear policy and of having "no respect for conventions and constitutional morality," and denounced the utter uselessness as well as the inopportunity of the treaty. "The alliance with Turkey is an insult to Piedmont and a disgrace to Italy. We have defied all sorts of privations, we have submitted to intolerable taxes, we have boldly faced the bankruptcy of the State in the hope of being able, one day, to return to the field with the cry: 'Out with the foreigner!' And now? We have done all this in order to squander our soldiers and our millions in the Crimea for the benefit of Italy's enemies." And he concluded: "If you approve this treaty, the downfall of Piedmont and the ruin of Italy will be an accomplished fact."

Cavour's own brother Gustavo, a deputy,[2] voted against it. It was on that occasion that Cavour made one of his best speeches.

The treaty was ratified, but sixty deputies voted against it, to one hundred and one in favour.

The Betrayal of Villafranca

The war of 1859 also aroused strong opposition. Cavour practically dismissed the Chamber and, at the last moment, called for extraordinary powers which were granted him by 110 votes to twenty-three. Everyone speaks of the terrible indignation, the wave of real fury which swept all Italy at the news of

[1] Cavour desired that Piedmont should enter into the Alliance with France and Great Britain as an equal, so that the Italian question should be brought up at the end of the war in the Crimea. However, when Austria entered into an agreement with the Allies in December, 1854, he hastened to join the Allies on their own terms, and despite opposition from the Cabinet, signed the treaty of alliance on January 25th, 1855. Italian intervention gained Italy recognition and a place at the peace conference (where the Italian question was discussed) but no territorial gains.

[2] Gustavo Benso Cavour, elder brother of Count Camillo Benso Cavour, with whom he often disagreed, especially on ecclesiastical policy.

the betrayal perpetrated by Napoleon III at Villafranca.[1] The polemics were exceptionally violent ; and yet Napoleon's betrayal was not on the same scale or of the same nature as that consummated by the House of Savoy on September 8th, 1943 ! And, in any case, he was a foreign monarch.

But the Italians will never forgive Napoleon, whose statue remained for years and years in the courtyard of the Senate at Milan, abandoned like a bit of worthless rubble.

The Shepherd's Prophecy

From a material point of view my captivity was not actually harsh, except at La Maddalena—and there because of the natural poverty of the island and the general difficulties. The officers and men always treated me very respectfully, too. From the beginning of September facilities even increased. I always took my meals alone, but in the evening I could now listen to the wireless, receive a few papers or play cards with my guard. All this began to look suspicious. I was reminded of the better treatment reserved for men condemned to death.

The rumours which came from L'Aquila were more and more confused. The war communiqués made it clear that it was now only a sham war.

On September 1st the Pope made a speech which I also heard ; the fervently pacifist tone of that oration, broadcast at such a time, was part of a spiritual preparation for the event now drawing to a close. At the Refuge Inn all went on peacefully. I left the building only in the early afternoon, and then only for a few hundred yards, always accompanied by an N.C.O. One morning machine-guns were placed each side of the gate. Another morning they carried out an exercise with heavy machine-guns on the neighbouring heights.

The Gran Sasso is really fascinating from the æsthetic point of view. The rugged profile of that mountain rising to over 10,000 feet in the heart of Italy cannot easily be forgotten. The rock is bare, but at the foot of the highest peak a great plateau extends to the south-east, the *Campo Imperatore*, at least 12½

[1] Napoleon III, after having announced that he would free Italy "from the Alps to the Adriatic," and having won several victories over the Austrian forces, entered into negotiations with the Emperor Francis Joseph, resulting in the treaty of Villafranca, signed July 11th, 1859. By this Austria ceded to France—and France to Piedmont—the whole of Lombardy, except Mantua and Peschiera ; Venetia, though remaining under Austrian sovereignty, was to become part of an Italian Confederation under the Pope's Presidency.

miles long, with gentle slopes, an ideal spot for winter sports.

At the beginning of September, many flocks which had come up from the Campagna in the spring and had been pasturing on this and the neighbouring plains were now slowly drifting away and preparing to go back again. Sometimes the owners of the herds appeared on horseback and then vanished along the ridge of the mountain, standing out against the skyline like figures from another age.

There is an indefinable something about the people and things—and even the air—of the Abruzzi which captures one's heart. One day a shepherd came up to me and said in a very low voice: "Excellency, the Germans are already at the gates of Rome. The Government is on the point of fleeing, if it has not already done so. We country people have all remained Fascist. Nobody has bothered us hereabouts. They have only closed down the local headquarters. People are always speaking of you. They say that you have fled to Spain, or that you have been killed, or that you died in hospital in Rome after an operation, or that they shot you at Fort Boccea. I believe that when they know where you are, the Germans will come and set you free. Now I am taking my sheep down, and I myself will tell them where you are. Nowadays it doesn't take long, the sheep go by train. When I tell my wife that I have seen you she will say I have gone mad. Now the sergeant is coming, so good-bye to you."

CHAPTER XIII

THE CROWN COUNCIL AND THE CAPITULATION

IT WAS 7 P.M. ON September 8th when news arrived that an armistice had been concluded ; people listened in to all the radio transmissions. From that moment vigilance was strengthened, and a sentry was posted outside my room by night as well. The inspector in charge of the guard arrangements seemed increasingly worried. The Army had received the Armistice declaration without excessive enthusiasm. From Rome came the first news of the King's and Badoglio's flight and of the beginning of the break-up of the armed forces and the whole nation. Barrack-room gossip let loose a non-stop flood of rumours.

Resolve Not to Give Myself up Alive to the Enemy

On the 10th, at 8 p.m., I went down to the drawing-room and switched on the wireless. As it happened I picked up Berlin, and I distinctly heard this announcement, date-lined Algiers, and saying : "Allied General Headquarters have officially announced that among the Armistice terms is included the handing over of Mussolini to the Allies." This started a discussion.

One of those present said : "An announcement of that sort has already been put out, but London later contradicted it." I was convinced, on the contrary, that the announcement corresponded to the truth. I was determined not to give myself up alive to the English, or, above all, to the Americans. The commander of the Carabinieri, who had been taken prisoner by the English in Egypt and who apparently loathed them profoundly, said to me : "An hour before that happens, you will be warned and will be able to escape. I swear this to you on the head of my only son."

These words, spoken in the accents of sincerity and accompanied with tears, expressed the man's feelings ; but who could guarantee that other factors would not intervene at the last moment ? Among the guards there were many young ones who did not conceal their sympathy for me ; but there were four or five with a furtive, uneasy look, who bore the internal and external aspect of real cut-throats.

On September 11th,[1] all the news and rumours from Rome went to show that confusion was at its height, while German troops were proceeding to occupy all our territory.

In the morning, the officers commanding the Gran Sasso detachment went down to L'Aquila, where they had a long conference with the local Prefect, and a no less long telephone conversation with the Chief of Police, who still remained at the Palazzo Viminale.

September 7th and 8th in Rome

Nothing definite was known about the Armistice terms ; but the surrender imposed had been accepted. Many versions have been given of the course of events on September 7th and 8th. The most probable is the following. It is a report by one who was present and lived through it. Here it is :

"On September 7th, in the late afternoon, the American General Taylor, young and sturdy, accompanied by an elderly colonel, also American, arrived at the Palazzo Caprara[2] in a motor-ambulance from Gaeta, where he had landed from an Italian monitor.

"My informant received him.[3] He already knew of this visit and first informed General Roatta, who declared that he did not wish to have any conversation with the above general ; then General Rossi, Deputy-Chief of General Staff, who also refused —the usual shirking of responsibility. Finally, he was received by General Carboni, who asked his Chief of Staff for the map

[1] The first edition has a wrong date, *September 15th.*

[2] Palazzo Caprara : General Staff Headquarters in the Via Venti Settembre, Rome.

[3] General Taylor and Colonel Gardiner were received by Colonel Giorgio Salvi, General Carboni's Chief of Staff. It seems very likely that he was one of the informants of Mussolini's source. Colonel Salvi's conduct and, by implication, the value of his testimony are vigorously attacked by his former superior, General Carboni, in his book "L'Armistizio e la Difesa di Roma," Rome, 1945, pp. 40-41. Italian accounts of the actual happenings are strongly

showing the disposition of the Italian and German troops in the Rome area.

"The American general was extremely irritated by the way he was kept waiting before being received by General Carboni."

An American General in Conference with General Carboni

"The conference lasted for over three hours. Apparently Carboni made it quite clear that the Italian forces could not hold the Germans in the Rome area for more than five hours. General Taylor replied that, on the contrary, General Castellano, when he signed the Armistice on September 3rd, had made it appear that the Italian forces were perfectly capable of coping with the Germans, and had declared that with Anglo-American aid with regard to the Rome area, or even without it, in Rome as in northern Italy the Germans would be decisively beaten, or, at least, brought to such straits that they would consider the Italian situation wound up, as far as the war with the Allies was concerned.

"On the strength of this, Eisenhower, fearing lest the Italians change their minds again and constitute (as in fact they were to do) a valuable aid to the Germans, insisted on the immediate signing of the Armistice on September 3rd, to which Castellano agreed, in view of the powers he had been given.

"Taylor was convinced by General Carboni's account and, after a dinner which seems to have been very sumptuous, according to the tradition of the Staff mess (as I know by experience), they went together to see Badoglio at his house, where they had a long conference, lasting till three in the morning.

"Badoglio requested General Taylor to make clear the difficult situation in which the Italian forces would find themselves if the Armistice were announced prematurely; and they agreed that no action to that effect should be taken prior to September 16th.

"No one knows why the American general and his adjutant did not leave until 4 p.m. on September 8th. They left in a

conflicting. They are all designed to exonerate one or other of the parties concerned, by blaming the other side for the failure of the Italian Armed Forces to resist the Germans; e.g., P. Monelli's "Roma 1943" (in favour of the King against Carboni), to which Carboni's book (attacking Badoglio, Roatta, Acquarone and, by implication, the King) is a reply. Another account, by David Brown, of Reuter's, is contained in the *Saturday Evening Post*, September 9th, 1944, and September 16th, 1944; it speaks of Carboni's pessimism and Badoglio's 'feebleness'.

special plane of the Royal Italian Air Force (my informant gave them civilian clothes to get to the airport).

"The announcement of the Armistice overtook the American general while still on his journey.

"Then why did General Eisenhower send him on this mission ?[1]

"After the announcement of the Armistice had been made on the Italian side, the troops were informed at 8 p.m. that a state of emergency existed.

"General Roatta, in an armoured car belonging to the Army, together with his adjutant, Lt.-Col. Fenazzi, took refuge at the Palazzo Caprara where, late at night, the chief Staff officers joined them.

"At four in the morning, General Carboni, who came out very pale from a talk with Badoglio at the War Office, gave orders for the motorised Army Corps to disengage and withdraw to Tivoli.

"His Chief of Staff pointed out the impossibility of carrying out such an order without compromising the fate of the units already partly engaged or in contact with the Germans.

"Carboni replied that the King was at Tivoli, and this argument convinced everybody. The written order was signed by General De Stefanis, the only one still there at five or six in the morning. Exit Carboni till the evening of the 9th.

"The troops found themselves in a tragic maze of orders and counter-orders. Calvi di Bergolo assumed command of the Army Corps and confirmed the order, which was carried out.

"Re-enter Carboni on the evening of the 9th, saying that he is in favour of negotiating with the Germans. Negotiations start, Caviglia intervenes. Negotiations broken off during the morning of the 10th. Carboni decides to fight. Fresh intervention by Calvi. Exit Carboni.

"The troops disband. Various generals flee in disguise."

5 p.m. on September 8th

"At 5 p.m. on September 8th, General De Stefanis received a

[1] According to various accounts from Allied correspondents and Carboni's book, *l.c.*, p. 28, the purpose of the Taylor mission was to arrange for an American airborne expedition to secure Rome with the help of Italian troops, a plan which had been suggested by General Castellano in Sicily after the signing of the Armistice. Mussolini's version ignores this fact and does not substitute any alternative object, with the result that both the Allies and the Royal Government are made to appear ridiculous. Mussolini's source either ignores the true facts, or else his version has been carefully edited by Mussolini for his own purposes.

telephone call from Badoglio's Cabinet to go at once to the Quirinal, in place of General Roatta, who was engaged with Marshall Kesselring in one of the normal operational conferences.

"General De Stefanis telephoned the Quirinal for confirmation of the request, as this urgent call to the royal palace seemed strange to him. They confirmed it.

"At 5.30 he reached the Quirinal and learned that an ultra-secret Crown Council had been convened.

"Almost without warning, he found himself in a drawing-room in the presence of the King. Badoglio, Acquarone, Ambrosio, Sorice, Sandalli, De Courten and Guariglia had been convened as well. General Carboni does not seem to have been present.

"Badoglio began to speak, and said that in view of the desperate situation, the King had convened them to learn their opinions. To the astonishment of all present, as their faces showed, Ambrosio said that on September 3rd an Armistice had been signed with the Anglo-Americans. He read its clauses, and said that the Anglo-Americans had suddenly announced it, contrary to the provisions made. So much for the timely knowledge of the Chiefs of Staff of the Army, Navy and Air Force.

"Guariglia protested at not having been informed of the signing which had taken place. De Stefanis made every possible reservation in view of Roatta's absence, asked them to wait for him, and expressed himself as personally against it. Acquarone pressed for the immediate acceptance of the Armistice.

"Badoglio was in a state of nervous depression.

"Most of them expressed themselves against it.

"Badoglio is said to have exclaimed: 'Then I can't carry on !'

"At 6.15 p.m. a radio message came from Eisenhower, conceived in terms of a two-hour ultimatum.

"Faced with this ultimatum, panic and indecision seized the minds of all present.

"It seems that Eisenhower, confronted with a new demand, had stated that guarantees for the future would be given with the most generous understanding of the conditions under which Italy and her government were now labouring.

"At 7 p.m. the King rose to his feet, stated that he had decided to accept the Armistice and asked them to compose an official Italian announcement to that effect, to be broadcast at 8 p.m., the time at which the Anglo-American ultimatum expired.

"De Stefanis was against the last part of the announcement, that is, the part concerning, 'from whatever Power hostilities may proceed. . . .' etc.

"His view was finally accepted by the King himself, and it was decided to leave out the last part of the announcement.

"At 7.30 p.m. the Council dissolved.

"At 9 p.m. De Stefanis, who was in the Monterotondo mess with Generals Mariotti, Utili, Surdi and Parone, expressed his astonishment and disappointment at the inclusion of the phrase concerning hostilities with Germany, which the King and Council had decided to omit.[1]

"Apparently Badoglio had put the phrase into the actual announcement at the last moment, on his own initiative.

"De Stefanis and the other Staff officers remained at Monterotondo until midnight.

"Meanwhile, in answer to a German request that they might evacuate Sardinia, taking with them the consignment of German 88 mm. A.A. guns which they had given our divisions there (the request was conveyed by our Command on the island), De Stefanis replied that we agreed and would let the Germans embark without interference.

"Afterwards, all of them removed to Rome, to the Palazzo Baracchini and the Palazzo Caprara.

The Flight

"At 6.30 a.m. on September 9th, De Stefanis and Mariotti left for the Abruzzi. At the meeting point at Carsoli they found an order from Ambrosio to proceed to Chieti. De Stefanis went on to Avezzano, where his family had arrived by car from Mantua, and from there, at 3.30, went on to Chieti, accompanied by Staff Colonel Guido Perone, saying he would be back the same evening.

"At 6 p.m. he reached Chieti, where Ambrosio held a review of the Staff. Generals Roatta, Mariotti, Utili, Armellini, Salazar and others were present, including Lt.-General Braida and Captain Barone, now at Rome.

"At 9.30 p.m., after dining in the garrison mess and after Roatta had given orders to General Olmi, Divisional Commander,

[1] In fact, Badoglio's announcement, broadcast by Rome Radio, September 8th, 1943, at 18.45 and 19.30 hours, ended as follows:

"Every act of hostility towards the Anglo-American forces on the part of the Italian forces everywhere must cease. The Italian forces will, however, *counter any attacks there may be from any other source whatever.*"

to take over command of Chieti, they all left in great haste and secrecy: lights out, machines a short distance one from another so as not to lose the way, destination unknown.

"At midnight the column of vehicles reached Ortona a Mare. Some hours later a few cars arrived from which the King, the Queen and Prince Umberto emerged, with a small suite.

"The Queen was distraught and kept sipping something. The Prince remained isolated and apart, racked by a severe cough.

"The King conferred with Ambrosio. Sandalli and De Courten were also present. A little later a tug arrived. A corvette was waiting in the offing. In thick darkness the embarkation of the fugitives was completed. The ship was the *Gleno*. Fifty thousand *lire* were distributed to the escort of Carabinieri. Some senior officers, among them General Cener, of the Transport Command, remained ashore."

That is an eye-witness account. One might add that the Royal family had been in hiding in the War Office, which they had hastened to leave as soon as news came that German armoured cars were about to enter the Piazza Venezia. Their flight was precipitous, and many maps and documents were left on the tables or shelves. The coffers containing money, however, had been thoroughly emptied.

By this complete desertion to the enemy—a case unique and without precedent—the Kingdom of the House of Savoy, born after the Treaty of Utrecht in 1713 through a diplomatic combination of the Great Powers (which gave them first Sicily and then, in exchange, Sardinia), was drawing to a dishonourable close.

History will not judge them otherwise than did the Italian people.

CHAPTER XIV

AN ECLIPSE—OR THE SUNSET?

DID THE AUTHORS OF the betrayal—primarily the King as head of the gang, together with his generals and councillors who had fled to Ortona—did they have the faintest conception of what they were doing? Were they conscious or unconscious criminals? Or a little of both? And yet the consequences might have been predicted with mathematical accuracy. It was easy to foresee that at the magic sound of the word "Armistice" all the armed forces would be pulverised; that the Germans, prepared for this, would disarm them to the last cartridge; that Italy, now split in half, would become a battlefield which would turn her into a "scorched earth"; that the plan for deceiving Germany and later betraying her would weigh, as it will, for an unconscionable period of time on Italy's future; that from now on it would be axiomatic that the words Italian and traitor were synonymous; and that the confusion and humiliation in every heart would be very great.

Once the immense cloud of dust raised by the hurling down of the whole structure of the State had subsided, and the military magazines had been plundered first by the troops and then by the mob, it became possible to discover two crystallisations of what remained of the national conscience.

The first consisted in considering the monarchy liquidated. A King who flees to the enemy, a King who (a case unique in history) gives the whole national territory over to the foreigner—enemy in the south, ally in the north—is a man who condemns himself to the vituperation of generations present and to come.

Second observation: the military magazines had been full. Mountains of equipment of all sorts, and piles of arms, the majority up to date, which had not been issued to the troops.

On April 2nd, 1943, barely three months before the crisis, the engineer Agostino Rocca, managing director of the Ansaldo works, sent me this report:

Duce,

I think I ought to give you certain information concerning the manufacture of artillery in the Ansaldo works. During the first thirty-nine months of war (July, 1940*–January,* 1943*) our works have manufactured* 5,049 *pieces of artillery. In the first thirty-one months of the last war (June,* 1915*–December,* 1917*) the famous old Giovanni Ansaldo works manufactured* 3,699.

The attached diagram shows that 15 *million working hours were needed to make these* 5,049 *guns, whereas, in the last war, six million working hours were needed for the* 3,699 *guns.*

The same diagram shows that the artillery of today, with high initial velocity and therefore more powerful propellants, takes more work than the artillery of the last war, despite the progress made in machinery and tools. The attached diagram D shows that at the beginning of the 1940 *war the industrial potential was higher than in June,* 1915, *because the measures adopted in* 1939–40 *were inspired by a broader vision than those of* 1914-15. *In this, as in every other branch of Italian industry, thanks to the autarkic and corporative provisions of the Régime, our state of preparation in* 1940 *was considerably better than that in* 1915. *The same diagram shows that production reached its height in* 1941 *and declined slightly in* 1942, *whereas the plant potential would allow of a production about double that of* 1941.

All that proves that the programme of productive exploitation of the industrial potential approved by you in 1939-40, *and carried out by the I.R.I.*[1] *concerns, has enabled us to meet the needs of the armed forces liberally.*

So one firm alone had manufactured five thousand pieces of artillery![2]

[1] The I.R.I., or *Istituto Ricostruzione Industriale* (Institute for Industrial Reconstruction), was formed in January, 1933, to provide State financial assistance to industrial enterprises through long-term loans financed through the issue of Government-guaranteed bonds. During the war it gave considerable financial assistance to the Italian armament industry.

[2] The quotation of this letter from Rocca is a good example of Mussolini's distortion of evidence to suit his purpose of the moment. In this Chapter, he wishes to prove that Italy had plenty of arms and that, consequently, the capitulation was due to treachery. In Chapter IV he quotes his own note of June 14th in order to prove the opposite, viz., that Italy had few arms, owing to the treachery and inefficiency of her generals.

A Vertical Drop

The crash was what the Spaniards call 'vertical.' When one compares the Italy of 1940 with what it is today, now that it has been reduced to an unconditional surrender such as no nation worthy of the name would ever have greeted with outbursts of rejoicing like those after September 8th (a fairly strong echo of which reached even the Refuge Inn on the Gran Sasso), it must be admitted that the comparison is heart-rending. Then, Italy was an Empire, today she is not even a State. Her flag flew from Tripoli to Mogadishu, from Bastia to Rhodes and Tirana ; today it has been hauled down everywhere. Enemy flags are flying over our home territory. Italians used to be in Addis Ababa ; today, Africans bivouac in Rome.

Italians of whatever age or class, young or old, man or woman, worker, peasant or intellectual, are asking themselves this question : Was it worth while surrendering and disgracing ourselves in the eyes of posterity, for this ? If we had gone on with the war instead of signing the capitulation, would Italy be in any worse a situation than she has been in since September 8th ?

Apart from the moral catastrophe, there is not a single Italian who is not feeling the fatal consequences of the decision. There is not a family in Italy who has escaped the storm, while the relatives of the 300,000 fallen are wondering whether the sacrifice of their blood has not been in vain.

By dint of repeating the word "betrayal" one runs the risk of making it lose its significance and of doubting even the existence of the fact. But was it not the blackest, the most classic example of all betrayals to plant a dagger in the back of an ally with whom, right up to the war communiqué of the previous day, we had been fighting side by side ? And was it not the blackest, the most classic example of deceit, when faced with our ally's doubts and legitimate enquiries, to lie to the last, to lie even when enemy stations were already broadcasting the announcement of the capitulation ? There is one burning question to which the attention of all Italians must be drawn, and that is, to their responsibility in the eyes of the world for their betrayal. If the actual responsibility for the betrayal can, in our country, be laid at the door of certain individuals and classes and made to redound on them, the shame of the betrayal redounds on all Italians. As far as foreigners are concerned, it is Italy herself who has perpetrated the betrayal, Italy herself as historical, geographical, political and moral entity. The atmosphere in which such betrayal was possible was Italian. Everyone contributed in greater or lesser degree to creating that atmosphere, including the many millions of assiduous listeners-in to London Radio, who were responsible for creating in themselves and others the present-day state of apathy. Even history possesses its debit and credit side or, if you like, its active and passive voice. It is only right that every Italian should be proud of belonging to the soil whence sprang such men as Cæsar, Dante, Leonardo da Vinci and Napoleon ; a ray of light from these stars reflects on every Italian. But the same holds good for shame and dishonour ; an element of these reflects on each and every one of us. There is only one way to redeem our disgrace, to re-establish the equilibrium, and that is by the sternest of all ordeals—the ordeal of blood.

Only through this ordeal shall we be able to answer another and no less grievous question : Are we faced with an eclipse or with a final sunset ?

Eternal Rome

In the history of every nation there are periods similar to the one through which Italy is now going.

Something of the sort was bound to happen, and in fact did, in Russia after the Treaty of Brest-Litovsk. The chaos from which Leninism emerged lasted nearly six years ; what happened later proved that it was a question of an eclipse, not of sunset.

Prussia suffered an eclipse after Jena, a battle in which the Germans had, as usual, fought heroically, and lost, mown down by death, what was called the "flower of the Prussian army," including the Commander-in-Chief himself, the Duke of Brunswick.[1]

The Italian intellectuals of today have adopted an attitude not very different from that of Johannes von Müller, the German Tacitus.[2] Hegel himself greeted Napoleon as "the Soul

[1] The disastrous defeat suffered by the Prussians at the battle of Jena and Auerstadt (October 14th, 1806) was hardly preceded by a heroic fight on their part. Nor was the Duke of Brunswick killed on the field.

[2] Johannes von Müller (1752-1809), the famous Swiss historian, was called to Berlin from Vienna in 1804, as Historiographer Royal, with the special task of writing the history of Frederick the Great. In Berlin he became one of the most violent of Napoleon's opponents, a prominent member of the War Party. When, after Jena, Napoleon entered Berlin, Johannes von Müller, who had stayed behind when the Court fled, changed his tune after an interview with the Emperor (November 20th, 1806), proclaiming that God had given him the Empire and the world. Summoned to Fontainebleau in 1807, he accepted the post of Minister-Secretary of State in the newly-founded Kingdom of Westphalia.

of the World," when the victor passed through Jena[1].

The standard-bearers of Enlightenment in Berlin were prodigal of their welcome to the "liberator." Was there not a Prince Doria Pamphili[2] in Berlin, in the guise of Count von der Schulenburg-Kehnert ?[3] But it was only an eclipse. The Prussian national conscience underwent a powerful and rapid awakening. The great traditions of Frederick the Great had only lain dormant.

Men such as Stein, Gneisenau and Scharnhorst were the champions of the recovery. So, above all, was the philosopher Fichte with his *Discourses to the German Nation*, which should be re-read. It is a heartening piece of reading for the Italians of 1944 as well. Listen to what this giant among German philosophers says of the Romans :

"What was it that inspired the noble Romans (whose ideas and way of thinking still live and breathe among us today in their monuments)—what inspired them to so many labours and sacrifices, to so much suffering endured for the sake of the fatherland ? They themselves give a clear answer ; it was the firm belief in the eternity of their Rome and the certain conviction that in that eternity they themselves would live eternally down the ages. And this hope, inasmuch as it was well founded and took the form in which they undoubtedly would have conceived it had they attained to knowledge of themselves—this hope did not deceive them. What truly was eternal in their Eternal Rome still

[1] On October 13th, 1806, i.e., on the day before the battle of Jena, Hegel wrote to his friend Niethammer immediately after the occupation of the town : "I have seen the Emperor, this Soul of the World ('*Den Kaiser, diese Weltseele, sah ich. . . .*') riding through the town to reconnoitre outside ; it is indeed a wonderful sensation to behold such an individual, who concentrated here in one point, sitting on a horse, embraces the world and dominates it." (Hegel, *Werke*, Supplement : K. Rosenkranz, *Hegels Leben*, Berlin, 1844, p. 229.)

[2] Prince Filippo Andrea Doria Pamphili—well known for his uncompromising stand against Fascism—was, after the liberation of Rome, appointed (June 11th, 1944) *Sindaco* (Lord Mayor) of the City by General Hume, Head of the Allied Military Government.

[3] Count W. F. von der Schulenburg, born in Kehnert (1742), Prussian Minister ; later, one of the leaders of the Peace Party, pleading for an understanding with the French. During the war of 1806, Governor of Berlin ; after Jena, he issued the famous proclamation to Berliners, "The citizen's first duty is to keep quiet." Dismissed after the peace of Tilsit, he entered the service of King Jerome.

lives today (and they therefore continue to live among us) and will live to the end of time."[1]

In consequence of the tremendous price paid today, it is essential that the feeling of the Romans should become the driving force of the Italians ; namely, that Italy cannot die. The Italians must ask themselves the questions which Fichte himself, in one of his lectures, asked the German people :

"We must come to an agreement," he said, "on the following questions. (1) Is it true or not that a German nation exists, and is there a threat to the possibility of its continued existence in terms of its own peculiar and independent nature ? (2) Does it or does it not deserve to be preserved ? (3) Is there a safe and efficacious means of preserving it, and if so, what ?"

Prussia answered these questions by sending Blücher's divisions to Waterloo. As far as Italy is concerned, we can answer that an Italian nation does and will exist, that it is worth preserving, and that to do this, it is essential that, of the two factors today weighing on its conscience—defeat and contemptibility—the most serious, that is the latter, should be wiped out in the only possible, the only irrefutable way : by returning to the fight, side by side with our ally, or rather allies : by hoisting the old flag of the Fascist Revolution once and for always, the flag for or against which the world has ranged itself in two opposing camps.

The war begun for lack of obtaining a German corridor through the Polish corridor is already over ; the war of today is a real war of religion, which is transforming States, peoples and continents.

In a sort of diary I kept at La Maddalena and which may one day see the light, I wrote :

"It is not to be wondered at, that people cast down the idols which they themselves have created. It is perhaps the only way of restoring them to the stature of common humanity."

And further on :

"In a short time Fascism will once more shine on the horizon. First of all, because of the persecution to which the 'Liberals' will subject it, showing that liberty is something to reserve to oneself and refuse to others ; and secondly, because of a nostalgia for the 'good old days' which will begin little by little to gnaw at the Italian heart. All those who fought in the European and,

[1] J. G. Fichte, *Reden an die deutsche Nation*, 8th Discourse. Coll. Works, Vol. VII, Berlin, 1846, p. 384.

especially, the African wars, will suffer particularly badly from this nostalgia. The 'African sickness' will carry off thousands."

One Day Perhaps . . .

"When Napoleon ended his career through being guileless enough to trust to the chivalry of the British, the twenty years of his epic struggle were foresworn and abused. A great many Frenchmen of that time—and some of today as well—condemned him as a villain who, in order to try and realise his wild dreams of conquest, had led millions of Frenchmen to the slaughter. Even his work in the political field was misjudged. The empire itself was considered an anachronistic paradox in the history of France. The years went by. The veil of time dropped over the former struggles and passions. France lived, and since 1840 has continued to live, in the shining furrow of the Napoleonic tradition. The twenty years of Napoleon are, rather than a historical event, a fact now inseparable from the French national consciousness. Perhaps something of the sort will happen in Italy. The decade between the Reconciliation[1] and the end of the war in Spain—a decade which raised Italy in a flash to the level of the great empires—the Fascist decade which enabled every man of our race, scattered all over the world, to hold his head high and to call himself Italian without blushing—the men of this decade will be exalted in the second half of this century, even though now, in the stress of the moment, people try and blot out its memory."

And elsewhere, still from my La Maddalena diary:

"To redeem oneself one must suffer. Many millions of Italians of today and tomorrow will have to experience in their own bodies and souls what defeat and dishonour mean, what it means to lose one's independence, what it means to be the object of foreign policy instead of determining it, what it means to be completely disarmed; the bitter cup will have to be drained to the dregs. Only by reaching the depths can one rise once more to the stars. Only the fury at suffering too great humiliation will give the Italians strength for recovery."

[1] The Reconciliation, i.e., the Lateran Agreements of February 11th, 1929, which regulated relations between the Italian State and the Holy See, and settled the question of the temporal power of the Pope.

CHAPTER XV

A "STORK" OVER THE GRAN SASSO

IN THE HISTORY OF every age and of every nation there are stories of flights and of dramatic, romantic and sometimes fabulous rescues ; but my own rescue appears even today, after a lapse of time, as the most daring, the most romantic and at the same time most modern, from the point of view of the means and method employed. Indeed, it has already become legendary.[1]

I had never nourished any hope of being liberated by Italians, even Fascists. That some of them thought about doing so, is certain ; that here and there the more spirited groups of Fascists even laid plans for it, is beyond question ; but nothing got beyond the planning stage. On the other hand, the groups or individuals capable of attempting such a plan were kept under strict surveillance and had not the means necessary to accomplish it.

From the very beginning I felt sure that the Führer would do everything to try and rescue me.[2] The Ambassador, von Mackensen, went to the King almost at once to obtain permission to visit me, according to the Führer's wish, but the request was refused with the following note :—

His Majesty the King has informed Marshal Badoglio of the Führer's desire. While confirming the excellent health enjoyed by H.E. Mussolini and his complete satisfaction with the treatment accorded him, Marshal Badoglio regrets that he is unable, in the personal interests of H.E. Mussolini himself, to consent to the proposed visit. He is however prepared to forward forthwith any

[1] Mussolini's narrative of his stay at the Gran Sasso and his liberation may be compared with the account given by the managers of the Hotel Campo Imperatore, in which he was interned. (See below, pp. 244-253.)

[2] But see below, p. 233.

L

letter which H.E. the Ambassador may have for him, and to transmit an answer.—July 29th, 1943.

The Chef de Cabinet of the Ministry for Foreign Affairs went to the German Ambassador and then reported to Marshal Badoglio.

Goering's Telegram

Given the situation of an Italian Government which pretended to be Germany's ally and to wish to continue the war, the Government of the Reich could not—by taking any formal steps, such as the request for my immediate release—compromise the relations between the two Governments or provoke a premature crisis in their relations. It is clear that Berlin mistrusted the trends and aims of Badoglio's policy. But diplomatic relations prevented that mistrust from becoming effective until the position had come to a head. Nobody gave me a thought on July 29th—with one exception. Reichsmarschall Hermann Göring telegraphed me as follows (the telegram was brought to Ponza by a Carabinieri officer):

"Duce,

"My wife and I send you our warmest and best wishes for today. Though circumstances have prevented my coming to Rome as I had planned, in order to offer you a bust of Frederick the Great as well as my congratulations—the feelings I express to you today of complete solidarity and brotherly friendship are all the more cordial. Your work as a statesman will live in the history of our two nations, destined as they are to march towards a common fate. I should like to tell you that our thoughts are constantly with you. I want to thank you for the charming hospitality which you formerly offered me, and I once more sign myself with invincible faith,

Yours, GOERING."

Even at La Maddalena I had noticed some German activity; they had a base on the opposite side of the Straits, at Palaù. In fact, the Germans had thought out a plan, consisting of a landing by a submarine camouflaged as an English one with the crew in English uniforms, which would take me off the island and set me free. The plan was just going to be tried out when I was transferred to the Gran Sasso.

On Saturday evening, September 11th, a strange atmosphere of uncertainty and expectation reigned on the Gran Sasso. It was now known that the Government had fled, together with the King, whose abdication had just been reported. The officials in charge of me seemed embarrassed, as if faced with the performance of a particularly unwelcome task. On the night of the 11th-12th, towards 2 a.m., I got up and wrote a letter to the Lieutenant,[1] in which I warned him that the English would never take me alive. After removing any remaining metal or other sharp objects from my room (in particular, my razor blades), Lieutenant Faiola repeated to me: "I was taken prisoner at Tobruk, where I was badly wounded. I witnessed the British cruelty to Italians, and I shall never hand an Italian over to the English." And he burst into tears.

The rest of the night passed quietly.

Sunday, September 12th

In the early hours of the morning of the 12th a thick whiteish mass of cloud covered the summit of the Gran Sasso, but it was nevertheless possible to observe the flight of a few aeroplanes. I felt that today would decide my fate. Towards noon the sun broke through the clouds, and the whole sky seemed to shine in the clear September air.

It was exactly 2 p.m., and I was sitting by the open window with my arms folded when a glider landed a hundred yards from the building. Four or five men in khaki got out, rapidly assembled two machine-guns and then came forward. A few seconds later, other gliders landed in the immediate vicinity, and the men from these carried out the same manœuvre. More men got out of more gliders. I never thought for a moment that they were English. There would have been no need for them to have recourse to such a risky undertaking in order to pick me up and take me to Salerno. The alarm was sounded. All the Carabinieri and police rushed out of the gate of the Refuge, weapons in hand, and arrayed themselves against the assailants. In the meantime, Lieutenant Faiola burst into my room and threatened me: "Shut the window and don't move."

Instead, I remained by the window and saw that another and more numerous group of Germans, having seized the funicular, had come up and were now marching compactly and resolutely

[1] The first edition has 'Captain.'

from the station square towards the inn. At the head of this group was Skorzeny. The Carabinieri had already got their guns at the ready when I noticed an Italian officer among Skorzeny's group whom, on approaching nearer, I recognised as General Soleti, of the Metropolitan Police Corps.[1]

Then, in the silence a few seconds before the order to fire, I shouted: "What are you doing? Can't you see? There is an Italian general there. Don't fire! Everything is all right."

At sight of the Italian general approaching with the group of Germans, the firearms were lowered.

This is what had happened. General Soleti had been carried off that morning by Skorzeny's detachment, having been told nothing of their motive and purpose. His revolver had been taken from him, and he left for an unknown destination. When, at the moment of the assault, he realised what it was all about, he was delighted. He declared himself happy to have contributed to my liberation and perhaps, by his presence, to have prevented a bloody conflict. He told me that it would not be advisable to return to Rome immediately, where there was an "atmosphere of civil war," and gave me some information concerning the flight of the King and Government. He was thanked by Captain Skorzeny, and when Soleti asked for his revolver to be returned, his request was granted, as was his further request to follow me wherever I might go.

Gueli had taken no part in the extremely rapid succession of events. He appeared only at the last moment. Skorzeny's men, after taking possession of the machine-guns at each side of the Refuge gate, came to my room in a body. Skorzeny, sweating and much moved, stood to attention and said: "The Führer, who, night after night, ever since your capture, has been thinking how to set you free, gave me this task. With infinite difficulty I followed your vicissitudes and peregrinations day by day. Today, in liberating you, I have the great joy of seeing the task assigned me crowned with complete success."

I replied: "I was certain from the beginning that the Führer would afford me this proof of his friendship. I thank him and I

[1] General Fernando Soleti, at the time Chief of the 'Public Security Police', wrote later, after the liberation of Rome, a narrative of events, to justify his conduct on the grounds of *force majeure*. A summary was published by the Rome Socialist paper *Avanti*, on July 19th, 1944. He does not, however, explain his requests to have his revolver returned (see also below, the Hotel manager's account) and to follow Mussolini.

thank you, Captain Skorzeny, as well as your comrades who faced the risks with you."

Then the conversation turned to other matters,[1] while my papers and belongings were collected.

On the ground floor the Carabinieri and police were fraternising with the Germans, a few of whom had been hurt on landing, though not badly. At 3 p.m. all was ready for departure. On leaving, I warmly saluted the men of Skorzeny's group, and all of them together—Italians included—went to a small plateau lower down where a Stork plane was waiting.

The "Stork" Takes Off

The captain piloting it came forward; a very young man called Gerlach, an ace. Before getting into the machine I turned to wave to the group of my guards; they seemed stunned. Many of them were genuinely moved. Some even had tears in their eyes.

The space in which the "Stork" had to take off was really very small, so it was dragged back to gain a few extra yards. At the end of the plateau there was a fairly deep drop. The pilot took his place in the machine, Skorzeny behind him and then myself. It was 3 p.m. The "Stork" started up. It pitched a little. Rapidly it covered the stony ground and then, a yard away from the precipice, with a violent haul on the joystick, took the air. There was still some shouting, some waving of arms; and then came the silence of the upper air. In a few minutes we passed over L'Aquila, and an hour later, the "Stork" came tranquilly to earth in the airport of Pratica di Mare.[2] There a large, three-engined plane was already waiting. I climbed into it. Our destination was Vienna, where we arrived late at night. A few people were waiting at the airport. From there we went to the Hotel Continental for one night. The next day, about noon, we set off again, for Munich, in Bavaria.

The next morning the welcome at the Führer's General Headquarters was simple and brotherly.

My liberation by German shock troops aroused a great wave of enthusiasm in Germany. One might say that the event was

[1] According to General Soleti's account (see above, p. 134, n. 1), Mussolini expressed his wish to return to his family; and he asked the Germans to accompany him, his intention being "to retire to private life at Rocca delle Caminate."

[2] A small village (the ancient Lavinium), about 16 miles due south of Rome.

celebrated in every house. The wireless had prepared listeners for some extraordinary news by repeated announcements, and they were not disappointed when, about 10 p.m., the news was made known. Everyone considered it an outstanding event.

Hundreds of telegrams, letters and poems poured in to me from all over the Reich. The event did not have similar repercussions in Italy. Those were the days of chaos and destruction, of looting and degradation. There, the news came as an unwelcome surprise and was received with vexation and rancour. And they began by denying it; rumours went round that the whole thing was a joke, that I had already died or been handed over to the English, and that the speech at Munich had been made by a double. This rumour went on circulating months afterwards even, the wish being father to the thought.

Hard to Kill

Although hundreds of people have seen me, that rumour has not entirely died out. The persistence of this phenomenon needs some explanation, for it was not due merely to the news given out by the enemy radio of my steadily failing health, or of continued attempts on my life, or of a flight into Germany either already achieved or about to take place. The phenomenon must be differently explained and referred to certain basic elements in the psychology of part of the Italian people: the part which is, perhaps, endowed with talent rather than intelligence.

From one point of view, I am a man who is "hard to kill." In fact, I have many times been on the point of death. At the hospital in Ronchi, in March 1917, with my body riddled with shell splinters, they thought I would die or, at best, have my right leg amputated.[1] Nothing of the sort. After the war, on my return from the Fascist Congress held in Florence in 1920, a formidable smash which splintered the bars of a level crossing outside Faenza only gave me slight concussion, as my shock-proof skull had brilliantly neutralised the blow.

The 'plane crash on the Arcore airfield was an extremely interesting experience. I observed then that the speed at which the

[1] Mussolini was wounded on February 23rd, 1917, when a trench mortar exploded by accident, during a firing practice. He spent some time in a field hospital at Ronchi, on the Carso front, where he was visited by his collaborators on the *Popolo d'Italia* and where his stay happened to coincide with a visit by the King. He made his wound an excuse to return to journalistic activities and, later, used it to build up a myth of heroism and Royal recognition.

machine fell was the same as the speed with which the thought, "We are going to crash" was formulated in words. It is no joke to fall like a stone from a height of 200 feet, even in a stout chassis like the unforgettable "Aviatik." The crash as we hit the ground was resounding enough, to say nothing of the creaking and groaning of the wings and fuselage. There was a rush from all parts of the airfield. The pilot-instructor, that enthusiastic and charming veteran of the air, Cesare Redaelli, was slightly hurt; as for me, I had merely bruised one knee, while my Panzer-like head only showed a light scar between nose and forehead.

The flight from Ostia to Salerno was fairly exciting on the day of the famous (and for some time unpublished) Eboli speech, in June, 1935.[1] It was in a howling storm. Just before we arrived, a flash of lightning struck the plane and burnt out the wireless. It must be admitted that not every common mortal gets struck by lightning at ten thousand feet above sea level and escapes unharmed.

We need not mention my many duels, which never got beyond the stage of innocent fun, even when the weapon employed was a rapier.

Less innocent, perhaps, and incredibly tedious, were the attempts made on my life in 1925 and 1926—a couple of bombs, a series of revolver shots, both masculine and feminine, native and British, besides a few other attempts the origin of which remains obscure.[2] Nothing out of the way.

We now pass from the—what shall I call it?—the realm of external injuries to that of my physique, or the organic side. For twenty years now, from February 15th, 1925, precisely, I

[1] Mussolini flew through a thunderstorm to deliver a speech on July 6th (not June as he says here) to four Blackshirt and two infantry battalions at Eboli. He exalted Italian heroism at Adowa and declared his determination to continue the struggle in Abyssinia to the end. The text of his speech, which was an improvisation, did not appear in the Italian press until August 4th, 1935, and it was published then in order to correct what the *Popolo d'Italia* called "apocryphal versions" which had appeared in the foreign press. The summary published by *The Times* on July 8th differed slightly in arrangement, but not in essentials, from the Italian version; there were rumours of other versions being circulated inside Italy.

[2] There were four attempts on Mussolini's life in 1925 and 1926: (i) November 4th, 1925, in Rome by the one-time Socialist deputy, Zaniboni; (ii) April 7th, 1926, in Rome, by Miss Violet Gibson; (iii) September 11th, 1926, in Rome by the anarchist Lucetti or Giovannini; (iv) October 31st, 1926, in Bologna. The alleged assassin, a boy named Zaniboni, was lynched on the spot by the Fascist leaders.

have been " blessed" with a delightful duodenal ulcer, whose exact and detailed history may be found (together with some other 70,000 case histories) in Professor Frugoni's archives. To see it on the X-ray plates, first taken by the very able and honest Aristide Busi, Dean of the Faculty of Medicine in Rome (now dead), was a cause of very understandable and very personal satisfaction.

From this description it will be seen that I may be considered hard to kill, so far at any rate.

How then can we explain the fact that public opinion, vague and amorphous as it is, believed I was dead ?

I have, if one may say so, different incarnations. Even from the political point of view I am hard to kill. In 1914, when I was expelled from the Italian Socialist Party at the memorable assembly at the Teatro del Popolo, all or nearly all the members considered me a dead man, beaten by the plebiscite carried out among the herd, to which, as usual, was added a "moral question."[1] A few months later Neutralist Socialism was completely defeated by the same herd.

When the war was over, Italy was swept by a wave of Bolshevism. In the 1919 elections, in which I had the honour of being on the same list as Arturo Toscanini (who was, therefore, one of the first Fascists), I obtained only 4,000 votes as against the millions obtained by my adversaries. The Red Flag fluttered triumphantly and menacingly. In the intoxication of victory they gave me a mock funeral, and a coffin containing my effigy and followed by a vociferous crowd, went past my home at No. 38, Foro Buonaparte, top floor.

I emerged from that coffin in the years 1921 and 1922. As in November, 1919, something of the same sort was tried in July, 1943. This time it was to be for good and all. And now, my political and physical death were to go hand in hand, with a well-calculated simultaneity. But He Who from the unsearchable heights rules the changing destinies of man had decided otherwise.

[1] Mussolini broke with the Socialist Party, which on September 9th, 1914, had declared itself in favour of neutrality at any cost, over the question of intervention. In October, he gave up the editorship of the Socialist organ, *Avanti.* The first number of his interventionist paper, *Italia del Popolo,* appeared on November 15th, 1914. His expulsion from the Party was decreed at a meeting of the Milan section on November 25th, 1914. Mussolini protested in a short speech, asserting that no "moral" grounds for his expulsion had been stated, and ending with a bitter attack on official Socialism. The decree was, nevertheless, ratified by the Party Executive Committee on November 29th.

There is a Mussolini who embodies the Mussolini of yesterday, even as the one of yesterday embodied the one of today, and this Mussolini, though no longer living at the Palazzo Venezia, but at the Villa delle Orsoline, has put his shoulder to the wheel with his usual determination. And so, O far from invincible phalanx of Doubting Thomases, if I work, then I must, to say the least, be alive.

The Greek philosopher, Thales, thanked the gods for creating him a man and not a beast, a male and not a female, a Greek and not a barbarian. I thank the gods for having spared me the farce of a vociferous trial in Madison Square, New York—to which I should infinitely prefer a regular hanging in the Tower of London—and for having allowed me, in company with the best Italians, to live through the fifth act of the terrible drama now being enacted in our tortured country.

CHAPTER XVI

ONE OF THE MANY: THE COUNT OF MORDANO

ON THE MORNING OF July 25th, Count Dino Grandi di Mordano made himself scarce. He was sought in vain at the Chamber, in vain at his villa—a fairly sumptuous one, apparently—in Frascati; even the telephone call to enquire for him at Bologna at the *Resto del Carlino* was in vain.[1] None of those questioned could give any information; at Frascati they said he had left by car straight for Bologna. In reality he had remained in hiding in Rome, awaiting the *coup d'état*. He remained at Rome in the days which followed as well.

As soon as he learned the composition of the Badoglio Government he wrote a letter to the Marshall to tell him that "it was a really solid Government" and that "the choice of men could not have been better."

After a few more days of fruitless waiting, he reappeared as the lawyer Domenico Galli, and slipped away to Spain. He did not stay there long, experiencing what might be termed an odd sort of hospitality from the Italian Consul at Seville; and not feeling safe under Franco's régime, he removed to near Lisbon, in Portugal—to Estoril, to be exact.

His former attitude, his speech in the session of the Grand Council, and his flight from Italy by 'plane with a Badoglio passport, remove the last shadow of doubt as to the part played by him in the carrying out of the conspiracy. He, who had been first Under-Secretary for the Interior, then Under-Secretary for Foreign Affairs, Minister for Foreign Affairs, Ambassador to London and finally Minister of Justice and, at the same time,

[1] Grandi's connection with the Bologna newspaper *Resto del Carlino* dated from 1913, when he started as one of its reporters. He long remained a contributor on economic questions.

President of the 'Chamber of Fasci and Corporations,[1] as well as a Count with the title of Mordano[2]. Was that not enough? No, it was not enough.

The "Collar"

At the beginning of March, 1943, he presented himself at the Palazzo Venezia, armed with the Year-book of the Ministry for Foreign Affairs, and addressed me as follows:

"It is not the first time that I have felt embarrassed in your presence, but on this occasion I feel it particularly. You know that after a certain period of time Ambassadors, especially if they have been accredited to the Court of St. James in London for many years, are decorated with the Collar of the Annunciation. I think I qualify for this. Would you speak to the King about it?"

This was the sort of talk that annoyed me frightfully. On a former occasion, so far as the Collar was concerned, I had renounced mine in favour of Tommaso Tittoni.[3]

"Very well," I replied. "I shall mention it at my next audience."

So I did. But at the outset the King did not seem in the least enthusiastic about it.

"First of all," he said, "it is not true that anyone who has been Ambassador in London is the senior Ambassador and has a right to the Collar. That reason won't wash. The other reason, extension of State territory, doesn't exist in Grandi's case. He can only be decorated with the Collar in the quality of President of the Chamber. But if I confer it on him I ought to give it to the President of the Senate, Count Suardo, as well, and there is no chance of that after the recent gossip about Senators giving information to the police."

I interrupted to point out that investigation had shown that the charges were unfounded.

[1] For *Fasci* and the 'Chamber of *Fasci* and Corporations' see below, Chapter XVII.

[2] Grandi himself admits (see below, pp. 198-201) that he owed his career to Fascism. The dates of his major appointments show the unbroken line of his services. (See the Who's Who.)

[3] The Collar of the *SS. Annunziata* ("Most Holy Annunciation") was the highest Italian Order. Its members were limited to twenty, and had the right to call the King "cousin." Tommaso Tittoni, born 1855, several times Foreign Minister, and one of the Italian delegates to the Versailles Peace Conference, became President of the Senate in December, 1919. He received the Collar in April, 1923. Mussolini did not receive this order until 1924.

At the following audience, the King raised no further objections. On the contrary, he admitted that, since the completion of the Codes, Grandi's services as Keeper of the Seals had earned him this high distinction.[1] Such a change of attitude in forty-eight hours seemed strange. As to the time, the Feast of the Annunciation was chosen, and shortly afterwards, on March 25th, 1943, Count Dino Grandi became cousin to Victor Emmanuel of Savoy.

The newspapers announced the fact without undue prominence. A few days later Grandi returned to the Palazzo Venezia and made such protestations of loyalty and devotion to me that the four walls of the building shook. Was the conferring of the Collar a part of the conspiracy, by any chance?

The Mask and the Face

Who indeed could have doubted Grandi's loyalty to Fascism? There were a few who did, but they were not listened to. Among the various thousands of files containing the life, death and miracles of 200,000 Italian citizens great and small, that of Grandi is unusually bulky. In order to avoid having to write several hundred pages, let us pass over the public manifestations, oral and written, from which it emerges that he gloried in calling himself an "orthodox" Fascist, one of my most faithful followers. Had I not raised him from the post of an obscure reporter on the *Resto del Carlino* to that of a politician of importance, first in the Party and then in the country?

"What should I have been," said Grandi, "if I had not met you? At the very most, an obscure provincial lawyer."

Let us glance through the file, which contains documents not meant for publication and, therefore, presumably, free from ulterior motives.

After the March on Rome, in March, 1923, to be precise, he was called to Rome to take up political activities, and on that occasion he wrote to me as follows:

Thank you for your words which have given me back in a flash all my old capacity for work and struggle. I have been reproaching myself for the time I have wasted, eating my heart out in sterile

[1] In 1925 a law was passed to authorise a revision of the Italian Codes of Law by a committee of jurists. The new Penal Code came into force on July 1st, 1931, and the new Civil Code on April 21st, 1942. Grandi was Minister of Justice from 1940–1943.

silence. No one knows and acknowledges his faults more than I do. They are very great, and infinite in number. But you, who are my Chief, will see me tested. You will see what an example of devotion and loyalty will be set by

Your

DINO GRANDI.

In May, 1925, I sent for Dino Grandi to take up the appointment of Under-Secretary to the Ministry for Foreign Affairs. Grandi had wanted that appointment badly and had not concealed the fact. He thanked me in these terms:

I tell you frankly, and without false modesty, that this unexpected appointment has flattered me greatly, the more so because your having chosen me for such an important function will enable me to be nearer you.[1] *This is my highest ambition and the greatest reward I could desire. On the other hand, you know how boundless and unquestioning my loyalty is, and how my one wish is to obey you, so pray do with me whatever you consider most opportune and most suited to the needs of the moment which you alone can know and appraise.*

"*You will See me Tested*"

On December 14th, 1927, he addressed me another letter containing the following words:

A few months ago you ordered me to resume my post. I have done so. And in resuming it, I can only repeat to you, with all my enthusiasm, an assurance[2] *which is an oath of loyalty. I can only say to you that my loyalty is blind, complete and indestructible. You have made the spiritual conquest of a man of silence and meditation.*[3] *You will see me when the test comes.*

[1] Two examples of faulty transcription. The translation follows Mussolini's text as found in both editions: ". . . this unexpected appointment (*nomina*) has flattered me greatly, the more so because your having chosen me for such an important function will enable me to be nearer you (*esserti piu vicino*)." The facsimile of this letter reproduced in the Appendix to the second edition reads, however: ". . . this unexpected news (*notizia*) has flattered me greatly, the more so because your having chosen me for such an important function will enable me to serve you more closely at hand (*servirti più da vicino*)". (See below, p. 198.)

[2] Again a faulty transcription. The facsimile of the letter reproduced in the Appendix to the second edition omits *only* (*che*) and reads: ". . . I will not repeat an assurance. . . ." (See below, p. 199.)

[3] Another example of faulty transcription. The translation follows the text which is the same in both editions: "You have made the spiritual

After directing the Ministry for Foreign Affairs for many years, he was replaced. Why? In assiduously frequenting Geneva he had become assimilated into those perfidious surroundings. From now on, his line was "The League." There is no doubt that he had made a certain name for himself in the international world. He had visited nearly all the European capitals, including Ankara. He was considered a man of democratic leanings, a man of the "Right" in Fascist foreign policy. The Government line altered after the failure of the Four-Power Pact. One day he was replaced and sent as Ambassador to London. It may well be that from that moment he began to cherish a grievance which was to carry him a long way. Nevertheless, he hid it well.

When there was a feeling in the air that something fresh was going to happen on African territory, he wrote from London on February 20th, 1935, as follows:

I have returned to my job with a vision of Fascist Italy as I never saw her before; the real Italy of your time, which goes forward to meet her fate, coolly appraising it, without anxiety on the one hand or a show of hysterical enthusiasm on the other, taking things as they are. The Romans, who understood such matters, would have called this the age of Fortuna Virilis.[1] *I think you should be satisfied with the way Italy has responded to your marching orders.*

From time to time the Ambassador to London deigned to return in order to keep in touch with the life of the nation and the Régime. Not a single reservation or criticism appeared in his public attitude, not a reservation in his private correspondence, but only loud hosannas of approval of everything.

The "Passo Romano"—the Roman Goose Step

After visiting a barracks of the Fascist Militia in February 1939, he wrote as follows:

conquest of a *man* (*uomo*) of silence and meditation." The facsimile of the letter reproduced in the Appendix reads: "It is my spiritual gain following a *year* (*anno*) of silence and meditation." (See below, p. 199.)

[1] Grandi has been misled if he supposed this to mean 'Manly Fortune'. *Fortuna Virilis* was the goddess to whom women prayed to conserve their charms for men. See Ovid, *Fasti*, IV, 145 ff.

The impression I brought back with me was profound. Guidonia[1] *is the most virile generator of power for our war of tomorrow and, of all your creations, is perhaps the one which affords in most sculptural form a feeling of Genius and Power.*

That was the year in which the "passo romano" was introduced for parades in the Italian Army, beginning with the Fascist Militia; that step concerning which so many otiose discussions then took place. It is a fact that the only army in the world which marched past without a certain style of step was the Italian Army. It is obvious that a parade step is the indispensable finish to training in close formation, and it is indisputable that such a step is of very great educational importance. The episode at Waterloo is well known. At one moment during the battle certain Prussian divisions wavered for a moment, surprised by heavy fire from the French artillery. Blücher marched them back to the lines in goose-step, and they then intrepidly resumed the fight.

When, during one of his periodic visits to Rome, Ambassador Grandi had occasion to assist at the first march past in "passo romano," he was simply electrified. He was quite carried away in beholding it, and interpreted the importance of the "passo" from the phonetic as well as the moral point of view, in this extract from a letter of apologetics addressed to me:

The earth shook beneath the thud, or rather the hammer-blows, of the feet of the legionaries. I saw these Blackshirts close to; when they marched with the "passo romano" their eyes sparkled, their lips straightened and hardened, their faces acquired a new expression which was not merely a martial air, but rather the air of satisfied pride with which a hammerer smites and crushes the head of his enemy. Indeed, after the first ten or twelve steps the thudding acquired a steadily growing power, as the echo of the hammer-blows in the ear of the hammerer himself redoubles their force. In the necessary revolution of our customs which you are making, the "passo romano" (together with the familiar "voi"[2]

[1] Guidonia, about 15 miles from Rome, on the slopes of the Sabine hills, was inaugurated by Mussolini on April 27th, 1935, as a large airport and modern experimental station for the Italian Air Force.

[2] The use of the pronoun, *Lei* (third person), as the polite form of address, a distinctive feature of the Italian language, was officially forbidden by a Party order issued by the Party Secretary, Starace, on February 15th, 1938. The form was regarded as undesirable, because of "foreign importation." Good

and the uniforms) is and always will be the most potent instrument of Fascist teaching of the young. That is why I am wondering whether music is not superfluous in the parade step. Whereas the drum "underlines" it, the music of the band (if you don't think me presumptuous for saying so) creates a spiritual distraction quite detrimental to that which should be exaggerated by the silence and the drums, I mean the echo and vibration of that rhythmic, powerful, united hammer of bronze.

The Changing of the Guard

Those were the years when the Party proposed to revolutionise traditions. With that object, the ceremony of the Changing of the Guard was introduced.

The Changing of the Guard had, with time, become the most slovenly of military ceremonies. Nobody watched it because nobody was interested in it. After improving the method of changing guard at the Quirinal, by detailing at least one company and a band to support the guard, an almost identical ceremony was performed in front of the Palazzo Venezia, before the eyes of an ever-growing audience of Italians and foreigners.

Grandi once had occasion to be present at the Changing of the Guard at the Palazzo Venezia, and having described the scene as *magnificent and formidable*, had continued as follows:

What I saw in Berlin formerly and what I see fairly often in London now, cannot be compared with this. The close formation which you have taught your soldiers is of superb and unique originality. These soldiers of yours this morning, in their steel-coloured uniform, marched with heart, muscles and sinews of steel. It was not the Anglo-Saxon "ballet," it was not the Teutonic "catapult." It was a single block of steel, a powerfully weighty mass like the German, but not of cast-iron but of vibrant metal. It is the most powerful instrument of popular pedagogy which you have ever created.

Who, in recent times, has not cast a stone at Party Secretary Starace? In the session of the Grand Council, Grandi was positively virulent. And yet in 1938, in a letter he wrote me after

Fascists were told to use the familiar *tu* when speaking to equals, and the slightly more formal *voi* to superiors. Female members of the Party were always to use *voi* when addressing their male comrades.

a visit to the Farnesina, he contrived to say: *Starace is doing wonders there,*[1] and, announcing his departure for London, declared that he would avoid going through France but would go via Germany because, as he said, *in the seven years I have been in London I have never, no, not once, stayed a single night in Paris, a city which I loathe.*

At the time of the occupation of Albania he wrote from London as follows:

Today's events have electrified my spirit. You, Duce, are making the Revolution move with the inevitable and ruthless motion of a tractor. After the vengeance for Adowa, the vengeance for Valona.[2] *Your faithful collaborator, who for eight years has had the privilege of being a daily witness of your work, knows that you have never relaxed your efforts even for a moment. This conquest makes the Adriatic a strategically Italian sea for the first time, and opens the ancient highways of Roman conquest in the East to Mussolini's Italy.*[3]

As for Count Grandi's attitude with regard to the present war, it was at first one of absolutely enthusiastic support. On August 9th, 1940, on presenting me with a photograph copy of one of his articles written twenty-six years earlier (December 1914), showing that the reasons for intervention in 1914 were the same ideological and political reasons for intervention twenty-five years later, he wrote:

From that time on, Duce, under your leadership, we believed that the real war, Italy's revolutionary war, was still to come, and that

[1] Grandi is here referring to Starace's reorganisation of the Fascist Youth organisations which he amalgamated in October 1937, to form the *Gioventu Italiana del Littorio* (Italian Youth of the Lictor's Emblem). Its headquarters and training centres at the Mussolini Forum, near the Monte La Farnesina, were often spoken of as the "Farnesina."

[2] (i) The battle of Adowa (March 1st, 1896) marked the abrupt termination of Italy's first attempt at colonial expansion, sponsored by Crispi. The Italian force, about 15,000 strong, was almost entirely destroyed by the Abyssinians under their Emperor Menelik. Fascist propaganda claimed that the shame of this defeat had been wiped out by Mussolini's successful campaign of 1935-6.

(ii) Italy occupied Valona on December 28th, 1914, in order to "protect her interests" in that area; she hoped to be given a mandate over Albania at the Peace Conference, and to be allowed to retain her sovereignty over Valona. Giolitti, however, wishing to encourage Albanian friendship, renounced these claims in the Tirana agreement of 1920, and all Italian troops were withdrawn.

[3] The facsimile letter given in the Appendix to the second edition adds, "in Albania."

it would be a war of the proletariat, with Italy, Germany and Russia on the one side, and France and England on the other. From then on we knew these latter to be our real enemies, even though we were preparing to fight on their side.

When he finally returned from London, where he had enjoyed a certain prestige in some circles, he was created Keeper of the Seals, and as such gave a strong stimulus to the completion of the Codes, which he wanted to call the Mussolini Codes. On being elected President of the 'Chamber of *Fasci* and Corporations,' while still remaining Keeper of the Seals, he wrote to me as follows on March 27th, XVIIIth year of the Fascist era:

I am deeply grateful for what you were good enough to tell me this evening. To become ever more one of the new Italians whom you are hammering into shape; that is the aim of my life, my faith and my soul, which have been yours for twenty-five years, my Duce.

A Woman Writes

On December 2nd, 1942, I addressed the Chamber on the political and military situation. Grandi presided. The assembly had a warmly cordial note which seemed to convey perfect unanimity. The next day a letter was sent me, signed *A Woman,* and containing the following:

You have at your side two or three officials who are plotting something. I followed the meeting yesterday from the press gallery and noticed Grandi's cryptic attitude. His applause was perfunctory. He has been too long in London. One who knows him warns you—beware!

The case of Grandi is not unique; it is one of many, and they are all alike. It is an historical fact that in times of great crisis the chiefs weaken or play the traitor, while the rank and file hold firm and remain faithful. It is therefore calculation (i.e., intelligence) that actuates the former, whereas in the latter it is the primitive and elemental force of feeling which guides them. Faced with spiritual changes of front such as are shown here by Grandi's letters (only a fraction of which has been quoted), one can understand my cynicism, which is also due to the fact that I have never had a friend in my life.

Was that a good thing? Or a bad one? I set myself this

problem at La Maddalena; but I did not solve it, because good or bad, it is too late now. There was someone in the Bible who cried: "Woe to him that is alone."[1] and someone in the Renaissance declared: "Be alone, and you will be your own master." If I had had friends today they would have had to "sympathise" with me, that is, literally, "suffer with me." As I have none, my affairs do not extend beyond the closed circle of my life.

[1] See *Ecclesiastes* 4, 10.

CHAPTER XVII

THE DRAMA OF THE DYARCHY (1)

From the March on Rome to the Speech of January 3rd

WHEN ONE IS FACED with historical phenomena of vast significance, such as a war or a revolution, the enquiry into first causes is extraordinarily difficult. Above all, it is difficult to give a date to the origin of these events. In tracing them back through the centuries one runs the risk of reaching prehistoric times, since cause and effect condition each other and follow each other in turn. To avoid this, a starting point must be chosen—a birth certificate, so to speak.

The first manifestations of Fascism go back to the years 1914-15, at the time of the first World War, when the "*Fasci* of Revolutionary Action" insisted on intervention.[1] On March 23rd, 1919, they were reborn as *Fasci di Combattimento* (Fighting Groups).[2] Three years later came the March on Rome. Anyone wishing to study the twenty years of the Régime up to July

[1] These groups founded by Mussolini to promote the entry of Italy into the war were more usually known as Interventionist *Fasci* and were so described by Mussolini himself in his speech at their inauguration in Milan on January 25th, 1915. They had little to do with the Fascist Party as it was later constituted.

[2] The basic unit of the fully developed Fascist Party was the *Fascio di Combattimento* (or, short, *Fascio*), i.e., the local 'Fighting Group.' There were over 7,300 of these *Fasci* (plural of *Fascio*), i.e., one in each Commune. The formation of the first *Fasci di Combattimento* at a meeting held in the Piazza San Sepolcro in Milan on March 23rd, 1919, marks the beginning of Fascism as a political movement. Former interventionists, syndicalists with nationalist leanings and above all, discontented war veterans, united by dislike of rational argument and by the cult of violence, banded themselves together against Socialism. However, the *Fasci* were not consolidated into a Party with a definite political programme until November 7th, 1921.

1943 and to retrace the first origins of the *coup d'état*, must take October 28th, 1922, as the starting point.[1]

What was the March on Rome? A mere governmental crisis, a normal change of ministers? No. It was something more than that. An insurrection? Yes. One which lasted on and off for about two years. Did that insurrection erupt into a revolution? No. Assuming that a revolution takes place when not only the system of government but also the constitutional framework of the State is changed by force, Fascism did not cause a revolution in October 1922. There was a monarchy before it, and a monarchy remained after it. I once said that when the Blackshirts were marching through the streets of Rome on the afternoon of October 31st, amidst the cheering crowds, there was a slight error in planning the itinerary; instead of passing in front of the Royal Palace on the Quirinal, it would have been better to go inside. Nobody gave it a thought because at that moment such a suggestion would have appeared untimely and absurd to everybody.

The Monarchy and the Republic

How could one attack the Monarchy which, far from barring the doors, had flung them wide? The King had effectually revoked the State of Siege proclaimed at the last moment by Facta; he had ignored the suggestions of Marshal Badoglio (or those attributed to him) which provoked a very violent article in the *Popolo d'Italia*; he had given me the task of forming a ministry which—by excluding those Left-Wingers still in the grip of anti-Fascist bias—was born under the signs of complete victory and national concord.[2]

[1] This passage is typical of Mussolini's methods of handling his material. In treating the origins of Fascism he can hardly omit all reference to the famous inaugural meeting of March 23rd, but he is careful to pass over in silence the programme there enunciated for a definitely republican and syndicalist state; a programme in direct variance with the thesis expounded a few lines further on that Fascism had never adopted the formal doctrines of republicanism. Ignoring this programme, he states that to understand the twenty years of the Fascist régime up to July 25th, 1943, the starting point is the March on Rome on October 28th, 1922; later, however, in discussing republicanism and the Party, he goes back far behind the March on Rome to the meeting of the Central Committee of the *Fasci* in Milan on August 28th, 1919, his reason being that this meeting can be twisted to support his own subsequent attitude to republicanism, while the meeting of March 23rd cannot.

[2] Although preparations for a Fascist march on the capital were nearly complete when Mussolini held a big meeting in Naples on October 24th,

If we had suddenly given a Republican cast to the March, it would have complicated matters. There had been the Udine speech of September 1922, in which Fascism's Republican tendency was set aside for the moment.[1] However, the attitude of Fascism to the form of the political institutions of the State had been laid down from the very beginning of the movement, in the declaration of policy by the first Central Committee of the Italian *Fasci di Combattimento* in 1919 (which had its headquarters at 37, via Paolo da Cannobio). Clause D of this declaration proposed "the convocation of a National Assembly for the duration of three years, whose first task will be to determine the constitutional form of the State." There was, therefore, no Republican formula or bias. A year later, at the National Congress held in the green room of the Lyric Theatre, Milan, on May 24th and 25th, 1920, a few guiding principles of Fascist action were formulated. These were summarised in the pamphlet "Technical Guides and Practical Postulates of Fascism" (central headquarters in via Monte di Pietà) which declared that the *Fasci di Combattimento* "are not on principle opposed to Socialism in itself and as such—as an arguable thesis and movement—but they are opposed to its theoretic and practical degeneration as summed up in the one word, Bolshevism." It then passed to the question of the political régime, declaring in the following precise terms:

> "For the *Fasci di Combattimento* the question of the régime is subordinate to the moral and material interests, present and future, of the nation, understood in its reality and its historical development; for this reason they are not prejudiced either in favour of or against existing institutions. This does not authorise anyone to consider the *Fasci* monarchists or supporters of the dynasty. If, in order to safe-

1922, the situation could still have been redeemed by a show of firmness. But the government was in a state of vacillating indecision and Badoglio's reported offer to scatter the Fascists with a "whiff of grapeshot" was ignored. At the eleventh hour, Facta (then Prime Minister) decided on energetic measures, and martial law was proclaimed on the morning of the 28th. He reckoned without the King who had already been negotiating with the Fascists. Victor Emmanuel first refused to sign the martial law proclamation and then offered the Premiership to Mussolini, who formed a Government.

[1] This speech of September 20th, 1922, has been described in the official edition of Mussolini's speeches (*Scritti e discorsi di Benito Mussolini*, Vol. II, Milan, 1934) as "the first act of the decisive phase of the Fascist Revolution." He said: "Our attitude towards political institutions is in no wise conditioned by any pledge . . . We must have the courage to be Monarchists."

guard the interests of the nation and to guarantee its future, a change of régime should appear necessary, the Fascists will be prepared for such an eventuality; but on the strength not of inalterable principles but of a concrete assessment of the situation. Not every régime suits every nation. Not every head can wear the Phrygian bonnet. A given nation needs a given form of state. The form of the state may rid itself of all its antiquated content and become democratic, as in England. On the contrary, there may and do exist republics which are fiercely aristocratic, such as the Russia of the so-called Soviets. Today, Fascists do not consider themselves in the least bound up with the fate of the present political institutions of monarchic type."

As may also be seen from the 1920 manifesto, the Fascist attitude might be described as "pragmatic." Nor did that attitude substantially change during 1921 and 1922. At the time of the insurrection, a republic was not present in the mind of the people either as an idea or as an institution. After the death of Giuseppe Mazzini and his fellow apostles (the last of whom, Aurelio Saffi, died in 1890[1]), the Republican party had lived on its "sacred memories," stifled by the reality of the Monarchy and weighed down by the new Socialist doctrines.

Three men stand out from the general greyness of that twilight: Dario Papa, Giovanni Bovio, and Arcangelo Ghisleri. The last of these was adamant in uncompromising faith which made him refuse ever to become a Deputy, in order to avoid taking the oath of allegiance. But the other party leaders—through parliament, that corrupting element *par excellence*—had become assimilated into the monarchic pattern to the point of assuming ministerial responsibility during the war. This sort of republicanism, democratic and masonic in sympathies, was represented by the Jew, Salvatore Barzilai.[2]

One might say that the Crown on the one hand and Freemasonry on the other had practically emasculated both the republican idea and the Republican Party. Against this, with

[1]Aurelio SAFFI, writer and politician, was born in 1819. Together with Mazzini and Armellini, he was proclaimed a triumvir of the Roman Republic of 1849. He remained faithful to Mazzini and to the Mazzinian ideal, sharing the master's exile and later editing his works.

[2] Salvatore BARZILAI: Minister without Portfolio in the Salandra Government, 1914–16. He had left the Republican group in 1911 owing to his support for the Libyan War. Deputy since 1890, he disapproved of the Triple Alliance and was an eloquent supporter of the Irredentist cause.

the 1915-18 war and the liberation of Trento and Trieste, the historical task of the party might be considered at an end. The dream of a century of sacrifices, of martyrs and of battles, had been realised. The credit for having kept that torch alight for so many years belongs unquestionably to the Republican Party. After the war, with the exception of the Red Demonstration at the opening of the first Chamber under the new electoral law in November 1919, no one mentioned a republic any more, not even the Left-Wingers.[1]

From the day when the King did Turati the 'honour' of summoning him to a conference at the Quirinal and Turati went (even though in a lounge suit and soft hat), it seemed an anachronism to speak of a republic in Italy, where the name of monarchy was associated with victory.

Of the 'quadrumviri' one, De Vecchi, was uncompromisingly monarchist and Savoyard; De Bono was at bottom no less monarchist; only Italo Balbo had gone through a republican phase in his youth; while Michele Bianchi, the political brains of the group (who had come to Fascism after syndicalist experience), did not consider the institutional problem in Italy to be practical politics.[2]

Given these historical conditions and political factors, the March on Rome could not establish a republic for which the nation was quite unprepared, while an attempt to do so out of season would probably have complicated, if not prejudiced, the outcome of the insurrectional movement.

The Dyarchy

The monarchy remained, but Fascism realised almost at once the need for creating institutions of its own, such as the Grand

[1] The elections in 1919, the first to be held under the new electoral law, resulted in an overwhelming victory for the Socialists. At the opening of Parliament, they left the hall in a body, singing the "Red Flag," when the King entered.

[2] The 'quadrumviri', the four leaders of the Fascist March on Rome of October 28th, 1922, ranked among the earliest and most ardent supporters of Fascism, and the fact that the two survivors voted against Mussolini at the last meeting of the Grand Council indicated the gravity of the dissensions within the Fascist Party.[3]

[3] Only one of them, Cesare Maria De Vecchi, Count of Val Cismon, is still thought to be alive. Having voted in favour of Grandi's motion, he was condemned to death *in absentia* by the Fascist Republican Special Tribunal at Verona in January, 1944. He took refuge in a monastery.

Council and the Voluntary Militia for National Security.[1]

At a meeting held in the Grand Hotel, Rome, in January 1923, not only were the Grand Council and the Militia born, but a political system which might be called a "dyarchy" was set up, the government of two, the "dual command." I am sometimes no end of a wit without meaning to be, and I said that the system was like a married couple's bedroom with separate beds: the worst possible situation according to Honoré de Balzac in his *Physiologie du Mariage*.

Little by little the dyarchy took on a more definite character, even though not always determined by special laws. At the top were the King and myself, and when the troops on parade cheered, they cheered each of us in turn. There was a moment after the conquest of the Empire when General Baistrocchi,[2] giving way to his volcanic exuberance, made them repeat the salute three times, until I requested him not to introduce the Litany into the regiments. Beside the Army, which was primarily

Marshal Emilio DE BONO, less fortunate than De Vecchi, was arrested by the Fascist Republican Government, sentenced to death at the Verona Trials and executed with Ciano on January 11th, 1944.

Italo BALBO, one of the most violent of the early Fascist *squadristi*, enjoyed, nevertheless, great popularity owing to the spectacular mass flights in which he led the Italian Air Force. He was often spoken of as a possible successor to Mussolini and was at the same time an intimate friend of the Crown Prince. He was killed in an air crash over Tobruk in June 1940 when his 'plane was "accidentally" shot down by the guns of an Italian cruiser in the harbour.

Michele BIANCHI, an ardent Socialist, followed Mussolini in his campaign for intervention in 1914, and assisted in the formation of the Interventionist Groups in 1915. He was the first General Secretary of the Fascist Party; after Fascism came to power, he became Minister for Internal Affairs. He died in 1930 before Mussolini had any need to accuse him of treachery.

[1] For the Grand Council of Fascism, the apex of the Party structure, see below, p. 161. By the law of December 9th, 1928, it assumed functions that infringed, as Mussolini points out in the next Chapter, the prerogatives of the monarchy under the Constitution of 1848.

The Voluntary Militia for National Security or Blackshirt Militia was founded in 1923 as a voluntary force whose members, in addition to being members of the Party, assumed special duties. Coming directly under the orders of the Duce, it was the ultimate guarantor of the security of the Fascist régime. It formed a parallel to the Royal Carabinieri, and Mussolini stresses the point that just as the King's bodyguard was specially picked from the Carabinieri, so he himself had a guard of Musketeers chosen from the Voluntary Militia.

[2] Under-Secretary for War, 1933–36. Arrested by order of the Commission for the Punishment of Fascist Crimes, April 18th, 1945.

loyal to the King, there was the Fascist Militia, primarily loyal to myself. The King had a bodyguard composed of specially tall Carabinieri, and one day Gino Calza-Bini created my own personal bodyguard, the "Musketeers."

The Council of Ministers derived from the Constitution[1], but the Grand Council exceeded it in importance because it derived from the Revolution[2]. On ceremonial occasions the martial and rousing anthem "Giovinezza" was coupled with Gabetti's noisy and tedious "Royal March" which, like a *moto perpetuo*, might be played until both the band and the audience were completely exhausted. In order to avoid the tedium of listening too long, only the first few bars of each anthem were played.

Even the military salute did not escape the dyarchic principle; with cap on, the old salute was retained; bareheaded, the Roman or Fascist salute was given (as if one had changed heads in the meantime !).

Of the three armed forces, the most Royalist was the Army, followed by the Navy, particularly the Naval Staff. Only the Air Force boasted the Lictor emblem under which it was born or, at least, reborn.

In the Army there was one branch especially which was exclusively devoted to the House of Savoy: the Carabinieri. This was the King's own corps. Even here Fascism tried to organise a police-force which would give some guarantee from the political point of view, and a secret organisation was added, the OVRA.[3]

But the Royal House itself even had its own police and an internal intelligence service which was carried out in the various

[1] The Council of Ministers is not specifically mentioned in the Constitution of 1848, although its existence, which was a fact, is implied. Its functions, defined later in a law of 1876, were considerably modified under Fascism by the creation of the office of Head of the Government whose powers were far more extensive than those of the former President of the Council. Mussolini himself said of the Council in its new form: "It does not waste time any more in useless discussions. The Ministers are soldiers. They stand or go where the leader tells them to go." Its authority was further weakened by the fact that it was customary for Mussolini to hold several Ministries at once.

[2] At the beginning of this chapter (p. 151) Mussolini denied that Fascism caused a revolution. Here the Fascist Revolution is invoked as the source of authority.

[3] The OVRA (*Opera Vigilanza Repressione Anti-Fascismo*) was the Italian counterpart to the Gestapo. Founded in 1929 by Arturo Bocchini, then Chief of Police, it concerned itself solely with political crimes. It had on its pay roll a vast variety of political spies, from impoverished society people to waiters in cafés.

provinces by former officials, civil or military, who had retired on pension. That the Crown had a diplomacy of its own, besides that of the Government, is certain ; not only through the diplomats who always came to report at the Quirinal when they returned to Rome but also through the connections of the royal or princely families, or through what was once the very numerous and powerful "International" of the reigning houses, now reduced to a circle of a few ghostly phantoms.

There is no doubt that the Army Staff was pre-eminently royalist[1] ; it formed a sort of highly circumscribed if not absolutely exclusive caste, on which the Royal House relied absolutely. If the Chamber seemed an emanation of the Party, specifically representing the Régime, the Senate, on the contrary, stressed its loyalty to the Royal House both by its royal nomination and by its very composition.[2] The percentage of generals, admirals and nominees of the monied class was always impressive. Rather than a material force, therefore, the Senate constituted a political and moral reserve in favour of the dynasty.

All the Italian aristocracy, first the "White" and then, after the Lateran Treaties, the "Black" as well, constituted another loyalist force.[3] Once the Roman question had been settled, the Curia and clergy joined the royal sphere of influence, so that the prayer for the King was enjoined for all religious ceremonies.

[1] The traditional devotion of the higher ranks of the army to the Crown, and in particular the special relation of the Piedmontese officer class to the House of Savoy, undoubtedly gave the King a body of loyal servants. On the other hand, the necessity for the professional officers to secure promotion and make a successful career, led to perpetual compromise and deference towards the Fascist hierarchs, with a resultant weakening of military morale and lack of independence and initiative.

[2] The final transformation of the Chamber of Deputies into the "Chamber of *Fasci* and Corporations" in 1939 made the Chamber an *ex-officio* delegation from the Grand Council of Fascism, the National Council of the Fascist Party and the National Council of Corporations. The Senate in theory continued to have a certain independence of the Party, through the royal nomination of the Senators. In practice, however, all new Senators were chosen on Mussolini's recommendation from devoted adherents of the Régime.

[3] The "White" aristocracy consisted of those noble families who, in 1870, after the establishment of Rome as the Italian capital, loyally accepted the former King of Sardinia–Piedmont as the King of Italy, including the Papal States. The "Black" nobility, on the other hand, still affected to regard the Pope as the legitimate sovereign of Rome and of the States of the Church. They refused to appear at Court, to hold any office in the State, or to take any part in national life.

Freemasonry and Jewry

The upper middle-classes, industrialists, landowners, bankers, though not in the front ranks, marched nevertheless under the royal banner. The Freemasons considered the King as one of their "honorary brothers." So did the Jews. A Jew, Professor Polacco, had been tutor to the Crown Prince.

In order for this dyarchic system, based on parallelism of power, to work, it was essential that the "parallel powers" should not cease to be such.

During the whole of 1923, the year of "full powers," there was not much change[1] except for the major incident of Corfu, which was settled at Geneva, to the entire satisfaction of the Italian government.[2]

1924, on the contrary, was a most critical year. The Régime had to face the consequences of a crime which, apart from any other consideration, was a political error both in method and in timing.[3]

In the summer of 1924 the pressure of the Aventine group on the King and his immediate entourage was very strong.[4] The

[1] After the formation of the first Fascist government in October 1922 Mussolini intimidated Parliament into granting him plenary powers for a year to reform the administration, the financial system and the judicial codes as well as to remodel the electoral law. It can, therefore, not seriously be maintained that there was no real change in 1923 except for the incident of Corfu.

[2] The Corfu incident was a presage of later lawless acts in Mussolini's foreign policy. In August 1923, all the four members of the Italian military mission charged with delimiting the Albanian frontier were murdered on Greek soil. Without waiting for action by the League of Nations, Mussolini bombarded and invaded the Greek island of Corfu. Athens appealed to the League of Nations and gained the support of Britain. Mussolini refused to recognise the League's right to interfere and threatened an Italian withdrawal from the League. The matter was finally settled by the award of an indemnity which saved Mussolini's face, although he had to relinquish Corfu.

[3] In this brief paragraph Mussolini makes his sole reference to the real crisis of Fascism, when its survival was placed in jeopardy by the murder of the Socialist Deputy Giacomo Matteotti. The election to the Chamber in April 1924 had been fought under the new and arbitrary electoral law, which had given Mussolini a large majority in the Chamber. On the opening day Matteotti and the Liberal, Giovanni Amendola, had courageously attacked the Fascists for corruption and terrorism at the polls and for the iniquity of the electoral law. Two days later, June 10th, Matteotti was kidnapped in the Lungo Tevere Arnaldo da Brescia, and his dead body was later found on the outskirts of the city. This was followed by an outbreak of popular indignation and a revulsion against Fascism which almost caused its collapse.

[4] The opposition deputies left the Chamber in protest against the murder of Matteotti, an act which was likened to the secession of the Roman plebs

opposition had made "formal" approaches to the Quirinal. The King had given certain general assurances as far as legal punishment of the crime was concerned, but hesitated in following the men of the Aventine into the domain of political responsibility.

Even Cesare Rossi's famous memorandum of the end of December (published on the Government's initiative, so as to anticipate their opponents) did not make much impression on the King.[1] The opponents of Fascism were henceforth bottled up in a moral question with no way out; and also, by going into exile, they had cleared the ground—that ground on which a counter-attack was to be launched at the right moment by the Régime. This was launched by the speech of January 3rd, 1925, and by the measures taken in the following forty-eight hours.[2] Although the King had shown some firmness in resisting the approaches made by the Aventinians in the second half of 1924—even when they had appealed to him more or less directly—he did not seem too pleased with the action taken on January 3rd which, by suppressing all political parties, laid the foundations of a totalitarian state.

That was the dyarchy's first "clash." The King felt that from that day onward the monarchy had ceased to be constitutional in the Parliamentary sense of the word. There was no longer any possibility of choice. The game of party politics and of alternating power was over. The Crown's *raison d'être* was fading away. Recurrent ministerial crises, apart from great national calamities and New Year greetings (later abolished)—these were the only occasions on which the King did anything to remind the Italian people that he was something besides an enthusiastic, not to say fanatical, collector of ancient coins.

to the Aventine hill. They failed, however, to lead the anti-Fascist movement and thus missed the great opportunity which public indignation had put in their hands.

[1] See above, p. 86, n. 2.

[2] Mussolini, after a period of apparent paralysis and hesitation, took courage from the failure of the Aventine parties to act with decision and seized fresh hold of the political situation. On January 3rd, 1925, in a speech which marked his acceptance of force as a political weapon, he challenged the Chamber to impeach him before the Senate in accordance with the Constitution and then took upon himself full responsibility for the crime committed. He went on to pillory the secession of the Aventine as unconstitutional and revolutionary and finally promised that Italy should be given peace and tranquillity by kindness if possible, or by force if this should prove necessary.

During a ministerial crisis the procession of candidates to the Quirinal had been an occurrence with the King as central figure. From 1925 onwards all that was over. From that year onwards, the changing of leaders assumed the character of a shift in internal arrangements within the orbit of the Party.

1925 was the year of special laws. 1926 was a year of constructive social laws.[1] But towards November the Chamber (henceforth called Fascist) expelled the Aventine fugitives from its midst, as guilty of secession. Nor did this hardening of the Régime's policy in a totalitarian sense pass unobserved in Court circles. From that moment they began to speak of the Crown as a prisoner of the Party, and they sympathised with the King, now relegated to second place compared with myself.

Notwithstanding, the two years 1925 and 1926 went by in peace.

[1] During the years 1925–6 a series of laws were passed on which the whole structure of the Fascist state was based. The special laws of 1925 included those restricting the liberty of the press, abolishing secret societies, and confiscating the goods of political exiles. They culminated in the law of December 24th, 1925, which defined the powers and prerogatives of the Head of the Government. 1926 saw the Fascist State still more firmly established by the law empowering the government to issue decrees having the force of law (January 31st); the reform of local government which was subjected to ever increasing central control (February 4th); the law on collective labour relations, which laid the foundations of the Corporative system (April 3rd); Special Tribunal for the Defence of the State (November 26th).

CHAPTER XVIII

THE DRAMA OF THE DYARCHY (2)

From the Grand Council Act to the July Conspiracy

THE LAW WHICH BROUGHT on the first serious clash between the monarchy and Fascism was the one legalising the Grand Council, making it the supreme organ of State and laying down its duties and prerogatives.[1] Besides the task of keeping a list of men worthy of becoming Head of the Government (and I once presented a list of this sort to the King), the Grand Council reserved the right of intervening in regard to the succession to the throne.[2] Dynastic circles were deeply shocked. This meant a mortal blow to the Constitution which settled this problem automatically. Some went as far as hinting that the article in question was of Republican inspiration and that in any case we wanted to prevent Prince Umberto's accession to the throne and to put forward the then Duke of Apulia.[3]

The Succession to the Throne

From that day on Victor of Savoy began to detest me and to nurse a profound hatred of Fascism. "The Régime," said the King one day, "should not meddle in these affairs, which have already been settled by the Constitution. If a party under a

[1] See above, p. 155, n. 1.

[2] The law of December 9th, 1928, laid down that as an organ of the State the Grand Council had to be consulted on constitutional questions among which the succession to the throne and the powers and prerogatives of the Crown were specifically included. This was a direct contradiction of the Italian Constitution as formulated by the "Statuto" of 1848 which stated in Article 2 that the throne was hereditary according to Salic law.

[3] The Duke of Apulia, later Duke of Aosta. (See the Who's Who.)

monarchic régime tries to decide who shall succeed to the throne, the monarchy will not be a monarchy any longer. The proclamation of succession can only be the traditional one of : 'The King is dead. Long live the King.' "

The crisis brought on by the Grand Council Act lasted several months, though relationships within the dyarchy remained cordial on the surface.

In 1929 the Reconciliation with the Holy See smoothed the irritation away, and relations returned to normal. At first, the King did not believe in the possibility of a solution to the "Roman Question"[1]; next he doubted the Vatican's sincerity; but finally he was flattered by the idea that the last mortgage held on Rome by its last deposed sovereign had been redeemed. Then, too, he was pleased at the prospect of an exchange of visits between the two neighbouring sovereigns. He saw in all this the strengthening of existing institutions. Nor did the Concordat displease him, although his notorious anti-clericalism made him suspicious of it. But when he saw the array of bishops filing past him in order to take the oath of fidelity he was convinced that even in the Concordat each concession made to the Vatican produced something in return.

1929 was therefore a lucky year. Some time after the signing of the Lateran Treaties the King said to me, at one of our usual bi-weekly conferences :

"You have succeeded in a task which others have never attempted and could never have carried out. By your speeches to Parliament you have corrected the wide interpretation given it in certain clerical circles.[2] That is excellent. I do not know how to give public expression to my gratitude. I really do not know. The Collar was given you after the annexation of Fiume. Perhaps a title . . ? "

"Oh, no," I interrupted. "A title would make me appear ridiculous at once. I should never dare look myself in the face again. I shall not say boastfully, '*Roi ne puis, prince ne daigne, Rohan je suis,*' but I ask you not to press me. Everyone should live in his own way."

[1] By the Lateran Agreements the open breach between the Pope and the Kingdom of Italy, known as the "Roman Question," which had been in existence since 1871, was healed.

[2] Mussolini explained and justified the Lateran Agreements in two speeches, one to the Chamber of Deputies on May 14th, 1929, and one to the Senate on May 25th, 1929.

The King understood and the matter was not followed up.

It would take too long now to relate all the incidents in which the dyarchy was put to more or less severe tests. The affair took on a more serious and sometimes grotesque aspect as soon as one penetrated the sacred and almost bewildering labyrinth of the "protocol" of court ceremonial. It came to a head during the Führer's visit to Rome. On that occasion the dyarchy revealed itself in all its plenitude before the public at large for a whole week, and there were incidents which surprised, irritated and sometimes amused the public. I had visited Germany in 1937. I had been given a memorable welcome in Berlin and Munich. Millions of Berliners foregathered at the Maifeld to listen to the Führer's and my speeches. The interest aroused all over the world by my visit was great. In May 1938 the Führer arrived in Rome. It was not always easy to decide on the formalities of the visit, but it was clear that the Führer chiefly intended to visit the 'Rome of Mussolini.'

When the German train reached the new and very handsome station of San Paolo, I was there to meet it as well as the King. But after that the Führer got into the State carriage with the King and went to the Quirinal. The crowd lining the Via dei Trionfi, the Via dell' Impero and the Piazza Venezia looked for me in vain. I had gone back to my office through the side streets of the Testaccio.

The Führer seemed offended by this. The following days we took it in turns to offer hospitality. In the morning the King accompanied the Führer to the various demonstrations, in the afternoon I did, or *vice versa*, according to the more or less political and Fascist nature of the demonstrations.

The Führer felt ill at ease in the frigid atmosphere of the Quirinal, partly owing to petty oversights of a material kind. At the grand military review in the Via dei Trionfi, the Führer's suite observed that, while the Queen and her ladies-in-waiting bowed deeply as the Army banners passed, they pretended not to notice the pennants of the Fascist Militia.

Protocol Differences

At ceremonies where the King and I were present together, I stood behind and left the foreground to the uniforms of the royal suite. That was specially noticed at a traditional festival in historical costume in the Piazza di Siena, one of the grandest and most picturesque spectacles of modern times in Rome. The Führer invited me to come next to him in the front row.

At last the stay in Rome came to an end. Having emerged from what one Berliner called "the atmosphere of the royal catacombs" and arrived in Florence, the Führer's mood lightened. If he had been deeply impressed by the majesty of Rome, he was enthusiastic over the grace of Florence. He would have liked to stay there longer. "It is my dream city," he said.

If the week of the Führer's visit to Rome revealed what may be described as the ceremonial aspects and differences attaching to the dyarchy, it was another incident which provoked the most serious crisis—the law creating the two First Marshals of the Empire. This happened at the spontaneous instance of certain groups of deputies and senators after a speech I had made[1], a speech which aroused great enthusiasm. The law having been passed by both chambers of Parliament, the King was on the point of refusing his signature that would make it law. In our talk immediately afterwards he was extremely agitated.

An Outburst of Fury

"Following the Grand Council Act," he said, "this law is a further mortal blow to my sovereign prerogatives. I could have given you any rank you liked, as a sign of my admiration, but this placing us on the same level puts me in an impossible position because it is another flagrant violation of the Constitution of the Kingdom."

"You know I do not care about these things, which are mere externals," I objected. "The sponsors of the Act held that in conferring that rank on me, you, Your Majesty, were automatically invested with it."

"No. The Chambers cannot take the initiative in such matters."

The King was white with rage; his lower jaw was quivering. "This is the limit! In view of the imminence of an international crisis I do not want to add fuel to the fire, but at any other time I would have abdicated rather than submit to such an affront. I would tear off this Marshal's braiding." And he looked with a disdainful eye at the braided double maeanders on his sleeve and hat.

[1] Speech of March 30th, 1938.

I was somewhat surprised at this outburst of fury and decided to ask Professor Santi Romano, President of the Council of State, for his opinion from a strictly constitutional point of view, as he was a very eminent expert on such matters. He sent in a memorandum of some few pages in which he proved in strict logic that Parliament was able to do what it had done and that in investing me with a rank not yet existing in the military hierarchy, the King must also be invested with it, in his capacity of supreme head of the aforesaid hierarchy. When I presented Santi Romano's memorandum to the King, Victor Emmanuel had a fresh outburst of rage. "Professors of constitutional law, particularly when they are cowardly opportunists such as Professor Santi Romano, can always find arguments to justify the most absurd theses. It is their job. But I am still of the same opinion. For that matter, I have not concealed my attitude from the two Presidents of the Chambers, who are to inform the people who sponsored this affront to the Crown that it must be the last."

From that moment Victor Emmanuel swore to himself that he would be revenged. It was now a matter of waiting for a propitious moment.

By the early summer of 1943 the relationship between the two forces of the dyarchy had profoundly altered. The whole Fascist structure—Government, Party, syndicates and administration—seemed to be suffering from the toll of war. Tens of thousands of Fascists had fallen on the field of battle, among them no fewer than 2,000 Party officials. That is a fact which it would be criminal to forget. Over a million Fascists were under arms, from the Var to Rhodes, from Ajaccio to Athens. Only a few members of the Party remained in Italy, and they had dedicated themselves almost exclusively to social service. To this must be added the unlucky course of military operations, with the loss of all the African colonies ; the terror raids on towns ; and the growing food difficulties.

The Vendetta

There then began the subtle and steady work of cleverly breaking down the nation's morale. Everything was used as a means to that end. And when facts were lacking they were invented or amplified. At the right moment the notion was spread abroad that the edifice of State was being undermined from within and that any shock would be enough to bring it crashing down. Nothing and no one was left untouched. The young people, particularly, had to be demoralised. Two forces, rivals indeed but akin, since they were both international, were particularly active in every field, from the political to the economic. Freemasonry, which had long lain dormant but had never died, realised that its moment had come, and set to work on the circles which had deferred to it in the past—members of the liberal professions, and civil and military State officials. A mysterious and untraceable sabotage began, which had immediate repercussions in all branches of the armed forces. The most absurd rumours were in circulation. Contact with the Anglo-Saxon Masonic forces was resumed via Lisbon. This reawakening of Masonic activity naturally did not pass unnoticed in the Vatican, which also entered the lists, though in a different field no less insidious and demoralising—that of supra-national pacifism which, preached in Italian and, above all, in Italy, acted as a depressing agent upon the people's spirit, especially in certain areas. To this manœuvre on the part of those two great organisations there was added the support of the old and new anti-Fascist parties, whose programme was one of revenge pure and simple.

With the landing in Sicily, the last hope of a military success had gone, and the crisis of the dyarchy was bound to explode in all its hideousness. Realising the toll taken of Fascism, the other force of the dyarchy, which had been holding itself in reserve and which also held in reserve all the forces which traditionally supported it, seized the right moment for going over to the attack.

In July, 1943, the Crown, which at last considered itself the stronger, was guided only by the instinct for its physical preservation. The war, the country, the future of the nation did not enter into its calculations in the least; the King's action was inspired by the most pitiable egotism, perhaps, even, by a purely personal self-interest. He wanted, according to one of his personal declarations from the grave at Bari, "to be done with Fascism."[1]

[1] On April 12th, 1944, King Victor Emmanuel declared that he was prepared to withdraw from public life as soon as the Allies reached Rome, and appointed Prince Umberto Lieutenant-General of the Realm in that event. He prefaced this announcement with the statement that eight months ago he "put an end to the Fascist régime and brought Italy, notwithstanding risk and danger, to the side of the United Nations in the struggle for liberation against National Socialism."

The King erred in his calculations, and the martyred nation is now paying the price of the royal betrayal.

Fascism—generous and romantic as it was in October 1922—has footed the bill for its mistake in not having been totalitarian right up to the apex of the pyramid, and for having believed that it was solving the problem by a system which, in its historical applications both recent and remote, has shown itself a difficult and short-lived compromise.

The Fascist revolution halted before the throne. That seemed inevitable at the time. Events have decided that the Crown should expiate, by its fall, the treacherous blow dealt to the Régime and the unpardonable crime committed against the nation.

The nation can arise again and live only under the banners of a Republic.

CHAPTER XIX

ANOTHER OF THE MANY: PORTRAIT OF AN EXECUTIONER

The Mask and the Face

On April 2nd, 1925, while barely convalescent, I made the Senate (which was discussing Di Giorgio's bill[1]) a speech of a military character, which had the honour of being posted up in all the towns and villages of the Realm by almost unanimous proclamation of the Senate. A few days later I assumed the direction of the Ministry for War.

On April 10th, 1925, the then General Pietro Badoglio sent me the following telegram from Rio de Janeiro (where he had been sent as ambassador):

On the occasion of your assuming direction of the Ministry for War I should like, Your Excellency, to send you my heartiest good wishes as General of the Army and soldier of our respected and victorious nation.

After the March on Rome, Badoglio had been sent to fulfil the task of Ambassador to Brazil. Just before the Fascist insurrection in October, declarations had been attributed to him which gave rise to a violent attack in the *Popolo d' Italia* on October 14th.[2]

Badoglio raised no objections of any sort when nominated ambassador, but left for his new destination, where he remained

[1]A plan presented to the Senate by General Di Giorgio, then Minister for War, for the reform of the Army.

[2]At the time of the March on Rome, Badoglio is believed to have offered to disperse the Fascists with a "whiff of grape shot." This offer is said to have been declined by Victor Emmanuel. According to another version, he told Roman business magnates: "These Fascist upstarts—give me a battalion of Royal Carabinieri and I will sweep them away. All Fascism will crumble at the first shot."

a couple of years without distinguishing himself particularly. When he returned, his loyalty to the Fascist Régime (which had meanwhile undergone the trials of 1924) seemed absolutely sincere. He went about saying: "Wherever I am ordered I shall go; Badoglio is always ready to go whenever you give the word."

In spring 1925 the question arose of creating the office of Chief of General Staff for the co-ordinated building up of all the armed forces. General Badoglio was the Court candidate and outstripped all the others; the King himself said that from the professional point of view he had "the best head."

The Man Responsible for Caporetto

At the moment it is not possible to discover what has become of the lawyer and ex-Senator Edoardo Rotigliano, who had come to Fascism via Florentine nationalism. His last public oration was a somewhat frondistic speech to the Senate in spring 1943, in which he recalled the King's attitude after Caporetto.

Now, on April 4th, 1925, the ex-Deputy Rotigliano sent the following symptomatic and, in some ways, almost prophetic letter to me, as Head of the Government:

His Excellency the President.

Today in the Chamber General Badoglio's name was repeatedly mentioned for the appointment of Chief of Army General Staff. I hope this rumour is unfounded. I had the opportunity of knowing General Badoglio during the war, and of following his actions closely. I can assure you that he has not the requisite gifts for being placed at the head of the Army. Many people know that Badoglio was the man chiefly responsible for Caporetto, but few know of his ignoble conduct on the morrow of the defeat, when he abandoned three of the four divisions of his 27th Army Corps without leadership on the left bank of the Isonzo, in order to rush to Udine and Padua to assure his own safety and to canvass for the appointment of Deputy Chief of Staff. He is a man of insatiable ambition. If he were once at the head of the Army I am sure he would profit by it to try and scale the ladder of government. I have no candidates to put forward, I would even assert that none of the generals most under consideration can, in my opinion, give a sufficient guarantee of loyalty to our Régime. But from that point of view Badoglio would certainly be the worst of the lot. Forgive me, Excellency, for thinking it my duty to express to you a conviction which is the fruit of my own personal knowledge of events, and of which, if you wish, I could give you proof. I assure you of my unchanging loyalty,

E. ROTIGLIANO.

This was followed by a typed P.S.:

By means of a faked telegram he tried to make it appear that he had been transferred to another command before the break-up of his Army Corps.

Rotigliano's letter did not pass unobserved, but provoked fresh discussions and further investigations. At a later meeting I received the impression that it was a question of polemical "taking sides." It was known that the Nationalists were going all out in support of Cadorna who, in his turn, had written as follows to the editor of *Vita Italiana* in a letter dated from Villar Pellice, September 12th, 1919:

The "Gazzetta del Popolo" yesterday published the findings of the enquiry into Caporetto.

After saying that he ought to write a book in reply, he continued as follows:

Responsibility is pinned on me and on Generals Porro, Capello, Montuori, Bongiovanni and Cavaciocchi, and yet there is not a word about Badoglio, whose responsibility was extremely grave. It was his very Army Corps (the 27th) which was routed in front of Tolmino, losing three extremely strong defence lines in a single day, although the day before (October 23rd) he had expressed to me personally his complete confidence in their resistance, confirming what he had already told Colonel Calcagno on October 19th when I had sent the latter to collect information on the state of that Army Corps and its requirements. It was the rout of that Corps which caused the rout of the whole army front. And yet Badoglio gets off scot-free! Here obviously Freemasonry and probably other influences have had something to do with it, in view of the honours with which he has subsequently been loaded. And that, I think, is that.

The other influence referred to by Cadorna was that of the Crown.

Still à propos of Caporetto, the War Museum in Milan contains

General Cavaciocchi's three unpublished manuscripts (presented by his daughter through General Segato fifteen years ago) which are to be published one day.

Army Chief of Staff

The battle taking place for and against Badoglio in political and military circles ended in Badoglio's favour, chiefly through the Duke della Vittoria's[1] support. In a letter dated May 1st, 1925, Badoglio, on taking up his appointment, and dealing with the choice of Deputy Chief of Staff, turned down Grazioli as slippery, Vaccari as not in the picture, and Ferrari as no longer enjoying prestige, and suggested General Scipioni, "despite the fact that he looked like an apothecary". He concluded:

What I have said above is exactly what I think.[2] *But I shall do the same with any Deputy Chief of Staff, and Your Excellency will get the army you want. I therefore resign myself completely to Your Excellency's decisions.*

The first problem to be faced at a series of meetings held at the Ministry for War, with myself presiding and Bonzani and Thaon di Revel present, was the organisation of the Air Force as an autonomous Service.[3]

After Zaniboni's unsuccessful attempt,[4] Badoglio sent me the following letter on headed notepaper, dated November 7th, 1925:

Your Excellency,

As Chief of General Staff and faithful collaborator of the National Government, in view of the fact that the ex-deputy Zaniboni was wearing a major's uniform of the Alpini at the time of his criminal attempt, I feel it my duty, in the name of as many as wear the uniform of a soldier of Italy, to protest indignantly against

[1] Duke della Vittoria, i.e., the title given to Marshal Diaz.

[2] As appears from the facsimile attached to the second edition, the original letter inserts "Because" (*perchè*) and omits "of Staff" (*di Stato maggiore*). It then reads: "I have said the above *because* it is exactly what I think. But I shall do the same with any *Deputy Chief.*" (See below, page 202.)

[3] After the 1915–18 war the Air Arms of the Army and Navy were amalgamated under a Commissioner for Air. Their autonomous status was confirmed by the law of May 14th, 1925, which created an Air Ministry. Bonzani was the first Under-Secretary for Air; Thaon Di Revel, Admiral of the Fleet, was Minister for the Navy at the time.

[4] See above, page 137.

this dastardly act by one who, forgetful of the dictates of honour, sought to make possible the perpetration of the vilest and most odious of crimes by means of the symbols of past distinction. God has protected Your Excellency and Italy !

In the heartbeats of the nation which, vibrant with emotion and exultation, has rallied affectionately to you at this time, Your Excellency will certainly have recognised and felt near you the heartbeats of all of us who bear arms in the service of our country ; and in the august name of the King, we remain your most obedient and loyal servants.

Your devoted

BADOGLIO.

It gives one a curious feeling, twenty years after, to hear the phrase "the dictates of honour" from the Marshal's lips. And it is odd that, among the first collaborators chosen for the Bari government born of the unconditional surrender, there should figure the would-be assassin of 1925 ! [1]

Having definitely assumed his command, Badoglio dealt with military problems very much from a distance, contenting himself with issuing directives of a general nature. He but rarely attended the grand annual manœuvres, so as to avoid meeting men he detested, such as Cavallero, for instance. That did not prevent him, on December 24th, 1926, from expressing *the most loyal and heartfelt good wishes to the Duce*, together with the hope that

. . . . under the energetic direction of the Duce the Army would attain to the maximum efficiency. I assure Your Excellency that in this grandiose task we shall be your most loyal and tireless collaborators.

PIETRO BADOGLIO.

The Governorship of Libya

In the autumn of 1928 Badoglio was nominated Governor of Libya in succession to De Bono, who had begun the agricultural development of the colony. It was agreed that Badoglio should keep his job of Chief of General Staff ; that, save for unforeseen

[1] i.e., Tito Zaniboni ; see above, p. 137, n. 2. Serving a term of 30 years' imprisonment at Ponza, he was released by the Allies in October, 1943. Elected Joint President of the first free congress of the six anti-Fascist Parties at Bari, January 28th, 1944, he was appointed by Badoglio High Commissioner in charge of the Purge of Fascists, February 25th, 1944.

developments, he should remain in Libya from January 1st, 1929, to December 31st, 1933; and that he should continue to draw his former salary as well as that of Governor, which Badoglio asked should be at least equal to what he had got as Ambassador to Brazil.

It was then that the Marquisate of Sabotino blossomed forth. In a letter dated September 12th, 1928, VI of the Fascist Era, Badoglio wrote:

Because Your Excellency's generosity in rewarding all your faithful collaborators is well known, I take the liberty of applying to Your Excellency to suggest to the King that he should grant me a hereditary title referring to my action on Sabotino.[1] *I should be most grateful if Your Excellency would confirm what I have had the honour of writing to you in this letter. As I told you verbally yesterday, Your Excellency can count on my most complete and absolute devotion now and always.*

PIETRO BADOGLIO,
Marshal of Italy.

This is not the place to examine Badoglio's political, military and economic achievements in the five years of his governorship of Libya. Maintaining the objectivity characteristic of this narrative, we may say that the work begun by De Bono was perfected on a greater scale. From time to time, in order to show that Libya "was not a liability to Italy," he sent me fruit, vegetables and grapes, the first-fruits of that earth which the industrious hands of thousands of Italians had rendered fertile.

In 1933, after the failure of the only logical and rational historical attempt to reach an understanding with the Western Powers so as to co-ordinate Europe's political and social evolution,[2] it became clear that if Italy wished to continue to exist, she would have to secure a larger and more fertile terrain in Africa. On December 30th, 1934, I sent my principal political and military collaborators a memorandum illustrating a plan for the conquest of Abyssinia.

This document is still in existence, as are the hundreds of

[1] Mount Sabotino formed a strongly fortified Austrian bastion for the defence of Gorizia. It was finally captured by Badoglio, then a Lt.-Colonel, on August 6th, 1916.

[2] The Four-Power Pact, signed on June 7th, 1933, between Great Britain, France, Germany and Italy, in which they pledged themselves to pursue, within the framework of the League of Nations, a policy of co-operation with a view to the maintenance of peace.

signed telegrams by which I directed all the preparations and the different phases of the campaign. Who of those who saw it could ever forget the national gathering on October 2nd, 1935? And those of May 5th and 9th, 1936?[1] Who does not swell with pride at the thought of the resistance to the blockade organised by the League of Nations? Who is not moved at the recollection of the "Wedding-Ring Day"?[2] No one can erase those great pages from the history of the Italian nation.

In my prefaces to the books written by the three conquerors of the Empire, I acknowledged the merits of each of them.[3] In view of the proportions the war might assume—over half a million Italians, military and civilian, had gone over to East Africa in spite of the English—I thought the task of directing it belonged to the Chief of General Staff. When the English fleet appeared in the Mediterranean in September, Marshal Badoglio had a bad attack of nerves and thought the game jeopardised. In a letter he implored me, "who had done so much for Italy, to do something to prevent a clash with Great Britain." I replied that Italy would not take the initiative in the Mediterranean, but would stand up to any blackmail and would defend herself, if attacked.

The English fleet arrived, cruised through the Mediterranean without firing a shot, and the dreaded crisis was averted.

Badoglio made no difficulties when he was ordered to Africa.

[1] On *October 2nd*, 1935, Mussolini spoke on the occasion of "national mobilisation" for the Abyssinian War. The Fascist invasion of Abyssinia began on the following day when Italian forces crossed the Mareb. On *May 8th*, 1936, Mussolini announced from the balcony of the Palazzo Venezia the capture of Addis Ababa by Marshal Badoglio. On *May 9th*, 1936, Mussolini announced the foundation of the Fascist Empire. "The territories and the peoples that belonged to the Empire of Abyssinia are placed under the full and entire sovereignty of the Kingdom of Italy. The title of Emperor has been assumed for himself and his successors by the King of Italy."

[2] The first "Wedding-Ring Day" was on December 18th, 1935, when, in response to an appeal from Mussolini, Italian women exchanged their gold wedding rings for iron ones to help finance the Abyssinian war. The anniversary of this sacrifice was religiously observed by the Fascists every year.

[3] Marshal De Bono, who was recalled for his mismanagement of the Ethiopian campaign in November 1935, afterwards wrote an account of his strategy: "Anno XIV. La Conquista di un Impero, La Preparazione e le Prime Operazioni," 1937. Marshal Badoglio, who replaced De Bono, published "La Guerra d'Etiopia" in the same year. (An English translation appeared under the title, "The War in Abyssinia" London, 1937.) Marshal Graziani, who was in command of part of the forces in the Ethiopian campaign, also wrote a book on the subject, which was published in 1938: "Il Fronte Sud."

Before leaving, he telegraphed me from Naples on November 18th, 1935, as follows:

On leaving Italy for Eritrea I wish to express to Your Excellency my feelings of profound gratitude for your having given me the opportunity of once more serving, under Your Excellency's orders, the cause of Fascist Italy in lands across the sea. The operation so happily begun will be brought to a conclusion according to the Duce's wishes, and with that strength which unites the people, soldiers and Blackshirts in one sole block of faith and enthusiasm.

The Duke of Addis Ababa is born

During the campaign in those exciting days of May 1936, Marshal Badoglio not only did not seek to conceal his Fascism, but made a parade of it on successive public occasions. Fascists accorded him honours everywhere. They considered him one of themselves. Meanwhile, he was sending in his various bills. First he demanded another title. He did that at once, the minute he returned from Addis Ababa in July 1936. The worthy Fedele, then Commissioner of the College of Heralds, although in favour of a dukedom, was against the title of Addis Ababa and against making it hereditary as the Marshal wished it to be, not only for his sons but for his daughter as well. He also asked to receive his wartime emolument for life and also that the expenses connected with the creation of the title should be borne by the Presidency of the Council. The King offered some opposition, particularly to the title chosen. But he ended by yielding. I contented myself with "putting the matter in hand." Thus the Duke of Addis Ababa was born.

Badoglio then resumed his old job, leaving others the thankless task of pacifying the Empire.

A sort of Badoglio clique had been formed in Rome which took upon itself the task of preserving the gilt on the Marshal's laurels. When, in the last part of his book, *Myself and Africa*, Sem Benelli[1] attributed the merit of the victorious and rapid conclusion of the campaign to me, Badoglio sent the author a letter of most lively protest, which was answered explicitly and exhaustively. Again, when Alberto Cappa's book *Total War*

[1]In *Io in Africa* ("Myself in Africa"; the title is misquoted), Milan, 1936, Benelli—a well-known playwright, recently President of the Association of Italian Writers—recorded his impressions as a volunteer in the Abyssinian campaign.

came out, in 1940, Colonel Gandin, Marshal Badoglio's chief secretary, pointed out the fact to my secretariat in these scornful terms:

In case you should not yet have noticed it, I draw your attention to the enclosed book in which some vile accusations against Marshal Badoglio are repeated. I consider it my duty to do this, since the Marshal does not propose to take any steps in the matter.

Your loyal and obedient servant.

The book mentioned the battle of Caporetto and contained a preface by Enrico Caviglia which said:

> "This is a study worthy of being read and meditated on by all who have to do with military science and politics in general. No one with any political or military responsibilitity can today ignore the principles of total war, which involve the forces of the whole nation."

Up to the whole of 1938–39 my relations with Badoglio were cordial, outwardly at least. So much so, that on September 21st, 1938, on the occasion of my visit to the province of Alessandria, the Marshal offered me the hospitality of his villa or, at least, a tea-party which *would be the greatest honour for him and a great satisfaction to the whole province.*

Badoglio accepted the war against France with apparent enthusiasm. He wished, however, to postpone it as long as possible. It is perfectly true that when Badoglio read out the French armistice terms at the Villa Incisa just outside Rome, he had tears in his eyes.[1]

Again, in 1940, the Marshal sent me "his hearty good wishes" on the anniversary of the founding of Fascism.

In this rapid retrospective glance over the twenty years of Fascism, the figure of the Marshal, a traitor several times over, has been subjected to the ordeal by fire and branded for all time.

He drew away from the Régime and began to premeditate his revenge after the start of the Greek campaign, when he was relieved of his appointment as Chief of General Staff.

[1] The Italo-French Armistice Convention was signed at the Villa Incisa all'Olgiata, near Rome, on June 24th, 1940, fourteen days after the Italian declaration of war.

CHAPTER XX

THE MEETING AT THE PALAZZO VENEZIA ON OCTOBER 15TH, 1940

AT THE RIGHT MOMENT, a rumour was cunningly circulated that Marshal Badoglio was against the war with Greece. It is time the truth was told. Marshal Badoglio was in favour of the war with the aim of occupying Greece entirely. Now, in view of the situation in which we have been placed, we can open the iron safes and publish, if not in their entirety, at least the essential points of many historical documents. And the meeting which took place on October 15th, 1940, at 11 a.m. in my study at the Palazzo Venezia may well be called historic. There were present Badoglio, Ciano, Soddu, Jacomoni, Roatta, Visconti Prasca,[1] and, as Secretary, Lt.-Colonel Trombetti, who took down the proceedings in shorthand.[2]

The War with Greece

After calling to mind the provocations which Greece, a fief of England, had offered us, and after going into the question of Italo-Greco-Albanian relations as a whole and, particularly, from the military and political angles, I explained the reason for

[1] Those present had, at the time, the following functions—BADOGLIO: Chief of General Staff. CIANO: Minister for Foreign Affairs. UBALDO SODDU: Under-Secretary of State for War. FRANCESCO JACOMONI DI SAN SAVINO: The King's Lieutenant-General (Viceroy) in Albania. MARIO ROATTA: Chief of Army Staff. SEBASTIANO VISCONTI PRASCA: Commander-in-Chief, Italian Forces in Albania.

[2] The Rome paper *Il Tempo*, July 13th, 1944, published the complete shorthand text of this meeting signed by Trombetti. (See below, Comment to Chapter XX.) The account of the meeting is distorted by Mussolini's deliberate omissions and an outright falsification. Some of the smaller omissions are indicated in the following footnotes.

the meeting, which followed many others held during the summer; and I invited Jacomoni, the King's Lieutenant-General in Albania, to review the situation.

JACOMONI spoke as follows: "In Albania this operation is being anxiously awaited. The country is impatient and full of enthusiasm; indeed, one may say that the enthusiasm is so great that there has lately been some disappointment because operations have not yet begun.

"We have provided very thoroughly for the provisioning of the country. The 'Durazzo harbour danger' exists, in the sense that if it were bombarded it would be difficult for us to get supplies. The question of road communications has made much progress but cannot yet be considered solved.

"What is the Greek situation like from the Albanian point of view?[1]

"It is very difficult to define. Public opinion is ostentatiously indifferent. We announced that the niece of the famous murdered Albanian patriot[2] had been killed, but they replied by denying the fact.

"From the information given by our agents it emerges that, while two months ago the Greeks did not seem likely to offer serious resistance, they now appear determined to oppose our operations.

"I believe that Greek resistance will vary according to whether our action is swift, determined and strong, or prudent and limited in scope.

"We have also to consider what help the Greeks may receive by sea, from the English."

DUCE: "I should most categorically rule out the sending of men."

JACOMONI: "The only worry might arise from a partial

[1] Mussolini omits here a remark interjected by himself: "This is just what we want to know."

[2] About the alleged murder of the 'Albanian patriot', the brigand Daout Hodja, see below, Comment to Chapter XX. As to the story of the murder of his niece, the *Agence d'Athénes* stated on September 28th, 1940: "The Agence Stefani has reproduced yet another chapter from the Albanian paper *Tomori's* fantastic serial story about imaginary crimes perpetrated against the Moslems in Epirus. . . . The third 'victim', a woman (sic) called Djemal Hodja, from the village of Karvounari, is also a fictitious personage, no murder having been committed in the above-named village since 1932, when a Moslem killed his wife for being unfaithful to him. It should be added that a certain Djemal Hodja (a man) was living in this village down to the year 1903. He died from natural causes in 1909."

occupation of Greece, because the English might launch an offensive against Southern Italy and Albania from the remaining bases, if they were in a position to send out powerful air support. The Greek Air Force has 144 'planes, which need not cause us serious apprehension."

DUCE: "What is the people's attitude like in Greece?"

JACOMONI: "They seem very depressed."

CIANO: "There is a clear cleavage between the people and the political and plutocratic governing class, which is the one that animates resistance and keeps the Anglophile spirit alive in the country. This is a very small class but very rich, whereas the rest are indifferent to whatever happens, our invasion included."

JACOMONI: "The news I let out of the high salaries in Albania has made a deep impression on the Greek people."

(The Duce then invited General Visconti Prasca, commander of the troops in Albania, to review the military situation.)

VISCONTI PRASCA: "We have planned an operation against Epirus which will be ready by the 26th of this month and which looks very promising.

"The geographical situation of Epirus does not favour the possibility of the other Greek forces intervening, because on the one side there is the sea and on the other an impassable mountain range. The Greek field of campaign enables us to carry out a series of enveloping movements against the Greek forces—reckoned at about 30,000 men—and it would make possible the occupation of Epirus in a short time, say ten or fifteen days.

"This operation—which might enable us to eliminate all the Greek forces—has been planned down to the last detail, and is perfect, so far as is humanly possible. The success of the operation would enable us to improve our position and would give us a safer frontier and the possession of the port of Prevesa,[1] which would completely alter our position.

"That is the first phase of the operation, which should be carried out thoroughly and in the best possible manner.

"The operation, however, depends on climatic conditions. In a few weeks the rainy season will raise serious difficulties for the conquest of Epirus and the base of Prevesa."

DUCE: "The starting date of the operations may be advanced, but not delayed."

VISCONTI PRASCA: "The morale of the troops is excellent,

[1] A port on the west coast of Greece, situated at the entrance to the gulf of Arta.

enthusiasm is at its peak. I have never had occasion to complain of the troops in Albania. The only sign of indiscipline I ever came across was the excessive eagerness of officers and men to go forward and fight."

DUCE: "What forces have you?"

VISCONTI PRASCA: "About 70,000 men, besides the special battalions. With regard to the troops against us—about 30,000 men—we have a superiority of two to one."

DUCE: "And with regard to enemy material—armoured cars and field defences?"

VISCONTI PRASCA: "The only worry is the help which the enemy might get from the English Air Force, since in my opinion a Greek Air Force does not exist.

"With regard to the Salonika front, certain reservations must be made because of the seasonal weather conditions.

"We could start our action against Epirus."

DUCE: "The action at Salonika is important because we must prevent it becoming an English base."

VISCONTI PRASCA: "This action will take a certain time. The port of embarkation is Durazzo, which is about 188 miles from Salonika. It will therefore take a couple of months."

DUCE: "In any case we can prevent the English landing at Salonika. It is important that two divisions should be sent to this front as well, because they may decide Bulgarian intervention."

VISCONTI PRASCA: "The basis of everything, even the beginning of the march on Athens, must be the occupation of Epirus and the port of Prevesa."

DUCE: "And the occupation of the three islands Zante, Cephalonia and Corfu."

VISCONTI PRASCA: "Certainly."

DUCE: "These operations should be carried out simultaneously. Do you know anything about the morale of the Greek soldiers?"

VISCONTI PRASCA: "They are not the sort of people to enjoy fighting.[1] The operation has been planned in such a way as to convey an impression of a crushing defeat in a few days."

DUCE: "By virtue of the responsibility which I take upon myself in this matter, I tell you not to worry yourself unduly

[1] A long passage is omitted in which Mussolini demands, and discusses with Jacomoni and Ciano, the creation of some incident which would serve as pretext for the Italians marching into Greece to establish order. (See below, Comment to Chapter XX.)

about possible losses, although from the human point of view you must consider the life of each separate soldier. I tell you this because sometimes a Commander halts in his advance on account of heavy losses."[1]

VISCOUNT PRASCA: "I have given orders for every battalion to go into action, even against a division."

Badoglio's Declarations

BADOGLIO: "The matter involves two questions—that of Greece and that of help from the English. I am completely in agreement with you, Duce,[2] in almost ruling out the possibility of an English landing. They are much more worried about Egypt than about Greece, and they are reluctant to embark troops in the Mediterranean. Therefore the only possible help would be from the air.

"To meet this contingency, the plan might be modified so as to make the attack on Greece coincide with that on Mersa Matruh. In that case it would be very difficult for them to withdraw 'planes from Egypt and send them to Greece.

"This would be feasible, because Graziani, too, will be ready by the 26th of this month.[3]

"Now, looking into the Greek problem, I believe that it will not meet the case if we stop short at Epirus. I don't exaggerate when I say that we must occupy Crete and the Peloponnesus as well, if we want to occupy Greece. The operation in Epirus as planned by Visconti Prasca is all right. With our left flank safe, the enemy forces should not give us much trouble. We have the Air Force. . . ."

DUCE: "We shall throw at least 400 machines into the operation, in view of possible English support."

BADOGLIO: "We shall have to occupy the whole of Greece if we want to get good results."[4]

ROATTA: "Taking everything into account, we can count on

[1] This paragraph has been omitted in the first edition.

[2] The word *Duce*, not found in the original stenographic report, has been added by Mussolini.

[3] Mussolini omits a long passage asserting that Graziani's attack on Egypt, projected to coincide with that on Greece, would result in the defeat of the British Empire. (See below, Comment to Chapter XX.)

[4] Mussolini omits the end of Badoglio's statement in which he declares that 20 divisions are needed instead of the 10 available. (See below, Comment.)

the equivalent of eleven divisions. In order not to stop at Epirus we shall have to intensify the despatch of troops, in order, also, to avoid giving the impression that we are too out of breath to go any further.

"We should therefore study the problem at once of occupying the whole of Greece."

DUCE: "If we fix the start of operations for the 26th of this month, and assuming we have eliminated the problem of Epirus by about the 10th or 15th November, we have another month for the despatch of fresh forces."

VISCONTI PRASCA: "The despatch of fresh forces depends on how the plan works out. And they can only be sent to Epirus when we have occupied it.

"It is not a question of carrying out a decisive action in the time, but of an operation for our own security. At this time of year we can only operate in southern Greece.

"If we retain Durazzo as a port of embarkation for Salonika we shall need a month for the despatch of each division."

DUCE: "To clarify our ideas on the subject we are now discussing, I would ask you how you propose to march on Athens after occupying Epirus."

VISCONTI PRASCA: "I don't think it will be very difficult. A group of five or six divisions would be sufficient."

BADOGLIO: "I think a march on Athens more urgent than a march on Salonika, because it does not seem likely that the English will land at Salonika."

CIANO: "The more so in view of possible Bulgarian intervention."

ROATTA: "What we need is pressure on that side, too."

DUCE: "Do you think two divisions would be enough?"

ROATTA: "Yes."

DUCE: "Our ideas seem to be crystallising. An attack on Epirus. As to Salonika: wait and see what follows if Bulgaria intervenes, as I think probable.

"I am in full agreement with the occupation of Athens."

VISCONTI PRASCA: "Then from Athens we shall cut Greece in half, roughly speaking, and we can start for Salonika from the capital."

DUCE: "How far is it from the borderline of occupied Epirus to Athens?"

VISCONTI PRASCA: "About 160 miles, over middling roads."

DUCE: "And what is the terrain like?"

VISCONTI PRASCA: "Rugged, steep, bare hill country."

DUCE: "And how do the valleys lie?"

VISCONTI PRASCA: "East to west, that is, in the direction of Athens itself."

DUCE: "That is important."

ROATTA: "That is only true up to a certain point, because we have to cross a range nearly 7,000 feet high." (Shows the Duce a map of the district.)

VISCONTI PRASCA: "There are a lot of mule tracks over it."

DUCE: "Have you been over these roads?"

VISCONTI PRASCA: "Yes, several times."

DUCE: "We now come to two further questions. Having settled all that, how many extra divisions do you think we shall have to send to Albania in order to occupy all the ground leading to Athens?"

VISCONTI PRASCA: "At first, three divisions equipped for mountain warfare would be enough; naturally, it depends on the circumstances. Now these troops could reach the port of Arta[1] in a night."

DUCE: "Another point is Albanian support either in regular troops or in irregular bands, which I consider fairly important."

VISCONTI PRASCA: "We have made a plan for this. We want to organise bands of 2,500-3,000 men under our own officers."

JACOMONI: "There are any number of applications. It would not do to send many Moslems in case they start a lot of vendettas."

DUCE: "But you could organise a certain number of bands?"

VISCONTI PRASCA: "Everything has been arranged. I have already sent off a telegram telling them to keep everything in readiness and to warn each individual."

DUCE: "How will you arm them?"

VISCONTI PRASCA: "With light machine-guns and hand grenades."

DUCE: "Now there is another aspect of the problem. What measures have you taken on the Yugoslav border?"

VISCONTI PRASCA: "We have two divisions and a battalion of Carabinieri and frontier guards. Altogether, quite good protection."

DUCE: "I don't think we shall be attacked from that direction, and in any case the troops will be supported by already prepared strong-points."

[1] This is not Arta in Greece, but Arta in Albania, near Valona.

VISCONTI PRASCA: "One might add that the terrain lends itself well to defence. A few small groups might achieve some penetration through the woods, but there would be nothing to fear because we have garrisoned the whole frontier. A frontier post every 600 or 700 yards."

JACOMONI: "In Albania they want us to call up a few classes."

DUCE: "How many men does each class produce?"

JACOMONI: "About 7,000."

DUCE: "We ought to consider that carefully. Although we must be careful not to neglect or repulse them, it would not do for these forces to make too large a contribution. We do not want it to appear that they have conquered Epirus.[1] A certain participation of Albanian elements would be opportune as long as it did not disturb the population. I should call up two or three classes. We should give particular attention to anti-aircraft defence, because we must, as far as possible, prevent raids on the oil-field districts or on Albanian cities, and prevent any comparisons being made with the superior defences of the cities in Apulia. We shall therefore need anti-aircraft defences on a large scale."

SODDU: "I have already arranged to send them the seventy-five 'Skodas' we got from Germany."

VISCONTI PRASCA: "The defence of Tirana is limited to two detachments, while there are barely five detachments for the defence of the whole of Albania."

DUCE: "Albania needs at least a hundred pieces of artillery because we must prevent the demoralising daylight raids. Send all the 'Skodas' and 'Oerlikons' out there."

SODDU: "We haven't received them all yet. I shall send them on the minute they arrive. I shall send the 'Oerlikons' by air."

DUCE: "We must have fighter 'planes as well as ground defences. Fortunately we have a large number of these available. In Albania on October 1st there were fifty-two front-line 'planes and fifteen second-line—sixty-seven machines altogether."

CIANO: "The 74th Wing is on its way."

DUCE: "I think we have now examined the problem from every aspect."

BADOGLIO: "The Army Staff will settle the details "[2]

[1] This paragraph has been left out in the first edition.

[2] Mussolini omits his concluding words on the "March on Athens." (See below, Comment.)

Yesterday and Today

Thirteen days later, after a fatal delay of two days, the war against Greece began ; not so disastrous a war as people now pretend it was. It was not overwhelming, as General Visconti Prasca thought it would be, but it is a fact that already by the end of December all Greek initiative was as good as spent, and it is certain that even without German aid (as the Führer himself loyally declared)[1] Greece would have been beaten in the coming battle in April, because even during the operations in the Klisura sector in March she had nearly exhausted her resources.[2]

When Valona was abandoned in 1920 during Giolitti's term of office, there was an outcry. Who does not recall my article "Farewell to Valona" ?[3] Then, twenty years later, the old route was retraced, the route laid down less by history than by the unchanging laws of geography. At a few minutes' distance by air from Bari or Brindisi one can see the lagoons of the Albanian coast beyond Valona, the Sinjëo range, the Trëbëshini mountains and the blood-stained Golico, while further away, always hidden in mist, the Tomor rears its stern and forbidding head. What a prodigious work was achieved in a few years in Albania, where the Albanians were given equal rights and the same duties as Italian citizens, in keeping with Roman tradition![4] Here one may see the great motor highway from Durazzo to

[1] Hitler's speech in Berlin on May 4th, 1941. In a letter to Mussolini, however, found among the latter's papers and quoted by the Milan Communist paper, *Unità*, May 24th, 1945 (see also *The Times*, May 25th, 1945), Hitler blames Mussolini for having attacked Greece.

[2] Far from being exhausted at the end of December, the Greeks retained the initiative throughout January and February 1941. After repulsing heavy counter-attacks at the end of January, they launched a successful offensive early in February and still retained sufficient resources to shatter desperate Italian attacks in the Klisura sector in March when Italian casualties were estimated (*The Times*, March 18th, 1941) at 48,000.

[3] See above, p. 147, for Valona incident. The article "Farewell to Valona" appeared in the *Popolo d' Italia* on August 5th, 1920, and consisted of a bitter attack on Giolitti's policy. It referred to the abandonment of Valona as "our Albanian disaster."

[4] The Italian annexation of Albania following the invasion on Good Friday, in April 1939, was the climax of a continuous process of penetration which had been going on since the Italo-Albanian treaty of "friendship" in 1927. After the complete occupation of the country, the exploitation of Albanian natural resources by Italian capital was intensified.

Tirana, the new buildings in the capital, the reclamation of the Musachia, the petroleum wells of Devoli (Italy's only source of this raw material), the iron mines near Elbassan, the bitumen, copper, coal and chromium mines ; there, the almost completed plan for a main railway from Durazzo to Elbassan which, had it been continued beyond Lake Ochrida, would have put us into direct communication with Sofia and the Black Sea. Industrial, commercial and agricultural enterprises and Italian banking concerns were transforming the face of that earth which for centuries had always gravitated towards the Italian west, from the time of Teuta, Queen of the Illyrians, down to Scanderbeg,[1] whose monument was recently erected in a square in Rome. Nothing is left of all that, absolutely nothing. Everything crumbled on that criminal 8th of September.

The men overseas who laid down their arms and surrendered instead of going over to the German side at once with flags flying and loyalty untarnished, committed an enormous crime, whether they did it in good or bad faith.

The flag of our country which waved over a land bathed in the blood and sweat of Italians should never have been furled. The soldiers of Italy should never have exposed themselves to the mockery or, worse still, the sarcastic pity of the Balkan peoples. They should never have left to their fate those thousands of Italian civilians, men, women and children, who had crossed the sea trusting in the protection of Italy's armed forces and who now find themselves abandoned to the often murderous violence of hostile mobs.

Of those who were the 9th and 11th Armies, there still exist only those interned in Germany, and groups of disbanded men in the mountains of Greece or pioneer divisions in Serbia.

Eight thousand Italians, defenceless, and looked at askance, are still in Albania and are now trying to pick up the threads of their life again (torn, as it has been, into a thousand shreds) with that eternal eagerness and persistence in "starting afresh" which seems at once the privilege and the punishment of the Italian people.

[1]TEUTA, Queen of the Illyrians in 230 B.C. Far from gravitating towards the Italian west, Teuta is known for her wars against the Romans in which she was finally defeated ; she sued for peace in 228 B.C. SCANDERBEG, the name given by the Turks to George Castrioti, the Albanian national hero who defended Albanian independence against the Ottoman invasion in the fifteenth century.

Besides the living, the dead also remain ; the forty thousand who fell in the Greek campaign.

Is there anyone still to look after the cemeteries where our comrades sleep ? Who takes care of that " holy ground "—really "holy"—on Height 731 ?[1] The hills where the battle raged are now enveloped in that strange, deep silence proper to places where man has met man in the tempest of iron and fire. Those are the places which still nostalgically haunt the 100,000 Italian soldiers who fought in Albania.

Let us set out on our way once more, looking ahead.

That which has been will, in the nature of things, come again. The stages in the life of a nation are counted in decades. Sometimes in centuries.[2]

[1] Height 731 at Monastir in Albania was the scene of desperate fighting throughout the winter months of 1941. It was captured by the Italians only after the German intervention, when the Italian XIth Army launched its last offensive on April 14th, 1941. The Italian press gave great prominence to the ' heroism' displayed on Height 731 by Mussolini's soldiers. It was referred to as ' holy ground' and by June 1942 had even become a place of pilgrimage, a symbol not only of "Italian heroism" but of "Italo-Albanian friendship."

[2] This marks the end of the first edition.

CHAPTER XXI

CALVARY AND RESURRECTION

AFTER THE RISE TO power of National Socialism in Germany, it was clear to me that the very unstable balance of power in Europe established by the Four Powers at Versailles was still more threatened and compromised. A new, powerful force had entered European life, entered it with a banner unfurled on which, in letters of fire, was written this watchword: "Revolt against the Versailles 'Diktat.' "

That the infamous "Diktat" had left in its wake a series of paradoxical and, in the long run, untenable situations, was admitted by the more clear-sighted politicians and by statesmen as well; that the revision of certain formulas must be faced seemed henceforth inevitable; and in the dilemma "Revision or War," it was the first alternative which nations hoped to see realised.

The Constitution of the League of Nations itself admitted the principle of revision of peace treaties. But the League of Nations had never considered the problem seriously. Entrenched in the unwieldy bureaucracy of that institution were the representatives of the territorial, political and plutocratic "status quo," belonging in the main to the smaller States which, having benefited substantially by the Versailles Treaties, wished to keep them inviolable for all eternity. It was obvious that not even a modest treaty revision would ever have taken place through the League of Nations. It was therefore necessary to face the problem in another place. Thus arose the idea of a Four-Power Pact.

Once, at the meeting in Rapallo on Christmas Day, 1926, Neville Chamberlain said to me: "It is important for the eagles to agree; the smaller birds will follow suit."

In my mind, the Four-Power Pact was to be the instrument of a steady, logical revision of treaties, and their adaptation to the new conditions of European life, and I had in view above all the supreme aim of conserving peace.

In one of the many articles which I published at that time in the American Universal Service press, and devoted to the study of the various aspects of the European situation, I pointed out the dilemma—either a minimum of European solidarity or else war, with the consequent crumbling of the common values of civilisation.[1]

When the Four-Power Pact was concluded and signed, it enjoyed great popular success. But later, opposition took shape; political: the initiative had come from Fascist Italy; territorial: Little Entente circles feared the loss of part of their States; and from the League: it was obvious that the functioning of the Four-Power Pact would depreciate the Geneva institution, depriving it of one of the tasks which it had allocated to itself but which it had never tackled. Some spoke of a new Holy Alliance; certain others found it absolutely intolerable and against the League of Nations that a directorate of Four Powers should calmly and thoroughly study the more urgent problems with regard to the development and future of the nations. They preferred the large committees and 'imposing' assemblies of Geneva, with their interminable series of speakers, few of whom were listened to with any attention.

After much talking and writing, the Four-Power Pact became silted up in the Parliamentary sand-dunes; it was, as they say in bureaucratic language, "filed," and, like other pacts, the Kellogg Pact,[2] for example, found its melancholy way to the graveyard of sensible initiatives which have failed.

I myself never spoke of it again. But the consequences of the

[1] Among the many syndicated articles by Mussolini published in summer and autumn 1933, deprecating "the system of Conferences," one headed "The Gravity of the Hour" (*Neue Freie Presse*, Vienna, 7.10.33) contained the following sentence:

"Germany . . . cannot entertain the thought of a war unless she wants to be punished by a new and perhaps irremediable catastrophe."

[2] Signed on August 27th, 1928, in Paris by representatives of fifteen nations (including Germany, Italy and Japan); formally proclaimed in Washington on July 24th, 1929, having then been ratified by 45 nations. Article I stated: "The High Contracting Parties solemnly declare in the name of their respective peoples that they condemn recourse to war for the solution of international controversies and renounce it as an instrument of national policy in their relations with one another."

event were momentous. A little later came the Stresa Conference. It has been said that this had an anti-German character, but not on the Italian side.[1] Italy once more attempted to open the door to German collaboration in the European field, while she reserved the right—and had already given clear signs of it—to solve her African problem ; à propos of which, on the occasion of Laval's visit to Rome and the relevant agreements (January 1935) Italy had been given "a free hand."

*

What could not be achieved by means of agreement, came to pass in 1936, when the Führer ordered and effected the military reoccupation of the Rhineland. Feeling ran high. One had the impression that Janus was about to reopen the doors of his temple. But France—which was in the throes of a political and moral crisis—and England, which was not yet ready, lay low. A few months later Austria ceased to exist as such, and became a boundary-province of the Greater Reich.[2] Feeling ran still higher, but the Western Powers said not a word. English political writers, and even a few Frenchmen who were loyal to the principle of nationality, admitted that Austria, being fundamentally a German nation, could not be denied the right of uniting with a people of the same race and language which, for centuries, had had a common destiny. The forceful dynamism of National Socialist foreign policy succeeded in forcing the Western Powers to recognise the new situation and to face the logical consequences of it.

[1]The author banks on the short memory of his public. At Stresa, April 11th–14th, 1935, after Germany had unilaterally denounced the military clauses of the Versailles Treaty, Mussolini signed with the Prime Ministers of Great Britain and France a resolution, confirming former joint declarations "in which the three Governments recognize the necessity of maintaining the independence and integrity of Austria, and which will continue to inspire their common policy." They "reaffirmed their intention to consult together as to measures to be taken in the case of threats to its integrity."

In Section 5 "it was regretfully recognised that the method of unilateral repudiation adopted by the German Government at a moment when steps were being taken to promote a freely negotiated settlement in the question of armaments had undermined public confidence in the security of a peaceful order. . . . Moreover, the magnitude . . . of German rearmament has shaken the hopes by which these efforts were inspired. . . ."

[2]When the *Anschluss* took place, March 12th–13th, 1938 (not "a few months," but two years after Germany, denouncing the Locarno Pact, reoccupied the Rhineland, March 7th, 1936), Mussolini sent Hitler the telegraphic message, "I congratulate you on the way you have solved the Austrian problem. I had already warned Schuschnigg." He received the reply, "Mussolini, I shall never forget this."

In reality, France and England wished simply to gain time. In 1938 the atmosphere was already extraordinarily lowering. The question of the Sudeten people, that is, of the Germans incorporated into Czechoslovakia, seemed at one point as if it must prove the famous spark which fired the powder. To prevent an explosion, the Big Four met, for the first and last time, in Munich. Italy's action was recognised as of prime importance in the peaceful solution of the question.

When it was known that an agreement had been reached, the nations breathed again. Daladier, the President of the Council, who had been accorded friendly popular demonstrations in Munich, was received in Paris by an enormous crowd and carried in triumph. The same happened to Chamberlain in London. Of the two opposite numbers, Daladier seemed the more anxious and desirous of finding a diplomatic solution which would exclude any recourse to force; Chamberlain followed the discussion very attentively, but then he very often found it necessary to consult with the personages of his suite. The atmosphere was cordial on the whole, and the faces of those present seemed brighter. On leaving the room a French journalist accosted me and said: "You have given a tube of oxygen to a sick man." I replied: "It is the normal practice in serious cases."

On returning to Rome I was received with perhaps the greatest popular demonstration of the whole twenty years of Fascism. The Via Nazionale was overflowing with crowds, hung with flags and strewn with laurels. I said a few words from the balcony of the Palazzo Venezia to announce that in Munich we had worked for "peace with justice." But a few weeks later the doors of the temple of Janus were no longer hermetically sealed, but rather ajar. One of the more absurd solutions which the Treaty of Versailles had given to the problem of Poland's outlet to the sea, namely the Danzig 'Corridor,' came to a head. One of the most difficult tasks for the historian is to establish the cause of a war and thence, also, to assign the consequent responsibility. The causes of a war are remote and immediate, direct and indirect. Proudhon, for instance, refused to enter into that sort of consideration, and maintained that war was a universal and eternal phenomenon, an "act of God." For the politician, on the contrary, the enquiry into immediate causes is a necessity. One may therefore say that the remote cause of the war which is soaking the world in blood was the Treaty of Versailles, and that the immediate cause was Poland's refusal to discuss any compromise solution, such as the "corridor within a corridor" proposed by the Führer; and that Poland's refusal was due to the guarantee which Poland herself had received from Great Britain and which served to stiffen her attitude to breaking point.

This is not the place to relate the diplomatic chronicles day by day during the first eight months of 1939. It will suffice to stress the appearance of Russia on the horizon. For some months London had been on its knees before the Kremlin, like Henry IV at Canossa, when, at the last moment, Stalin came to an agreement with Ribbentrop, so that the first phase of the war was conducted in common, or nearly so, on Polish territory and therefore, in point of fact, by Russia also against England, who could do nothing but stand impotently by at the hundredth partition of a Poland protected to no avail—now as then—right up to today, Autumn 1944.

In August things began to move. Events were striding swiftly towards war. During the last ten days of August, Italy made what might be called a desperate effort to try and avert the catastrophe. This was acknowledged by all parties in books and speeches, even by our present enemies. I did not want war. I could not want war.[1] I saw it approaching with the deepest anguish. I felt that it was a question-mark hovering over the whole future of the nation. Three military undertakings had ended successfully: the Abyssinian war in 1936; the participation in the Spanish Civil War of 1937–39; and the union of Albania with Italy in 1939. I thought that a pause was now necessary in order to develop and perfect the work. From the point of view of human loss the figures were modest, but the financial and administrative strain had been enormous. Nor must one forget the nervous strain of a people which, save for short intervals, had been at war since 1911! It was therefore high time to give

[1] On the day of Italy's entry into the war, June 10th, 1940, Mussolini declared: "We have of our own will burned the bridges behind us." On February 23rd, 1941, he added in his address to Blackshirts: "If we had been 100 per cent ready, we should have gone to war in September 1939, and not in June 1940." This statement was repeated, in a modified form, two years later, by the official Stefani Agency, June 7th, 1943: "It is three years since we entered the war, when we were not fully prepared. If we had been, we should have come in in September 1939."

The war itself was described by Mussolini, on June 10th, 1940, as "the logical development of our revolution." Echoing this statement his Minister for Italian Africa, General Teruzzi, asserted on May 9th, 1943: "This is, therefore, for us an intrinsically Fascist war. As loyal followers of Mussolini, we proudly claim the honour of having wanted it and carried it out."

people's nerves a rest, it was high time to apply the nation's energy to works of peace.

The programme for the works of peace was imposing. With the great Pontine reclamation completed and the colonisation of the Foggia plain well under way, it was time to tackle the Landed Estates of Sicily, for which the construction of no less than 20,000 cottages was envisaged. Other no less important works were planned for Sardinia, with the reclamation of the waste lands of Campidano and Macomer and with the intensified exploitation of the island's raw materials.

The start of work on the great Po-Rimini irrigation canal was imminent which, tapping the water from the river near Boretto, would have stretched along the Via Emilia to the extreme limit of the Po plain, in a short time tripling agricultural production[1]. The great plan for a self-sufficient industry was in course of realisation, with establishments for the production of liquid fuel, rubber and bauxite, as a result of which, for example, aluminium production had risen from 7,000 to 52,000 tons in five years ![2] Also in process of achievement was the multiplication of the agricultural colonies in Libya by means of which, little by little, the vast empty region was changing its native appearance to adopt that of the homeland. The new housing of the Italian universities was already well advanced and the construction of 20,000 elementary schools had been begun. Together with the cleaning up of the old quarters of many towns, the construction was planned of very many hospitals, of modern prison establishments, and of rural water supplies. Much energy and enterprise was directed towards Albania ; much also towards the Empire,

[1] It will be noted that apart from the reclamation of the Pontine marshes, completed at enormous cost, Mussolini can point to hardly any Fascist achievement in the field of national economy. Most undertakings were envisaged for the future—an indirect admission that they had advanced little in the preceding years of Fascist rule and that promises, such as those concerning the reclaiming and improving of the Sicilian *latifundia*, had remained unfulfilled.

[2] The plan for industrial 'autarky,' a cardinal point in the Fascist programme, was doomed from the start owing to Italy's inevitable dependence on foreign sources for such essentials as coal, petroleum, ferrous minerals and precious metals. The only figures quoted by Mussolini concern aluminium, with regard to which Italy is in an especially favourable position. And even here the figures are wrong. According to the official *Annuario Stastistico* for the years obviously in question, production in the period from 1935 to 1939 had risen from 13,776 to 34,236 tons. Absurd hopes were held out of self-sufficiency in such products as liquid fuel and lubricants ; cf. e.g. Mussolini's speech of 15.5.1937, *Scritti e Discorsi*, Vol. XI, p. 104.

whither many thousand families had already emigrated and, under the protective shade of our victorious flag, had created a Romagna, an Apulia and a Veneto in Africa.[1] Together with a station which would have been the finest and the most modern in Europe, there arose—between the Colosseum and the sea—to which the Romans had been led back by Fascism—numerous buildings of the World Exhibition which was to have opened in October 1942, and which would have constituted the solemn and imperishable consecration of Fascism's twenty years' work.

Italy was a regular hive of industry in Spring, 1939, and I felt that one ought not to tempt fate too often—that a long period of peace was absolutely necessary for Europe in general and for Italy in particular, and that war, once it had broken out, would hold up everything, jeopardise everything, perhaps ruin everything completely. In my opposition to the war there were motives of a political and moral nature also, that is, the feeling that the fate of Europe as a continent creative of civilisation was at stake.

During the latter days of August 1939, work to avoid a conflict took on a rhythm which might be called frenzied. From Rome went out the proposal of an immediate second meeting of the Big Four which would consider, as well as the 'Corridor' question, other questions no less urgent. During the 30th and 31st, and the 1st September, dozens of telegrams went out from the Palazzo Chigi. The telephones in the Palazzo Venezia rang almost uninterruptedly, in communication with London, Paris and Berlin. There was already the feeling in the air that "the guns would go off by themselves," but nothing was to remain untried from the moment the life of the finest youth in Europe was at stake; and everything was indeed tried, even when the guns outside the 'Corridor' had already made themselves heard. The Führer would have halted on the line which his troops had reached, but Great Britain put forward the demand that they were to retreat to their starting-point, and presented other claims more difficult to accept. The die had already been cast. There was nothing further to be done. The war took its course, liquidating Poland in three weeks, while in the West, in the shelter of the useless Maginot Line, all was quiet. Italy, with

[1]From 1938 onwards batches of emigrants were sent to Abyssinia under the ægis of the three regional emigration boards of Romagna, Apulia and Veneto. The land where they were settled—in the zone west of Harrar—was called after their region of origin.

the Führer's telegraphed consent, proclaimed her non-belligerency and, though convinced that *pacta sunt servanda* (pacts are to be kept) and that at some point intervention at the side of her ally would be inevitable—in accordance with a pact which was called, and had to be of, 'steel'—she was able to enjoy another ten months of difficult and troubled peace.

In September, on receiving the Fascists of the 'Tenth Legion' of Bologna, I had already foreseen that the war would spread across continents and that it would by degrees take on the character of a war of religion, a clash of civilisations.[1]

The events of the war up to the Armistice are graven on the Italian heart, but the unconditional surrender of September 1943 was the greatest material and moral catastrophe in the three thousand years of our history. From that fatal month onwards, the sufferings of the Italian people have been indescribable and surpass anything human, to enter the realms of imagination. Never did nation climb a more dolorous Mount Calvary!

All Italy in successive stages has become a battlefield. The tragic truth is this: Italy has been largely destroyed. First, it was the cities which underwent the still continuing savage and ferocious raids by the Anglo-Saxon liberators, then it was the turn of the smaller towns, the villages and hamlets. After the urban agglomerations had been reduced to rubble, came the destruction of the land as regards its natural products. Where thousands of armoured vehicles pass, nothing remains. Millions of trees have been bodily uprooted by tank tracks or cut down for defence works. Areas where centuries of share cropping had made a sort of agricultural masterpiece out of the farms, are now as desert as the steppes of Cyrenaica. Not a man remains, not a beast, not a tree, not a sign of life.

More than once in her changing and troubled but none the less glorious history Italy has been overrun by invaders; but all—except for the Arabs—were of European extraction. Today what may well, without rhetorical platitude, be called the sacred soil of our nation is being overrun by every race in the world. To the south of the Apennines are men of the United States of America, Brazilians, English, New Zealanders, Canadians, Australians, South Africans, Moroccans, Algerians, Frenchmen, Greeks, Poles and indeterminate blackamoors.

[1]The version of the speech of September 23rd, 1939, published at the time, contains no reference to a war of religions or a clash of civilisations.

It is well known that Moroccans have the right to loot and lodging. By the unconditional surrender everything representing the Armed Forces was pulverised, if it did not, like the Fleet, pass into enemy hands. Not a gun remained, not an aeroplane, not a rifle, not a lorry, not an armoured vehicle, not a cartridge. Then began the Odyssey of the demobilised men and of the military internees in Germany—over half a million men who, at bottom, were guiltless, and who were the victims but not the cause of the events by which they had been overthrown. Thousands, nay, tens of thousands of Italian soldiers stationed in the Balkans have merged themselves with the civil population, putting their hands to the most menial tasks ; or they have joined bands of partisans where, compelled to do forced labour, they are considered "cheap labour" in the most terrible sense of the word. One fact sheds light on the situation—Italian ex-soldiers are serving in the baggage-trains of Mihailovic's bands ! The origin of the partisan movement which is scourging Italy dates back to the 8th September, when hordes of soldiers could not regain their homes and so joined the anti-Fascist fugitives, escaped convicts and those set free from concentration camps.

Besides the war between armies, civil war has thus broken out, with episodes of savagery such as, until yesterday, would have been thought impossible on Italian soil. But that is not enough. These sufferings are accompanied by a wave of abuse from all parts of the world.

Churchill began it, with his unforgettable phrase "the stick and the carrot,"[1] but there is not an author or journalist who does not load Italy and the Italian people with insults, making no distinction between those who betrayed and those who were betrayed. It is a time when the envenomed lance of contempt may be thrust with impunity into the side of crucified Italy, because Italy cannot defend herself. And when, as often happens, the contempt is accompanied by a hypocritical compassion, the suffering is all the greater.

Speaking objectively, one may avow that there is no proportion between the crime committed by a minority and its punishment, unless our enemies wish to punish the whole Italian people more for their virtues than for their errors. Could the world perhaps not forgive her for having in these last few years attempted to

[1] See Editorial Foreword.

solve the problem of her existence ? Well, this is the time when the Italian people should get their second wind, and set themselves as watchword the ancient *fare da sè* (do it by yourself). Little by little Italy will once more become a 'Power.' What has been done in this period since the capitulation, amidst unheard-of difficulties, is the necessary preliminary. Before the war the conception of a 'Great Power' was demographic and military. The 'Great Powers' were the United States of America, Great Britain, Japan, Germany, Russia, France and Italy. The present war will produce an alteration in order of rank. Great Britain, for instance, is destined to become a second-class Power, in view of the disclosure of Russian and American strength. If the military criterion continues to be the determining factor in establishing the greater or lesser strength of a nation, Italy, like all nations even when victory is won, will have a long period of crisis before her. This once overcome, she will again become a Continental and Mediterranean Power, both European and African. And therefore a Great Power. She will once again sail the thousand-year-old highways of that sea in which she is set, whence she has drawn and will, through the peaceful labours of future generations, continue to draw, the springs of life and of her renewed creative greatness.

APPENDIX TO CHAPTER XXI: DOCUMENTS[1]

I. LETTERS FROM GRANDI TO MUSSOLINI

1 *Under-Secretary of State for the Interior.*

May 3rd, 1925.

Dear President,

Yesterday morning Contarini and, later, Federzoni, spoke to me of a nomination of myself as Under-Secretary for Foreign Affairs, to which you had given favourable consideration.

I tell you frankly and without false modesty that this unexpected news has flattered me greatly, the more so because your having chosen me for such an important function will enable me to serve you more closely at hand. This is the highest ambition and the greatest reward I could desire.

With equal frankness and honesty I must point out to you—as I have already done to Federzoni and Contarini—that I doubt whether I possess the qualifications—outwardly, especially—or the preparation necessary for a function such as you wish to entrust to me.

On the other hand, you know how boundless and unquestioning my loyalty is, and how my one wish is to obey you, so pray do with me whatever you consider most opportune and most suited to the needs of the moment which you alone can know and appraise.

Awaiting your orders, I remain,

Your devoted

DINO GRANDI.

[1] The documents given in this Appendix first appeared, as facsimile reproductions, in the second edition. They relate to Chapters XVI and XIX.

2 *Rome,* December 14th, 1927.

Dear President,

I cannot return to Bologna—after the decisions of the National Directorate—without having first told you this, with all the sincerity of my twenty-eight years :

I have always considered that in politics, rancour is the worst of counsellors, and for this reason I conscientiously feel able to say that the battle fought by me now is not a miserable battle of factions and personalities. It is the epilogue to a struggle between State Fascism and an anti-State pseudo-Fascism, demagogic and rebellious. A struggle, in short, between one sort of Fascism which would like to make an attack on the State through a poorly conceived and badly digested Syndicalism, and *our* Fascism, which desires nothing else and must not be anything else but *an organ of internal State policy, that is, of your government.*

A few months ago you ordered me to resume my post. I have done so. And in resuming it with all my enthusiasm I will not repeat an assurance that is an oath of loyalty. I can only say to you that my loyalty is *blind, complete and indestructible.* It is my spiritual gain following a year of silence and meditation.

You will see me when the test comes.

DINO GRANDI.

3 *Italian Embassy, London.*
April 7th, XVII (1939).

Duce,

Today's events have 'electrified' my spirits. Our troops in Valona! In a few hours *the whole* of Albania will be ours, it will be a '*Province*' of the Empire ! After the vengeance for Adowa, the vengeance for Valona. You, Duce, are making the Revolution move with the inevitable and ruthless motion of a tractor whose tracks take hold, crush, and relinquish hold only when the next track has already begun to crush.

I remember having once read, whether in Tacitus or Suetonius I don't know, that Augustus would not celebrate the victory of the Empire until the day Tiberius sent him the news that Illyria, the bastion of Rome, had been definitively conquered.

The Roman Empire was born of two wars ; Scipio's war in Spain, and Caesar's war in Albania. Today it is Caesar's legions

—your legions—who are crossing the sea again, at exactly the same spot, for the first time for two thousand years.

Your faithful collaborator who for eight years has had the privilege of being a daily witness of your work in Albania, knows that you have never relaxed your efforts, even for a moment, that your marching-orders were *one alone* and that one alone was the definitive solution for which you were preparing, *the definitive and permanent military conquest of Albania.*

This conquest makes the Adriatic a strategically Italian sea *for the first time*, and opens the ancient highways of Roman conquest in the East to Mussolini's Italy.

But the conquest of Albania means not only security in the Adriatic ; the pincer which immobilises Belgrade for good ; and the starting-point for a march through the Balkans and the East. It is much more ; it automatically means a fresh military defeat for England in the Mediterranean, because it puts Greece at our mercy ; Greece, which the English Admiralty has hitherto considered the natural and indispensable stronghold of England in her naval war in the Mediterranean.

You once said in the Grand Council that one of the *decisive* reasons for our African victory was our having *forced* the English, through sending the two motorised divisions to Cyrenaica, to *land warfare.* And that, Duce, was one of your profoundest truths. Your two divisions in Cyrenaica, on the Egyptian frontier, were the key to your strategic plan and the preliminary to victory in Africa.

Your legions in Albania—which means, whenever you wish, in Greece—denote another 'land war' which you have imposed on the English, with the latter's automatic loss of the two naval bases and our complete domination of the Eastern Mediterranean.

In 1928, on returning from Albania, I brought on purpose for you a bust of Dea Roma[1] then excavated at Butrinto and known by the name of the 'Goddess of Butrinto.' You had it placed in one of the rooms of the Palazzo Venezia, because that was where it should be. Then there arrived the usual nuisance from the *Belle Arti* and took the Goddess of Butrinto to bury it in one of the usual graveyards that museums are. Have it brought back to the Palazzo Venezia, in the ante-room of the Sala del Mappamondo. It is there that it should be.

GRANDI.

[1]Whatever goddess the so-called "Dea di Butrinto" represents, it is certainly not a "Dea Roma."

4 *Keeper of the Seals, Minister of Justice.*
March 27th, XVIII (1940).

Duce,

I am deeply grateful for what you were good enough to tell me this evening. To become ever more one of the new Italians whom you are hammering into shape—that is the aim of my life, my faith and my soul, which have been yours for twenty-five years, my Duce.

I have thought over the question of the dual function and I have also consulted several authoritative experts on constitutional law, who are on the legislative side. I think the difficulty may be surmountable even from the strictly formal point of view and within the ambit of our constitutional law itself.

I enclose a short minute.

At your orders, Duce,
GRANDI.

II. LETTERS FROM BADOGLIO TO MUSSOLINI

1 *Senator of the Realm, Rome.*
May 1st, 1925.

Excellency,

During the discussion with Marshal Diaz on the choice of a Deputy Chief, the best solution was found to be that of choosing an Army Corps Commander. But having studied the various names, the following conclusions were reached:

1. *Grazioli.* Extremely intelligent—but not made for constant and heavy work—extremely ambitious—character slippery and not straightforward.

   I don't know whether Your Excellency knows the contents of the two letters written to Balbo and Farinacci on the Blackshirt Militia. Clerici knows about them.

   A man therefore in whom one can have little confidence.
2. *Vaccari.* Not in the picture.
3. *Ferrari.* A good man—but too much under the thumb of the Minister Di Giorgio—no longer enjoys any prestige.

Among the Divisional Generals the choice is easier. There is Scipioni, who isn't much to look at, as he looks like an apothecary, but he has the qualities of a worker and organiser, and more intelligence than any of the other officers. He would be a real comfort to me ; in the sense, that is, that I could absent myself from manœuvres and inspections, sure that my orders from the centre would be carried out, and carried out well. It would however be necessary to give the future Air Force Chief the rank of Divisional General only, like that of the Navy, and equivalent to the rank of Deputy-Chief of General Staff.

I have said the above because it is exactly what I think. But I shall do the same with any Deputy-Chief, and Your Excellency will get the Army you want. I therefore resign myself completely to Your Excellency's decisions.

Your most devoted

BADOGLIO.

2

Chief of General Staff, Rome.

December 24th, 1926.

Excellency,

The Army Staff sends Your Excellency the warmest and most heartfelt compliments of the season, expressing the hope that, under Your Excellency's energetic direction, the army may attain to the maximum efficiency. I assure Your Excellency that in this grandiose task we shall be your most loyal and tireless collaborators.

Marshal of Italy,

PIETRO BADOGLIO.

3

Chief of General Staff, Rome.

June 26th, 1936—XIV.

Excellency,

I have received a letter from H. E. Fedele, His Majesty's Commissioner at the College of Heralds, in which he informs me that the title of Duke of Addis Ababa is transmissible, minus the style of Addis Ababa, to all my children. I take the liberty of drawing Your Exc.'s attention to the fact that H.E. Marshal Diaz was granted the title of Duca della Vittoria, transmissible with its relative style, to his children.

I have the honour, therefore, to ask Your Excellency to accord me the same treatment as that which, in 1921, was accorded H.E. Diaz. Having two sons, the elder would inherit the title of Duke of Addis Ababa, the second that of Marquis of Sabotino.

Your Excellency has already granted me that treatment with

regard to the title of Marquis of Sabotino, which is inheritable, together with the style chosen, by both my sons.

I take this opportunity of pointing out to Your Excellency that, by the special law of 1920, Their Excellencies Diaz and Thaon di Revel were granted the special remuneration which they had received in time of war.

I would ask Your Excellency to accord me parallel treatment.

Your always devoted

BADOGLIO.

4

Marshal of Italy, Pietro Badoglio del Sabotino,
Duke of Addis Ababa.

San Marzanotto d'Asti.

September 21st, 1938—XVI.

Excellency,

The Federal Secretary of Asti informs me that on October 21st you will remain for 4 hours in Asti—from 3 p.m. to 7 p.m. to be exact.

Your Excellency's visit to Alessandria has been announced for the 22nd. I take the liberty of suggesting to Your Excellency that you should spend the night of the 21st–22nd at the villa presented me by the Province of Asti, a villa which is three miles out of the town.

If Your Excellency cannot stay the night, I would ask Your Excellency to give me the pleasure of coming to tea at the villa, after 7 p.m. In this case, the time needed would be one hour.

It would be a very great honour to me and a great satisfaction to the whole Province.

Your most devoted

BADOGLIO.

To H.E. Cavaliere Benito Mussolini,
Prime Minister and Head of the Government,
Rome.

EYE WITNESSES

DOCUMENTS

RELATING TO

MUSSOLINI'S LAST YEAR

I

WHAT MUSSOLINI TOLD ME

by Admiral Franco Maugeri

FOREWORD BY THE EDITOR

The following account appeared in 1944, in the August-September and October numbers of the Rome periodical *Politica Estera.* It was subsequently issued as a pamphlet,[1] with the addition of notes and a separate chapter[2] written up by the editors of the periodical from information supplied by Vero Roberti, special correspondent of the Bologna paper, *Resto del Carlino.*

The contrast between the two sections is obvious. The editors, and their journalist source, seem now and then to have been guided by the thought that

> "Small sands the mountains, moments make a year,
> And trifles life."

However, as the detailed attention they accorded to their subject has preserved the local colour as well as some characteristic anecdotes, their few pages have been left unabridged.

Admiral Maugeri, on the other hand, has a clear eye for the significant. His narrative combines a sailor's terseness with the discriminating judgment of a man accustomed to sifting and weighing evidence.

Born in Gela, Sicily, in 1898, Franco Maugeri went through the Royal Naval Academy at Leghorn, and had a distinguished record in the First World War. His later career included service

[1] In the series *Quaderni di "Politica Estera,"* Rome, 1944. As a sub-title was added "Mussolini's Confession during his Internment at Ponza and La Maddalena."

[2] Chapter II, "In the Ras's House." (See below, pp. 225-230.)

as head of a section in Naval Intelligence, as member of Marshal Badoglio's staff, and as instructor in the Naval War College. At the beginning of the Second World War, as may be gathered from his account, he commanded the *Giovanni dalle Bande Nere*, a light cruiser, in which he took part in the action north of Crete. known as the battle of Cape Spada (July 19th, 1940). In command of the heavy cruiser *Bolzano*, he fought at Cape Teulada (November, 1940), and witnessed the defeat of Cape Matapan (March 27th, 29th, 1941). From May, 1941, till September, 1943, he was head of the *Servizio Informazione Segreto* ("Secret Information Service"), that is, Chief of Naval Intelligence, holding the rank of Rear-Admiral from 1942.

During the German occupation of Rome, in the months between the Armistice and the liberation of the city, he took a leading part in the underground Resistance Movement, doing outstanding work in the fight against Germans and neo-Fascists. In May, 1945, he was put in charge of La Spezia, Italy's principal base on the Tyrrhenian Sea, his coastal command extending from the French border to the South of Tuscany. By his tact, skill and energy, he achieved remarkable success in difficult salvage operations.

In December, 1946, Admiral Maugeri was promoted to the highest post in the Italian Navy, that of Chief of the Naval Staff.[1]

[1] He has since written an account of the war in the Mediterranean, the Armistice and subsequent events, under the title *From the Ashes of Disgrace* (ed. by V. Rosen; Reynal and Hitchcock, New York, 1948). Both as an historical and as a human document it ranks far above the numerous other narratives which have been published about this period.

Raymond Klibansky

1. FROM GAETA TO PONZA

IT FELL TO MY lot to accompany Mussolini, who, after July 25th, 1943, was no longer Head of the Government, to Ponza, the first place chosen for his captivity, and later to La Maddalena, the second. We talked together during his two transfers by sea. The following pages were written immediately after my return to Rome from these two missions, from notes taken on the spot, and they record our conversations with almost stenographic fidelity. I have also added a few of the immediate impressions I received in my dealings with him.

On the second mission, especially, I often found myself instinctively sitting in judgment on his actions and ideas ; I was an Italian who had lived through the whole epoch of the Régime, and it seemed to me that I was representative of all the Italians who rightly held, and still hold, him responsible for our country's ruin.

*

At about 5 p.m. on July 27th, 1943, Aliprandi, the Chef de Cabinet of the Ministry for the Navy, rang me up to warn me that I should probably have to go on a short mission outside Rome—"a little escort duty," and that I should be back by noon next morning. By the time I went to see him, half an hour later, I had made a pretty good guess as to what it might be about. Aliprandi confirmed this, and told me that they were awaiting the decision of the Cabinet, which was in session at that very moment.

At seven o'clock I went home and got into my uniform ; the mission had been decided on, and was to be carried out by the corvette *Persephone*, starting from Gaeta. I went to General

Cerica, Commander-in-Chief of the Carabinieri, who told me that Mussolini, accompanied by Chief Inspector Politi[1], by a senior officer of the Carabinieri and by an armed escort, would leave Rome by car for Gaeta about ten p.m. Cerica was responsible for the journey by land, and I was to take him to Ventotene. The General's chief worry was that some of those on board might get "cold feet" as he expressed it, force my and the Captain's hands, and compel us to alter course. I reassured him decisively on that point, and I was quite sure in my own mind that somehow or other I should keep the situation in hand and carry out my task.

I returned to the Ministry, where the Minister, de Courten, wanted to give me his oral instructions. Together we looked at a map of Ventotene, to see what difficulties might be expected in landing, because of the sirocco ; and we both agreed on the fitness of Captain Tazzari, Commander of the corvette *Persephone*, to fulfil such a delicate mission. By 8.45 p.m. I was already on my way to Gaeta by car, where Commander Marino Salvatori, of the Ministry, had preceded me, to assist me. Naval Headquarters in Gaeta had been given orders to hold the corvette in readiness for midnight ; I had suggested to the General that the cortège of cars should not arrive before midnight but, preferably, half an hour after, so that there should not be the slightest delay between Mussolini's arrival and our departure.

We drove swiftly along the Appian Way, although we were very often stopped by extremely strict control-posts. By 11.15 I had arrived at Gaeta Naval Headquarters. I sent for Commander De Martino, Captain Tazzari, the commander of the *Persephone*, and Commander Salvatori. I told them we were to go to Ventotene, carrying important personages implicated in a serious case of espionage. They told me afterwards that if they had not actually seen him on board, they could never have imagined that it was a question of Mussolini, and of him alone ! One of them (the good Commander Fecia di Cossato, who was at Gaeta with a corvette, and whom I was later to see on board the *Persephone* before we left) thought I might be having a meeting at sea with enemy envoys, in order to start peace preliminaries.

I ordered the tug *Tino* to put to sea, and proceed to Ventotene, in order to be of possible assistance during the mission.

We went aboard the *Persephone*. I gave Tazzari strict orders

[1] The name of this high Police official should read Pòlito.

that only he and his second-in-command were to be on the quarter-deck to receive the people we were expecting ; all the crew were to remain forward. Once we had embarked, the crew were to go to action stations.

I drank a cup of coffee. In my haste I had not had dinner. Now it was too late. Quarter-past twelve, half-past twelve, one o'clock. It was stiflingly hot in the little ward-room. With all the control-posts, the cortège would certainly be late. We went on to the quay, we continued to talk as we walked up and down, then we got into my car. Endless cigarettes, war reminiscences from each of us, our hopes and difficulties.

A few minutes after two. On the road from Formia two, four, six car headlights came rapidly into view. I sent my car away, and despatched Salvatori to make sure they halted the column at the right place and directed it to the Costanzo Ciano Wharf, where we were.

*

The foremost car draws up in front of me, a few yards from the gangway leading on board. Lt.-Colonel Pelaghi of the Carabinieri, an old acquaintance, approaches. Chief Inspector Politi and Mussolini emerge from the following car. I salute, I meet his enormous eyes as they come nearer to me, shining in the surrounding darkness.

"This way, Excellency, please. I shall go first."

I lead the way and take him as far as the threshold of Tazzari's quarters, followed by Politi, Pelaghi, and another police officer. Mussolini pauses to look at the barograph, while I go on deck. Here, the lieutenant of the corvette is seeing to the escort—six Carabinieri armed with machine-guns. There is also a man-servant ; not Mussolini's, but Politi's.

We weigh anchor and leave Gaeta astern. There is some trouble with the starboard engine ; then it starts up, throwing out a cloud of smoke which lasts the whole journey, together with a rain of sparks. I notice that Tazzari is active and on the alert. Slight sirocco, low cloud, damp heat, visibility poor. I am very happy at being on board again. I reflect that if there is an attack by aerial torpedoes, or by bombers or submarines, it won't be such fun.

We reduce speed before Ventotene and reverse our course, to wait for daybreak. At quarter-past five we drop anchor a few hundred yards from the shore.

Colonel Pelaghi and Chief Inspector Politi go ashore, to

see about suitable accommodation. I remain on deck a little to see where the motor-launch will land, in view of the surf I can see breaking on the shore. I make out a small, red buoy marking the channel to a minute inlet where it certainly is calmer. I reflect that in an hour's time my mission will be over, when I have accompanied Mussolini ashore. Then I go below to make sure that everything is going on all right. I am also impelled by a feeling of curiosity. I enter the cabin.

Mussolini raises his great eyes to mine, as I say : "Excellency" (what else could one call him ?) "do you want anything—a hot drink or a cup of coffee ?"

"No, thank you, I don't want anything. Only a piece of information. How large is this island ? "

I give him the data which I know from memory, then I send for the chartbook.

"Ah, a small island," he said, smiling ; his thoughts—and mine—turn to another small island[1].

I stand in front of him, while the little police official sits and dozes. Mussolini looks like a corpse ; he is emaciated.

"This is a corvette, isn't it ?" And the talk turns on corvettes and the present programme of construction.

"I know," observes Mussolini, "that Admiral de Courten has been made Minister. I think highly of him, partly because he knows German and the Germans well, which is very important just now. I, too, had thought of making changes in the composition of the Government ; but I wanted to carry them out when a better moment came along, when things were going well."

Conversation flows easily along ; the theme is the war at sea, the trials we have undergone, the battles in which I have

[1] Note 1 in Original : *Mussolini was obsessed by Napoleonic delusions. He himself was to tell the sergeant-major of the Ponza Carabinieri : "In the car which took me from Rome to Gaeta I was told by the General accompanying me that I was to be taken to one of the islands in the Pontine archipelago. 'You must be joking,' I replied to the General, 'I'm not Napoleon, am I ?' "*

He adopted another typical Napoleonic attitude towards General Ferone, who visited him the day after his arrest.

"General," said Mussolini, "we have met once before, have we not ?" As a matter of fact, it was in reality the first time the General had ever spoken to him. He had been presented to him in Albania where Ferone commanded the 'Bari' division, but the encounter had been very fleeting and Mussolini, surrounded by an enormous following, had not paid the slightest attention to the General. However, the latter replied that he had met him in Albania, and at once Mussolini, opening his eyes wide, said : "Quite right, General. Don't forget that I always appreciated you !"

taken part. We acknowledge technical superiority of the English Navy, particularly in night fighting—with the help of radio-location—and in their Fleet Air Arm. I spend some time explaining the advantages of being able to open range at night from such a distance that the target is still invisible.

He recalls the destruction of Brivonesi's convoy. "Yes, I read Brivonesi's report, and I am convinced that he could not have done more."[1]

I say to him: "In reality, Excellency, the main reason for the superiority of the English Navy lies in the fact that they are at sea for two hundred and sixty-five days out of three hundred and sixty-five. That is the whole secret. All problems of manning, administration, modernisation, and training are automatically settled by that formula." He agrees.

On my deploring the fact that we had always lacked aerial reconnaissance and air support during a battle, he says to me: "You are right, Admiral. The English, whether on land or sea, have succeeded in obtaining perfect co-ordination with the Air Force. I remember Cavagnari saying to me: 'I cannot understand why naval officers, who are charged with the most various tasks, cannot take observations at sea.' And the Air Ministry replied: 'Send them to us; we will teach them, and they will then be perfectly competent.' But obviously the solution was faulty, and the consequences have been grave."

I relate my battle in the *Bande Nere*[2] in detail. Then that of Cape Teulada.

"It was a brilliant engagement on the whole, wasn't it?" says Mussolini.

The fluctuation of tactical situations at sea; the battle of Jutland.

"I read a French book of some two hundred pages, which at last gave me a clear idea of how it all happened. The English admiral ought decidedly to have taken more of a chance."

I say: "It was Admiral Beatty, who commanded the vanguard, who should have kept him better informed."

My part in the last war as an airman. "My pilot's licence—an international one—bears the number 72."

[1]But see above, p. 91, and below, p. 247.

[2]Short for *Giovanni dalle Bande Nere*, a 6-inch gun light cruiser of 6,000 tons. Named after the Florentine *Condottiere* famed for his exploits against the Imperial armies in the early sixteenth century.

"Ah, you are a pioneer. Did you see the battle in the Adriatic on May 15th, 1917, from the air ? "

"No, Excellency, on that occasion I was carrying out an anti-submarine reconnaissance patrol."

He asks for details of the battle, about how Admiral Horthy exercised his command, and about Admiral Acton, who was in command on the Italian side.

"Is the battleship *Roma* ready ?" asks Mussolini. "What magnificent floating fortresses those ships have shown themselves ! And Admiral Bergamini ? He is a sound man, and if he is called upon to act he will certainly lead his squadron well[1]. I know he was displeased at the Fleet's inactivity during the landing on Sicily and at the remarks the enemy made about it, but we went into the matter thoroughly and decided that the risk was too great without air protection, especially in the Straits of Messina, where you need what the English call an 'umbrella.' "

Then Mussolini asks me my opinion of the American Navy, then of the French, then of the Japanese. He speaks of the way of life in the United States and in Japan.

"They recently showed me a film of a Japanese School of Naval Aviation, and I noticed that the Japanese were much taller than is generally believed. Why is that ?"

"A lot of sport, and also, in the last few years, a number of intermarriages with Russians and Koreans."

"The children are very pretty. So my daughter, who has been there, told me. I saw the Japanese Ambassador last

[1] Note 2 in Original: *As is well known, Admiral Bergamini, Commander-in-Chief of the Fleet in War, died when the battleship* Roma *was sunk by German air bombardment on September 9th,* 1943, *in the waters of the Straits of Bonifacio. The squadron was proceeding to a base in Allied hands, in accordance with the Armistice terms, but it is not devoid of interest to observe that Mussolini, not wishing to retract his opinion of Admiral Bergamini, whom he considered one of his supporters, later wrote an article about him in his* "Corrispondenza Repubblicana,"* *in which he upheld the singular thesis that if Bergamini had not been killed—by German bombs, be it noted—he would certainly have ended by ordering his squadron to proceed to a German-controlled port. . . . The commentary was entitled "The Bergamini Case," and if one can speak of a 'case' with regard to that valiant admiral, one must admit that he was the only man who, at the very moment that the Badoglio Government was asking the King to bestow a very high military decoration posthumously on him, was also claimed by the Nazi-Fascists, who promoted him 'in the field' for war service, with a malice aforethought which is really too absurd even to be deemed an insult to his noble name.*

*The official news-sheet of the Fascist 'Social Republic.'

Saturday, the 24th, when he brought me a message from the Prime Minister Tojo. I have the impression that the Japanese are finding enormous difficulty in digesting and exploiting the immense resources they have conquered. The chief reason is lack of transport. Only imagine that at this moment, when they are in possession of the richest part of the globe, they have had to cut the ration in the mother country. I know they are building large craft of toughened rubber, which are used for a few voyages and then destroyed, the rubber being re-used." Then he asks me: "How important have the last naval engagements been? I think it will be very difficult to defeat Japan."

Little by little, as our talk goes on, his voice strengthens, he loses his ashen colour, and his eyes no longer have the fixed stare I had noticed at first, they are almost sparkling now. We speak of America again, of her capacity for absorbing the various races, and of the great progress achieved in the field of technical and scientific research.

Tazzari comes into the cabin and announces that there is no sign of the motor-launch, and the sirocco is rising. I go on deck to see. It will still be possible to make communication with the shore in spite of the swell. I go below again. Mussolini says to me: "I beg your pardon, Admiral, if I have unintentionally done you an injustice. I understood your name was Malgeri, the former editor of the *Messaggero*, a man I do not care for."

I reply: "He is a friend of mine.[1]"

He asks Tazzari his name, and Tazzari, in replying, adds: "I am a son-in-law of Professor Frugoni."

Mussolini's face lights up: "Ah, dear old Frugoni! I think so very highly of him. Give him my regards and tell him how very highly I think of him."

The attendant brings coffee and milk, Mussolini pours himself out a cup and asks me to do the same, but I refuse.

The motor-launch returns from the shore. Pelaghi informs me that there is not the slightest possibility of any accom-

[1] Note 3 in Original: *Captain Tazzari reported that during Maugeri's short absence, Mussolini had asked him: "Who is that admiral?" "Admiral Maugeri."*

"Maugeri, Maugeri . . ." repeated Mussolini. "I remember his reports. Maugeri, not Malgeri. The latter is a worthless fellow; he is a journalist."

modation at Ventotene and that we must go to Ponza.[1] Without more ado, Tazzari and I go on the bridge. It is 8.15 a.m. when we start. The sirocco is dropping, and the sky, too, is clearing little by little. It is very hot. Now I give my attention to navigation, in view of the danger of a possible submarine attack. I notice that the corvette, though outwardly in bad order, is well organized for action ; watches set and guns ready. On the centre platform of the pom-poms I notice a sailor who gives me a broad grin. He was with me in some ship or other. I call him. He was with me in the *Bande Nere*, he fought with me at Crete. He was also on board when my dear *Giovannino*[2] was torpedoed and sunk.

I reflect that this is my first job at sea as an admiral. I could never have imagined that it would be what it is. What was the name of the English admiral who took Napoleon to St. Helena in the *Bellerophon* ? Is the comparison disproportionate ? For a moment I have qualms lest, in my conversation of just now, I should have gone beyond the limits of my task. But I only have qualms for a moment, they are wiped out at once by the clear conviction that humanity and chivalry are the tradition of us sailors. Above all, to the loser ; and Mussolini is now definitely a loser.

Ponza comes clearly into view. We drop anchor a few hundred yards from the shore and the small mole. It is greener than Ventotene, and larger.

Once more, Politi and Pelaghi go ashore.[3] I remain on deck, to smoke. I do not feel tired. After a few minutes Tazzari comes up and says Mussolini wishes to speak to me.

[1] Note 4 in Original: *According to Roberti's account, Chief Inspector Politi had barely landed before asking the Police Commissioner of Ventotene whether it would be possible to house Mussolini in a fisherman's cottage some way out of the town. The Commissioner, after a moment's reflection, replied, stammering, that the island was too small, that the presence of political exiles there might give rise to serious complications for which he could not accept responsibility, and that the houses on the island were not fit to receive a guest of such importance. Chief Inspector Politi agreed as to the precarious conditions of security on Ventotene and therefore suggested proceeding to Ponza.*

[2] Nickname for the *Giovanni delle Bande Nere* (see above, p. 213, n. 2.) After the battle of Cape Matapan, March 28th, 1941, the British Admiralty, March 31st, mentioned this ship as "possibly sunk."

[3] Note 5 in Original: *At Ponza the Ventotene scene was repeated. While the inspector and the Carabinieri colonel made for the shore in the motor-launch, a launch set out from the mole in Ponza harbour, with the Police Commissioner Vassallo, the Commander of the Base and the Garrison Commander on board. The two boatloads met, and the Ponza authorities transferred*

I find him agitated, although he is making a visible effort not to be or to appear so. He rises to his feet and then says to me: "Admiral, why all these pointless annoyances? Since last Sunday I have been cut off completely, I have had no news of my family, I haven't a penny, I've only got the clothes I stand up in. I have got a letter from Badoglio here in which he speaks of a serious plot against me." He reads Badoglio's letter to me, which is written in the third person: "The Head of the Government informs you, etc., etc."

Mussolini has doubts about the plot. "I had a guarantee from someone in a position to give it me. They asked me where I wanted to go, they promised me I should be able to go to Rocca delle Caminate. Yesterday the colonel commanding the Carabinieri legion, an extremely nice fellow, told me that all preparations had been made in this respect. I asked if I might go by air so as not to be seen; they replied, no. When I got into the car yesterday I was certain that we were leaving for Rocca delle Caminate.[1] Although the blinds were drawn I saw

to the motor-launch of the Persephone. *The discussion on the problem of receiving Mussolini was continued at the end of the mole, near the lighthouse, the islanders meanwhile gazing out of every window of every house in Ponza, agog with curiosity. Then the Commissioner sent for the sergeant-major of the Carabinieri and ordered him to take five men to Santa Maria, a village in Ponza, in a bend of the coast, and to see to it that within half an hour the so-called "Ras's House," that is, the house where Ras Imeru used to live, was ready to receive an exalted personage. At nine o'clock the sergeant returned to the end of the mole. The order had been carried out. In the meantime the Commissioner had prepared a tasty meal of lobster and rock salmon in honour not of Mussolini but of his own superior, Chief Inspector Politi.*

[1] Note 6 in Original: *In the Carabinieri barracks, the day after his arrest, Mussolini had received a visit from Divisional General Ernesto Ferone, who was attached to the War Office for special duties. The General handed him Badoglio's missive concerning the plot, used as justification for the measures taken, and asked him where he would prefer to go. Mussolini replied somewhat contemptuously that he could not give the slightest indication since he had no property, either houses or villas, and would therefore be a guest wherever he went, which might cause annoyance. The General then mentioned Rocca delle Caminate, and Mussolini agreed at once, with satisfaction, saying that he had not suggested it himself simply because he did not consider it as his own but as belonging to the office he had filled. At Mussolini's dictation the General then wrote down a declaration containing four points:* (1) *Thanks to Marshal Badoglio for having thought of his personal safety;* (2) *Full agreement with the choice of Rocca delle Caminate as a place of banishment;* (3) *A solemn promise to abstain from any political activity directed against Marshal Badoglio's government;* (4) *An offer to collaborate with the Marshal's government, to which he wished every success. General Ferone asked Mussolini if he did not wish to add a word for the King. Nodding, Mussolini wrote a few words of homage to the Sovereign in his own hand and after signing the document, wrote underneath: "Long live Italy!" General Ferone*

we were going past the Santo Spirito, along the Appian Way instead of the Salarian. I asked where we were going but they were not allowed to tell me. I thought it was to the fortress of Gaeta ; you know, Fieramosca[1] and Mazzini[2] came to my mind, although I am not nearly as great as they. Now you are taking me all round the islands, you are taking me to Ponza where Zaniboni is, who made an attempt on my life, and whom I pardoned. Why are you doing all this to me ? I did not behave like this in '22. I left Facta at liberty and actually made him a Senator. I left Bonomi at liberty ; I remained friends with Orlando, whom I respect and admire.[3] This is not chivalrous, it is not generous, it is not the thing, it is pointless. After all, I have worked twenty-one years for Italy, twenty-one years. I too have a family, I have given a son to the motherland. And besides, Badoglio has worked with me for seventeen years."

His voice grows calmer. He sits down. I sit down too. I say to him : "Excellency, I was ordered on this mission because the Navy thought it right that an officer of high rank should accompany you on your journey by sea. I have no sort of authority or right to answer you."

"Yes, I quite understand ; but you know what I have done for the Navy in twenty-one years. It was I who made the Navy. It is ungenerous to treat me like this, it is not a good thing, it will greatly displease Hitler, who has a very strong sense of friendship. This may do a lot of harm. What are they afraid of ? I am

took the document to Badoglio ; and the Prefect of Forli, the Squadrista *Marcello Bofondi, was warned by telephone that Mussolini would be brought to Rocca delle Caminate. Bofondi, however, very strongly advised against this ; he said that the people of Romagna had broken loose since the fall of the Régime, and that not even a powerful array of forces would be able to guarantee that Mussolini's fellow-countrymen would not succeed in invading Rocca to lynch the prisoner. A decision was therefore taken to send Mussolini out to the Archipelago of Ponza.*

[1] Popular hero, leader of the thirteen Italian knights who, in 1503, defeated the thirteen French knights of Bayard's army in the famous *Disfida di Barletta.* Imprisoned for a short time, in 1505, by the King of Naples at Gaeta.

[2] For Mazzini at Gaeta see above, page 87.

[3] Note 7 in Original : *According to Tazzari's account, Mussolini also said disconsolately : "Today, at nearly sixty years of age, I realise that I am still as guileless as a child." The "nearly" was, in fact, superfluous because the very next day, July 29th, was Mussolini's sixtieth birthday.*

politically defunct.[1] I don't want to land by daylight. I don't want people to see me."

I try and think of some device. I tell him that everything will be done to ensure that the landing takes place unobserved. I ask him where his family is.

"My wife and one son are in Rome. My son is transferring from bombers to fighters. The two children—they're not children any longer, one is sixteen and the other fourteen—are at Rocca. And goodness only knows what they are going through now."

I say a word or two of sympathy for his sorrow as a father. Then the conversation gradually turns on the course of the war, on the mistakes, both political and strategic, which we, and still more, the Germans, have made.

"The wheel of fortune," he says, "turned on June 28th, 1942, when we halted before El Alamein. We ought not to have advanced so far without the certainty of reaching Alexandria. But Rommel was pig-headed. While I was in Libya he told Bastico that he was going ahead, and so much the worse for the Italians if they didn't want to come too. His great virtue was remaining in the midst of his troops, in an armoured car. A good battalion commander, excellent in the tactical sphere, but without any breadth of vision. And again, when he had twice attacked unsuccessfully, before Montgomery's offensive, he should have withdrawn at once—the attack having failed—to Mersa Matruh. We should still have had a month's time to strengthen the defences. When I left Libya, I gave orders to strengthen the Halfaya-Sollum line as much as possible; its configuration and height lend themselves well to defence, far better than those twenty or twenty-five yard trenches round which so much blood has been shed."

I observe that even if the whole of Egypt had been occupied it would not have solved the problem of sea-borne supplies for our expeditionary force; that it would rather have aggravated it, by adding to the length of our supply lines; I explain that the only way of solving it would have been to occupy Malta, not too difficult an operation after the tremendous softening up it had had through the ceaseless air offensive. Mussolini agrees, and says forcibly: "The Germans have never grasped the importance of the Mediterranean, never. I told them we ought to

[1] Note 8 in Original: *At Ponza, too, Mussolini repeated to the Carabinieri sergeant-major who was in charge of him: "I have been betrayed .... Now I realise that my political career is over."*

occupy Egypt; we should then have linked up the Middle East with the East. By the grace of God, and completely unexpectedly, they were able to rout the French army in a very short time and in a spectacular manner, that army which Churchill had inspected a few months earlier and adjudged the best in Europe—and then they went and started a Russian front! And that, after they had won the great political battle of the alliance with Russia, snatched from under the noses of the English who had been there for more than five months. I told them to create an independent Poland; but they maintained and still maintain that Russia is a deadly peril to Western and European civilisation. I tried in vain to convince Hitler that that was a meaningless phrase, *sinnlos*, like that of the New Order. Stalin has killed Bolshevism, by putting to death men of the first water, real 'big guns' like Kamenev. In contrast to Trotsky, he has completely renounced world revolution. To this day Hitler is anchored to his convictions. I was the first to recognize the U.S.S.R., I asked Litvinov to Rome and we signed a pact of friendship."

Mussolini reflects a little and then continues: "The Germans thought they could liquidate Russia in a few months. They fell into a diabolic trap which I wouldn't have believed if I hadn't been told it by Hitler himself. The German Intelligence Service was offered the Russian mobilisation plan, a document complete down to the smallest details. The Germans thought it too thorough to be genuine, but they bought it just the same. The Russians arrested the agents, whom they themselves had sent, and put them to death. When that was learned in Germany, the Germans were sure that the plan was genuine. The whole thing was a fake; where they had written '50 cavalry brigades,' there were really 50 armoured brigades, and so on.

"I advised Hitler to come to an agreement with Russia and, latterly, to do so at any price, giving up everything he had conquered, the Ukraine included. I tried to turn his mania to good account; to play upon his superstition; the first campaign did not succeed, then they had that terrible winter, then the Stalingrad disaster. It was no good. I told him we had lost the initiative from June 1942 onwards, and that a nation which had lost the initiative had lost the war. In Salzburg[1] I told him: 'We can't get back into Africa again,

[1] April 7th-10th, 1943. The object of the meeting was the "total mobilisation of Europe."

the Italian islands will be invaded ; there is only one last hope, and that is to make peace with Russia and switch your whole potential over to the Mediterranean. You can't help us, not because you don't want to, but because you cannot do so until you have made peace with Russia.' The talk at Feltre[1] did not go off well. It was supposed to last three days and it lasted three and a half hours. I was very vexed at not having been in Rome during the raid. As usual, none of the questions on the agenda were dealt with at all, but only quite different ones. I repeated my old theme ; peace with Russia. Impossibility of the Germans giving us any substantial aid."

"Don't you think, Excellency, that it would have been a good thing to have shared the mastery of the Mediterranean with the English on equal terms, after the conquest of Ethiopia, rather than have a war ? "

"I tried, as you know, but it didn't come off."

"Then wouldn't it have been a good thing to have waited a few more years ? "

"Certainly, and after the Pact of Steel[2] I tried to restrain Hitler. I wrote him at great length, telling him that we could not be ready earlier than 1942. I had to make full use of Ethiopia's resources, replace the artillery and armoured cars and complete the battleships. I wanted to solve the question of the Great Estates, which I would have reclaimed by building 15,000 or 20,000 houses. I wanted to get up the World Exhibition in 1942, partly to show the world our new Italy, partly to attract foreign currency. Finally, I said in my letter that the tender shoot of the Italo-German alliance was too young, and that time would be needed for the spiritual and sentimental revision of pre-existing relationships. When Hitler declared war I succeeded in gaining ten months by the formula of non-belligerency, which saved our alliance and left all possibilities open to us. Then I had to intervene, otherwise we should have had to renounce all hope of any claims against France, while I was certain that the Germans would invade England successfully, where all they had were two hundred brass carronades. The invasion might not have reduced the English to a surrender, because they would

[1] See above, p. 51.

[2] The ten years' military alliance between Germany and Italy, signed in Berlin, May 22nd, 1939.

have shifted the Government to Canada or Australia, but we should have been in an immensely strong position."

"And Gibraltar ?"

"I suggested that to Hitler, too. But he replied that he was not sure of Franco's attitude. We ought to have told Franco that we would go there with or without his permission. All we would have had to do was succeed in showing ourselves in La Linea and the English fleet would have abandoned the base."

"So many mistakes," I observe, "both strategic and political. And fancy not having occupied Tunisia !"

"In the presence of France the Germans feel like provincials in the presence of the aristocracy, and their vision becomes completely distorted."

Now the conversation turns on the repercussions which his fall has had in Germany and England. "Was Churchill very harsh about me ? There is a lot of feeling against me personally, in England."

I tell him of the colourless German comments and of the trend of English propaganda, which is telling us to drive out the Germans if we hope for an honourable capitulation.

And once more we revert to the subject of war and peace.

"We must throw off the German yoke," says Mussolini. "We have a right to tell them that we have been at war for three years and more, lost our mercantile marine and almost all our fleet, and had a large number of towns destroyed. They won't help us. There is nothing else to be done."[1]

"And the Hungarians and Roumanians will follow suit."

" The Hungarians can't go on any longer."

I ask him what he thinks of the internal situation in Germany.

"Not too good. Every day the German people are beginning to realise more and more that what happened in the last war is repeating itself ; great conquests of territory, advances of hundreds of miles, millions of tons of enemy shipping sunk, but no sign of victory. The people have the feeling that history will repeat itself—another Napoleonic campaign in Russia. The Japanese have been and are treading much more cautiously with Russia, and their Ambassador also confirmed this to me. I think it will be

[1] Note 9 in Original: *Two days earlier, however, Mussolini had said to General Ferone : "Don't forget to tell Marshal Badoglio that we must go on resisting ; a month, or six weeks at most, and victory will be ours !" Elsewhere, too, speaking to Maugeri, Mussolini changes his opinion again.*

extremely difficult to defeat Japan ; for that matter, the Americans already have an idea that the war will last till 1949.

"Germany is a steel cable, we are a hemp cable, more elastic, giving more under tension. A steel cable snaps all of a sudden. And then there is the dissension with the Vatican, religious internally, but having grave international repercussions. Marvellous, those bishops who spoke so courageously at Cologne."

"Perhaps, Excellency, we in Italy wanted to bite off more than we could chew. What I mean is, that you made the same mistake as Crispi,[1] who thought he could branch out overseas before he had a strong people behind him."

"Yes. As far as the Italians are concerned, it is a question of moral courage. They have every other virtue—endurance, sobriety, intelligence ; but moral courage, no. For that we need generations and generations, and terrible trials like these. The Sicilians stood up splendidly to the hammering they got, which caused havoc, and a shortage of food, water, relief work and schooling. The authorities disappeared ; the only one who stuck to his post was the Prefect of Catania.

"If the 'Goering' division had resisted more strongly the Americans would have been thrown back into the sea at Gela, and that might have changed a lot of things."

I say: "I come from Gela."

"Ah, I know it, I spent a delightful day there. We even danced, and I told the parish priest that our dances were innocent.

"I know that in some towns in the island the Sicilians would have nothing to do with the English. In Sicily, too, there was military unpreparedness and indecision in the Command. Imagine that I was only able to speak to Guzzoni once ! And then, the Commands are too far away from the troops and they lose touch. I decreed that army commands should not have their headquarters more than sixty miles behind the lines, so that a despatch rider could always maintain contact. For fifteen days we thought a battalion of the 'Napoli' division had been wiped out. Finally we discovered that it was still fighting, together with a German detachment. Unpreparedness everywhere."

"The Navy was prepared."

[1] Francesco Crispi, 1819-1901. His imperialist ambitions during his Premiership eventually led to the catastrophic defeat of the Italian Army by the Abyssinians at Adowa, May 1896.

"Yes, very much so, and Cavagnari did a splendid job, especially with regard to oil."

Mussolini once more speaks of the invasion of Sicily. "I had arranged to make a tour of the island. At first the Staff were against it, because they thought my presence would attract heavier air raids. Rubbish. Then two itineraries were prepared, one for a fortnight and one for about a month. Starting from Messina, I wanted to make a complete tour and inspect platoon by platoon, post by post. My health prevented my doing so. I had attacks of the most violent pain. I, of all people, who have a really exceptional resistance to pain, had once to have recourse to a numbing injection. I lost nearly four stone, and Frugoni warned me that if I had not stopped losing weight I should have wasted away. When the journey to Sicily had been arranged I had another attack. Pozzi, Frugoni's assistant, Milani, the radiologist, and Puccinelli, the surgeon, said that I needed at least three weeks' complete rest and then an operation. So I couldn't do anything more."

The talk turns on the campaign in Ethiopia. "We lost the Empire with 1,500 dead. Too few. There, too, poor generalship. They had magnificent reserves of food and fuel, I read the English report. Italian Somaliland was not defended at all. In Eritrea, on the contrary, the English themselves acknowledged that we fought extremely well."

He mentions the repatriation of Italians from the Empire; the endless accusations of one against another, of plunder and treachery. "I ended by authorising the third journey, the one going on now, because of the pressure of Coppola, the Academician, who had relatives out there."

It is now time to land. Mussolini goes on deck, and pauses a moment to look at the panorama of the island.[1] He says goodbye to me and repeats: "Please pass on what I have told you." He smiles sadly and salutes with outstretched arm. He takes his place in the landing craft with his escort. The motor-launch draws away from the ship. The sailors remain at their work or on watch; not a word, not a sign.

[1] Note 10 in Original: *According to Roberti, it was at this moment that Mussolini asked which was the house that was going to receive him. He was answered with a host of details which he brushed rapidly aside: "I understand," he said, "it is that little house above the sailing-boats, with the two green windows." The house—which Mussolini did not yet know had been Ras Imeru's—was of two storeys, isolated, light grey in colour, with two windows opening on to a narrow inlet between two high rocks. There, seven sailing-boats were laid up one beside the other.*

II. IN THE RAS'S HOUSE[1]

A FEW minutes before ten o'clock, Mussolini landed on the small beach of Santa Maria, in front of the Ras's House. Surrounded by his gaolers and escorts, he remained for a few moments looking across the sea to the horizon, towards the East, where there appeared the high mountains of Ischia and the cliffs of Santo Stefano and Ventotene. The *Persephone* was anchored in the roadstead near the ancient grottos of Pilate, where the Romans used to rear lampreys in order to extract oracles and prophecies from them.

Emerging from his melancholy contemplation, Mussolini said suddenly: "I am tired. I should like a bed to rest on."

They accompanied him to the door of the house and asked him to go up to his room, which was all freshly whitewashed. He looked about him and saw, in that clear, clean light, a wretched iron bedstead with only the bare slats, a chair with the stuffing out, and a table from a public-house, greasy and scored by knives. He clenched his fists with rage and said, turning towards the window: "I have had enough of this!" Then he took up the chair, carried it into the middle of the room, and sat down, saying: "And enough of this, too!" He bowed his head and covered his face with his hands.

When he came to himself, he saw the sergeant-major of the Carabinieri at the door. The sergeant entered, saluted him, and remained standing at attention. It was obvious that the sergeant was feeling the whole strangeness of the situation. He could not believe that the man who had been master of Italy for

[1] This chapter is not by Maugeri but compiled by the Editors of *Politica Estera*. (See above, p. 207.)

more than twenty years was now his prisoner. Mussolini rose and took him by the shoulders, saying: "Courage! I know what you are feeling . . . I need rest."

His voice was tired, and the sergeant, apologising, said that he would go at once and look for a mattress, some sheets and something to eat. "We didn't know you were coming to Ponza, Excellency. I was told barely half an hour ago." "Don't worry, sergeant," rejoined Mussolini.

The sergeant left the room to go to the nearest house, where one of his men lived, to collect the things he had promised Mussolini, and in an hour he was able to return with a mattress, sheets and a pillow. The wife of a Carabiniere brought a cup of broth, an egg and two pears.

The sergeant knocked at the door. Mussolini, who had been stretched out on the slats of the bed, with his head resting on his rolled-up jacket, got up. "I have brought a few things," said the sergeant, and set about making the bed, while another Carabiniere put the food on the table.

On the following day, July 29th, Mussolini's birthday, the sergeant returned, to give him four peaches. Mussolini was sitting by the window. He turned and said: "Sergeant-major, you are too kind. I hope this doesn't mean that the population will go short of this fruit." "No, no," the sergeant assured him. "Good," rejoined Mussolini, "then I shall eat them between now and tomorrow. Thank you."

On the third day Mussolini did not speak to anyone, because a Lieutenant-Colonel of Carabinieri, who arrived unexpectedly from the mainland, gave extremely strict orders that no one was to speak to him. Mussolini was approached only by two Carabinieri who were detailed to tidy his room and prepare his food. On this subject the sergeant-major went to see Commendatore Vassallo, Police Commissioner of Ponza, to ask him for the necessary funds for the prisoner's keep, and to get himself refunded for the few *lire* he had spent. The Commissioner went off the deep end and threw the poor N.C.O. out, saying that if Mussolini "had any money" he could eat whatever he liked, but that he personally would not "fork out" a penny, because he had had no authorisation to do so.

*

Mussolini's life in Ponza was made up as follows: He rose at 7.30 in the morning and took a little milk and an egg. At noon he had lunch, consisting of tomato salad, an egg, a little bread and a little fruit. As soon as night fell he went to bed. In the ten days he spent in Ponza, the two Carabinieri never once lit the fire to make him anything hot to eat.

On the fourth day, the sergeant-major was able to see Mussolini again, having been officially detailed to watch his movements, and he exchanged a few words with him about the high Party officials of the former régime. The cause of the conversation was the water-tap over the wash-basin in the room. Mussolini demanded: "Tell me, sergeant-major, why is there never any water in this tap? I spent a pretty penny on getting the Ponza aqueduct built." "Excellency," replied the sergeant, "you spent a pretty penny all right, but the water from the spring still runs into the sea." "Are you speaking the truth, sergeant?" "Yes, Excellency." "Ah, these Prefects, these Prefects!" said Mussolini. "And these Federal Secretaries!" added the sergeant-major.[1]

"Why? Tell me, sergeant." The N.C.O., encouraged by Mussolini's curiosity, began to relate the main incidents in his life as a Carabiniere, and ended by saying that he was in Ponza as a punishment for having denounced the Federal Secretary of Littoria, who had been stealing grain from the State pools.

On the fifth day, August 1st, the motor-auxiliary *Maria Pace*, belonging to Totonno, the lobster catcher, came into the little harbour at Ponza (since Mussolini's arrival, civil communications between the island and the mainland had been suspended). Besides six cows destined to feed the islanders, and eight detectives, green with seasickness, Totonno's auxiliary carried two trunks, a small crate of fruit and a package for the prisoner. At last Mussolini was able to change—for he had worn the same clothes since the day of his arrest. He took immediate advantage of the outfit which had been sent him from home, and appeared at the window dressed in white. A few minutes later, however, he appeared stripped to the waist and wearing his characteristic yachting cap. Suddenly he vanished again, to reappear dressed once more in white; then he retired yet again, and reappeared in shirtsleeves.

When he opened the packet, the sergeant-major was standing beside him. There were three letters, one from his wife, one

[1] A Prefect, the Head of a Province, is a *State* official. Under the Fascist régime, a Federal Secretary was the Prefect's opposite number in the *Party* organisation.

from Edda and one with some money. Mussolini first of all read the one from his wife, who also sent him a photograph of their son Bruno. Then he opened the letter from his daughter, which also contained a photograph, this time of his granddaughter. He glanced rapidly through this letter and, with a gesture of disgust, threw it and the photograph under the bed.

On August 2nd he had an attack of his old complaint. It was a very serious bout, so much so, that they feared for his life. The Ponza doctor was immediately sent for, Doctor Silverio Martinelli, who said as soon as he reached the bedside: "Excellency, I know your complaint, I have brought you this draught. I believe it to be the only remedy to stop the pain. I can't do more than that, because you ought to be operated on." "Everyone in Italy knows my complaint," said Mussolini in an emphatic, scornful voice. "Give me the draught!" The doctor poured the whiteish liquid into a glass and handed it to Mussolini, who said: "Doctor, that is too little, please. Twice as much, twice as much! My body is already accustomed to this medicine." He drank it and then, after a few minutes' pause, related the case history of his illness to the doctor, concluding: "So you see, those are the Duce's physical sufferings!"

During the following days, as he recovered physically, he became more cheerful. He twice bathed on the beach at Frontone, going there by sea in Luigi Parisi's boat, accompanied by the Lieutenant-Colonel of Carabinieri and two lance-corporals. Later he also made a trip to the "Serpent's Grotto," halting to see the Roman remains—a small amphitheatre and a reservoir; but in order not to excite the islanders' curiosity and, above all, not to necessitate too large an escort of Carabinieri and detectives, he generally preferred to remain shut up in the Ras's House until the day of his departure for Maddalena Island. He read Father Ricciotti's *Life of Jesus Christ*,[1] and translated Carducci's poems into German. On August 4th, towards evening, he wrote a letter to the parish priest of Ponza. It said:—

Reverend Father,

Saturday 7th is the second anniversary of the death of

[1] First published in January, 1941 (Rizzoli, Milan and Rome), it achieved such success that by Easter 1943 it had gone into seven editions. Its fame attracted Fascist high-ups such as Federzoni, Bottai and Ciano, one of whom may have called Mussolini's attention to it. The author is now Professor of History of the Christian Orient at Rome University.

my son Bruno, killed in air combat over Pisa.

Will you please say a Mass for his soul? I enclose 1,000 *lire for you to dispose of as you think best.*

I should like to make you a present of Giuseppe Ricciotti's book, "The Life of Jesus Christ," which I have just finished reading these last few days. It is an uplifting book which one really has to read at a sitting.

It is a book in which science, history, religion and poetry are marvellously blended.

Through Ricciotti's work Italy may perhaps have achieved pre-eminence in yet another field.

With best wishes,

MUSSOLINI.

Ponza, August 5th, 1943.

Roberti[1] later succeeded in seeing Ricciotti's book in the nervous and trembling hands of the parish priest (who was deeply agitated because the news that Mussolini had written him a letter and given him a book had already spread to the mainland, whence he feared reprisals). Many passages in the book had been marked by the learned reader, and these marks show the two different states of mind in which Mussolini read that *Life of Christ*, besides showing an attempt to draw a monstrous parallel between himself and Our Saviour.

Mussolini began reading the volume while he was still Head of the Government. The parts that interested him most then were those respecting the customs and habits of the Jews in the time of Jesus. The lines and arrows, drawn in red pencil, are firm and almost violent, and it is not hard to see that they are inspired by anti-Semitic feelings and, in consequence, by racial policy.

The second part of the book, that is, the part read in Ponza, is easily recognisable. The underlining and the words in the margin of the page are fainter; they show a more agitated hand, and the passages marked no longer refer to the wicked deeds of the Jews, but mainly to the arrest of Jesus. In fact, when Mussolini finds it written that the Jewish elders, with the object of destroying Jesus, had described him as a common agitator, he notes in the margin: "Only too true," meaning that he had been preceded by another victim of calumny. Then there

[1] The journalist whose notes are the basis of this chapter. (See above, p. 207.)

is the scene of Our Saviour's arrest, followed by a sentence of Ricciotti: *The Master was led away like a common criminal,* and in the Mussolinian gloss an arrow points to the last word. Again: *Jesus left Gethsemane surrounded only by gaolers; not a single friend stood by him.* Here the words *gaolers* and *friend* are glossed by the single word: "Prefect." Mussolini had found an illustrious predecessor for the happenings of his own life.

III. FROM PONZA TO LA MADDALENA

At one p.m. on August 6th, just as I was shutting up my office, I was sent for by the Minister, De Courten, who ordered me to be ready to leave at five o'clock ; Mussolini to be transferred from Ponza to La Maddalena. They were waiting for a telegram of confirmation from Carabinieri Major Bonitatibus, who had left by air that morning to look for accommodation ; in any case, I was to go to Gaeta in the afternoon, where the destroyer F.R.22 was ordered to proceed at seven p.m.

I had had a presentiment the evening before, of what was going to happen, while I was on duty at Naval Headquarters. Two rather important naval actions were in progress, and the Chief and Deputy-Chief of Naval Staff, *i.e.*, De Courten and Sansonetti, had been in the War Room. Admiral De Courten had sent for maps of the Maddalena estuary and had asked the officers on duty if there was anyone really familiar with the island. Nobody was. The examination had to be limited to maps. At one point I said to him under my breath : "Excellency, shall I have to go on another voyage, by any chance ?" He replied by a smile.

And now, at 6.50 p.m., Major Bonitatibus's telegram of confirmation having arrived, I was once more *en route* by car for Gaeta, this time accompanied by a Carabinieri officer, Major Pontani. The Minister had given me instructions to tell Admiral Brivonesi, Naval Commander-in-Chief in Sardinia, that Mussolini's person was, indeed, entrusted to a military guard, but that he was to keep the strictest watch on all arrivals and departures in the estuary. In reality, the reason for Mussolini's transfer from Ponza to La Maddalena was to put him out of reach of a possible kidnapping by the Germans, to whom the fall of Mussolini and Fascism had been a great blow. The extremely delicate situation which had arisen, and the continual and growing influx of German land forces into Italy (designed without doubt to prevent us by force from making a separate peace) bore out such a supposition. It remained to be seen whether the place chosen were really the most suitable.

No incidents on the journey. Reflections about the mission to be carried out. Certainty in my own heart that this too would go off all right. By 9.20 p.m. I was in Gaeta, and immediately after visiting De Martino, Commander of the Naval Base, I went on board the F.R.22. Once again I had left without having dinner, but this time I was able to get a bite while the F.R.22 was putting to sea. Then on the bridge. Fine firework display round Naples because of air attack. At 11.30 we drop anchor in front of Ponza. I send an officer ashore to look for Colonel Meoli of the Royal Carabinieri, Military Commander in Ponza, who at once comes on board. We make our arrangements ; he is to go and fetch Mussolini and bring him aboard at once, while the embarkation of the escort (eighty Carabinieri and Metropolitan Police, plus their paraphernalia) is to be carried out simultaneously. The motor-launch takes Meoli ashore. A few minutes later a rowing-boat approaches which, I must say, manœuvres extremely badly in order to come alongside. "Who goes there ?" the look-out shouts repeatedly to the boatman.

"We are bringing somebody." It is Mussolini. He comes on deck. I salute him and give my name. "Ah, again !" I lead him below to the commander's messroom. He looks at me, smiling : "And where are we going, Maugeri ?"

"To Maddalena Island."

"More and more inaccessible !"

He reflects. Then he tells me to sit down. It is about one o'clock in the morning. We talk till quarter-past three, until all the escort are on board, and we can up anchor. He looks bolder, has more colour, less flaccid (they let him bathe in Ponza). Still the same suit, still the same hat, both blue. He is wondering what the reasons are for this new transfer, and asks me.

"Ponza," I say, "lends itself too easily to a *coup de main.*"

"True. I said to Meoli: 'If two English submarines arrive with a hundred Commandos, what will you do?[1]' "

I mention the fact that suspicion may also arise as to a German *coup de main*. He is up in arms. "That is the greatest humiliation that could possibly be inflicted on me. And do they really think I might go off to Germany and try to seize the reins again, with German aid? Ah no, I should think not!" His indignation seems sincere. I tell him that the Germans might also kidnap him against his will. He reluctantly admits this, but thinks it would be very difficult.

"Farinacci is in Germany, he succeeded in escaping, and he has apparently spoken on the Munich radio," I tell him.

This news greatly interests him, and he asks what the German *Stimmung* is like with regard to us. I mention the extreme delicacy of the situation, the natural mistrust of the Germans and the influx of their divisions, and the difficulty our Government finds in withstanding them and in continuing the war against the wishes of the nation.

"There is nothing else to be done except to continue the war," asserts Mussolini (he has changed his opinion from what he said during our first meeting—"we must throw off the German yoke.") "The English are making a great mistake in not offering us an acceptable peace."

I speak of the two tendencies which seem to run counter to one another in the field of British foreign policy; one fearing Russian expansion and the other proposing to rely on Russia both now and in the future. We speak of the English politicians.

"Eden told the Commons," I inform him, "that he was sorry to have to squash a journalistic sea-serpent, the one which had given such credence to the rumour that he had had a personal clash with you at the Palazzo Venezia."

"No clash at all," he replies. "We saw each other twice. I explained to him the absolute necessity of Italy's having some territory where she could find raw materials and labour. He replied that England was not against our expanding. The next

[1] Note 11 in Original: *Roberti's account shows that on August 3rd, when Mussolini received the Carabinieri sergeant-major in Ponza, he had expressed his alarm at the precarious state of security on the island, from the point of view of an English attack, which he thought probable. He learned then that Sicily was about to fall into Allied hands entirely and said, by way of comment: "One fine day the English will come to a halt, won't they?" "Let us hope so," replied the sergeant cautiously. And Mussolini added, to round off and, in a sense, to modify his remarks: "I am not afraid of England, or of America either!"*

day he came again and offered me the port of Zeila, in British Somaliland.[1] 'No,' I replied, 'I have had enough of receiving territorial presents from third Powers. And besides, Zeila doesn't get us anywhere.' 'Don't you think,' said Eden to me, 'that any undertaking of yours in Ethiopia might lead to serious clashes with England?' 'I quite understand,' I replied, 'but you, too, should think it over.' I accompanied him as far as the door and we parted perfectly calmly. Not a sharp word, far less a vulgar gesture, which I should never have dreamed of making." He continues: "They have dissolved the Fascist Party, haven't they?"

"Yes."

"And what have they done about the Fascist Federations?"[2]

[1] An obvious perversion of the facts. On July 1st, 1935, Mr. Eden, reporting to the House of Commons his conversations with Mussolini of June 24th and June 25th, 1935, stated: "I expressed to Signor Mussolini the grave concern of His Majesty's Government at the turn which events were taking between Italy and Abyssinia. Our motives were neither egoistic nor dictated by our interests in Africa, but by our membership of the League of Nations. I said that British foreign policy was founded upon the League. His Majesty's Government could not therefore remain indifferent to events which might profoundly affect the League's future. Upon this issue public opinion in this country felt very strongly. It was only through collective security that in our judgment peace could be preserved, and only through the League that Great Britain could play her full part in Europe. It was for this reason that His Majesty's Government had been anxiously studying whether there was any constructive contribution which they could make in order to promote a solution.

"I then described to Signor Mussolini the kind of contribution which His Majesty's Government had in mind and which I was authorised to make to him as a tentative suggestion. This suggestion was broadly speaking as follows:

"To obtain a final settlement of the dispute between Italy and Abyssinia, His Majesty's Government would be prepared to offer to *Abyssinia* a strip of territory in British Somaliland giving Abyssinia access to the sea. This proposal was intended to facilitate such territorial and economic concessions by Abyssinia to Italy as might have been involved in an agreed settlement. His Majesty's Government would ask for no concession in return for this arrangement save grazing rights for their tribes in such territory as might be ceded to Italy. This suggestion was not lightly made, and only the gravity of the situation could justify the cession of British territory without equivalent return.

"I much regret that this suggestion did not commend itself to Signor Mussolini, who was unable to accept it as the basis for a solution of the dispute."

On July 8th, 1935, the then Secretary of State for Foreign Affairs, Sir Samuel Hoare, made it clear that the territory which it had been tentatively proposed to cede to Abyssinia comprised the port of Zeila and a corridor through British Somaliland.

[2] The national unions of employers or workers, according to trade or profession, which formed the basis of the Fascist Corporative System, dissolved by decree of 4.8.43 (the Fascist Party having been dissolved on 28.7.43).

"Closed down. There is going to be an enquiry into the wealth acquired by the high Party officials."

"That is a good thing. And the Militia? I know it has been incorporated into the Army. For that matter, it already was, in fact, if not in name. Haven't they left it any distinctive badge?"

"None. In place of the Lictor's rods they have put Army stars."

"They might have left something; the fez, for instance."

And we now come to the thorny question of the fall of the Régime. I point out how surprising it was that everything should have collapsed in so few hours, without anyone—without even a single solitary soul—attempting to defend the Régime, without a single soul dying as he waved aloft the banner of the Régime and called on the name of Mussolini.[1]

He repeats what he had said to me in our first discussion: "It is the Italians' lack of moral courage. But Fascism has done some great things; many of these things can never be destroyed, much less denied. I am positive"—and his face takes on its well known expression of a Roman mask—"that there are more Fascists in Italy today than there were yesterday. Time will pass and the days of Fascism will be regretted.

"The session of the Grand Council took a far less stormy course than they said. Naturally, of all those present, extremely few realised the importance of the session. People like Cianetti, Rossoni and others really thought that it was a question of handing back the command of the Armed Forces to the King, who, for that matter, had never lost it. There was a lot of criticism over my assuming the command of the Armed Forces, but I asked Badoglio for his opinion, and I have a letter in which he agrees with me about its advisability, and says that the command assumed by the King in the last war was purely nominal. For that matter it is an entirely academic question;

[1] Note 12 in Original: *During his stay in Ponza, Mussolini had asked the Carabinieri sergeant-major who was his guard: "Tell me, Sergeant, didn't the* squadristi, *my followers of '21, do anything?" "No, Excellency," the sergeant had replied. Mussolini added: "I asked the Chief Inspector who accompanied me to Ponza, what the popular demonstrations had been like on the night of July 25th. He replied sarcastically—I remember it exactly—that there were no demonstrations like those in the Piazza Venezia, but a lot of small demonstrations in every quarter of every town in Italy; a lot of small demonstrations, but spontaneous . . . Sergeant, is all that true?" "Yes, Excellency." The exact words of the dialogue may not have been remembered by the witnesses, but we can well believe it to be true in essentials.*

in every country, democratic or Bolshevik, the direction of the war is necessarily in the hands of the Head of the Government. [1]

"Grandi's behaviour was diabolically astute. Naturally he thought that he himself would become Head of the Government and heaven knows what else besides. The very day before, he came and implored me not to convene the Grand Council ! I refused ; by then it was essential to make an end of such a critical situation. Scorza, too, played an ambiguous rôle from the first moment he took up his appointment."

"It was generally thought," said I, "that Scorza, in taking up position in his speech in the Adriano Theatre[2] against the many mistakes Fascism had made, was in agreement with you. An attempt at an internal clean-up by Fascism itself."

"No. The only really sane man in the Grand Council session was Federzoni.[3] He supported Grandi's motion, but he also pointed out the consequences that would have to be faced. The session was long—nearly ten hours—and animated, but there was no unsuitable language or quarrelling. What are all these gentry doing now ?"

"Nothing. They are disappointed that the formation of the Government is not as they had foreseen it."

"You might call it 'the Conspiracy of the Collars.'[4] And Count Ciano ?"

"He has been dismissed from his Ambassadorship."

"A truly wretched figure." Mussolini's voice is decided and scornful.

"But you kept him as Foreign Minister for seven years ! How could one help seeing how frivolous and superficial he was ? His private life, too, had so little to recommend it."

[1] Note 13 in Original : *At this point there begins Mussolini's indictment of the traitor Party chiefs* (*the extreme harshness of which may be seen exemplified in the speech of the Public Prosecutor in the Verona trials*). *For that matter, one day when the Carabinieri sergeant-major in Ponza had told him a few home truths, he had already said solemnly : "Sergeant, you have told me some important things. If only my collaborators had done as much ! Instead, I have been betrayed ! I did not know I had so many jackals round me ! Even the Grand Council betrayed me, even Count Ciano !"*

[2] Speech of May 5th, 1943.

[3] But condemned to death by Mussolini's Italian Social Republic. (See the Who's Who.)

[4] I.e., the holders of the Collar of the Most Holy Annunciation. (See above, p. 141, n. 3.) Of members of the Grand Council who voted against Mussolini, the following four held the Order : Grandi, Federzoni, Ciano, De Bono. (See also the King's reference to this fact, above, p. 81.)

"Yes, golf with his girl friends every day. At last I threw him out."

"Too late. I had an interview with him last December. I came out from it really demoralised, at the thought that our foreign policy was entrusted to such a man."

Every now and again, silence falls. Mussolini pursues his own thoughts, I wait quietly for him to continue his analysis of what has and had happened. More and more the disconcerting impression takes shape in my mind that he is looking at events as a historian does, that he is putting himself, as it were, years away from it all, that he is considering himself as a third person and not as the principal actor in the gigantic tragedy of our nation. And then my mind perceives the immediate necessity of not acquiescing in this way of his of seeing things, in this attitude of his which, as I reflect, goes back years and is perhaps the prime cause of his failure.

Then, too, his ever more marked tendency to blame others, especially the heads of the armed forces, for what has happened, will be opposed more and more strongly on my part.

Yet another word of acknowledgement for the Navy:

"What Sirianni and Cavagnari told me about the quantity of fuel oil and coal in the ships always corresponded absolutely to the truth. But when Valle and Pricolo spoke to me of 1,500 'planes ready for action, they included the training machines, those under repair and those becoming obsolete. Things happened as they did, too, because of our mistake in not building aircraft-carriers or torpedo bombers. I took the airmen's word for it, who, after all, were the experts who ought to have known more than I did.

"For that matter, even Marshal Badoglio, who was Chief of General Staff for seventeen years, never pointed out these mistakes or that situation to me. He no longer took any part in the manœuvres, either.

"All our campaigns failed owing to lack of preparation. Look at the campaign in Greece. A meeting was held. All the Army Staff, Badoglio included, were convinced that the campaign would be a success. Visconti Prasca was positively lyrical. The information they gave me about the enemy armed forces was such that victory seemed assured in a few days, if not in a few hours."

"I was there in the *Bande Nere*, Excellency, to take part in the operation. It is impossible to describe to you the state of confusion among the various commands ! Imagine, an order had already been given for the bombardment of Janina ; it was held up because the following day we were supposed to enter, received by the Greeks with open arms."

Once more the talk turns on the internal situation in Italy and on what Fascism has done.

"Excellency," I say to him, "no one could put you and the Régime on trial better than you yourself, who are in possession of all the facts. I must, however, tell you what the general feeling is. Take the average person's opinion, my wife's, for instance. A woman who looks after her children and her home, who comes of an honest Italian stock ; her father was the Prefect Bonfanti Linares, whom you will certainly remember. My wife says : 'We are ruined. What has he brought us to ?' She points to you, the head, as the person really responsible. And so, believe me, does all Italy."

"But Fascism has done so much and so many good things that no one will be able to destroy. Everything went well up to 1937. Marvellous achievements. We created an Empire, conquered perhaps at too little cost—only 1,537 dead. I gave Albania to the Crown. It would have been greatly to my advantage if my complaint had got worse in 1937 and I had died then. They will regret the days of Fascism. No other régime has done what Fascism did for the workers.

"And now imagine what prestige Stalin, Marshal Stalin, will have, if Russia wins the war. Hitler considers Stalin his real enemy, the one worthy of his steel.

"Churchill and Roosevelt are secondary figures, in Hitler's view ; according to him, Churchill is not worth much and Roosevelt still less—he is too rich."

Mussolini returns to the subject of his own fate : "I did not realize the law of contraries, which dogged me ever after June 28th, 1942. I wanted to have a great celebration for our twentieth anniversary,[1] which would have made a great appeal to the masses, when the disaster in Libya began. I was present at every air alert in Rome, but absent during the first raid. I had said that in Sicily we would throw them back into the sea, I had spoken of the 'water-line'[2] and instead everything went wrong."

[1] For the World Exhibition in Rome, planned for October, 1942, in commemoration of the twentieth anniversary of the March on Rome, see above, p. 221.

[2] See above, p. 37, n. 1.

There is a long pause ; then once more we talk about the war.

It is a quarter past three. The commander of the destroyer, Bartolini Baldelli, comes into the cabin to announce that the embarkation of the escort has been completed. I introduce him to Mussolini. I order him to up anchor and shape course for Point B. I follow him on to the bridge almost at once.

By 3.25 a.m. we are under way.

*

The sun has already intensified every hue. A fresh wind from the west. It is quarter-past seven when I leave the bridge to go to my cabin for a moment. Mussolini is sitting at the table, without a coat ; he must have been sleeping on the couch, where there is a cushion. He says to me : "Have you had a little nap, Admiral ?" On my replying : "No, I have been on the bridge," he makes a gesture of surprise. "Even the eye of an old admiral may come in useful," I say. He smiles. And we begin to talk about the Navy. The Naval Academy, that great mother who brought us all up in the same way, whatever our origin.

"Ours," I remark, "is an exclusive caste, and I advise future generations to keep it so, with its inevitable defects but also with the immense power of its traditions." He agrees, and acknowledges that the special character of our training gives excellent results : "The Navy will come out of this war with very great prestige, which it has already acquired all over the country."

"And yet, Excellency, they say that it was the Navy's treachery which caused the fall of Augusta and Pantelleria ! If I put myself in Admiral Pavesi's shoes, I ask myself what more I could have done. I might have emerged from the shelter and got myself killed by a bomb splinter, but that is all, and that wouldn't have saved Pantelleria. The reason for the fall of Pantelleria is because we let it be bombed so systematically, day after day, and entrusted its defence to A.A. batteries instead of to air opposition. Plane against plane ; that would have been the only way to prolong—greatly to prolong—resistance." Once more Mussolini agrees with me. As for Augusta, his definition is : "a regrettable incident" ; he asserts that much can be attributed to the lack of communications and to Guzzoni's weak and vacillating command.

He says: "They decided to send Guzzoni there." I interrupt him immediately: "It was you who sent him, because it was you who were Minister of War."

"Ah, true. But the General Staff goes by seniority, and so it is always the same names that crop up.

"The first mistake was forming that army with Sicilians; how could they fight calmly or heroically with the immediate knowledge of the destruction of their villages and homes, the probable death of their families and their immense sufferings? Besides, they have a right to say: 'When the Veneto was invaded, we Sicilians were there to defend it; now that our homeland is invaded, the soldiers from other parts wash their hands of us.' To say nothing of that most unfortunate expression with which Roatta's ill-chosen proclamation ended (for which I had to recall him): 'You, Sicilians, and we Italian and German fighting men!'

"And then Guzzoni, I remember him well, and his indecision at the time of the conquest of Albania, when he halted on the road to Tirana, on Sciac Sciac bridge."

"I was at Durazzo, commanding the *Pola*. I remember your telegram: 'You have lost too much time.'"

"Exactly. When I sent him to Sicily I wrote him a letter of encouragement which ended like this: 'A Marshal's baton is in readiness for you.' But instead, everything went so badly."

Mussolini is speaking, but it seems as if he were not speaking of himself at all, it seems as if he had nothing to do with the matter.

And he continues his tirade against the Army Staff, and the impossibility of filling the commands except by seniority. "Italy is the only nation which in wartime maintains a Central Committee for Promotion! In England, Churchill gives the commands to the men he thinks best. In Germany they give Divisional Commands to colonels, on trial; if they do well they are promoted generals. What a lot it took to persuade the Staff to give the Supreme Command of the Carabinieri to a Carabinieri general!"

Then, once again, the lack of preparation for the war.

"Don't you think, Admiral, that besides the unpreparedness of the Army there was a spiritual unpreparedness, too?"

"Certainly. The whole education of youth has been falsified."

"This is a war of reason, not of feeling. We were far readier for the first World War."

"Yes. For years, when we were children, we had chanted: 'Trieste and Trento.' But the present-day youth has not had the same driving-force. The orientation and spiritual education of youth have been a failure. Here, too, your collaborators have not been equal to their task. I believe that of all those who worked with you, those who were honest and straight, can be counted on the fingers of one hand."

"There were some straight ones. Paolo Revel, for instance."

"But then, look how much harm Farinacci has done you, with that newspaper of his."[1]

"I have confiscated it so many times! Incorrigible. The whole campaign against the Vatican completely mistaken. He is an illiterate. Latterly, too, he was really too much of a busybody."

"You ought to have kicked him out."

"He had a certain following among Fascists. But everything to do with the Vatican was mistaken. Imagine, Scorza wanted to give the Pope a million *lire* out of Party funds for the rebuilding of San Lorenzo. I told him not to do it, as the Vatican had no desire to be placed in an embarrassing position."

*

I go back on the bridge. The west wind is blowing harder and the choppy sea is breaking on deck, over the bows, the spray flying as far as the bridge. The tang of that salt water gives me great pleasure; it is months since I last had the taste of it. With the sea dead ahead of her, the destroyer rides it splendidly, and maintains her twenty-two knots without effort. By eleven o'clock we ought to be at the entrance of the channel between Cape Ferro and Le Bisce. This "Point B" is about eighteen sea-miles from Cape Ferro; visibility is poor. The mountains of Corsica begin to come into view, but Sardinia shows only very faintly. We proceed right up to the danger limit of the barriers, in the hope of being able to take our bearings properly. But there is nothing to be seen except Cape Figari, and we are not quite sure even of that. We proceed southwards then, keeping outside the limit of the minefields until we can see Tavolara clearly. In doing this we have lost two hours before we are sure of the entrance to the estuary.

[1] i.e. The *Regime Fascista*, published in Cremona.

A motor-boat pilots us through the channels at four knots. Now that the worries of navigation are over, I feel calmer. I see Mussolini on deck, at his side the Carabinieri officers. This vexes me. Colonel Meoli ought to have avoided this ; one can't be sure that the crew may not shout : "Down with him !" or "Three cheers for him !" However, the ratings behave extremely well ; they look discreetly and without staring at the man who was their Head for so many years.

I move off, in order to go below and wash. Mussolini stops me and says : "I was thinking about what we said a little while ago about luck. But a man whose luck is running badly must be given time to recoup. Look at Stalin ; for two years he had nothing but failures, he did nothing but lose territory. Now his luck is running well again."

I reply : "That is true, Excellency ; but Stalin has had the growing support of all his people. You, on the contrary, have had less and less support, and at a given moment no one followed you any longer."

"True enough, that is the crucial point. When we make our third voyage together, Admiral—for we certainly shall—we must continue our conversation." We make fast to a buoy in front of the little town of Maddalena proper.

The motor-launch comes alongside with Admiral Brivonesi and Major Bonitatibus. They come aboard and Mussolini at once gets into the motor-launch, Brivonesi, myself, Meoli and Bonitatibus accompanying him.

We go alongside a landing-stage at Padule, where Brivonesi has left his car without even a chauffeur as precaution. The journey is a short one, and we arrive at the new residence—Villa Webber, the only possible and decent one. During the night it has been evacuated by E-boat officers, who were billeted there. It has a fairly large garden, it looks on to the sea, it is surrounded by pines—a belt of greenery, which is very rare in these islands. We go over the rooms ; there are a number of them. The one Mussolini is to inhabit is decently furnished. "A Senior Officer's room," says Brivonesi to me. While Mussolini and the two officers are still looking round and are lingering on the terrace, Brivonesi and I remain by ourselves, to talk. I give him Minister De Courten's orders : strictest surveillance in the estuary, to prevent any German *coup de main*. Brivonesi points out the great difficulty in controlling the traffic of German craft. Mussolini comes in from the terrace and says to the Admiral: "You will see, Brivonesi, I shall not give you much trouble." His face is gloomy, his expression once again disgusted. He goes to his room, barely nodding a farewell to the two of us. We go downstairs, and depart.

My mission is over. For a long time the impression remains with me—and I shall make mention of it in my official report, too—that Mussolini does not entirely consider himself "politically defunct," as he had declared to me in the course of his transfer to Ponza.

II

WITH MUSSOLINI AT THE CAMPO IMPERATORE

Extracts from accounts given by Flavia Iurato, Manageress of the Campo Imperatore Hotel up to September 11*th,* 1943, *and Domenico Antonelli, Manager from the* 11*th onwards.*

IT WAS TOWARDS the end of August 1943, and in the Campo Imperatore Hotel, alive with tourists, life was going on as usual. During the last few days, however, word had gone round among the guests and staff that an important personage was shortly to arrive.

On August 27th the staff was sent down to the bottom of the funicular railway, where there was a small inn called "La Villetta," and told to put everything in perfect order there. Preparations went on up to the morning of the 28th, and in the afternoon, when all was ready, a column of cars arrived in the square. Among them, strangely enough, was a Red Cross motor-ambulance. From it emerged a heavily-built man in a dark suit, overcoat and black hat—Mussolini. There was no longer anything of the well-fed, self-assured dictator about him. Instead, he looked anxiously about him as if he feared some trap, rolling his eyes, which stood out from his emaciated face.

In the "Villetta" he was given the best room on the second floor. By not keeping the prisoner on a lower floor there began the series of "precautions" which—according to our detectives—were to prevent Mussolini's escape at all costs. His batman was Private Francesco Grevetto, who had already been in his service prior to July 25th.

The presence of such a man could not escape the notice of the guests at the other hotel farther up ; in fact, in the course of a few hours it became the chief subject of conversation and, as a result, the Campo Imperatore Hotel was closed down the following day. That was the second, and really rather belated, precautionary measure taken. Having been turned out, the guests who went down by funicular, saw Mussolini walking up and down a few yards from the "Villetta," and thus obtained direct confirmation of the rumours which had been circulating the day before.

The prisoner took his meals in his room, and Police Inspector Gueli and Lt. Faiola of the Carabinieri, who were in charge of him, were always present. At the end of the meal Gueli and Faiola hastened to remove the knives and even the forks as well, in order—according to them—to forestall any attempt at suicide by Mussolini.

Not a week had gone by since Mussolini's arrival at the "Villetta," when a serious incident occurred, which ought to have opened his guardians' eyes. On September 4th, the Carabinieri at a road-block above the village of Assergi halted a small car with two German officers aboard. The car turned back, but the two Germans hid it in a bend of the road and tried to reach the starting-point of the funicular by a short cut on foot. When the Carabinieri discovered them, they were put to flight by rifle fire; and despite the immediate employment of numerous police-dogs—which, together with a hundred Carabinieri, made up the guard—the two officers succeeded in reaching their car and getting away in safety. As if that were not enough, a German reconnaissance plane flew over the "Villetta" every day at a low altitude and for a long time. . . .

Gueli and Faiola decided to take Mussolini a little farther up, to the Campo Imperatore Hotel. This they did on September 6th at five in the afternoon. Mussolini was not keen on moving, still less on travelling by funicular. On getting into the carriage he asked the station-master: "Is this funicular safe?" adding: "Not for my sake, because my life is over, but for those who accompany me."

But the journey, which took exactly ten minutes, went off well, and he reached his destination. Here—again because of the great precautions we mentioned before—he was lodged in a suite on the second floor, consisting of a hall, sitting-room, bedroom and bathroom.

The suite was luxuriously furnished, and the sitting-room was transformed into a study. In between was Room 203, occupied by Private Grevetto. Mussolini thought that if he was going to be considered a prisoner there was no need for such comfort. With his own hands he rolled up the rugs covering the floor in the study. Then, as the hotel staff and the Carabinieri detailed to look after him treated him with great respect, he exclaimed Spartanly: "If I am a prisoner, treat me as such. If not, I wish to go to Rocca delle Caminate."

After that he raised no more objections, but made the best of things instead, and seemed to benefit by the mountain air. For that matter, everyone seemed to expect a long stay there; many police-agents, in fact, had brought their skis and other mountain paraphernalia.

At his own request, Mussolini took his meals in his own rooms, in the sitting-room, to be exact. He was on a strict diet, due to his illness, that is, almost entirely plain rice, eggs, boiled onions, very little meat, some milk and a lot of fruit. Indeed, he really did a "grape cure," because he ate about seven pounds of them every day. . . .

Mussolini's day became that of any peaceful citizen on holiday. He rose at nine and breakfasted in his room. Then he went down to the dining-room and chatted a little with Gueli and Faiola. At 12.30 he went upstairs again to have lunch—always the same rice, the same fruit, the same onions. About two o'clock Sergeant-major Antichi, who had been in his personal service for about eight years and who was nevertheless allowed to remain at his side, accompanied him on a walk in the neighbourhood of the hotel. Towards 4.30 he returned, and often lingered to talk with the policemen on guard at the gates. He was often to be seen at the window, looking at the majestic Gran Sasso with field-glasses, or sitting on the low wall by the square, gazing abstractedly into the distance like the traditional oleograph of Napoleon on St. Helena.

Punctually every afternoon Gueli went up to Mussolini's rooms and had a long talk with him. These talks were, as Gueli said in his own words, "the best hours of my life," since he found himself in contact with a man "of such brain." In these talks Mussolini often spoke of politics, and was not above confiding in the police inspector, and recounting scraps of his domestic affairs. Gueli repeated many of these confidences to the manager of the hotel.

For instance, Mussolini once said that after France had

surrendered he had advised Hitler to attack England immediately, "even if the landing cost a million men." Another time he said he had advised Hitler against attacking Russia who, in Mussolini's words, had become "a running sore" to Germany.

One of his favourite subjects was that of betrayal; according to him, he had been betrayed by the very people for whom he had done most. His resentment was chiefly directed against Ciano, Grandi, Farinacci and various generals and admirals. A propos of betrayal, Lt. Faiola said: "When we left Maddalena Island, Mussolini said to me, pointing to the commander of the base[1]: 'There is the chief culprit responsible for our defeat. He was supposed to escort a convoy laden with petrol to Africa; the non-arrival of those vital supplies was the cause of our retreat from El Alamein.'[2] To which I replied: 'Why didn't you shoot him, Excellency?' And Mussolini said: 'I was wrong not to,' and relapsed into silence. . . . ."

Mussolini dined at seven o'clock. Then he went down to the dining-room of the hotel, to play the usual game of *Scopone*. This card game had become a habit since his captivity, and the four was made up by Gueli, Faiola and Antichi. He did not spend his time in either reading or writing; only sometimes, when he saw he was being observed, he composed his face in a thoughtful expression. He showed neither sorrow nor humiliation. The only things that really roused him were the talks with the police-agents round about, and the card games.

After the game he was also allowed to listen to the wireless —German and Italian as well as Allied stations. He did not show any embarrassment when the transmissions mentioned his name . . . .

The day after the Armistice, on the morning of September 9th, he told his attendant that he was feeling ill. This created a certain disturbance. Faiola was extremely worried, and immediately sent for an Army doctor, Lt. Masciocchi, who discovered that there was a slight worsening of his old complaint, but that was all. Mussolini liked to buttonhole the police attendants and the hotel staff, and talk about his health.

Once when the chambermaid, Lisa Moscardi, who looked after his laundry, complained of a swollen ankle which hurt her, the Dictator stepped forward with bandages and ointment, and

[1] i.e. Admiral Brivonesi.

[2] Not long before Mussolini had expressed the conviction that Brivonesi could not have done more. See above, p. 213.

said smilingly to her: "Be brave, my child! Remember that I have been in pain for eighteen years!" He continued to enquire after her ankle the following days. . . . .

On the afternoon of September 10th, the Prefect of L'Aquila telephoned twice on end to Inspector Gueli, who went down to the town about seven o'clock to confer with the Prefect. Meanwhile, Faiola stationed his men, got out weapons and hand-grenades, posted various sentries on the look-out, and sent a platoon, under an N.C.O., to the "Duca degli Abruzzi" Inn on the top of Mount Portella, which commanded the whole slope to the north of the Gran Sasso range. A German attack was expected. At 8.30 p.m. an aeroplane, powerfully illuminated, flew low over the hotel. Mussolini said it was a German Red Cross machine. About an hour later, at ten o'clock, Gueli returned to the Campo Imperatore. According to him there was no need to worry; the only thing he had learned in L'Aquila was that a German column had been observed advancing on the town. Together with Gueli, the new manager of the hotel arrived at the Campo Imperatore, to replace Signora Iurato. This was because it was not deemed prudent to leave a woman in charge of the hotel, in case the Germans attempted any violence.

Mussolini remained tranquil and asked no questions.

On the morning of the 11th he showed great coolness. One would have said that for some reason he was in a good humour. He chatted with the new manager and, on learning that he was a war casualty, asked him where he had been wounded. "In Albania, on Tomori."

Mussolini said: "The Alpini who fought in Greece curse me, but they are wrong. There too I was betrayed." Then, his voice altering, he thrust out his lips in his usual gesture, and said: "Serena built this hotel; I like it very much. Some years ago my children came here too, to ski. I was also invited several times, but I never had the time to come . . . ."

Just before dinner-time an Abruzzi shepherd came up to the hotel to buy some wine. As civilians were forbidden to cross the threshold, a dispute arose between the shepherd and the Carabiniere on guard. Mussolini, passing by, heard what it was about and gave orders for the shepherd to be admitted. He then led his guest to a table and ordered some wine. First of all he asked him what improvements Fascism had brought about in the sheep-farming industry. But the shepherd had not noticed any improvement and answered instead, addressing him with the familiar "*tu*" and putting a horny hand on Mussolini's shoulder: "You are wrong; you taxed us too heavily and you let them steal too much from us for the wool and cheese State pools."

Mussolini seemed amused at this account, and continued his questioning: "What do you think of this war, which has ended so badly?"

"Too many thieves about," said the shepherd. "The bread had to fatten too many people before it got to the soldiers' mouths."

Finally the hillman rose and said a familiar goodbye, shaking Mussolini by the hand and saying, as he would have said to an old friend: "Take care of yourself, Mussolini, and thanks for the wine."

After that, Mussolini went upstairs to supper in his rooms. Just before the usual card game the prisoner said a few words which, by their easy tone, gave the impression that he still thought his stay in the mountains would be a long one. Turning to the manager of the hotel he said: "They tell me you are a ski-ing expert. When do you think we shall get the first snow? I should love to put on my skis again."

On learning that they sometimes had snow up there at the beginning of October, he looked pleased, and added: "Let us hope it snows soon. You must give me some lessons."

That evening the terms of the Armistice signed by Badoglio were put out on the wireless. Late at night, towards three o'clock, Mussolini's servant brought Lt. Faiola a letter containing the following:

In the few days you have been with me I have realised that you are a true friend; you are a soldier, and know better than I what it means to fall into the hands of the enemy. I learned from the Berlin radio that one of the Armistice terms speaks of handing me over alive to the English. I shall never submit to such a humiliation, and I ask you to let me have your revolver.

Faiola immediately sprang out of bed and rushed into Mussolini's apartment. When he reached the bedroom he found the would-be suicide awkwardly waving a Gillette razor-blade as if he were trying to slit the veins of his wrist. Poor Faiola, desperately agitated, tried to cheer up his charge, and finally, having taken the razor-blade away from him, returned to bed.

The following morning, September 12th, while Mussolini was breakfasting with Gueli and the hotel manager, he expressed his great astonishment at the fact that the Italian troops had let the Germans occupy Rome without resistance. If he had been there, things would have gone differently. Supposing, for instance, that the Germans tried to come to the Campo Imperatore ! "We should make corpses of the lot," said Faiola proudly. With regard to the Duce, the order which Badoglio had given his guards, according to Faiola, was : "The Germans must not take him alive."

It was 1.30 p.m. when there came a deafening roar of engines. Everybody rushed outside. About ten machines were visible, with gliders in tow. At that very moment the gliders were cast off and began to plane down. Here, all was confusion. No one thought of giving orders. The police left their machine-gun posts without the slightest attempt at firing, and took shelter in the hotel. The rifles and hand-grenades distributed two days earlier were not used. The platoon at the "Duca degli Abruzzi" Inn went running down the northern slope. They did not return till the following morning, when all had been quiet for some time. Faiola, too, ran into the hotel and rushed up to the second floor, shouting like a madman : "Excellency, the Germans !"

While this ridiculous and regrettable scene was taking place, the gliders began to land undisturbed. From the first one, which landed about two hundred and fifty yards from the hotel, the people in the doorway saw an Italian General of Police, Soleti, emerge, followed by a German officer who was pressing the muzzle of a machine-gun into his ribs. Meanwhile a German N.C.O. emerged from another glider and calmly began to film the scene. Soleti came towards the hotel, shouting: "Don't shoot !" and the officer following him asked for Gueli.

Gueli was standing in the lodge. Faiola had also come downstairs again. The German at once asked them : "Is the Duce alive or dead ?"

"Alive," was the reply. And that was the end of the strict order which, only an hour earlier, Lt. Faiola had sworn to carry out at all costs.

Meanwhile, the gliders, eleven in all, had come to earth,

together with a Stork. The latter machine, as the papers later announced, had been specially constructed and adapted from the original model, so as to carry six people instead of two. A hundred and thirty Germans, commanded by a captain, had come down from the air. There was also a lieutenant who spoke perfect Italian, and a few N.C.O.'s. They were all armed with a machine-gun, two revolvers and a number of hand-grenades.

The Germans surrounded the hotel, in case of resistance.

But Mussolini leaned out of the window and shouted in Italian and German: "Stop! Don't shoot! Don't shed any blood." And in fact not a shot was fired. The Germans, on seeing Mussolini on the balcony, organised an enthusiastic demonstration, to the cry of "Du-ce! Du-ce!"

Immediately afterwards, the German commander was accompanied by Gueli and Faiola to Mussolini's apartment, where the latter shook his hand and embraced him. A friendly conversation ensued, in the course of which Mussolini was informed that his household had been taken to Vienna and were all in the best of health. If he wished, he could join them that very day. But he declared that he would rather spend the night at Rocca delle Caminate. The German commander, radiant with satisfaction, recounted the details of the enterprise. He added that they had had to hurry the preparations on, because there had been a hint that a similar *coup* was being prepared by the United Nations.

Meanwhile, the Germans were blocking all the roads leading to the Campo Imperatore. Another Stork landed at the bottom of the funicular, and forty parachutists descended at the same time. A column composed of six armoured cars reached the road-block at Assergi. Here was made the only attempt at resistance by the Italian Carabinieri, one of whom was killed. The column advanced on the Campo Imperatore. The Germans, too, had a few badly wounded, but only because of a mishap to one of the gliders on landing. The wounded were carried to the hotel on mattresses. To celebrate the success of the enterprise, the German lieutenant who spoke Italian ordered wine for all the soldiers.

General Soleti, meantime, was relating his adventures. He had been seized by two German officers, disarmed, and taken to Pratica airport, from which the expedition had then started. The German captain had told him to warn the Carabinieri guarding the Campo Imperatore not to shoot. At that point

Soleti turned to the German officer and said: "And now give me back my revolver. Rest assured that I shall not use it against the Duce or you."

The lieutenant took a revolver from his belt and handed it to the general, saying: "I give it to you in remembrance of an enterprise which will go down in history for its audacity."

Mussolini in the meantime had already assumed the manners of a dictator; he moved with more confidence, he spoke with emphasis, he thrust out his jaw.

He decided to take Inspector Gueli and Lt. Faiola with him. Gueli accepted, but Faiola came hesitatingly towards him and said: "Excellency, I should like to speak to you alone for a moment."

Mussolini at once re-established the distance between himself and the poor little lieutenant whom, the evening before, he had honoured with the title of friend, and he replied shortly and impatiently: "Go on, go on, then."

Summoning all his courage, Faiola said: "Duce, I have a wife and child. If you don't mind, I would rather stay here."

Mussolini replied harshly: "Very well then, stay."

By 4.30 the baggage was ready, and departure was imminent. Mussolini stood on the threshold of the hotel. Beside him were the German captain and lieutenant, Inspector Gueli and Lt. Faiola. All the hotel staff followed at a respectful distance. Mussolini stopped and shook hands with each of them, saying a few words in farewell: "Thank you very much, I shall never forget you." Then, with a youthful, elastic step, he went towards the Stork and got in, together with the pilot and the commander of the expedition. Meanwhile, the police who had had charge of the prisoner, and the German soldiers who had liberated him, stood stiffly at the Fascist salute, shouting loudly: "Duce! Duce!"

The Stork bumped for a time along the somewhat rugged slope. It seemed about to crash, then it rose. It took off. Immediately after the machine's departure the Germans began to descend by the funicular, and on each trip they took an Italian with them as hostage. At the bottom of the funicular a number of armoured cars, which had arrived in the meantime, awaited them. Once aboard these, the Germans made for the National Highway.

On the 13th, all the men forming the prisoner's guard were to go down to L'Aquila. But Faiola, together with the N.C.O.'s., preferred to remain, for fear of being deported to Germany. On the 14th, the Germans sent a platoon to collect the arms and various material left behind by the police. Faiola, knowing that the Germans were already at the base of the funicular, fled at once with the N.C.O.'s through the Portella pass and down the slope of Teramo. And so vanished the last actor in that tragi-comedy.[1]

[1]According to an account current in Northern Italy, it was Badoglio's own Minister of the Interior who had instructed the Chief of Police that it would be futile and harmful to resist by force of arms a possible attempt to liberate Mussolini. (See below, *List of Sources*, A 63.)

III

MY LAST MEETING WITH MUSSOLINI[1]

by Cardinal Ildefonso Schuster, O.S.B.
Archbishop of Milan

"At noon on April 25th, 1945, Mr. Bruni (who was then in contact with the officers of the Prefect of Milan), came to inform me that Mussolini would pay me a visit. Mr. Bruni had been sent to me by Fr. Marinelli, a member of the religious order of the Barnabites and by Professor Strachettio. It was Mussolini's desire that I should arrange a meeting between him and General Cadorna, Commander in Chief of all the partisans in Northern Italy, and Signor Marazza, Secretary of the National Liberation Committee and also Secretary of the Christian Democratic Party.

"At the appointed time the Duce arrived, and was at once ushered in by my secretaries. He entered the reception room with such a dejected look that the impression he gave me was that of a man nearly benumbed by an immense catastrophe. I received him with episcopal charity, and, while waiting for the arrival of the persons whom he had wanted to meet, I tried to cheer him a little by starting a conversation.

"I began by assuring him that I fully appreciated his personal sacrifice in accepting, with capitulation, a life of expiation in prison in order to save the rest of Italy. I assured him that all honest men would appreciate the value of his gesture. I did not want him to retain any illusions. I reminded him of the fall of Napoleon ; he answered that he also saw his second empire of a hundred days coming to an end. All that was left to him was to accept his fate with resignation. I assured him that the Church in Italy would not forget what he had pledged himself by the Lateran Treaty to do ; if his intuition had not been fulfilled—to give Italy to God and God to Italy—this was due

[1] Translated by Don Alberto Castelli, Professor of English Literature, University of the Sacred Heart, Milan.

in great part to misfortune. He had been served very badly by his 'gerarchi.' I had conveyed a warning to him as long ago as June, 1931, through his brother Arnaldo. 'It is too true,' said the Duce, 'when we come to know our men it is always too late.' 'Indeed,' I rejoined, 'to know men is the most difficult of all the arts.'

"We went on to speak of ecclesiastical policy in the last few years. The Duce insisted on excusing himself a good deal, and said that he had nothing to do with the anti-clerical movement of the 'Crociata Italica,' and indeed was against it. [This movement was started by some priests who believed blindly in Fascism; they had established its headquarters in Cremona, under the protection of the Fascist leader, Farinacci. They also published a weekly, the reading of which was banned by the bishops.] 'Moreover,' the Duce added, 'I have always resisted when others tried to induce me to take measures against the Church, or indeed to take any action not in accord with the pacts of the Concordat.' I let the subject drop, because this was not the moment to start a discussion, particularly as I had already let him know, some months before, that I was convinced of his own full responsibility.

"Seeing him very dejected, I insisted on his taking some refreshment. Out of politeness, he accepted a small glass of elixir and a biscuit. I kept him company, and I thought of St. Benedict, who ordered the abbot to do the same when receiving a guest in his monastery; he himself must have done so when meeting Totila at Monte Cassino. Taking my cue from this episode, I asked Mussolini whether he knew my recent History of St. Benedict. He answered, no. Then I offered him the last copy which I possessed, advising him to keep it, so that it might give him comfort in the sad days which lay before him. I insisted that he should consider his Calvary as an expiation before God, just and merciful. Devoutly, he took my hand.

"Then we began to speak of Monte Cassino and its destruction. As the conversation continued on the theme of religion, he disclosed to me that, when he was a prisoner on the island of La Maddalena, a good priest of Pausania had undertaken to begin his training anew in the practice of the Catholic life. He had made progress, and they had even appointed the following day for him to attend Holy Mass. But that same day he was ordered to leave the island. I then reminded him that Napoleon, when he was at St. Helena, had also sought comfort in the faith of his fathers; Pius VII had been so generous as to plead his cause with England, and had succeeded in sending a priest, Abbate Vignali, to St. Helena to bring him comfort and to serve as chaplain to him in his exile. Let Mussolini likewise appeal to the Holy See, which would certainly try to help him as best might be.

"The conversation had already been going on for an hour, and General Cadorna and Signor Marazza had not yet arrived. I left the room for a moment to make sure that they would come, and returning, I asked Mussolini to wait for a few more minutes. Afterwards I learned that the Committee of National Liberation had met to decide whether General Cadorna should accept Mussolini's invitation.

"When we resumed our conversation, Mussolini seemed extremely tired. I begged him again to spare Italy useless havoc and to accept the honourable surrender which was offered him. He answered that his programme was twofold and would be carried out in two moves. The Army and the Republican Militia would be dissolved. He himself would retire into the Valtellina with an escort of some thousands of Black-shirts. 'So,' I asked, 'you intend to continue the war in the mountains?' The Duce assured me: 'Only for a short time; then I shall surrender.' I ventured to remark: 'Duce, do not have any illusions. I know that the Black-shirts who are going to follow you are rather three hundred than three thousand, as some would have you believe.' He answered: 'Perhaps a few more; not many, though. I have no illusions.' Seeing him resolute in his determination, I did not reply.

"Our conversation continued with a sense of tiredness. The Duce was like a man bereft of will, listlessly facing his destiny. We spoke of the resolute opposition of the whole clergy of Northern Italy to the war, and of the great influence they had upon the people. He asked me why the clergy of Northern Italy and of Lombardy lived in more prosperous conditions, had a more profound influence than, and seemed superior to, the clergy of other regions of Italy. I explained to him how excellent was the intellectual and spiritual state of the Ambrosian clergy. I noticed that the Duce was interested in the subject; he asked what had led to such good clerical training. I spoke of the reforming work of St. Charles, whose spirit has still so great an influence on the hierarchy as well as on the faithful, that all feel it their duty to follow and imitate him. Afterwards, Mussolini asked me whether the Ambrosian rite, at least in its essential dogmas, is in accordance with the Roman Church. At such a strange question I felt a sense of surprise, perceiving how scanty was the religious knowledge of a man who had tried to guide the destiny of Catholic Italy. I answered him that it was not in theological dogma, which is the same throughout the Catholic Church, but only in prayers and ceremonies that the Ambrosian rite differed from the Roman. This old Ambrosian rite has retained its formative influence on the faithful, and contributes in no small degree to the unity of the Ambrosian clergy, who are one family of strenuous workers under their Archbishop, the humblest servant of the diocese.

"From the Ambrosian rite we passed on to discuss the Slavonic East, and the Duce put some questions about the Orthodox Russians. My answer was, that Jesus Christ had founded His One Church on the Rock of Peter. Outside it, one could put up stately buildings as beautiful as one might wish ; but they would never be the true Church of Christ, and they would be subject to the inevitable vicissitudes of all human foundations. At this point Mussolini hinted at the less than benevolent disposition of the Patriarchate of Moscow towards the Vatican. I said that the breaking-off of the Orientals from Rome represented for them a real dogmatic revolution against the most sacred traditions of the Fathers of their churches, and of the venerable traditions of the old Christian East. From Russia our conversation turned to the Western front, and to England. Mussolini praised above all her genius and ability, 'sine ira et studio.'

" 'You see,' he told me, 'for 15 million German soldiers fallen in battle, and for many millions of Russians, England has lost only 260,000 Englishmen and 300,000 soldiers from all her large possessions ! England knows the secret of commerce very well ; and she has saved the lives of her men.' Explaining his idea of English policy in a better way, Mussolini recalled the old saying: 'England is like a ship, anchored in Great Britain, but always ready to sail the Oceans.'

"The Duce was of the opinion that, after the present war, there would not be another for many years, because Germany would no longer be in a condition to fight again. I related a conversation I had had with Pius XI, some ten years ago. As I was speaking of my fears concerning a new European conflagration, the Pope had recalled Napoleon's saying: 'To make war one needs, above all, money.' 'Now,' the Pope concluded, 'Mussolini has no money, and therefore he will never make a war.'

"Unfortunately, he was no prophet! 'A war,' Mussolini rejoined, 'may be made without money, but not without men and raw materials. At present, Germany, after its conquest by the Allies, will be left with neither. Therefore, she will not be in a position to wage war for many years. Unfortunately,' he added, 'England has now given up her traditional policy, and is letting Russia gain the upper hand in Europe, too.'

"In the meantime, General Cadorna and Signor Marazza had arrived. I ended my conversation with the Duce, reminding him that one day history would remember how, to save Northern Italy, he had taken the way to St. Helena and spared Lombardy from ruin. I exhorted him to put his trust in God, who cares for us all. Mussolini's answer was: 'History? You speak of history? I believe in ancient history, which is written without passion, and a long time after the event.' I said that I agreed with him because of the difficulty of judging contemporaries with dispassionate serenity. I quoted St. Jerome who, when he comes to speak of St. Ambrose in his book on Ecclesiastical Writers, refuses to pronounce judgment on his literary production, lest it should be attributed to envy or flattery.

"The entry of the representatives of the two belligerent parties broke up our conversation. Mussolini put my History of St. Benedict into an envelope and placed it on the table in front of him.

"At first, the two parties faced each other very stiffly: but soon the discussion became animated, and the Liberation Committee, while requiring from Mussolini simply an unconditional surrender, pledged themselves to respect the following conditions:

"(1) The Fascist Army and Militia, and all the armed groups attached to them, were to surrender their arms, and be taken prisoner with military honours, in accordance with the rules of The Hague Convention; (2) The families of Fascists were not to be victimised; (3) Diplomats were to be treated in accordance with international law.

"These conditions seemed to satisfy the Duce; so much so that I asked the Committee to grant me, as Archbishop of Milan, the right to visit prisoners' camps in order to continue my work of Christian charity.

"At this moment, Marshal Graziani rose and told Mussolini

that they had no right to negotiate a capitulation independently of the Germans if they did not want to repeat the betrayal of September 8th. There was a moment of surprise. All the previous discussions had been of no use. Then some of those present remarked, that the German authorities, through myself, had already started negotiations. Professor Bicchierai had revealed the secret in the ante-room. I, who had kept it up to that moment, felt annoyed. I could not deny the news. On the other hand, I wanted to save the country from the ruin which Marshal Graziani's objection inevitably entailed. I therefore declared that I strongly deplored the indiscretion of those who had violated a diplomatic secret. As, however, it was useless to keep a secret which had become common knowledge (and not only through Professor Bicchierai's revelation), I explained that in fact General Wolf, Chief of the SS in Italy, was negotiating with me through the German Consul-General and through Colonel Rauff. Mussolini, giving way to a sudden impulse of indignation, declared himself to have been betrayed by the Germans, who had always treated us as their servants. He threatened to resume his freedom of action since, he said, 'they have also acted behind my back.'

"To prevent a diplomatic incident, which would have led the Germans to repudiate the negotiations now nearing completion, and which might also have driven them to a desperate defence of their position in Lombardy, I reminded the Duce that we had not yet reached any final conclusion. 'That does not matter,' Mussolini replied, 'simply to have begun negotiating without letting me know is a betrayal. I shall ring up the German Consul and tell him that I resume complete freedom of action.' Marshal Graziani tried to calm the Duce so that we could continue the discussion on the conditions of surrender. At length the Duce asked the Committee for an hour's time to make up his mind, and they granted it to him. I saw the Duce to the ante-chamber of my apartment. He answered my leave-taking with no special interest. After he had gone, I took Marshal Graziani aside and besought him to prevent Mussolini from taking any inconsiderate step that would leave Lombardy once more as a target for the anger of the Germans, the more so since — according to General Wolf's promise — they had decided by that time to sign an unconditional surrender in my presence.

"When Marshal Graziani had gone I went back to my reception room, where the representatives of the various parties and other members of the Liberation Committee had remained to talk things over. An hour and a quarter later, they insisted on ringing up Mussolini, so that he might either give his decision or be present for the surrender. To our surprise we were told that the Duce had left Milan after ordering a negative reply to be given.

"What had happened? General Wolf had asked me for an escort to Milan where on the evening of the 26th he was to sign his capitulation. He was expected in vain, for on the previous day he had gone to Switzerland. And Mussolini, yielding to panic, hoped to find refuge in Switzerland, himself. Breaking his word, he gave orders to inform me that he would not return; and he took flight towards Como, only to be arrested — and, a day or two later, killed. The newspapers of the following day published accounts of the last vicissitudes of his tragic odyssey.

"Had he accepted my humble advice, indeed my urgent prayer, he would have saved Milan — for capitulation would have spared it the guerrilla warfare of those last days — and he would also have saved himself, protected, as he would have been, by the terms of The Hague Convention."

APPENDICES
by Raymond Klibansky

I

THE ATTACK ON GREECE

A Comment on Chapter XX

THE ACCOUNT OF THE meeting at the Palazzo Venezia, at which the attack on Greece was finally decided upon, vividly illustrates both Mussolini's handling of political affairs and his method of writing history. It deserves closer examination, by setting it into its historical context.

Italy's relations with Greece

(1) FRIENDLY DECLARATIONS AND PERSONAL MESSAGES

Italo-Greek relations had been settled in a detailed Treaty of Friendship, signed by Mussolini and Venizelos in Rome on September 23rd, 1928. Fascist Italy's ruthless policy in the Dodecanese, in the following decade, prevented any cordial understanding. Relations, however, remained correct until Italy's *coup* against Albania on Good Friday, 1939, which caused profound alarm in Greece about Italian ambitions at her expense.

Aware of this reaction and of the dismay felt in the capitals of the West, Mussolini immediately issued a "solemn declaration," in which he "affirmed his belief that nothing could disturb the existing friendship between Italy and Greece." This was followed by a personal message to Metaxas, the Greek Dictator and Prime Minister: "Fascist Italy categorically reaffirms her intention to respect the integrity of both the Greek mainland and islands. Fascist Italy desires to continue and develop still further the friendly relations existing between the two countries and is ready to give concrete proof of these intentions." Similar assurances were conveyed, at the same time, to the British Government.

The Greek Dictator, on his part, had obligingly assured the

Italian Government, the day after the invasion of Albania, that all necessary steps would be taken to prevent King Zog from engaging in any political activity on Greek territory ; replying to Mussolini's message, he expressed the conviction that a new era of cordiality and peaceful collaboration between Italy and Greece was now about to begin.[1]

In the summer months of 1939 there was no lack of Italian provocation. The Greek Government learnt that high officials —the Minister of Education and Marshal Badoglio, Chief of the General Staff—had made speeches to Albanians, promising extensions of their territory. Italian soldiers, on their way to the Dodecanese, boasted in Greek ports that they would soon land at the Piræus and conquer the Ægean. Large concentrations of troops were observed at the Greek frontier. However, the time for action had not yet come ; and shortly after the outbreak of the German war, Mussolini addressed a personal note to Metaxas, reaffirming his peaceful intentions :

"(i) Italy has already declared on September 1st that she does not intend to take the initiative in resorting to military action of any kind. (ii) The above decision of the Italian Cabinet, which is valid in a general sense, applies more especially to Greece. (iii) Even in the event of Italy entering the war, a contingency which she, as a Great Power, cannot exclude, Italy will not take the initiative in resorting to any military action against Greece. (iv) In order to give a more concrete form to the Italian Government's and especially the Duce's friendly feelings towards Greece, orders will be issued for the withdrawal of the Italian troops from the Greek frontier to a depth of 20 kilometres. (v) Notwithstanding the present situation, the Duce does not exclude the possibility of resuming and stabilizing the policy of an Italo-Greek entente, which had been previously established by special diplomatic agreements."

Soon afterwards, on September 20th, a joint Italo-Greek communiqué was issued, testifying to the spirit of complete and mutual confidence guiding relations between the two countries and announcing, as practical proof of their feelings, the decision of both Governments to withdraw their military forces from the

[1]For this and the following, cp. R. Greek Ministry for Foreign Affairs, *The Greek White Book*, London, 1942, Documents 19 ; 22 ; 27 f. ; 42–50 ; 55. Emanuele GRAZZI (late Italian Minister to Athens), articles in : "Il Giornale del Mattino," Rome (see below, *List of Sources*, B 16).

Greek-Albanian frontier. A few weeks later, on November 3rd, the same principles were emphasized once more in an exchange of notes and the firm hope was expressed "that the development of the international situation would present to the two Governments, in the nearest future, the opportunity to give their relations a more concrete form, with a view to fertile collaboration based on mutual confidence, in all fields."

(2) THE WAR OF NERVES

Further mutual expressions of good-will were issued until the spring of 1940, when the atmosphere suddenly changed. In March, after his meeting with Hitler at the Brenner, Mussolini had made up his mind to take part in the war in a not too distant future—as soon as German successes would give him the "mathematical certainty" of achieving victory in a short time. In April, rumours of an impending Italian occupation of Corfu began to circulate in many Italian towns as well as in neutral countries. They were reported simultaneously from Greek representatives in Rome, Trieste, Brindisi, Geneva and Sofia. The first campaign of the nerve war against Greece had begun.

At the same time, more drastic methods of Fascist political warfare were being considered by Mussolini's Minister of Foreign Affairs. In Rome, while the King of Greece was believed to be Anglophile, his brother, the Crown Prince, was supposed to be in favour of the Axis Powers. Would it not be possible to find some Albanian who would remove the King?[1]

However, no action was taken. More important issues were at stake in the weeks preceding the German lightning war in the West. Thus, when Sgr. Grazzi, the Italian Minister to Athens, returned from one of his visits to Rome at the beginning of May, he brought the assurance that "Italy was not at all inclined, at any rate for the present, to be involved in war. As far as the Balkans were concerned, her desire was that peace should on no account be disturbed." After a few days he was instructed to repeat the same statement, adding that "Italy as a Great Power has her own claims which she will put forward in due time ; but she is prepared to give the assurance that these claims do not concern either Greece or the Balkans generally. Should Italy be involved in war against Great Britain, she would not attack

[1]This question was actually put by Ciano to Sgr. Grazzi ; see Grazzi's account, *Politica e affari a Palazzo Chigi*, in "Il Giornale del Mattino," Rome, 12.8.1945.

Greece, provided the latter was not converted into a British base."[1]

A month later, a German victory seemed certain. When Mussolini, obsessed by the fear that he might miss a share in the booty, hastened to declare war on Britain and France,[2] he gave Greece yet another assurance of Italy's peaceful intentions. In his speech of June 10th, announcing his declaration of war on the Western Powers, he stated :

"Now that the die is cast and we have of our own will burned the bridges behind us, I solemnly declare that Italy does not intend to drag other peoples who are her neighbours by sea and by land into the conflict. Let Switzerland, Yugoslavia, Turkey, Egypt and Greece take note of these words of mine, for it will depend entirely upon them if they are fully confirmed or not."

Whatever misgivings were felt in Greece about Italy's entry into the war, they found no official expression. On the contrary, General Metaxas informed the Italian envoy that this war would clarify the atmosphere in the Mediterranean and render possible that more intimate collaboration between Italy and Greece which he, as well as the King, had always desired; and he concluded by expressing his good wishes for Italy.[3]

The Greek Dictator's accommodating attitude was of little avail. Hardly a week had elapsed before Italian propaganda began to prove that Greek bases were used by the British Navy. The refutation of this charge was promptly followed by another accusation of the same kind. However, it was conclusively demonstrated by the Greek Government that the warships in question were not British, but Greek. Moreover, the Italian Minister received the assurance from Metaxas that any British attempt to land on Greek territory would be resisted by force.[4]

[1] *The Greek White Book*, Document 64 ; E. Grazzi, *loc. cit.*

[2] On April 20th, he had declared that he would not act before the end of August, "that is after improving preparations and after the harvest." On May 10th, after learning of the invasion of the Low Countries, he decided for quick action "within a month." On May 26th, the date of intervention was postponed to the latter part of June ; but on May 28th, "the events of the night (the Belgian capitulation) led him to speed up his planning as he was convinced that things were now coming to a head and he wanted to create enough claims to be entitled to his share of the spoils." Thus June 10th was fixed. See Galeazzo Ciano, *Diary* (below, List of Sources B 6) pp. 236-56

[3] E. Grazzi, *Chiaroscuri dell' aggressione alla Grecia*, in "Il Giornale del Mattino," Rome, 14.8.1945.

[4] *The Greek White Book*, Documents 79–82 ; 87–93. E. Grazzi, *loc. cit.*

(3) PROVOCATIONS

Meanwhile, the idea of a *coup* against Greece had taken shape in Mussolini's mind. His attack on an almost defeated France, far from bringing the Italian Army any laurels, had revealed its parlous state; it had resulted in high losses, and the slice of territory gained was so insignificant as to make the expectation previously raised appear ridiculous. Any further advance to the West was barred by a German veto. With bitterness the Duce began to feel that in his partnership with Hitler he was in danger of playing a secondary role. As Ciano observed at the time, he now "feared that the hour of peace was drawing near, and he saw fading once again that unattainable dream of his life: glory on the field of battle." More than ever he now wanted to fight. And he expressed his joy when, a few weeks later, the threat of a premature peace had vanished.[1] For the time being, the only chance of securing easy booty seemed to lie in the East. Thus, in July, Mussolini tentatively conveyed to Hitler his intention to land on the Ionian islands: and his Minister for Foreign Affairs asked the Commander of the Italian troops in Albania to hold himself ready to strike.[2]

At the same time, the Italian Government began to resort to more active measures. On several occasions, their 'planes attacked Greek ships in Greek territorial waters. The Greeks, anxious to avoid any pretext for hostilities, answered with restrained protests.

(4) THE ATROCITY CAMPAIGN

After a few weeks, the sequence of diplomatic pinpricks and military provocations was followed up by a new campaign of a different order. On August 11th this statement was issued in Rome by the official Stefani Agency:

" A deep impression has been produced on the Albanian

[1] Galeazzo Ciano, *Diary*, entries for 18.-19.6, and 22.7.1940 (see below, List of Sources, B 6). In his bitter mood, Mussolini made a strange prediction; speaking to Ciano about his conference with Hitler, "he concludes by saying that the German people have in themselves the germs of a collapse; a formidable internal clash will come that will smash everything." (*Diary*, *l. cit.*, p. 266.)—On 1.9.1940, "he declares he is glad that the war will last beyond this month and, perhaps, beyond the winter, because this will give Italy time to make greater sacrifices and thus enable him better to assert our rights." (*Ibid.*, p. 289.)

[2] Galeazzo Ciano, *Diary*, entry for 5.7.1940; E. Grazzi, *Moventi dell' attacco alla Grecia*, *loc. cit.*, 18.8.1945.

population under Greek rule by a terrible political crime committed on the Greco–Albanian border.

"The great Albanian patriot, Daout Hodja, born in the unredeemed region of Tsamuria[1], has been savagely murdered on Albanian territory close to the frontier. His body was found headless. According to later information, the murderers were Greek agents who carried the head back into Greek territory and delivered it to the authorities, who had already set a price on this Albanian patriot's head many years ago. It is also learned that his head was paraded about from village to village by order of the Greek local authorities and exposed to public view so as to terrorize the unredeemed Albanian brethren in the abovementioned district. Daout Hodja had been compelled some time ago to leave Tsamuria secretly in order to escape from the persecutions of the Greek authorities, who could not forgive his untiring propaganda among his compatriots for the annexation of Tsamuria to the Mother-country. He fled to Albania, where he again and again received messages threatening him with death, This murder, which has deeply affected the Albanians of Tsamuria, is not the only recent incident in the Greek policy of oppression.

"A few months back a small note was found pinned on the corpse of an Albanian murdered in Tsamuria, saying that the same fate awaited all those Albanians who hoped to liberate their country from Greek rule.

"This ancient Albanian territory is situated between the present Greco–Albanian frontier and the Ionian coast and extends as far as the outskirts of Preveza and to the borders of the province of Yannina. It is inhabited by some fifty thousand pure-blooded Albanians, who form the vast majority of the population . . . ."

There followed a history of Greek rule over this territory, alleging that the Greeks "decimated the inhabitants of the region by means of confiscation, massacre and deportation."

"Today, blind tyranny is weighing more heavily than ever on this population, so that many of the inhabitants of Tsamuria are compelled to seek refuge in Albania in order to escape these ruthless persecutions. According to several reliable statements, the Greek authorities have gone so far as to declare in public that the Italians will shortly be expelled from Albania.

[1]The region between the rivers Pavla and Mavropotamo, on the Greek side of the frontier.

"But the population of Tsamuria is less than ever disposed to yield to Greek oppression. If her devotion to the Albanian Motherland was sufficient to sustain Tsamuria's faith in those dark days of Albania's destiny, today the Albanians of Tsamuria will find even stronger grounds for hope in the renewed fortunes of their Mother-country."

On instructions from the Ministry of Popular Culture, this statement was published on the front page of all Italian papers, under sensational headlines. The following day, the Greek 'Agence d'Athènes' issued a detailed refutation of the story:

"About two months ago, two Albanians, who had managed to penetrate into Greek territory, were arrested, and when examined admitted having killed the individual named Daout Hodja in a quarrel. The latter was a notorious brigand on whose head a price had been set twenty years ago by the Greek Government on account of murders and other ordinary crimes committed by him on Greek territory. The Greek Government placed the murderers under arrest and ordered that the usual procedure in such matters should be followed. On July 25th, the Italian Legation in Athens informed the Hellenic Ministry for Foreign Affairs that a regular demand for their extradition would shortly be made by the Albanian Ministry of Justice.

"The Greek authorities, who continue to keep the said Albanians in custody, are still awaiting this extradition demand. It should be observed that the Italian Note, which is couched in the ordinary terms employed in administrative affairs of a current nature, states that Daout Hodja had settled in Albania twenty years ago.

"To sum up: (i) There is no question of an Albanian patriot but just of an ordinary criminal. (ii) The murderers were not Greeks but Albanians. (iii) Daout Hodja committed his crimes, and was outlawed, twenty years ago. (iv) The Italian authorities were in possession of all the facts at least twenty days ago.

"We should like to add that: (i) The alleged parading of the head from village to village is a pure myth. (ii) So also is the story about the murder of another Albanian and the finding on his dead body of a note containing threats of similar murders. We are moreover obliged to affirm in the most categorical terms that the allegations of a more general nature contained in the said Agency's statements are not founded on fact . . . ."

Neither this nor any of the subsequent communiqués of the

official Greek Agency—adducing the list of Daout Hodja's previous convictions for murder—were published in the Italian Press. Instead, a full-scale Press campaign was launched to show that the murder of 'the great Albanian patriot' was "a link in a chain of terrorism against Albania, forged in Athens, where support from England was counted upon."

A few days later, on August 15th, when pilgrims from all parts of Greece had gathered at the shrine of Tinos in the Cyclades to celebrate the Feast of the Holy Virgin, the Greek light cruiser *Helle*, which was lying at anchor a short distance outside the mole of Tinos harbour, was torpedoed by an "unknown submarine." While the cruiser sank, two other torpedoes exploded against the mole, which was crowded with pilgrims. Though the nationality of the submarine was not mentioned in the official communiqué,[1] no Greek was in doubt about it, and Greek opinion reacted accordingly.

Suddenly, on August 23rd, the Press campaign against Greece stopped as abruptly as it had started. Why this switch-over from clamour to silence? Puzzling to observers at the time, its cause will emerge later.

In the next few weeks, the two stock accusations—of rendering help to Britain and of persecuting Albanians—reappeared sporadically, but were given far less prominence than before. Suddenly again, on October 14th, without any fresh incident having occurred and for no reason connected with the Greek situation, Mussolini fixed the date for the attack and convened for the next day the meeting which was to decide upon the plan of campaign[2]—the meeting described by Mussolini in this book.

Mussolini's Account of the Meeting

The official minutes of the meeting have recently come to light.[3] Their comparison with Mussolini's version reveals his method of treating documentary evidence.

[1] Orders had been issued to the Press Censors forbidding all mention of the submarine's nationality; see *The Greek White Book*, Document 130.

[2] Galeazzo CIANO, *Diary*, entry for 14.10.1940 (see below, List of Sources, B 5 & 6).

[3] Published in "Il Tempo," Rome 13.7.1944; see below, List of Sources, B 17. The official account bears the following subscription: "The present verbal report has been approved by the Duce at Palazzo Venezia on October 16th, 1940–XVIII at 14.00—The Secretary, Lt.-Col., attached to the Supreme Defence Committee (sgd.), Trombetti." Copies of the report were ordered to be sent to: "(i) His Majesty the King-Emperor; (ii) The Duce; (iii) The Minister for Foreign Affairs; (iv) The Chief of General Staff; (v) The Chief of Army Staff; (vi) The Chief of Naval Staff; (vii) The Chief of Air Staff; (viii) The Lieutenant-General of Albania."

The document, marked "Secret," is headed as follows: "Verbatim report of the meeting held in the study of the Duce at the Palazzo Venezia on October 15th, 1940—XVIII at 11 o'clock. (Stenographic account)."

(1) The text begins with Mussolini's opening speech:

DUCE: "The object of this meeting is to lay down in broad outline the procedure to be followed in the attack I have decided to launch against Greece.

"This attack will have, first of all, to aim at both sea and land objectives.

"Our land objectives must be designed to give us possession of the whole South Albanian coastline. They are, therefore, the occupation of the Greek islands of Zante, Cephalonia and Corfu; and the capture of Salonika.

"When we have reached these objectives, we shall have improved our position in the Mediterranean with regard to England.

"Either simultaneously or later, Greece must be occupied completely so as to get her out of the fighting and ensure that, whatever happens, she remains within our political and economic orbit.

"Having thus defined the problem, I have also settled the date which, in my opinion, should not be postponed even for an hour—namely, the 26th of this month.

"This is an operation I have been planning for a long time, for months and months, before we came into the war—before the conflict began, even.[1]

"Having settled these essential points, we must now consider how to put this operation into effect. I have therefore sent for the Lieutenant-General of Albania and for the Commander of our Army to give us a picture of the political and military situation, so that we may decide on all the measures needed to attain our ends in the best way and in the shortest possible time.

[1]Signor GRAZZI, *loc. cit.*, calls this statement a lie, on the grounds that in September 1939 Mussolini had disclaimed any aggressive intention against Greece and was even willing to sell Metaxas aeroplanes and weapons. This, however, in no way disproves the truth of Mussolini's admission. His policy, in theory determined by cold 'Machiavellian' calculation, was in fact time and again dictated by momentary emotions. Hence its inconsistency, to the point of self-contradiction.

"I should add that I foresee no trouble from the North. Yugoslavia has every interest in keeping quiet, as may incidentally be seen from public declarations from official sources, which rule out the possibility of complications arising except where the defence of the country is concerned.

"As to Turkish complications, I should discount them, especially now that Germany has planted herself in Roumania, and Bulgaria has strengthened her position. The latter might be a pawn in the game, and I shall take the necessary steps to see that she does not lose this unique opportunity of realizing her claims to Macedonia and an outlet to the sea.

"Having fixed our objectives and the date, we must now look at the other aspects of the situation, so as to decide, on the basis of these, the measures to be taken and the means of carrying them out."

In the summary of this speech which Mussolini gives in his own version, he asserts that he began by "calling to mind the Greek provocations to Italy." There is no mention of this in the verbatim account. To use this pretext would have been waste of time. All of those present, whether military or civilians, knew its futility. Besides, none of them required an excuse, when it was a case of attacking a weaker opponent.

On the other hand, references to Mussolini's aims, then clearly stated, are now passed over in silence. Nor does he mention that he had contemplated some such action long ago, even before the outbreak of the European war.

(2) Jacomoni's answer has also been tampered with. After having remarked that the Greeks "now appear determined to oppose our operations," the King's Lieutenant-General in Albania added this reassuring observation: "The clandestine radio station, which we have installed in Argyrocastro, was to carry out a vigorous propaganda campaign. It is much listened to; we know that good results are obtained."

About this station, the Greek Vice-Consul at Argyrocastro reported on September 18th to Athens: "Two days ago a new radio station was inaugurated here. It broadcasts a programme of Greek music, news bulletins and propaganda in Greek. The latter is addressed to the Greek people and it attacks H.M. the King and the Greek Government."

(3) In his estimate of Greek morale, General Visconti Prasca had characterized the Greek soldiers as "not the sort of people

to enjoy fighting." After this comforting statement, Mussolini raised another point, which, though suitable for his audience at Palazzo Venezia, he took good care to conceal from his readers :

DUCE : "Now there is still another thing. Now the date has been settled, the question is, how to make this action appear necessitated by events. We have a general justification in the fact that Greece is an ally of our enemies, who use her bases, etc.; but there ought to be an 'incident' to enable us to say we are coming in to keep order. If you can provoke this incident, well and good—if not, it doesn't matter."

JACOMONI : "I could manage something on the frontier—incidents between the Tsameri[1] and the Greek authorities."

VISCONTI PRASCA : "We have already got French weapons and bombs ready for a feint attack."

DUCE : "All that does not matter to me in the slightest ; the thing is to provide a little smoke. However, it would be a good thing for you to furnish a pretext for us to touch off the fuse."

CIANO : "When do you want the incident to occur ?"

DUCE : "On the 24th."

CIANO : "An incident will occur on the 24th."

DUCE : "No one will believe in this coincidence, but by way of metaphysical justification one might say that matters were bound to come to a head.

"What you need in operations of this kind is to act with the maximum resolution, for that is the secret of success, with regard, also, to any outside help.

"Now we must provide an alibi in such a way that people will be able to say, 'There is nothing to be done. What is the use of going to the help of people who have been defeated already ?' That is an argument which the Turks might well use, and which even the English might find it convenient to invoke."

It will be seen that the incidents here demanded were duly created.

(4) Marshal Badoglio suggested a modification of the plan of campaign : If the attack on Greece could be made to coincide with Graziani's attack on Mersa Matruh, it would be difficult

[1] An Albanian tribe on the Greek side of the pre-war frontier ; see above, p. 266.

for the British Command to divert aircraft from Egypt to Greece. Graziani, too, he asserted, would be ready by the 26th.[1]

At this point Mussolini interrupted with the following statement:

DUCE: "I should be in favour of advancing Graziani's attack by a few days. Then the conquest of Mersa Matruh would make the possibility of such help still more remote, especially in view of the fact that we shall not stop there. Once the corner-stone of Egypt has been lost, the British Empire will fall to pieces, even if London can still hold out. India is in a state of unrest, and the English could no longer get help from South Africa or by the Red Sea lifeline.

"There is a consideration of morale to be added, to the effect that a success in Africa would give a fillip to our men in Albania. For this reason, too, I should like operations to be synchronized, the African slightly preceding the other."

Writing in 1944, Mussolini did not think his reference to the destruction of the British Empire altogether appropriate. It is, therefore, omitted from his 'verbal account.'

(5) Marshal Badoglio, in summing up his appreciation of the plan of campaign, pointed out the necessity of occupying, not only a part, but the whole of Greece. Mussolini left out the end of his statement:

BADOGLIO: "To do this we need about twenty divisions, while in fact we have nine in Albania, plus a cavalry division. It is obvious that in the circumstances we shall need three months."

The reason which had prompted Mussolini to include the account of the meeting at the Palazzo Venezia in his book was to show that Badoglio had been in favour of the war with Greece. By omitting Badoglio's statement that twenty divisions were needed instead of the available ten, he tries to create the impression that Badoglio had also agreed to the plan of campaign then decided upon. In fact, it is confirmed from other evidence that

[1] Graziani later accused Badoglio of having grossly misrepresented the facts. According to his own version, Graziani had declined to commit himself to the attack before clearly assessing the chances of its success. Independent evidence shows, in fact, that he had given repeated warnings against the disastrous consequences of a premature attack. At the beginning of October, he insisted, in spite of great pressure from Mussolini, that two more months' preparation were needed. (And even then, far from being ready to strike against Egypt, he was, after weeks of waiting, decisively routed in Wavell's December offensive.) Whatever his faults in other respects, in this case he seems justified in complaining of Badoglio's misstatement. Cp. CIANO, *Diary*, entries for 3.5; 2.-20.8.; 9.9.; 2.-16.10., 1940.

Badoglio viewed it with considerable pessimism. Yet, whatever misgivings Badoglio may have felt, it cannot be said that they were strongly expressed at the decisive meeting. Rather, as Chief of the General Staff, he explicitly approved of Visconti Prasca's plan of operation in Epirus. He emphasized, it is true, that the plan of campaign had to be widened and that for the occupation of the whole country more troops and more time were required. As far as the attack itself was concerned, he raised no objection.

Shortly after the meeting, on October 17th, he spoke "very seriously" to Ciano about the projected action. The next day he declared to the Under-Secretary for War that, in the event of a move against Greece, he would resign. However, as Ciano remarked on that day, "Mussolini is planning to move at any price, and if Badoglio presents his resignation, it will be accepted immediately. But Badoglio not only does not present it, he does not even repeat to Mussolini what he told me."

When, after the failure of the attack, Badoglio resigned his command he was, shortly afterwards, vehemently taken to task by the uncontrollable Farinacci, for spreading " in drawing-rooms, on the hunting field, and in the circles of his protégés" that he had not favoured the Greek operation and that he had, in any case, demanded more troops. Badoglio replied with no less feeling, castigating amateurish interference with the decisions of the High Command and criticizing, by implication, Italy's unpreparedness for modern war.[1] It would be misleading, however, to infer from this that the Marshal had, in principle, been opposed to Fascism and its ways. Only a short while before, immediately prior to Italy's entry into the war, he had declared when prefacing a book on the Armed Forces of Fascist Italy[2]: "In the present work, particular stress has rightly been laid on the achievements of Fascism with regard to the military striking power of the nation. The idea of the *fascio*, grandiose in its simplicity, could not fail to radiate its light in the military

[1] Badoglio's resignation as Chief of the General Staff was announced on 6.12.1940. Farinacci's attack appeared in "Regime Fascista," Cremona, 12.12.1940. Badoglio's reply (said to have been published in an immediately confiscated issue of the Rome "Tribuna," 23.12.) was in March 1941 broadcast by Athens Radio. Several copies were circulated in Rome; extracts are given in R. & E. PACKARD, *Balcony Empire*, London, 1943, pp. 120 ff.

[2] *Le Forze Armate dell' Italia Fascista* ed. Tomaso Sillani. *Prefazione del Maresciallo d'Italia Pietro Badoglio, Capo di S.M.*, sec., revised ed., Rassegna Italiana, Rome, 1940, p. VII f.

field and to bestow on it that inflexible energy which it irresistibly releases . . . Side by side with the Armed Forces, through the formations and institutions of the Régime, the entire nation prepares itself militarily, growing with the Armed Forces into one single formidable fighting body."

Serving the Duce and the Fascist cause as long as success was on their side, he withdrew and turned against them once their fortune declined.

(6) A last omission occurs at the end of Mussolini's account. The meeting was concluded as follows:

DUCE: "To sum up: An offensive in Epirus; a watch and pressure on Salonika; and, at the next stage, the march on Athens."

It would be difficult to find a parallel, in the history of modern warfare, to this plan of campaign. Whether it was "the excessive eagerness of the Italian troops to go forward and fight" or the "enthusiasm of the Albanians" or the indifference of the mass of the Greek population or Marshal Graziani's readiness to strike against Egypt—all the relevant factors forming the basis of the plan were misrepresented. As to the number, strength and morale of the enemy's fighting forces, none of the military chiefs present thought it worth while to refer to the reliable estimates given them by their Military Attaché in Athens[1]; and without demur they accepted the Duce's advice "not to worry unduly about possible losses." The cynicism of the political leadership was well matched by the feckless subservience of the High Command.

The Staging of the Attack

The start of operations, irrevocably planned for October 26th, had for lack of preparations to be postponed for another two days. Its *mise en scène* shows a mixture, in poor taste, of the tragic with the burlesque.

[1] At the beginning of October the Italian Minister had signalled that the Greeks had 250,000 men under arms, a large part of whom were deployed along the frontier. A few days later, the Military Attaché, Colonel Mondini, indicated that 16 divisions were fully mobilised. (See Signor Grazzi's well-documented account, *loc. cit.*, 22.8.1945.) Yet neither the Chief of the General Staff, Marshal Badoglio, nor any other military leader contradicted Visconti Prasca's repeated assertion that the enemy forces amounted only to 30,000 men. Nor did they take any action when, in the days preceding the attack, the Military Attaché announced a further increase both of the Greek forces as a whole, and of the number of divisions deployed along the frontier.

The newly reconstructed Athens State Theatre was to open, on October 25th, with a performance of "Madame Butterfly." The Greek Government had, as a friendly gesture, invited the son and daughter-in-law of the composer to attend the performance; the offer had been officially accepted by the Italian Ministry for Popular Culture, who arranged the visit of Signor and Signora Puccini. The gala performance, designed as a tribute to Italian art, and attended by the King, members of the Government and the whole of Athens society, was followed the next evening by a big reception at the Italian Legation. While Signor Grazzi, the Minister, was receiving his guests, telegrams containing parts of the Italian ultimatum—which Ciano had begun drafting four days before—started coming in. At the same time the Greek Government learned that the Italian Air Ministry had ordered the suspension of the air service between Athens and Rome. It also heard of two Stefani communiqués announcing two grave incidents: armed Greek bands had attacked Albanian frontier posts with guns and hand-grenades, and bombs had been hurled at the office of the Italian harbourmaster at Porto Edda in Albania, the perpetrators being Greek or British agents.

The reception, however, took its course until the early hours of the 27th, with secretaries rushing in and out to decipher further parts of the Italian note. During the day, the official Greek Agency refuted both stories, proposing an inquiry into the incidents. No reply came. Instead, at 3 o'clock on the morning of the 28th, the Italian envoy called on Metaxas to hand him the Italian ultimatum. It repeated the old charges against Greece of systematic violation of her own neutrality—her help to Britain and "her provocative attitude to the Albanian nation by her policy of terrorism"—and ended:

"Italy is unable to tolerate any further such conduct. Greece's neutrality from today has tended to become purely nominal. The main responsibility for this state of things falls on Great Britain and her persistent endeavour to draw other countries into the war.

"To the Italian Government it is patent that the policy of the Hellenic Government has tended and is tending to convert Greek territory—or at least to permit Greek territory to be converted—into a base for warlike activities directed against Italy. This was inevitably bound to lead to an armed conflict between Italy and Greece, a conflict which the Italian Government have every desire to avoid.

"The Italian Government have therefore decided to demand from the Hellenic Government as a guarantee alike of the neutrality of Greece and the security of Italy, the right to occupy with her armed forces, for the duration of the present conflict with Great Britain, a number of strategic points in Greek territory. The Italian Government demand that the Hellenic Government shall not oppose any resistance to this occupation nor impede the free passage of the forces destined for this purpose. The forces in question do not come as enemies of the Greek people, nor have the Italian Government, in proceeding to this temporary occupation of certain strategic points—an occupation rendered necessary by the circumstances and of a purely defensive character—the least intention of prejudicing the sovereignty and the independence of Greece.

"The Italian Government demand that the Hellenic Government instantly issue the necessary orders to the military authorities, so that the occupation may be carried out peacefully. Should the Italian forces meet with resistance, the resistance will be crushed by force of arms, and in that case the Hellenic Government will bear the responsibility for whatever may ensue."

When asked by Metaxas which strategic points Italy demanded to occupy, the Italian Minister was unable to reply. His masters had taken care to word the ultimatum so as to exclude any possibility of acceptance. As Ciano noted, frankly and cynically, "Naturally it is a document that allows no way out for Greece. Either she accepts occupation or she will be attacked." At 5.30, before the three hours' time-limit for the answer had expired, Italian troops began to attack.[1]

The Failure

The quick "March on Athens" which was to start on this anniversary of the March on Rome soon became a retrograde movement, of increasing rapidity, into Albania. Those troops which had advanced some way into Epirus fared even worse. The Armoured Centauro Division ran into a well-prepared trap, and the Third Alpini was decisively routed in the gorges of the Pindus.

The valour displayed in these actions by the Greek Fighting Forces is too well known to need any comment. Another, less

[1] See E. Grazzi, *loc. cit.*, 25–26.8.1945 ; Galeazzo Ciano, *Diary*, entries for 22. and 27.10.1940 ; *The Greek White Book*, Documents 171–178.

obvious, factor should not be forgotten. The Greeks were not caught unprepared. The high quality of their Diplomatic Service in the period preceding the war can hardly be exaggerated ; the despatches of their representatives abroad, from the skilful précis of their Minister in Rome down to timely messages from Vice-Consuls in obscure provincial towns, are models of accurate reporting of significant events.[1] And the information they conveyed was listened to and put to good use by their Government.

When it could no longer be concealed that things had gone wrong, Mussolini made, on November 18th, one of his public pronouncements :

"After long and patient waiting, we have torn the mask from a country guaranteed by Great Britain, a perfidious enemy, Greece. It was an account which demanded settlement. One thing has to be said, and it will perhaps surprise certain out-of-date classical scholars. The Greeks hate Italy with a hatred which seems inexplicable at first sight ; but it is general, profound and incurable, in all classes, in the cities, in the villages, everywhere. The reason why is a mystery. Nevertheless, the fact remains. To this hatred, which can be described as absolutely grotesque, Greek policy adapted herself during recent years. It was a policy of absolute complicity with Great Britain. . . . This complicity, shown in many ways which will be irrefutably proved in due course, was a continuous act of hostility against Italy. From maps discovered by the German General Staff in France, it has been established that as early as May, Greece had offered to the English and French all her naval and air bases. It was imperative to put an end to this situation ; and that was done on October 28th, when our troops crossed the frontier between Greece and Albania."

The tale of captured documents, adopted from familiar German propaganda technique, is aptly characterised as not worth a refutation by a man well qualified to judge—the late Italian Minister to Athens. In his recent account this diplomat leaves no doubt that all the allegations of Greek breaches of

[1] See e.g. *The Greek White Book*, Documents 161 ; 163 ; 165–171. After the failure of the attack, it was whispered in Rome that large sums had been spent on bribing Greek generals who, accepting the money, transmitted it to Metaxas for the Greek war chest. A good story which, however, through the memoirs of American correspondents, threatens to be accepted as historical fact. In reality, there was hardly any attempt to bribe any highly placed Greek military leader ; see Sgr. Grazzi's account, *loc. cit.*

neutrality, contained in the ultimatum he had to present in such dramatic circumstances, were but shameless lies.[1]

Mussolini continued:

"The rugged mountains of Epirus and its muddy valleys do not lend themselves to a lightning war, as the incorrigible experts of a comfortable armchair strategy would suggest. No deed or word by myself, or the Government, or any other responsible quarter suggested a lightning war. . . . .

"Comrades, there are some among you who remember the unpublished speech I made in July 1935, before the Abyssinian War. I said that we would break the back of the Negus. Now, with the same absolute, I repeat absolute, certitude, we shall break the back of the Greeks, whether in two or twelve months makes little difference."

But the further course of the campaign, with the many mishaps it brought to Italian arms, proved that the situation could not be retrieved without German intervention.

Hitler, Mussolini and the Greek War

How had the Germans viewed the whole episode? It has been maintained, from authoritative Greek quarters[2], that the Italian attack tallied with German interests, and was, therefore, launched with German approval. However, in the light of recently published documents[3] it is manifest that the contrary was the case. Mussolini's intimations in July of a move against the Ionian Islands had not met with an encouraging response from Berlin. When, in the following month, the Fascist campaign on the murder of the 'great Albanian patriot' and the torpedoing of the cruiser *Helle* made it obvious that Mussolini was determined on going ahead with his projects, he was informed in no uncertain terms that Hitler was opposed to any action against Greece. As a result of this strong intervention, the Press campaign on Greek atrocities was immediately toned down and came, a few days later, to a sudden stop.

To leave no doubt on the subject, the German Government shortly afterwards emphasized once more to their ally that peace

[1] E. GRAZZI, *loc. cit.*, 4. and 14.8.1945.

[2] General METAXAS, Memorandum of 15.1.1941, in *The Greek White Book*, p. 17; Emmanuel TSOUDEROS, Prime Minister, *ibid.*, Preface, pp. 9–13.

[3] See below, List of Sources, B (1)–(6).

in South-Eastern Europe should on no account be disturbed.[1] To avoid a conflagration in the Balkans was, at that time, one of the main objects of Hitler's policy. With the Vienna arbitration between Hungary and Roumania, on August 28th–30th, he hoped to eliminate any danger of conflict on the Northern fringe; his formal representations to Rome were to prevent his Axis partner from embarking on an adventure which might lead to complications in the South.

Mussolini was well aware of this and, on the eve of the Vienna negotiations, hastened to assure Hitler that the measures he had taken on the borders of Greece and Yugoslavia were merely in the nature of a safeguard against possible hostile acts on the part of these countries. He acknowledged his agreement with Hitler to preserve peace in the Balkans as binding upon him; Italy would make no military move in that direction.

At the next meeting of the two leaders, at the Brenner on October 4th, Hitler had shown himself strongly anti-Russian and had, moreover, been more ready than before to acknowledge the great importance of the Mediterranean Theatre. Full agreement on all issues was maintained. Never had the Führer seemed so frank, and Mussolini left in a mood of high satisfaction.[2] Rarely had a greater harmony been achieved between the two dictators.

Less than a week later, on October 10th, the Germans marched into Roumania. This unexpected move filled Mussolini with rage. Hitler's method of staging all his *coups* without ever taking him into his confidence had long rankled. Now resentment came to a head. It would be his turn next, he vowed, to present Hitler with a *fait accompli*. "Next time, Hitler will learn from the papers that I have attacked Greece."[3] And thus the attack on Greece was decided upon.

[1] Galeazzo CIANO, *Diary*, entries for 17, 22, 26, 28.8.1940.

[2] *ibid.*, entry for 4.10.1940.

[3] *ibid.*, entry for 12.10.1940. Porfirio, *Il Diario di Ciano*, "Risorgimento Liberale," Rome, 22.7.1944. For the German habit of keeping the Italians in the dark, see Ciano's speech at the meeting of the Fascist Grand Council, 25.7.1943 (in *La Fine del Fascismo* [see below, List of Sources, A 34] p. 12): "It is now evident from the documents that, while we were signing the Alliance with Germany on this implicit undertaking on Hitler's part (*i.e.* not to raise issues which would provoke a war), the German General Staff had already fixed the date of the attack against Poland. We were in no way forewarned or consulted. . . The Germans prematurely set fire to the powder cask, in defiance of every pact and understanding with us. And they did not give up this method during the course of the war. All the attacks which followed that on Poland were likewise communicated to us at the last minute:

In August, Mussolini would still have been content with some such gain as Corfu and the border region of Tsamuria. Now, in revenge for Roumania, nothing less than the whole country would satisfy him.

Eager to spring a surprise on Hitler, Mussolini saw to it that no time was lost. It now becomes clear why, suddenly, on October 14th, without any fresh factor in the Greek situation having arisen, the date for the attack was fixed and the 'historic meeting' convened.

The unexpectedness of this decision is confirmed by several independent witnesses, well placed to judge, of whom two may be quoted. Only a few days before, the then Chief of Army Staff, Marshal Graziani, had been to Rome, from his African Command, to report on the situation. No plan for an attack on Greece was discussed. "Thus, on October 5th, I left Rome, without having been informed, as Commander-in-Chief of the Army, of what was afoot."[1] He could account for this silence only by assuming a conspiracy of his rivals, Badoglio and Roatta. In fact, they knew no more than himself; for nothing had been "afoot" against Greece before the Duce's impulse of the 14th.

The Italian Minister in Athens, on his part, was left with the impression, after the Press campaign of August had suddenly died down, that normal relations had been restored. Since in the following weeks no new issue was raised, he congratulated himself on the improved situation, convinced that, from any rational point of view, the danger of war was now, at this advanced season, far removed. Not until October 23rd, and then only by chance, did he learn to his bewilderment and dismay that the attack was imminent.[2]

A few days before the start of the attack, Mussolini felt some scruples about concealing from Hitler his intention to act against their agreement. On the other hand, he feared lest a renewed veto might spoil his game. To satisfy his scruples without having

that on Belgium and France, which Mackensen, German Ambassador in Rome, with whom I had been until past midnight, announced to me at four in the morning, actually at the very moment when German troops were crossing the frontiers, and that on Russia, announced to me in the same manner by Prince Bismarck."

[1] He asserts that he learned of the attack only over his wireless at Cyrene. If this is true, it would be a further striking sign of the haste with which the operation was planned. (Marshal Rodolfo GRAZIANI, letter to the Editor of "Vita Italiana," March 1945, quoted in Fascist papers and broadcasts of the time.)

[2] E. GRAZZI, *loc. cit.*, 21.8.1945.

to renounce the projected surprise, he hit upon the expedient of sending Hitler—who was then on his way to meetings with General Franco and Marshal Pétain—a letter intimating the move he planned. Written on October 22nd, the letter was ante-dated the 19th; and care was taken that it should not reach Hitler in time.[1]

In fact, only on October 28th, when Hitler arrived in Florence to meet Mussolini, did he learn that the attack had started that very day. Mussolini had gained his point.

Hitler, concealing his annoyance, raised no objections. A few weeks later, however, when the failure of the campaign had become apparent, he sent Mussolini in the guise of a solemn epistle of condolence a crushing indictment of his action. He had gone to Florence, he now revealed, to discuss the Greek situation, to make the Duce postpone the attack and to work out a plan of campaign, which, if executed at a later stage, would, with German help, ensure rapid success. Not to spare him any humiliation, he mercilessly and almost with relish enlarged, by contrast, on the grave dangers—psychological and strategic—which the unsuccessful *coup* against Greece had provoked; dangers which might well affect the outcome of the war as a whole.

Mussolini immediately replied, in the meek manner of a schoolboy who knows he has done wrong but seeks to evade responsibility by shifting the blame on forces beyond his control. He did not forget to express his regret that his letter of October 19th had not reached Hitler in time for the latter to give his advice, which would, as always, have been followed.[2]

This exchange of letters marks a turning point in the relationship between the two Axis chiefs. Mussolini who, conscious of his status as 'senior dictator,' had previously, before Italy's entry into the war, felt able, from time to time, to volunteer some guidance,[3] was henceforth relegated, once and for all, to the degrading position of a subordinate.

[1] The ante-dating of the letter becomes evident from a comparison of its text with Ciano's diary, entry for October 22nd, 1940. The delay in the transmission is pointed out in the commentary given in "Libera Stampa," Rome, 9.10.45. See below, List of Sources, B 1.

[2] The text of Hitler's letter of 20.11. and Mussolini's reply of 22.11. is printed in "Libera Stampa," Rome, 9. and 11–12.10.1945. See also List of Sources, B 1.

[3] A characteristic remark is noted by CIANO, *Diary*, entry for 17.1.1940: "They (the Germans) should allow themselves to be guided by me if they do

From now on, in Hitler's eyes Mussolini was branded with a serious defect : lack of success. His action might be condoned ; his failure could not be forgiven. Hitler had no illusions about the effect which this check to Axis arms would have on all those rulers who would join his side only when victory was assured. And he had no doubt of how the disturbance of the equilibrium in the Balkans would affect Russia. His plans in that direction, then maturing, had been gravely perturbed, and his much cherished Spanish project had been completely upset. The picked paratroop divisions trained for the purpose of storming Gibraltar had to be used for other tasks, and the design to close the Mediterranean, fundamental to Hitler's strategy, had to be abandoned.

His resentment never subsided. Years afterwards, at the end of December 1944, when Allied armies were fighting on German soil, he sent Mussolini this bitter message, in reply to a letter of congratulation[1] :

". . . . It is not my wish now, Duce, to look back and to examine all the possibilities which, in one case or another, might have brought an improvement in the military situation ; but let me add the following explanation of my conduct :

"In 1940 and in January 1941 I had decided, Duce, to close the Western outlet to the Mediterranean. My meeting with the Head of the Spanish State was calculated to bring about this end, and the agreement reached could have been put into effect. Then, unexpectedly and with many misgivings, I received the news that Italy intended to declare war on Greece. This was the reason for my sudden visit to Florence on October 28th, 1940.

"The ill-omened opening of that campaign encouraged the English to launch a successful offensive in Libya and, for the first time, made Franco hesitate.[2] All subsequent efforts to induce

not want to pull unpardonable boners. In politics it is undeniable that I am more intelligent than Hitler." A year later, 16.1.1941, Ciano writes: "Mussolini is concerned about his trip to Germany. He feels that he will meet Hitler under conditions of obvious inferiority."

[1] The German original of the letter and an Italian translation were among the documents which Mussolini carried at the time of his capture by the partisans. The translation was published by the Milan paper, "L'Unità," on 25.4.1945. It may well be that in a few places the Italian translation did not adequately render Hitler's involved sentences. However, until the original is available, it is our only source for this important document.

[2] The Italian text reads: . . . "encouraged the English . . . *to make* Franco hesitate . . ." which is obviously faulty.

the Spaniards to enter the field none the less, proved futile. . . . The spring of 1941 provided the last chance of putting pressure on Spain, but that could only have succeeded if German and Italian policy had been in perfect harmony, and above all, if there had been a supreme common effort.

" In spite of that, I wished to take up a position before Gibraltar in January 1941 ; and I have no doubt whatever that the *coup* would have succeeded thanks to the enormous numerical superiority we then possessed in men and materials, armaments and air strength, and also in view of the excellent condition and equipment of our troops. In 1943, Duce, we were aware, without being able to point to details, of the treason being hatched by your enemies in Italy. In addition to this there were the heavy counter-strokes in the East, the loss of an Army at Stalingrad, the loss of all our allies on the Eastern Front and the catastrophe in North Africa, necessitating the continuous creation of new armies, in order, for example, on the Eastern Front alone, to close a breach of over 700 kms. Moreover, defence in the West had to be seriously considered and for that purpose still more divisions to be formed. Finally, our positions in the Balkans, where the hostility of many of the Italian authorities was by then beyond doubt, caused serious concern. We were thus obliged to take precautionary measures with our forces, to face up to the possibility of a betrayal in Rome. After mature examination of all the military Commands, whose conclusions I was obliged to share, it seemed clear that a move against Spain at that time would have, to say the least of it, extremely uncertain results.

"At that time the question of whether Franco would have offered any resistance or not was no longer of decisive importance. Instead, the crucial problem was whether we, without any positive help from Spain, would have been in a position to occupy, and to guarantee the military security of, so vast a territory in addition to facing a still graver threat to the German positions on the Atlantic coast, and especially in Belgium and Holland. That England already planned to effect landings is proved by the Dieppe attempt. I am therefore convinced that, though the occupation of the English positions at the entrance to the Mediterranean was possible in the spring of 1941 even without the concurrence of Spain, in 1943 it could no longer succeed without her active participation. But unfortunately in the first instance it was not possible to obtain Italy's full support, while in the second the plan could not be carried out for lack of forces.

"If in 1941 Italy, instead of attacking Greece had together with Germany resolved the Spanish problem, the development of the war might have taken a different course.[1] . . . ."

The true effect of Mussolini's *coup* may now be gauged. It compelled Hitler to march on Athens and to land in Crete, instead of investing Gibraltar, and thus decisively shaped the course of events. How the Yugoslav and Greek campaigns affected the outcome of the first year of war in Russia has long since been noted by Allied and neutral observers.[2] The importance of Mussolini's action is thus admitted by both sides. Unaccountable in terms of any generalizing doctrine of history, his fateful move appears as the result of the tension between two men ; a tension which led an ambitious gambler suddenly to throw away all caution, in his desire to assert himself before a fanatical and far more powerful rival.

[1] This passage was twice underlined by Mussolini.

[2] See e.g. Mr. Eden's statement to the House of Commons, 8.1.1942, pointing out that the Greek campaign, prolonged by the British decision to transfer troops from the African theatre to Greece, delayed the German attack against Russia for six vital weeks. Neutral critics are quoted in *The Greek White Book*, p. 15 f. [The fact has recently been confirmed to the Editor by several German participants in the Russian campaign, who were well placed to judge.]

II

NOTE ON THE GRAND COUNCIL MEETING OF JULY 25TH, 1943

The following voted:

For Grandi's motion:	Grandi, Acerbo, Albini, Alfieri, Balella, Bastianini, Bignardi, Bottai, Cianetti, Ciano, De Bono, De Marsico, De Stefani, De Vecchi, Federzoni, Gottardi, Marinelli, Pareschi, Rossoni (19 votes).
Against Grandi's motion:	Biggini, Buffarini, Frattari, Galbiati, Polverelli, Scorza, Tringali-Casanuova (7 votes).
Abstention:	Suardo.
For Farinacci's motion:	Farinacci.
Scorza's motion:	Withdrawn.

THE SEQUEL AT VERONA

On January 8th–10th, 1944, the nineteen members of the Fascist Grand Council who had voted for Grandi's motion were tried for high treason by the 'Special Extraordinary Tribunal' of Mussolini's German-controlled 'Italian Social Republic' at Verona. Of the nineteen accused, six only were present, the others being tried *in absentia.*

Only one of the accused, Cianetti—one of those present—was granted extenuating circumstances, for having recanted immediately after the vote, and condemned to thirty years' imprisonment. The other eighteen were all condemned to death.

On January 11th, the day after the announcement of the sentence, Ciano, De Bono, Gottardi, Marinelli and Pareschi were executed near Verona Prison.

Cianetti was released soon afterwards.

Of the remaining thirteen, Grandi found his way to Portugal soon after the *coup d'état,* when he saw that his hope to play a part in the new Government was thwarted. Acerbo was arrested by the Bonomi Government, and, in May, 1945, condemned by the High Court of Justice to thirty years' imprisonment. Alfieri and Bastianini eventually found refuge in Switzerland. De Vecchi is reported to have become a monk. Bottai, Federzoni and Rossoni were, in their absence, condemned by the Italian High Court of Justice (under the Bonomi Government) to lifelong imprisonment and are still in hiding. [While this book was in print, Bottai, one of the intellectual leaders of Fascism, was able to return to Italy a free man, enjoying the publicity of a journalistic welcome.]

III

SELECT LIST OF SOURCES

In the short time that has elapsed since the fall of Mussolini, numerous publications have appeared, purporting to tell the inside story of the last meeting of the Fascist Grand Council and of events leading up to the Armistice, the flight of the King and the Marshal's Government, and the surrender of Rome to the Germans. Nearly all these accounts are inspired by a tendency to indict one, and to exonerate another, of the principal actors concerned. While one would thus look in vain for objective treatment in records tinged with the passions of political strife and personal feuds, they have, through their nearness to events, a certain value. If such narratives are often of little use in determining the facts, by their very bias they throw light on the nature of the parties whose interests they are designed to serve. They, too, will therefore prove of help for any historical estimate of the *coup d'état* and of the leading figures concerned in the preparation and execution of an act which resulted in the sudden and complete breakdown of a dictatorship of twenty years' standing.

Furthermore, a certain number of documents relevant to events described in this book have lately come to light. They illustrate the circumstances of Italy's entry into the war ; Mussolini's increasing subservience to Hitler after the failure of his attack on Greece ; the various plots aimed at the Duce's overthrow once the desperate nature of the military situation had become manifest ; and, finally, the factors which caused the procrastination of the Armistice and its tragic effects. These documents have appeared scattered, mainly in the Italian press. Their publication in this ephemeral form has made it desirable to list those which have come to our notice.

The Editor wishes to thank the staff of the Press Archives of the Royal Institute for International Affairs, London, for their help in tracing newspaper publications.

A. NARRATIVES

(*a*) *General*

(1) Luigi PASTORE, *Crollo del Fascismo e invasione tedesca.* Tip. Consorzio Nazionale, Rome 1944. (Based on Badoglio's account.)

(2) Paolo MONELLI, *Roma 1943.* Migliaresi Ed., Rome 1945.

(3) Vitantonio NAPOLITANO, *25 Luglio.* Ed. Vega, Rome 1944.

(4) A. FAVOINO, *'22–'43.* Ed. Roma, Rome 1944.

(5) Filippo BOJANO, *In the Wake of the Goose-step.* Cassell, London 1944.

(6) "Comandante X dello Stato Maggiore," *La caduta del Fascismo e l'armistizio di Roma.* Azione letteraria Italiana, Rome 1944.

(7) G.M., *Dal 25 luglio al 10 settembre. Nuove testimonianze.* S.A.I.G., Rome 1944.

(8) Federico COMANDINI, *Breve storia di cinque mesi.* (Events from July 20th–December 20th, 1943.) Ed. Partito d'Azione, 1944.

(9) Agne HAMRIN, *Diktatorns Fall.* Bonniers, Stockholm 1944.

(10) Mario ROATTA, General. *Otto milioni di baionette.* Mondadori, Milan 1946.

(11) Giacomo ZANUSSI, General. *Guerra e catastrofe d'Italia.* Corso, Rome 1946.

(11*) Quirino ARMELLINI, General. *La crisi dell'Esercito.* Rome 1945.

(11**) M. CARACCIOLO DI FEROLETO, General, "*E poi?*" *La tragedia dell' esercito italiano.* Corso, Rome 1946.

(12) Carlo FAVAGROSSA, General, *Perché perdemmo la guerra. Mussolini e la produzione bellica.* Rizzoli, Milan 1946.

(13) Carmine SENISE, *Quando ero Capo della Polizia* 1940–43. Ruffoli, Rome 1946.

(13*) Curzio MALAPARTE, *Kaputt.* E. P. Dutton, New York 1946.

(14) Ivanoe BONOMI, *Diario di un anno.* Garzanti, 2nd ed., Milan 1947.

(15) "Iuvenalis," *Mussolini alla luce infrarossa.* Ed. Lazzaro, Rome 1944.

(16) Clara PETACCI, *Il mio diario.* Ed. Assoc., Milan 1947.

(17) Quinto NAVARRA, *Memorie del cameriere di Mussolini.* Longanesi, Milan 1946.

(18) [Edgardo SULIS], *Mussolini e il Fascismo.* Istituto Naz. per le relazioni cult. con l'Estero, Rome 1941. (With useful bibliography of Fascist publications).

(19) Francesco FLORA, *Ritratto di un ventennio.* (With a letter by B. CROCE). Macchiaroli, Naples 1944.

(20) Luigi SALVATORELLI, *Vent'anni fra due guerre.* Ed. Ital., 2nd ed., Rome 1946.

(21) Carlo SFORZA, *L'Italia dal* 1914 *al* 1944 *quale io la vidi*, Mondadori, Rome 1944.

(21*) Stefano JACINI, *Il regime fascista.* Garzanti, Milan 1947.

(22) Luigi SALVATORELLI, *Il Fascismo nella politica internazionale.* Guanda, Rome 1946.

(22*) Mario DONOSTI, *Mussolini e l'Europa. La politica estera fascista.* Leonardo, Rome 1945.

(23) Giacomo PERTICONE, *La politica italiana nell'ultimo trentennio.* Rome 1945.

(23*) Elizabeth WISKEMANN, *The Rome-Berlin Axis.* Oxford 1949.

(24) [Amedeo GIANNINI], *I rapporti italo-inglesi.* Ist. per gli Studi di Politica Internaz., Milan 1940.

(24*) Virginio GAYDA, *Italia e Inghilterra. L'inevitabile conflitto.* Rome 1941.

(24**) M. H. H. MACARTNEY, *One Man Alone.* Chatto & Windus, London 1944.

(25) Ulrich v. HASSELL, *Vom andern Deutschland.* Atlantis, Zurich 1946.

(25*) Leonardo SIMONI, *Berlino : Ambasciata d'Italia* (1939–1943). Migliaresi, Rome 1946.

(26) Luigi SALVATORELLI, *Casa Savoia nella storia d'Italia.* Cosmopolita, Rome 1945.

(26*) Ernesto ORREI, *La monarchia fascista.* Rome 1944.

(26**) Pietro SILVA, *Io difendo la Monarchia.* de Fonseca, 3rd ed., Rome 1946.

(27) Domenico BARTOLI, *Victor Emmanuel.* Sfelt, Paris 1946.

(*b*) *The months before and after Italy's entry into the war*

(28) Galeazzo CIANO, *L'Italia di fronte al conflitto.* (Speech of 16.12.1939.) Ist. per gli Studi di Politica Intern., 2nd ed., Milan 1940.

(29) Sumner WELLES, *The Time for Decision.* Hamilton, London 1944. (pp. 64–73 ; 108–118: Welles's conversations with Mussolini and Ciano in February and March 1940, in the course of his mission to Europe as President Roosevelt's personal representative.)

(30) [Sumner WELLES], "*Welles describes talks in Rome while on mission for Roosevelt.*" (Comment on Ciano's account of his Rome conversations.) "New York Herald Tribune," 11.7.1945.—See also below, B (10).

(31) André FRANCOIS-PONCET (French Ambassador to Rome, 1940), *Ciano et les derniers mois de l'avant-guerre.* In: "Le Figaro," Paris, 17.7.1945.

(32) "Dario," *L'Italia fu costretta a entrare in guerra?* (Contains report on conversation between Mussolini and King Victor Emmanuel on June 8th, 1940.) In: "Il Giornale del Mattino," Rome, 17.6.1945.

(33) UMBERTO, Prince of Piedmont, Interview with the correspondent of "The Times" (on his "Role in Italian Affairs" and the responsibility for Italy's war). In: "The Times," London, 20.4.1944; "Manchester Guardian," same date. Translated in "Gazzetta del Mezzogiorno," Naples, 12.5.1944.

(34) Benedetto CROCE, *L'intervista del principe di Piemonte.* In: *Per la nuova vita dell' Italia*, p. 74 f. Ed. Ricciardi, Naples 1944.

(34*) Badoglio Government, Declaration of 11.5.1944 against Prince Umberto's statement to "The Times." In: "The Times," London, 15.5.1944.

(35) Herbert L. MATTHEWS, *The Fruits of Fascism.* Harcourt, Brace and Co., New York 1943.

(36) John T. WHITAKER, *We Cannot Escape History.* Macmillan, New York 1943.

(36*) Richard J. MASSOCK, *Italy from Within.* Macmillan, London 1943.

(36**) Reynolds and Eleanor PACKARD, *Balcony Empire.* Chatto & Windus, London 1943.

(37) Camille CIANFARRA, *The Vatican and the War.* Lit. Affairs Inc., E. T. Dutton, New York 1944.

(*c*) *Activities of anti-Fascists*

In the absence of a comprehensive account cp., *e.g.*:

(38) *New Move to oust Mussolini.* Statement from anti-Fascist leaders in Rome, announced by Carlo SFORZA. In: "New York Times," 28.6.1942.

(38*) [Carlo SFORZA], *Sforza Predicts Revolt of Italians.* In: "New York Times," 3.7.1942.

(38**) Montevideo Declaration, August 1942, In: Carlo SFORZA, *La guerra totalitaria e la pace democratica.* Ed. Polis, Naples 1944.

(39) "Italian Socialist Party," *Manifesto: Call to Civil Disobedience.* In: "Manchester Guardian," 1.12.1942.

(39*) Articles in the clandestine "Italia Libera" and other clandestine papers, Spring–Summer 1943.

(39**) Articles (*Lettere dall'Italia*) in "Quaderni Italiani," vol. I ff., Boston, January 1942 ff.

(39***) *Quaderni di Giustizia e Libertà.* Published by the organization "Giustizia e Libertà" in Egypt and France, 1942–43.

(39****) The Manifesto of the Liberalsocialist Movement (1940) in: Guido CALOGERO, *Difesa del liberalsocialismo.* Atlantica, Rome 1945.

(40) Palmiro TOGLIATTI, *Per la salvezza del nostro paese.* (Collection of broadcasts from Moscow, 1941–43, and newspaper articles). Einaudi, Rome 1946.

(41) Guido MIGLIOLI, *Con Roma e con Mosca.* Garzanti, Cremona 1945.

(42) Benedetto CROCE, Political writings of February–June 1943 [circulated in typescript], published in *L'idea Liberale.* Laterza, Bari 1944; *Per la nuova vita dell'Italia*, pp. 87–97, Ricciardi, Naples 1944.

For the strikes of spring 1943 in Northern Italy see *e.g.*:

(43) Umberto MASSOLA, *Premesse e sviluppi degli scioperi di Marzo-Aprile 1943.* In "Risorgimento" (Monthly) I no. 1. Rome, April 1945.

(*d*) *Discontent within the Fascist Party*

(44) Dissatisfaction with the Party: reflected in articles in "Critica Fascista" (Fortnightly), ed. by Giuseppe BOTTAI, Rome 1942–43; and in the papers of the Guf (Fascist Student Groups), e.g. of Bologna.

(45) Dissatisfaction with the German "New Order": Francesco ORESTANO, *La vita religiosa nella nuova Europa.* In: "Gerarchia" (Monthly, founded by Mussolini), Milan, December 1942.

(*e*) *The various plots leading to the coup d'état*

(46) On Badoglio's part: Guido CASSINELLI, *Appunti sul 25 luglio 1943. Documenti di azione.* Ed. S.A.P.P.I., Rome 1944.

(47) On the Generals' plot: Marshal Ugo CAVALLERO, *Memoriale*, written at Fort Boccea, 27.8.1943. Broadcast by Rome Radio, 11.1.1944. Published in "Comandante X" [see above, A (6)], pp. 42–45; "Giornale di Sicilia," Palermo, 4–5.10.1945; "Avanti," Rome, 9–11.10.1945.

(48) On the part of the Court: Duke Pietro ACQUARONE, ex-Minister of the Royal Household, Defence before the High Court of Justice (Purge Commission), in: "Il Tempo," Rome, 13.11.1945—*Das ital. Königshaus und der Sturz Mussolinis*, in: "Neue Zürcher Zeitung," 15.2.1946.

(49) On the Fascist plot: the accounts of CIANO, DE BONO, CIANETTI, ALFIERI, FARINACCI and other members of the Fascist Grand Council, below, B (26), Acts of the Verona trial—Colonello TRAVI, *Agonia di un regime.* In: "L'Italia Libera," Rome, 17.2.–25.2.1946.

(50) Grandi's version: George KENT, *The Last Days of Dictator Benito Mussolini.* ("Story . . . obtained from Dino GRANDI and from other members of the Grand-Council") in: "Reader's Digest," November 1944, pp. 19–23.

(50*) [Dino GRANDI], *Dino Grandi Explains.* In: "Life," Philadelphia, vol. 18 no. 9, 26.2.1945; "Daily Express," London, 19–23.2.1945.

(51) Lorenzo BARBARO, *Come si giunse al "25 luglio."* In: "Risorgimento Liberale," Rome, August (1; 8; 10; 14; 19) 1944.

(51*) Lorenzo BARBARO, "*Sono l'uomo più odiato d'Italia.*" In: "Risorgimento Liberale," Rome, 22.8.1944.

(*f*) *The Feltre meeting between Hitler and Mussolini*

(52) *Il convegno di Feltre.* (Based on "Official stenographic account.") In: "Il Popolo," Rome and Milan editions, 28.10.–4.11.1945; "Il Giornale del Mattino," Rome, 31.10.–3.11.1945—Official reports in *Hitler e Mussolini*, (see below, B1), Milan & Rome, 1946, pp. 165–90.

(*g*) *The Meeting of the Fascist Grand Council*

(53) *Official account* (Badoglio Government), Stefani Agency, 27.7.1945; quoted in the Rome and Swiss press, 28–29.7.1945.

(54) *Anonymous account*, in: "Nuova Antologia," Rome, August 1945; quoted by "Neue Zürcher Zeitung," Zurich, 16.8.1945.

(55) *Anonymous account* (based on information from a member of the Grand Council) in: "Gazzetta Ticinese," Lugano, 9.9.1943. Reproduced *e.g.* in: (i) *Gli ultimi giorni del Fascismo*, Biblioteca del Popolo Siciliano, Ed. Etna, Catania 1944; (ii) *Come cadde Mussolini . . . Con una nota di Abele sulla storica notte romana.* Ed. Messaggerie Meridionali, Bari 1944. (iii) The same account, differently worded—said to be transl. from "Neue Zürcher Zeitung," n. 140, August 1943"—in *L'ultima seduta del Gran Consiglio del Fascismo*, Rome 1944; contained also in "Comandante X" [see above, A (6)], pp. 5 ff.

(56) *Anonymous account*, based mainly on information from BOTTAI, in: *La fine del Fascismo. L'ultima seduta del Gran Consiglio*, Rome, 1944. (Reprint of articles in the Monarchist "Italia Nuova," Rome, 9–25.7.1944.) —P. SAPORITI, *La dernière séance du Grand Conseil du fascisme révélée par le procès-verbal de G. Bottai.* In: "Le Monde," Paris, 25.–26.7.1946.

(57*) For the accounts of CIANO, DE BONO, BASTIANINI, FARINACCI, and other members of the Grand Council, see below, B (26), Acts of the Verona Trial.

(58) Frederick G. PAINTON, *How Mussolini Fell*, in: "Harper's Magazine," January 1945, pp. 137–144 ("based upon a secretarial script in which all speech and actions were recorded"). [From other sources it appears that no minutes were taken of the meeting !] Inaccurate. Transl. in "Domenica," Rome, 25.3.5 1945.

(*h*) *Arrest, internment and liberation*

(59) Lorenzo BARBARO, *La giornata degli inganni. Come fu arrestato Mussolini a Villa Savoia.* In: "Risorgimento Liberale," Rome, 25.7.1944.

(60) Benito MUSSOLINI, First broadcast after his liberation, 20.9.1943. Text in G.M., *Dal 25 luglio* . . . [see above, A (7)], pp. 50 ff.

(61) G. MURATORE and C. PERSIA, *I dodici giorni di Mussolini a Ponza.* Vallecchi, Rome 1944.

(62) *Come Mussolini fu liberato da Campo Imperatore.* (Based on General Soleti's account.) In: "Avanti," Rome, 19.7.1944.

(63) *Zur Befreiung Mussolinis am* 12 Sept. 1943. In: "Neue Zürcher Zeitung," Zurich, 16.11.1945.

(*i*) *The Armistice and the flight of the Government*

(64) General Giacomo CARBONI, *L'Armistizio e la difesa di Roma. Verità e menzogne.* Universale De Luigi, Rome 1945.

(65) General Giuseppe CASTELLANO, *Come firmai l'Armistizio di Cassibile.* ("How I signed the Armistice of Cassibile.") Ed. A. Mondadori, Milan 1945.

(66) [Baron Raffaele GUARIGLIA, Minister for Foreign Affairs in the first Badoglio Government], *Intervista con l'Ambasciatore Guariglia.* (On the diplomatic negotiations preceding the Armistice). In: "Il Popolo," Rome, 18 and 20.11.1945.

(67) David BROWN, *The Inside Story of Italy's Surrender.* In: "Saturday Evening Post," Philadelphia, 9. and 16.9.1944.

(68) Francesco ROSSI, *Come arrivammo all'armistizio.* Garzanti, Milan 1946.

(69) Clark LEE (Corresp. of the International News Service), Account of the Armistice negotiations. In: "Cosmopolitan," New York, February 1944.

(70) Ivanoe BONOMI, *E se armistizio non ci fosse stato?* In: "Il Giornale del Mattino", Rome, 24.11.1945. (on the resolutions of the Anti-Fascist parties against continuation of the alliance with Germany, 3.8 and 2.9.43.

(71) Marshal Enrico CAVIGLIA, *Memorie.* (Severe criticism of Badoglio). In: "Corriere d'Informazione," Milan, 20–29.9.1945.

(72) Emilio LUSSU, *La difesa di Roma.* A cura del Partito d'Azione (Clandestine publ. during German occupation), Rome 1944.

(73) *La catastrofe del Settembre '43. Chi sono i responsabili della resa di Roma?* In: "Risorgimento Liberale," Rome, 14.7.1944.

(74) Achille CORONA, *La verità sul 9 settembre.* With Preface by Pietro NENNI. Ed. Avanti, Rome–Milan, 1945.

(75) Giacomo PERTICONE, *Settembre '43.* Ed. Roma, Rome 1944.

(76) Nino BOLLA, *Dieci mesi di Governo Badoglio.* Ed. La Nuova Epoca, Rome 1944.

(77) Eyewitnesses' reports about Rome, July–Sept. 1943, in "Mercurio" (Monthly) I No. 4, Darsena, Rome, December 1944. Contains Corrado ALVARO, *Quaderno* (Extracts from Diary); Adriano BARACCO, *La capitale perduta*; Vittorio GABRIELI, *Settembre* 1943; etc.

(78) [Anonymous], *Via Rasella.* Azione Letteraria Ital., Rome 1944.

(79) Paolo ALATRI, *Roma tradita.* In "Aretusa" (Monthly), Rome, October 1945, pp. 78–86.

(80) Benedetto CROCE, *Quando l'Italia era divisa in due.* (*Settembre* 1943–Giugno 1944.) *Estratto di un diario.* In: Quaderni della Critica, fasc. VI ff., Laterza, Bari 1946 ff.

(81) Emilio SERENI (Chairman of the "Committee of National Liberation" for Lombardy). "*C.L.N.*" (History of the Committees of National Liberation for Northern Italy.) Ed. Percas, Milan 1945.

(*j*) *Edda Ciano's account*

(82) Interviews with Edda Ciano on Lipari island: (i) Jader JACOBELLI, *Rottami e spettri del passato,* in "Il Giornale del Mattino," Rome, 21.9.1945, f. (ii) C.L., *Edda Mussolini a Lipari,* "L'Italia Libera," Rome, 21–22.9.1945.

(83) *La correspondance de la contesse Ciano.* In: "Le Soir," Brussels, 10.1.1946.

(*k*) *Mussolini's last days, capture and death*

(84) *L'esecuzione di Mussolini.* (First-hand account.) In "L'Unità," Milan, 30.4.1945.

(85) *Le ultime giornate dell'ex-duce Mussolini.* In: "Popolo e Libertà," Bellinzona, 4–14.7.1945

(86) *Il mistero di Dongo.* In: "Risorgimento Liberale," Rome, 8.7; 15.8; 21.9.1945.

(87) Nicola VACCARO, *Ultime ore di Mussolini sul Lario.* In: "Il Popolo," Rome and Milan, 24–26.10.1945.

(88) *Come finì Mussolini.* In: "Corriere Lombardo," Milan, 24.10.ff. 1945; "Gazzettino", Venice, same dates.

(89) *Enthüllungen über Mussolini.* In: "Neue Zürcher Zeitung," Zurich, 22.10.1945.

(90) *Ultime confessioni di Mussolini, 400 milioni al giorno per pagare i tedeschi.* In: "Libera Stampa," Rome, 20.10.1945.

(91) Don Enea MAINETTI, Parish priest of Musso (Province of Como), Report to the Bishop of Como about Mussolini's capture and death. Extract in: "Reynolds News," London, 28.10.1945.

(92) Colonel 'VALERIO' (i.e. Walter AUDISIO), *Come giustiziai Mussolini.* ("How I executed Mussolini.") In: "L'Unità," Rome and Turin, 18.11.15.12.1945; "La Voce della Sicilia," Palermo, same date. Repeated in Communist publications of many countries.

(93) Ferruccio LANFRANCHI, *Nostra inchiesta sui fatti di Dongo.* In: "Corriere d'Informazione," Milan, 23/24.10—2/3.11.45. (Contains, 31.10/1.11, *L'ultimo 'colloquio' fra Mussolini e la folla.*)

(94) *Le premier récit authentique de la mort de Mussolini.* (Based on the account of the non-Communist partisans "Bill" and "Pedro".) "Le Figaro," Paris, 27.–30.4.1946.

(95) *La'Vérité vraie' sur la fin de Mussolini.* "Le Soir," Brussels, 5.7.1946.

(96) *Der Befehl zur Erschiessung Mussolinis.* (Prime Minister Parri's account.) In: "Neue Zürcher Zeitung," Zurich, 13.3.1947.

(96*) *Dichiarazioni di Togliatti sull'esecuzione di Mussolini.* (The Communist leader's account.) In: "Risorgimento Liberale," Rome, 14.3.1947.

(97) On Mussolini's "treasure": *De l'exécution de Mussolini au trésor de Dongo.* In: "Le Soir," Brussels, 29.–7.5.1947.—*Der Nibelungenschatz von Dongo.* In: "Neue Zürcher Zeitung," 7.3.1947.—Italian press of Jan.–March 1947.

(98) On Mussolini's archives: Emilio RE, *Storia di un archivio.* Ed. del Milione, Milan 1946.

(98*) *Gli archivi segreti di Mussolini nelle mani della Commissione Alleata.* In: "Corriere della Sera," Milan, 15.12.1946—*Chi prese le carte di Mussolini?* In: "Risorgimento Liberale," Rome, 3.4.1947.

B. DOCUMENTS

(*a*) *Mussolini's correspondence*

(1) *Correspondence Mussolini–Hitler*:

(i) Nineteen letters from *Mussolini to Hitler*, dating from 4.1.1940 till 22.5.1943. (ii)Ten letters from *Hitler to Mussolini* (Ital. transl.), dating from 20.11.1940 till 2.5.1943. In: "Risorgimento Liberale," Rome, 4.10—16.11.1945; "Libera Stampa," Rome, same dates; "Corriere d'Informazione," Milan, same dates; "Giornale di Sicilia," Palermo, 7.10—27.11.1945. Extracts translated in "Sunday Chronicle," London, 28.10.1945 ff.

(i) and (ii) Collected in: *Hitler e Mussolini, Lettere e documenti.* Rizzoli, Milan and Rome 1946.

(iii) *Mussolini to Hitler*, 27.9.1943. In: "L'Unità," Milan, 28.5.1945.

(iv) *Hitler to Mussolini*, 27.12.1944. In: "L'Unità," Milan, 24.5.1945.

(2) *Correspondence Mussolini—King Victor Emmanuel.* Three minutes from Mussolini to the King, 30.8.1941—3.5.1943 (concerning correspondence with Hitler); one letter from the King to Mussolini, 28.3.1941. Published above, B (1).

(3) *Mussolini to Field-Marshal Kesselring*, undated (1944, after August). In: "L'Unità," Milan, 28.5.1945.

(*b*) *Marshal Badoglio's account*

(4) Marshal Pietro BADOGLIO, Speech to Italian Officers in S. Giorgio Ionico, October 1943. Published as pamphlet, *La caduta del Fascismo e l'Armistizio*, Rome 1944; also in Luigi Pastore, see above, A (1); and in "Comandante X," see above, A (6).

(4*) Marshal Pietro BADOGLIO, Interview with British and American war correspondents, October 1st, 1943. In: "The Times," London, 6.10.1943; "Manchester Guardian," same date; "New York Times" and "N.Y. Herald Tribune," 5.10.1943.

(4**) Marshal Pietro BADOGLIO, *L'Italia nella seconda guerra mondiale.* Mondadori, Milan 1946. French transl., Paris 1947; Eng., Oxford 1948.

(*c*) *Ciano's diaries and conversations*

(5) Galeazzo CIANO, *Diario.* Preface written in Verona prison, 23.12.1943, and parts covering events from 1.1.1939—3.2.1943. In: "Il Tempo," Rome, 14.7.1945 ff. First published in translation, not at all accurate, in "Chicago Daily News," 18.6—23.7.1945. A few excerpts, very abridged, in "New York Times," 18.6—23.7.1945, and other papers.

(5*) Extracts were first published by 'PORFIRIO,' to whom Ciano read his diary in August 1943, in: "Risorgimento Liberale," Rome, 18–28.7.1944, "*Il diario di Ciano.*"

(5**) Galeazzo CIANO, *Diario politico.* Covering events of the same time as (5), published under this title in "Il Tempo," Rome, 1.11.1945 ff. "La Libertà," Milan; "Il Gazzettino," Venice; "Il Lavoro Nuovo," Genoa; and other papers of the same dates.

Collected in: *Diario*, 1939–1943, 2 vols., Rizzoli, Milan 1946.

(6) [Galeazzo CIANO], *The Ciano Diaries, 1939–1943.* Edited by Hugh GIBSON. Introduction by Sumner WELLES. Doubleday, Garden City, New York, 1946. (Translation, based on that of the "Chicago Daily News").

(6*) [Galeazzo CIANO], *Ciano's Diary*, 1939–1943. Ed. with Introduction by Malcolm MUGGERIDGE. Foreword by Sumner WELLES, Heinemann, London and Toronto 1947. [Transl., based on B (6), "but again revised and where necessary anglicised", yet still not free from mistakes.]

(7) Edda CIANO, Letter to Mussolini of 11.1.1944. (*Documenti segreti. Edda ricatta Mussolini.*) In: "L'Unità," Milan, 23.6.1945.

(7*) [Marchese Emilio PUCCI], *Le memorie del Marchese Pucci.* (On Mussolini, Ciano, Edda Ciano, and the diaries.) In: "Giornale di Sicilia," Palermo, 6–22.9.1945; "Libera Stampa," Rome, same dates.

(8) Galeazzo CIANO, *L'Europa verso la catastrofe.* Verona 1948 (Palazzo Chigi papers). Transl., *Ciano's Diplomatic Papers.* London 1948.

(*d*) *The Holy See's activities to avert Italy's entry into the War*

(9) *L'Opera di pace della Santa Sede e l'Italia.* Appunti. (Vatican, Secretariat of State), Tipografia Poliglotta Vaticana, Vatican City, 1945.

(10) F. CAVALLI, S.I., *Documentazione dell' opera di Pio XII. per preservare l' Italia dalla guerra.* [Contains, *inter alia,* Cardinal Luigi MAGLIONE (Vatican Secretary of State), Memorandum on conversation with Mr. Sumner Welles, March 17th, 1940]; published in: "La Civiltà Cattolica," Rome, June 1945.

(*e*) *Meetings of the Italian High Command*

(11) Mussolini's meeting with the Chiefs of Staff, 29.5.1940. (Stenographic report.) In: *Un impressionante documento di cinismo e d'irresponsabilità*, "L'Italia Libera," Rome, 9.1.1945; *Storia segreta della guerra,* "Milano Sera," Milan, 11.9.1945.

(12) Meetings of the Chiefs of Staff under Badoglio's command, before and after Italy's entry into the war: 30.5, 5.6 and 25.6.1940. (Stenographic reports.) In *Documenti della guerra* and *Storia segreta della guerra,* "Milano Sera," Milan, 12–18.9.1945.

(*f*) *Telephone conversations, April 6th–July 24th*, 1943, *intercepted at Mussolini's orders*

(13) Conversations of prominent Italians : *Che cos'era la "spia acustica."* In : "Il Tempo," Rome, 11.11.f.1945.

(13*) Conversations of the German Command in Italy with Berlin and G.H.Q. : *La spia acustica.* In : "Il Tempo," Rome, 18.11.f.1945.

(*g*) *The Propaganda Ministry's daily directives to the Press*

(14) Claudio MATTEINI, *Ordini alla stampa.* Ed. Polilibreria Italiana, Rome 1945.

(*h*) *The attack on Greece*

(15) Royal Greek Ministry for Foreign Affairs, *The Greek White Book. Diplomatic documents relating to Italy's aggression against Greece.* With Preface by E. TSOUDEROS, Prime Minister of Greece. Hutchinson, London etc., 1942.

(16) Emanuele GRAZZI, Italian Ambassador to Athens in 1940, Series of articles on the diplomatic pre-history of the Italian aggression, in : "Il Giornale del Mattino," Rome, 28.7—30.8.1945. Collected in : *Il principio della fine.* Ed. Faro, Rome 1945.

(16*) Col. Luigi MONDINI, Italian Military Attaché in Athens, 1940, *Precisazione* (to Grazzi's publication). In : "Il Giornale del Mattino," Rome, 30.8.1945.—*Prologo del conflitto italo–greco.* Garzanti, Rome 1945.

(17) [Minutes of the meeting of 15.10.1940 at Palazzo Venezia], *Rivelazione su una tragicomica seduta di Palazzo Venezia.* In : "Il Tempo," Rome, 13.7.1944.

(18) Carlo DEL BUFALO, *L'umiliante avventura greca nelle rivelazioni di un combattente.* In : "Il Tempo," Rome, 14.7.1944.

(18*) S. VISCONTI PRASCA, General, *Io ho aggredito la Grecia.* Rizzoli, Milan 1946.

(*i*) *The Armistice*

(19) President ROOSEVELT and Prime Minister W. CHURCHILL, Quebec telegram on the Armistice conditions; in the hands of the Allied representatives at the Lisbon meeting, 19.8.1943. Published (Italian translation) in : General G. CASTELLANO [see above, A (41)], pp. 109–112 ; "Il Tempo," Rome, 10.11.1945.

(20) Minutes of the meeting of Allied and Italian representatives at the British Embassy, Lisbon, 19.8.1943. Italian translation in : General G. CASTELLANO [see above, A (41)], pp. 211–18.

(21) Minutes of the meeting of Allied and Italian representatives at Cassibile, Sicily, 31.8.1943. Italian translation in : General G. CASTELLANO [see above, A (65)], pp. 219–23.

(22) British White Paper, Cmd. 6693. *Italy No. 1 (1945), Documents relating to the Conditions of an Armistice with Italy* (September–November 1943). *With Commentary.* H.M. Stationery Office, London, 1945.

(23) Marshal Pietro BADOGLIO, Letter to President Roosevelt and Prime Minister W. Churchill on the Armistice Terms, 20.11.1943. In : "Affari Internazionali," Rome, November 1945 ; "Il Popolo," Rome, 10.11.1945.

(24) Winston CHURCHILL, Speeches to the House of Commons and broadcasts. E.g., Speech of 21.9.43 in : Parliamentary Debates, House of Commons, Official Report, vol. 392, No. 102, London, 21.9.1943 ; Speech of 24.5.1944, etc.

(25) Collection of documents. *Dall'Armistizio alla liberazione di Roma,* in : "Politica Estera," Vol. I, No. 6, Rome, July 1944.

(j) *The trial of members of the Fascist Grand Council by the Special Tribunal of the "Italian Social Republic" at Verona*

(26) Acts of the Verona Trial, 8–10.1.1944. *La verità sul processo di Verona* in: "Avanti," Rome, 8.9–12.10.1945; "Giornale di Sicilia," Palermo, 11.9.1945 ff. (Contains, *inter alia*, the defence of Ciano, De Bono, Cianetti, and apologetic memoranda by the absent Bastianini and Alfieri.) A shorter selection in "Comandante X" [see above, A (6)], pp. 41–56.

(26*) Domenico MAYER, *La verità sul processo di Verona*, Mondadori, Milan 1945.

(k) *Mussolini's internment and liberation*

(27) [Benito MUSSOLINI, Letters to his wife]. "The letters which the Duce wrote to his wife during his internment at La Maddalena and the Gran Sasso have been found and confiscated by the Como Police. They contain interesting appreciations of the situation at the time and also judgments of men and affairs. Among the papers found were a number of enthusiastic letters from supporters complimenting Mussolini on his escape, also the manuscript of his book *Storia di un anno* and several historical essays." (Reported by "Risorgimento," Naples, 25.11.1945.)

(l) *Mussolini's last days and death*

(28) *Dai documenti segreti del "fondatore dell'impero"* (Mussolini's attempts to save himself by offering conditional surrender to the Socialist Party, April 23–25, 1945) In: "L'Unità," Milan, 25.5 and 1.6.1945.

(29) Cardinal Alfredo Ildefonso SCHUSTER, Archbishop of Milan, *Record of his last meeting with Mussolini and of the negotiations, at the Archiepiscopal Palace, between Mussolini and the representatives of the Committee of National Liberation of N. Italy, April 26th,* 1945. In: *Gli ultimi tempi di un regime.* 2nd ed., La Via, Milan 1946.

(29*) Cardinal Alfredo Ildefonso SCHUSTER, *La Chiesa in Italia nell'ora presente.* Pastoral letter of October 28th, 1945. Contains a reference to the meeting with Mussolini. In: "L'Osservatore," Milan, 28.10.1945.

See also the interview with the Cardinal, *Cardinal on his last vain appeal*, in *The Times*, London, 6.5.1945.

(30) Renato SALVADORI, *Nemesi, Dal* 25 *al* 28 *Aprile* 1945. (Collection of eyewitness accounts and documents). B. Gnocchi, Milan 1945.

(31) Ermanno AMICUCCI, *I 600 giorni di Mussolini dal Gran Sasso a Dongo.* Ed. Faro, Rome 1948. (Neo-Fascist account.)

(32) The physicians' autopsy, proving the absence of any serious illness: A. ASTUNI, *Parla il dottore che misurò il cadavere di Mussolini*, in: "Avanti", Rome, 18.5.1945. (Prof. CATTABENI and Prof. CAZZANIGA), *Die Autopsie der Leiche Mussolinis*, in: " Neue Zurcher Zeitung, " 26.7.1945. A. POZZI, *Come li ho visti io*, Milan 1947.

IV

WHO'S WHO

Biographical particulars are provided only of those Italians mentioned in this book who played any part in Italian history during the Fascist era and its aftermath. Following recent judicial proceedings, most of the officials and dignitaries who, at the time of writing, had been punished for their former Fascist or pro-German activities, may, at the time of publication, have been granted amnesty or, as in the case of Senators, been reinstated.

ACERBO, BARON GIACOMO, b. 1888. Early member of the Fascist Party and one of its ablest organizers. Founder of Fascism in the Abruzzi. Created Baron of Aterno by the King, 1924. Minister of Agriculture, 1929–35; of Finance, 8.2.–25.7.43. For having voted against Mussolini (25.7.43), condemned to death in absentia by Republ. Fascist Tribunal at Verona, 10.1.44. Arrested by Bonomi Government and, in May 1945, condemned to 30 years' imprisonment for Fascist crimes.

ACQUARONE, DUKE (originally COUNT) PIETRO, b. 1890. Genoese patrician. Senator since 1934. Minister of the Royal Household, 1939–44; created a Duke for his merits in handling the King's finances. A member of the Fascist Party since 1921 and (as stated in *The Golden Album of Fascism*, Novara 1937) "a fervent admirer of the Duce and the Régime, showing his firm adherence to Fascism not by words but by deeds," he played a leading part in the *coup d'état* of July 1943, acting as the King's chief adviser and go-between, and co-ordinating the actions of the Generals with those of the Court. Member of Badoglio's 'provisional Cabinet,' 1.10.43. Appeared before High Comm. of Court of Justice, but retained title and privileges of Senator, 1946.

ALBINI, UMBERTO, b. 1895. Early member of the Fascist Party; took part in the March on Rome. Holder of high Party offices and Prefect of various provinces, 1925–43. Under-Secretary of the Interior, 8.2–25.7.43. For having voted against Mussolini (25.7.43), condemned to death in absentia by Republ. Fascist Tribunal at Verona, 10.1.44. Suspended from Civil Service by Bonomi Government, under provision of 1.9.44.

ALFIERI, DINO, b. 1886. Early member of the Fascist Party. Minister for Press and Propaganda, 1936–39, Oct.; Ambassador to Holy See, 31.10.39.–16.5.40; to Berlin, 16.5.40–43, July. Had the reputation of a playboy and Don Juan. After voting against Mussolini (25.7.43), did not return to Berlin; escaped to Switzerland, Oct. 1943. Though trying to ingratiate himself again with Mussolini, condemned to death in absentia by

Republ. Fascist Tribunal at Verona, 10.1.44. Dismissed from Diplomatic Service by Bonomi Govt., 19.7.44.

ALIPRANDI, Giovanni, b. 1893. Naval Captain. Chef de Cabinet to Minister for the Navy, 1943.

AMBROSIO, general Vittorio, b. 1879. As G.O.C., II. Army, led the Italian forces against Yugoslavia, 6.4.1941–20.1.1942. Chief of Army Staff, 20.1.42–31.1.43. Chief of General Staff of Armed Forces (succeeding Marshal Cavallero), 31.1.–22.11.43 ; member of Badoglio's "all-military provisional Cabinet," 1.10.–beg.11.43. Accused of war crimes (execution of hostages) by Yugoslav Govt., Oct. 43 ; subject of questions in House of Commons, 13.10.43. Appointed by Badoglio Inspector-General of Italian Army, 22.11.43–July 1944, when the post was abolished.

ANSALDO, Giovanni, b. 1895. Editor of the Leghorn "Telegrafo" (closely connected with Ciano), 1932–43. One of the Fascist Party's star radio commentators ; well known for his "woe, woe" broadcast after the defeat in Libya, Jan. 1941. Accused of defeatism by the Republ. Fascist Govt., May 1944, and deported to Germany. After his return, Sept. 1945, arrested by Parri Govt. at request of High Commissioner for Sanctions against Fascism. Released soon afterwards.

AOSTA, Amedeo, duke of, b. 1898 ; d. 1942. Son of a cousin of King Victor Emmanuel III. Had the title of Duke of Apulia until the death of his father, 1931, when he became Duke of Aosta. Viceroy of Abyssinia, 1937–41. C.-in-C., East Africa ; surrendered at Amba Alagi, 19.5.41 ; died in captivity, 3.3.42.

APULIA, duke of. *See* AOSTA, duke of.

ARMELLINI, general Quirino, b. 1889. Corps Commander at Spalato (Split), 1942. Appointed by Badoglio Commander of the former Fascist Militia, to carry out its absorption into the Army, 26.7.43.

BADOGLIO, Pietro, marshal of italy, marquis of sabotino, duke of addis ababa, b. 1871. After the defeat of Caporetto, 1917, Deputy Chief of Army Staff. Chief of Army Staff, 1919–21. After the rise of Fascism, Ambassador to Brazil, 1924–25. From 1925, Chief of General Staff of Armed Forces. Governor of Libya, 1928–33. Taking over command of Abyssinian campaign, 28.11.35 ; Governor-General and Viceroy of Abyssinia, 5.5.36 ; created Duke of Addis Ababa when relinquishing these posts and resuming his duties as Chief of General Staff, 11.6.36. Awarded by King Order of Most Holy Annunciation ("Cousin of the King"). President of National Research Council, 1937. Resigned his post as Chief of Gen. Staff after unsuccessful beginning of Greek campaign, 6.12.40. Nominated by the King Head of Govt., 25.7.43. Left Rome immediately after announcement of Armistice, 8.9.43. Formed an "all-military provisional Govt.," 1.10.43 ; a new Cabinet at Bari, 17.11.43 ; a "Cabinet of National Union," 22.4.44. Resigned after liberation of Rome, 9.6.44. Removed from list of Senators by decision of High Court, 29.3.46.

BAISTROCCHI, general count Federico, b. 1871. Under-Secretary for War, 1933–36. Senator since 1939. Suspended from service by Purge Commission (Bonomi Govt.), Oct. 1944. Tried, and acquitted, Sept. 1946.

BALBO, air-marshal Italo, b. 1896 ; d. 1940. Member of the Quadrumvirate of the March on Rome. Minister for Air, 1929–33. Popular for the spectacular mass flights across the Atlantic which he directed, 1931–33. Gov.-General and C.-in-C. Libya, 1933–40. Sometimes regarded as possible successor to Mussolini. Anti-German. Killed over Tobruk, June 1940, when his plane was shot down by guns of Italian battle-cruiser.

BALOCCO, general Riccardo, b. 1883. Took part in the campaign against Yugoslavia, 1941. Placed on the retired list, Jan. 1945.

BARBASETTI DI PRUN, GENERAL COUNT CURIO, b. 1885. Chief of Staff, Italian Forces in North Africa, 1942. Commander of XIV. Army Corps and Mil. Gov. of Montenegro, July–Sept. 1943. Accused of war crimes by Yugoslavs, April 1944.

BASSO, LT.-GENERAL ANTONIO, b. 1881. Mil. Gov. of Sardinia, 1940–Nov. 1943. Commander of Italian Armed Forces in Campania, 9.11.43. Right-wing Monarchist.

BASTIANINI, GIUSEPPE, b. 1899. Since the early days of Fascism filled many posts in Party, Govt. and Diplomatic Service. Boasted of being Fascist first and Italian afterwards. Vice-Secretary of the Party, 1921–23; Sec.-General of Fascists abroad till 1927. Minister to Athens, 1929; Ambassador to Warsaw, 1932–36; Under-Sec. for Foreign Affairs, 1936; Ambassador to London, Sept. 1939–June 1940. Gov. of Dalmatia, 1941–Feb. 1943. Under-Sec. for Foreign Affairs, 8.2–25.7.43. Voted against Mussolini, 25.7.43. Appointed by Badoglio Ambassador to Ankara, beg. August 1943; this shortly afterwards denied, owing to unfavourable reactions. Though in a letter to Mussolini protesting his loyalty to Fascism, sentenced to death in absentia by Republ. Fascist Tribunal at Verona, 10.1.44. Escaped to Switzerland, April 1944. Classed by Yugoslavs as war criminal for crimes committed as Gov. of Dalmatia.

BASTICO, ETTORE, MARSHAL OF ITALY, b. 1876. For his leadership of Fascist forces in Basque campaign of Spanish Civil War called 'hero of Santander.' Made Senator, 1939. Gov. of Dodecanese, Dec. 1940–July 1941. Gov. of Libya and C.-in-C. Italian Forces in North Africa (replacing Gariboldi), July 1941–Jan. 1943 (replaced by Messe). Dismissed from office as Senator (under Bonomi Govt.), Dec. 1944.

BENCIVENGA, GENERAL ROBERTO, b. 1878. Liberal Deputy, 1924–26. Accused of active opposition to Fascism and interned at Ponza, 1927. Released after Mussolini's fall, July 1943, he took part in clandestine anti-German activities before the liberation of Rome. Later, opposing the anti-Fascist parties, became supporter of "Front of the Common Man" ("Uomo qualunque") movement.

BENELLI, SEM, b. 1877. Well-known playwright. One of the leading propagandists for incorporation of Fiume, 1918–19. Volunteer in Abyssinian war. Attacked by Fascist press for his play "L'Orchidea," 1938. Wanted by Republ. Fascist police, Dec. 1944. President of Ital. Writers and Authors Assoc., 1945.

BERGAMINI, ADMIRAL CARLO, b. 1888; d. 1943. C.-in-C. Naval Battle Forces, April 1943. Killed on board battleship *Roma* when making for Allied port after the Armistice, Sept. 1943.

BIANCHI, MICHELE, b. 1882; d. 1930. Member of Quadrumvirate of March on Rome. Formerly an ardent Socialist, he became the first Secretary of the Fascist Party. Under-Sec. of the Interior, 1928–39. Minister of Public Works, 1929–30.

BIGGINI, CARLO ALBERTO, b. 1902; d. 1945. Member of Fascist Party since 1920. Professor of Law; Rector of Pisa University, 1940–43. Minister of Education, 8.2.–25.7.43. Voted for Mussolini, 25.7.43; reappointed Min. of Education in Republ. Fascist Cabinet, 23.9.43–April 1945. Tried in absentia (under Parri Govt.) for collaboration with the Germans, Oct. 1945. His death announced, Nov. 1945.

BIGNARDI, ANNIO, b. 1907. President of National Fascist Confederation of Agricultural Workers. Voted against Mussolini, 25.7.43; though trying to ingratiate himself again with Mussolini, sentenced to death in absentia by Republ. Fascist Tribunal at Verona, 10.1.44

BOFONDI, MARCELLO, b. 1896. Member of Fascist Party since 1921; took part in March on Rome. Prefect of Udine, until 1943; Prefect of Forlì, 1943.

BONGIOVANNI, GENERAL LUIGI, b. 1866; d. 1941. G.O.C. Italian Air Force, 1918. Gov. of Cyrenaica, 1924. Sectional President of Supreme Colonial Council since 1925. Senator since 1928.

BONITATIBUS, MAJOR SILVIO, b. 1895. Carabinieri officer; guarded Mussolini on his way to internment at Ponza and La Maddalena.

BONOMI, IVANOE, b. 1873. Lawyer and politician. Expelled from Socialist Party for approving the war against Turkey, became co-founder of Socialist-Reformist Party, 1912. Prime Minister, June 1921–Feb. 1922. Retired into private life after breakdown of truce between Fascists and Socialists; awarded Order of Most Holy Annunciation ("Cousin of the King"). Chosen as President of clandestine Rome Committee of National Liberation, beg. 1944. After liberation of Rome, succeeded Badoglio as Prime Minister, June 1944; presided over a second Cabinet, Dec. 1944–June 1945.

BORDIGA, AMEDEO ADRIANO, b. 1889. Secretary of Ital. Communist Party, 1921; expelled from the party as "Trotskyist," after April 1925; under Fascism, interned, later released under strict police surveillance. Freed, 1943.

BOTTAI, GIUSEPPE, b. 1895. Journalist and Univ. Professor; one of the leading Fascist intellectuals. Joint founder of Rome Fascio, 1919; led detachment in March on Rome. Played, after Rossoni, leading part in organizing the Fascist "Corporate State"; Under-Sec., 1926, and Minister of Corporations, 1929. Gov. of Rome, 1935. Minister of Education, 1936–8.2.1943; responsible for Fascist 'School reform.' Increasingly critical of Mussolini since 1941. For having voted against Mussolini (25.7.43), sentenced to death in absentia by Republ. Fascist Tribunal at Verona, 10.1.44. Under Bonomi Govt., tried in absentia for Fascist crimes, sentenced to life imprisonment and one year's solitary confinement, May 1945. In hiding. According to unconfirmed reports, joined French Foreign Legion. Returned to Italy a free man, 1948.

BRIVONESI, ADMIRAL BRUNO, b. 1886. Commander of naval base at La Maddalena, summer 1943.

CADORNA, COUNT LUIGI, MARSHAL OF ITALY, b. 1850; d. 1928. Chief of General Staff, 1914–17. Ordered retreat of Caporetto and established resistance line on the Piave; relinquished his command, nominated representative at Allied Supreme Council at Versailles. Placed on retired list, 1919; recalled, 1924; promoted Marshal, 1926.

CALVI DI BERGOLO, GENERAL COUNT GIORGIO, b. 1887. Son-in-law of King Victor Emmanuel III. Commander of the Centauro Division of Armoured Corps; took over command of Rome, after Badoglio's flight and Caviglia's withdrawal, 10.9.43. Conducted negotiations with German command. Resigned end Sept., after formation of Republ. Fascist Govt. with which he refused to collaborate.

CALZA-BINI, GINO. One of the founders of Rome Fascio and of the "Musketeers of the Duce"; Lt.-General of the Fascist Militia.

CARBONI, GENERAL GIACOMO. Commander of Armoured Corps stationed near Rome; in addition, appointed by Badoglio Head of the S.I.M. (Italian Military Intelligence Service), 18.8.43. Later strongly attacking Badoglio, Ambrosio, Roatta, for their failure to prepare resistance against Germans and their flight from Rome. Suspended from service, 1945.

CASATI, ETTORE, b. 1873; d. 1945. President of Supreme Court of Appeal before the fall of the Régime, appointed by Badoglio President of the Commission for the investigation of illicit Fascist gains, 14.8.43. Minister of Justice under Badoglio, Feb.–April 1944; President of High Court of Justice for Sanctions against Fascism, Aug. 1944.

CASTELLANO, GENERAL GIUSEPPE, b. 1893. Gen. attached to Army Staff, 5.2.42; to General Staff (Ambrosio), 3.2.43. Badoglio's emissary to the Allies, conducting negotiations in Madrid and Lisbon, Aug. 1943. Signed Armistice of Cassibile, 3.9.43.

CAVAGNARI, ADMIRAL DOMENICO, b. 1876. Under-Sec. for Navy, 1933–40; Chief of Naval Staff, 1936–40. Resigned both posts, 8.12.40.

CAVALLERO, COUNT UGO, MARSHAL OF ITALY, b. 1880; d. 1943. Under-Sec. for War, 1925; left office after being involved in financial scandals, 1928. C.-in-C., East Africa, 1937. Replaced Badoglio as Chief of General Staff, 6.12.40. Considered incompetent and a tool of the Germans. Resigned and returned to business interests, end Jan. 1943. Arrested under Badoglio, 26.7.43. Alleged to have committed suicide after his 'release' by the Germans, 16.9.43.

CAVIGLIA, ENRICO, MARSHAL OF ITALY, b. 1862; d. 1945. Victor of battle of Vittorio Veneto, 1918. Minister of War, 1919; Senator s. 1919. Holding aloof from Fascism. By chance in Rome at time of Armistice, found himself senior officer in command, the day after Badoglio's flight, 9.9.43. Seeing the defenceless state in which the Govt. had left Rome, arranged truce with Germans and withdrew.

CERICA, GENERAL ANGELO, b. 1885. G.O.C. Carabinieri Corps, 19.7.43.

CHIERICI, GENERAL RENZO, b. 1895; d. 1944. Lt.-Gen. of Fascist Militia. Chief of Police (closely collaborating with Himmler), 16.4–26.7.43.

CHIRICO, LT.-COL. ETTORE, b. 1896. Carabinieri officer, guarding Mussolini on his way to internment.

CIANETTI, TULLIO, b. 1899. Fascist Syndicate leader. Under-Sec., 1939; Minister of Corporations, 1943. Voted against Mussolini, 25.7.43, recanting the same day. In view of "extenuating circumstances" sentenced not to death but to 30 years' imprisonment by Republ. Fascist Tribunal at Verona, 10.1.44; said to have been released soon afterwards. After liberation of Italy, in hiding; came forward as witness at second Matteotti trial, Feb. 1947.

CIANO, COUNTESS EDDA, b. 1910. Mussolini's daughter; dabbled in politics. At time of her husband's trial placed by Gestapo under surveillance in nursing home near Parma; escaped to Switzerland, with Ciano's diaries, 9.1.44. Interned in nursing home in Valais; expelled from Swiss territory. Aug. 1945. Interned in Lipari island. Charged with having supported Fascist foreign policy leading to war, maintained friendly relations with prominent Nazis, and sold her husband's diaries for publication. Sentenced to two years' further internment, Dec. 1945. Under the amnesty of 22.6.46, set free on 2.7.46. Lives in Italy.

CIANO, COUNT GALEAZZO, b. 1903; d. 1944. Took part in March on Rome. Diplomatic service since 1925. Marriage with Edda Mussolini, 1930, followed by dazzling career and accumulation of wealth. Minister for Press and Propaganda, 1935. Carrying out bombing raids in Abyssinian war. Minister for Foreign Affairs, 1936—Feb. 1943. Awarded Order of Most Holy Annunciation ("Cousin of the King"), 1939. Suspicious, and strongly critical, of German policy. Bent on war against Greece. Holding court on golf links. Ambassador to Holy See, Feb.–July 1943. Voted against Mussolini, 25.7.43. Placed under mild surveillance by Badoglio. Escaped to Germany, Aug. 1943. Arrested in Munich and transferred to Verona. Sentenced to death by Republ. Fascist Tribunal; executed, 11.1.44.

CLERICI, GENERAL AMBROGIO, b. 1868. Under-Sec. for War, 1924–25. First aide-de-camp to Prince of Piedmont.

CONTARINI, SALVATORE, b. 1867; d. 1945. Senator s. 1921. Secretary-General of For. Affairs, 1919–26. Resigned, disagreeing with Grandi's handling of Balkan questions.

COPPOLA, Francesco, b. 1878. Former Nationalist leader, advocating fusion of Nat. Party with Fascists ; publicist and University Professor (Rome), specializing on foreign policy. Appointed member of It. R. Academy, 1929.

DE BONO, Emilio, marshal of Italy, b. 1866 ; d. 1944. Leader of Army circles supporting Fascism before its rise to power. Member of Quadrumvirate of March on Rome. First Fascist Chief of Police and C.-in-C., Blackshirt Militia. A failure in all subsequent posts. Senator s. 1923. Minister of Colonies, 1929–35 ; Min. of State ; High Commissioner for It. East Africa and C.-in-C. in the first stage of the Abyssinian war, before being replaced by Badoglio. Awarded by the King Order of Most Holy Annunciation ("Cousin of the King"). For having voted against Mussolini (25.7.43), sentenced to death by Republ. Fascist Tribunal at Verona ; executed, 11.1.44.

DE CESARE, Nicolo. Vice-Prefect. Private secretary to Mussolini since 1941.

DE CICCO, Attilio, b. 1894. Former Federal Sec. of Fascist Party. Head of Dept. for Italians abroad, in Min. of For. Affairs, 1943.

DE COURTEN, admiral Raffaele, b. 1888. Inspector of submarines, 1942–43. Minister for Navy in first Badoglio Govt., 26.7.43 ; retained this post through successive Govt. changes (Bonomi, Parri, De Gasperi), until July 1946. Chief of Naval Staff July–Dec. 1946. Resigned.

DE MARSICO, Alfredo, b. 1888. Professor of Law (Rome). Member of Nat. Directorate of Fascist Party, 1924. Nat. Councillor, representing Corporation of professional classes and artists. Minister of Justice, 8.2–25.7.43. For having voted against Mussolini (25.7.43), sentenced to death in absentia by Republ. Fascists at Verona, 10.1.44.

DE STEFANIS, general Giuseppe, b. 1885. Deputy Chief of Army Staff, Sept. 1943. Placed on retired list (Bonomi Govt.), 1945.

DE VECCHI, Cesare Maria, b. 1884. Pugnacious Fascist and member of Quadrumvirate of March on Rome. Senator s. 1925, and created by the King Count of Val Cismon. Ambassador to Holy See, 1929–35 ; Minister for Education, noted for harshness, 1935–36. Gov. of Dodecanese, famed for repressive measures and discrimination against Greek religion, 1936–7.12.40. Active warmonger. Given divisional command in Italy, summer 1943. For having voted against Mussolini (25.7.43), sentenced to death in absentia by Republ. Fascist Tribunal at Verona, 10.1.44. Took refuge in monastery ; became monk, Aug. 1945.

D'HAVET, general Achille, b. 1888. First general to fall in Allied hands in Sicilian campaign, 13.7.43.

DIAZ, Armando, marshal of italy, b. 1861 ; d. 1928. Succeeded Cadorna as Supreme Commander after Caporetto, 1917. Created Duke della Vittoria. Minister for War, 1922–24.

DI GIORGIO, general Antonino, b. 1867 ; d. 1932. Minister for War, 1924–25.

DORIA-PAMPHILI, prince Filippo Andrea, b. 1886. Head of main branch of House of Doria. Well known for his uncompromising stand against Fascism ; penalized in many ways under the Régime. After liberation of Rome appointed Sindaco (Lord Mayor) of the city by Allied Mil. Govt., 11.6.44 ; held office until 1947.

ELENA, queen of italy, b. 1873. Princess Petrovic Niegos of Montenegro ; married Victor Emmanuel III (then Crown Prince) in 1896 ; *q.v.*—After his abdication, 9.5.46, leaving Italy with him for Egypt.

FACTA, Luigi, b. 1861 ; d. 1930. Prime Minister, Feb.–Oct. 1922. A proverbially weak man ("Non Facta, sed verba"). However, at time of Fascist March on Rome tried to obtain King's signature for decree of martial law ; the King refused and made him revoke decree at once. F. obeyed and withdrew, thus giving way to Mussolini.

FAIOLA, lieut. One of Mussolini's guards on the Gran Sasso.

FALDELLA, col. Emilio. Chief of Staff to Gen. Guzzoni, C.in-C. Sicily, summer 1943.

FARINACCI, Roberto. Railway clerk, later lawyer. Fascist Party leader at Cremona, b. 1892 ; d. 1945. Editor of extremist "Regime Fascista." One of the most brutal Fascist bullies. Defended Matteotti's murderers, 1926. Party Secretary, 1925–26. Minister of State. Violently anti-Semitic ; pro-German ; anti-Vatican. Closely co-operating with Nazis, fled to Germany after 25.7.43. Became leader of extreme wing of Republ. Fascists. Shot after summary trial by partisans in course of liberation of North Italy, end April 1945.

FECIA DI COSSATO, Carlo, b. 1908. Reputed to be daring submarine commander ; decorated by Doenitz, 1943.

FEDELE, Pietro, b. 1873 ; d. 1943. Prof. of Mediæval History (Rome). Minister for Education, 1925–28. Senator. Commissioner for College of Heralds, 1930. Minister of State s. 1933.

FEDERZONI, Luigi. Joint founder and leader of Nationalist Party, 1911. Leader of "Blue Shirts" (rivalling Fascist Black Shirts), 1919–22. After Mussolini's rise to power, made Nationalists merge en bloc with Fascist Party ; rewarded with high offices : Minister of Colonies, 1922–24 ; of Interior (intoducing many measures to strengthen hold of Fascism ; suppressing freedom of Press), 1924–26 ; of Colonies, 1926–28. President of Senate, 1929–39. Given Order of Most Holy Annunciation ("Cousin of the King"), 1932. Ed. of high-brow "Nuova Antologia," 1931–43. President of R. Ital. Academy, 1938–43. For voting against Mussolini (25.7.43), sentenced to death in absentia by Republ. Fascists at Verona, 10.1.44. For Fascist crimes sentenced, in absentia, to life imprisonment by High Court (Bonomi Govt.), May 1945. In hiding.

FERRARI, general Guiseppe Francesco, b. 1865. Chief of Army Staff, 1927–28. Vice-Pres. of Senate, 1928. Min. of State.

FOUGIER, general Rino Corso, marshal of air force, b. 1894. In command of Italian air corps operating with Germans against Great Britain from Channel coast, 1940—41. Chief of Air Staff and Under-Sec. for Air, Nov. 1941–25.7.1943. Put on retired list under Bonomi Govt., Aug. 1944.

FRATTARI, Ettore, b. 1896. Fascist since 1919 ; Commissioner for speeding up deliveries to grain pools, 1939. President of Confederation of Farmers and Member of Grand Council. Voted for Mussolini, 25.7.43. Witness at Verona trial, 8–10.1.44.

FRUGONI, Cesare, b. 1881. Professor of Medicine, Rome ; Vice-Pres. of Academy of Medicine. For many years Mussolini's physician.

GALBIATI, general Enzo, b. 1897. Fascist since 1919. C.-in-C., Fascist Militia, 1941–43. Member of Nat. Directorate of Fascist Party and Member of Grand Council. Voted for Mussolini, 25.7.43. Arrested under Badoglio ; released after Armistice, Sept. 1943. Supposed to be one of the organizers of the underground 'Squadre Azione Mussolini,' Dec. 1945.

GALLI, Domenico. *See* GRANDI, Dino.

GANDIN, col. Aldo, b. 1895. Gen. Staff Officer ; Badoglio's secretary, 1940. Author of report on conditions of Italian troops in Russia, 1941.

GARIBOLDI, general Italo, b. 1879. Gov. Gen. of Libya and C.-in-C., Ital. Forces in N. Africa (replacing Graziani), March–July 1941. C.-in.C., Ital. VIII. Army in Russia, 1942–43. Arrested by Republ. Fascists for treason, Jan. 1944.

GIGLIOLI, GENERAL EMILIO. Deputy Chief of Staff, Ital. Armed Forces in N. Africa, 1942–43. Placed on retired list under Bonomi Govt., Dec. 1944.

GIURIATI, GIOVANNI, b. 1876. Lawyer. 'Chef de Cabinet' to D'Annunzio in Fiume expedition. President of Chamber of Deputies, 1929–34. Secretary of Fascist Party, 1930–31. Declared that if the Duce ordered him to throw himself out of the window he would do so. Awarded by King Order of Most Holy Annunciation ("Cousin of the King"), 1932. Senator s. 1934. Imprisoned by High Court of Justice, 1945.

GRANDI, DINO, b. 1895 at Mordano (Bologna). "A true Fascist of the first hour" (eulogy in German paper, March 1943). Journalist, lawyer, and one of chief organizers of Fascist Party in Emilia. Founder of the "Assalto" (Attack); leader of Fascist squads in many "punitive expeditions," hunting down political opponents in Bologna district. Chief of Staff to Quadrumvirate of March on Rome. Member of Party Directorate, 1921–24. Under-Secretary of Interior, 1924–25; of Foreign Affairs, 1926. Minister of For. Affairs, 1929–32. Ambassador to London, 1932–39. President of Chamber of Fasci and Corporations, 1940–43; Minister of Justice, 1940–6.2.43. Created Count of Mordano. Awarded by King Order of Most Holy Annunciation ("Cousin of the King"), 25.3.43. Organized plot of members of Grand Council against Mussolini, 24–25.7.43. Surprised by Badoglio's action, left for Portugal under name of Domenico Galli. Sentenced to death in absentia by Republ. Fascists at Verona, 10.1.44. Did not follow invitation of Bonomi Govt. to return to Italy to answer charges brought against him by Nat. Purge Commission, June 1944. —Speaking in Germany, Nov. 1940, declared: "The common ideals which our two great leaders have roused . . inevitably brought our two revolutions together, leading them along the same path towards the same glorious future. . . . National Socialist Germany and Fascist Italy . . . supplement each other and contribute to each other's improvement . . . difficulties and victories will be shared by them together in life, in history and in fame." Writing in Portugal, 1945, tried to prove to Britain and U.S.A. his consistent opposition to Germany and to Mussolini's foreign policy.

GRAZIANI, RODOLFO, MARSHAL OF ITALY, MARQUIS OF NEGHELLI, b. 1882. Succeeded Badoglio as Gov. of Abyssinia, 1936–37; an attempt against his life followed by ferocious reprisals, 1937. Created Marquis of Neghelli, 1937. Chief of Army Staff, 1939–25.3.1941. Gov. of Libya and C.-in-C., North Africa, July 1940–25.3.41. Relieved of command after his defeat by Wavell. Under Republ. Fascist Govt., C.-in-C. and Minister for Nat. Defence, 23.9.43-April 1945. Surrendered to Allies, 29.4.45. Trial by Italian Court prepared, beg. 1946. Was handed over to Italians, Feb. 1946. Trial postponed several times, on account of his illness. Imprisoned at Procida, where writing his memoirs. Now released.

GRAZIOLI, GENERAL FRANCESCO SAVERIO, b. 1869. Deputy Chief of General Staff, 1925–27. Senator s. 1928.

GUARIGLIA, BARON RAFFAELE, b. 1889. Prominent diplomat. Ambassador to Paris, 1938–40; to Holy See, 1942–Feb. 1943; to Ankara, Feb.–July 1943. Minister for For. Affairs in Badoglio's first Cabinet, 26.7–8.9.1943.

GRAZZI, EMANUELE, b. 1896. Dir-Gen. of Foreign Press, Min. for Press and Propaganda, 1935–36. Dir.-Gen. of Transocean. Affairs, Min. of For. Affairs. Minister to Athens, April 1939–Oct. 1940. After return to Rome, in disgrace with Ciano.

GUELI, POLICE INSPECTOR. One of Mussolini's guards on the Gran Sasso.

GUZZONI, GENERAL ALFREDO, b. 1877. C.-in-C., Albania, 1939. Commander of IV. Army in 'campaign' against France, 1940. Dep. Chief of Gen. Staff and Under-Sec. for War, 1940–May 1941. C.-in-C., Italian forces in Sicily, May–Aug. 1943. Arrested by Republ. Fascists, held responsible for 'disaster' in Sicily, Oct. 1943; released after few weeks.

JACHINO, ADMIRAL ANGELO, b. 1889. C.-in-C., Navy, Dec. 1940–43.

JACOMONI DI SAN SAVINO, FRANCESCO, b. 1893. Minister to Tirana, 1936–39. After King Victor Emmanuel 'accepted' the Albanian crown, Lieutenant-General (Viceroy) in Albania, 22.4.1939–March 1943. Wanted by Albanians as war criminal, March 1945. Sentenced by Ital. High Court (Bonomi Govt.) to 24 years' penal servitude, March 1945.

MARRAS, LT.-GENERAL EFISIO, b. 1888. Military Attaché in Berlin, 1939–43. Interned there after Armistice, Sept. 1943.

MAUGERI, ADMIRAL FRANCO, b. 1898. Head of Naval Intelligence, 1943. *See* above, p. 207.

MEOLI, LT.-COL. CAMILLO, b. 1897. Carabinieri officer, in command of Ponza at the time of Mussolini's internment.

MESSE, GIOVANNI, MARSHAL OF ITALY, b. 1883. C.-in-C., Ital. Exped. Corps in Russia, Sept. 1941. Made C.-in-C., First Army (Ital. forces in N. Africa), Jan. 1943; surrendered, May 1943; created Marshal. Released by Allies, Nov. 1943; replaced Ambrosio as Chief of Gen. Staff. Relieved of this post, April 1945.

MONTEZEMOLO, COL. GIUSEPPE CORDERO DI, b. 1901; d. 1944. Attached to Supreme Command. After July 1943, Badoglio's secretary. Relinquished post, disapproving of manner in which Supreme Command handled Armistice negotiations. After Armistice, stayed in Rome; attempted to save Bank of Italy's gold reserves. Under many disguises, organized resistance against Germans. Hero of clandestine struggle; captured, Jan. 1944; tortured by Gestapo for two months; revealed nothing. Killed by Gestapo, March 1944.

MUSSOLINI, BRUNO, b. 1919; d. 1941. The Duce's second son. Air force pilot; bombed Abyssinians. Director-General of 'Lati' air line to S. America. Killed on test flight near Pisa. In *I speak with Bruno*, publ. soon afterwards, his father said: "My 'live dangerously' was fulfilled in your life."

MUTI, ETTORE, b. 1902; d. 1943. Fascist air pilot, credited with many hundreds of bombing raids against Abyssinians and Spaniards. Acted as bodyguard to Mussolini's sons. Secretary of Fascist Party, 31.10.39–29.10.40, replacing Starace. For his death, *see* above, p. 95, n. 1. Glorified as hero and martyr by Republ. Fascist propaganda, 1944.

ORLANDO, VITTORIO EMANUELE, b. 1860 at Palermo. Prof. of Law, prominent Liberal politician (Deputy s. 1897) and Minister in various Cabinets (s.1903). Assumed Premiership after Caporetto disaster, 1917, rallying the country and leading it to victory. One of the Big Four at Versailles, faced with opposition to Italy's territorial claims (incl. Fiume), withdrew from Peace Conference, 1919. President of Chamber, 1919. Opposed to Fascism, resigned his seat as Deputy, 1925, resuming legal practice. Supported war against Abyssinia. After liberation of Rome, nominated (by Bonomi Govt.) President of Chamber, July 1944. Resigned his seat as Deputy in protest against Peace Treaty; resuming it shortly afterwards, 1947.

PAVESI, ADMIRAL GINO, b. 1888. Gov. of Pantelleria at time of its surrender, 10.6.1943. Sentenced to death in absentia by Republ. Fascists, May 1944.

PELAGHI, LT.-COL. ANTONIO, b. 1897. Carabinieri officer, guarding Mussolini on way from Rome to Ponza.

POLACCO, VITTORIO, b. 1859 ; d. 1926. Prof. of Law, Univ. of Padua and Rome. Tutor of Prince of Piedmont.

POLITO, BRIGADIER-GEN. SAVERIO. Acting Insp-Gen. in Ministry of Interior, 1942–43. Head of Military Police, 1943.

POLVERELLI, GAETANO, b. 1886. Journalist and joint founder of Rome Fascio. Took part in March on Rome. Head of Mussolini's Press Office, 1932–33. Member of Nat. Party Directorate. Under-Sec. (1941–Feb. 1943), then Minister (Feb.–26.7.43) for Popular Culture (*i.e.* Propaganda). Voted for Mussolini, 25.7.43. Arrested (under Bonomi Govt.), June 1944.

PRICOLO, GENERAL FRANCESCO, b. 1891. Chief of Air Staff and Under-Sec. for Air, Oct. 1939–Nov. 1941.

PUNTONI, LT.-GENERAL PAOLO. First A.D.C. General to the King, 1940–44.

RICCARDI, ADMIRAL COUNT ARTURO, b. 1878. Senator, 1939–44. Under-Sec. for Navy and Chief of Naval Staff, 8.12.40–26.7.43. Placed on retired list under Bonomi Govt., 1945.

ROATTA, GENERAL MARIO, b. 1887. Head of S.I.M. (Mil. Intelligence Service), 1934–36. Commanded Italian forces in Spanish Civil War, 1936–37. Mil. Attaché in Berlin, 1939. Deputy Chief of Army Staff, Nov. 1939–March 1941. Chief of Army Staff (replacing Graziani), March 1941–Jan. 1942. C.-in-C., II. Army, occupying Yugoslav territory, Jan. 1942–Feb. 1943. C.in-C., VI. Army (Sicily), Feb.–June 1943. Again Chief of Army Staff, June 1943 ; continued to hold this post under Badoglio, with whom he abandoned Rome immediately after announcement of Armistice ; included in Badoglio's "provisional, all-military Cabinet," 1.10.43, until removed, at Allied request, 12.11.43. Indicted as war criminal by Yugoslav Govt. Arrested on order of Dep. High Commissioner for Punishment of Fascist Crimes, Nov. 1944. During trial before Rome High Court, escaped and vanished, 7.3.45.

ROCCA, AGOSTINO, b. 1895. Director of Ansaldo Company. One of leading Fascist industrialists. Pres. of Committee for Metallurgy. National Councillor, representing steel and metal industry.

ROMANO, SANTI, b. 1875. Prof. of Constitut. Law, Rome Univ., and member of R. Ital. Academy ; President of Council of State, until 1943.

ROSI, GENERAL EZIO, b. 1881. G.O.C.,VI. Army (Sicily), until 1.2.43. Chief of Army Staff, 1.2–1.6.43 (replaced by Roatta).

ROSSI, CESARE, b. 1887. Intimate collaborator of Mussolini in early days of Fascism. Implicated in Matteotti murder. *See* above, p. 86, n. 2.

ROSSI, GENERAL FRANCESCO, b. 1885. Deputy Chief of General Staff, 1943.

ROSSONI, EDMONDO, b. 1884. Extreme Left-wing Socialist and active agitator in revolutionary syndicalist movement in U.S.A., before 1915 ; returned to Italy during war as propagandist for intervention. Founded Italian Union of Labour ("uncompromising war against capitalist system"), 1918. Went over to Fascism, becoming chief organizer of Fascist 'syndicates' ; made employers recognize Fascist unions as only representatives of labour, 1925. Wielding great power as President of confederation of all employees' unions, 1926–28. After period of eclipse, Under-Sec. of State, Pres. of Council, 1932–35. Minister of Agriculture, 1935–39. Min. of State and Member of Grand Council ; voted against Mussolini, 25.7.43. Sentenced, in absentia, to death by Republ. Fascists at Verona, 10.1.44 ; to lifelong imprisonment for Fascist crimes by High Court (Bonomi Govt.), May 1945. In hiding.

ROTIGLIANO, EDOARDO, b. 1880. Lawyer. Took part in D'Annunzio's Fiume exploit. Deputy s. 1924. Nat. Councillor. Senator, Feb. 1943.

SANDALLI, RENATO, AIR MARSHAL, b. 1897. Chief of Techn. Dept., Min. of Air, 1943. Minister of Air and Chief of Air Staff under Badoglio, 27.8.43–9.6.44.

SANSONETTI, ADMIRAL LUIGI, b. 1888. Dep. Chief of Naval Staff, July 1941. Vice-Pres. of Navy Council, April 1945.

SCIPIONI, GENERAL SCIPIONE, b. 1867. Commander of Military Training Schools, 1924–28. C.-in-C., Sicily, 1928–32. Senator, 1933.

SCORZA, CARLO, b. 1897. Journalist. Played prominent part in early days of Fascism in Tuscany, leader of armed gangs, notorious for brutality. Member of Party Directorate, 1926. Organizer of 'Young Fascist' groups. 1930. Pres. of Fascist Press organization, 1940. Vice-Sec. of Party, Dec. 1942–April 1943. Sec. of Party, April–July 1943, carrying out ruthless purge of 'defeatists' inside and outside the Party. Played ambiguous part in plot of members of Grand Council. Voted for Mussolini, 25.7.43. Arrested (under De Gasperi Govt.), while hiding as librarian in the Jesuit convent at Gallarate, but escaped, Dec. 1945. Supposed to be head of underground neo-Fascist movement. [Granted amnesty, July 1949.]

SCUERO, GENERAL ANTONIO, b. 1885. Under-Sec. for War, May 1941–Feb. 1943.

SENISE, DR. CARMINE, b. 1883. Prefect and Vice-Chief of Police, 1932–40. Succeeded the notorious Bocchini as Chief of Police, 1940. Too mild for Himmler's liking, superseded by Chierici, 16.4.43. Reappointed by Badoglio. 26.7.43.

SERENA, ADELCHI, b. 1895. Dep. Sec. of Fascist Party, 1933. Minister of Public Works, 1939. Sec. of Party, 1940–Dec. 1941.

SIRIANNI, GUISEPPE, ADMIRAL OF THE FLEET, b. 1874. Senator, 1926. Minister for Navy, 1929–1933. Attempted to oppose encroachment of Fascism on Navy; placed on reserve list, 1936.

SODDU, GENERAL UBALDO, b. 1883. Chef de Cabinet to Min. of War (Mussolini), 1934–36. Under-Sec. for War, Nov. 1939, and C.-in-C., Ital. forces on Greek front (succeeding Visconti Prasca), 11.11.40; after defeats, resigned for reasons of health, 13.1.41.

SOLETI, GENERAL FERNANDO, b. 1891. Commander of Mil. Division of Police, later of Security Police, 1943. Accompanied Germans rescuing Mussolini from Gen. Sasso. Went with Mussolini to Vienna. *See* above, p. 134.

SORICE, GEN. ANTONIO, b. 1897. Councillor of State, 1938. Under-Sec. of War, Feb.–26.7.43. Minister of War (under Badoglio), 26.7–8.9.43. Suspended from service by Purge Commission (Bonomi Govt.), May 1945.

STARACE, ACHILLE, b. 1889; d. 1945. Secretary of Fascist Party, 1931–1939. Responsible for increasing regimentation of Party members and for campaign against 'bourgeois spirit.' Fond of uniforms and medals. C.in-C., Fascist Militia and member of Party Directorate, 1939–41. Shot by partisans in course of liberation of N. Italy, end April 1945.

SUARDO, COUNT GIACOMO, b. 1883; d. 1946. Took part in March on Rome. Lt.-Gen. of Fascist Militia. Under-Sec. in various Ministries. President of Senate, 1939–43. Abstained from voting for or against Mussolini, 25.7.43. His application to join Republ. Fascist Party rejected, Dec. 1943.

TABELLINI, COL. DINO, b. 1892. Carabinieri officer, commanding Training School in Trastevere, Rome, summer 1943.

TERUZZI, GENERAL ATTILIO, b. 1882. Vice-Sec. of Fascist Party, 1921; holding position of command in March on Rome. C.-in-C., Fascist Militia, 1928. Commander of Blackshirt Division in Abyssinian war, 1935. Minister for Italian Africa, 1939–43. Arrested (under Bonomi Govt.) and sentenced to 30 years' imprisonment, April 1945.

THAON DI REVEL, GRAND ADMIRAL PAOLO, DUCA DEL MARE, b. 1859. Chief of Naval Staff, 1913–15; Minister of Navy, 1922–25. Senator; holding Order of Most Holy Annunciation. Held various posts in Royal Household. Appointed President of Senate by the King, 26.7.43.

THAON DI REVEL, MARQUIS PAOLO, b. 1888. Nephew of the Grand Admiral. Senator s. 1933. Minister of Finance, 1935–Feb. 1943.

TOGLIATTI, PALMIRO, b. 1893. One of the founders of Italian Communist Party. Working underground after 1926, directed clandestine Communist movement. Later, represented Italian Communists on the Comintern in Moscow. Returning from Moscow to Italy, March 1944, made Communists accept office under Badoglio, thus ending deadlock caused by refusal of anti-Fascist parties to co-operate with Badoglio régime. Minister without Portfolio in Badoglio Cabinet, March–June 1944; Vice-Pres. of Council in Bonomi Govt., June 1944–45; Min. of Justice in Parri and De Gasperi Govts., 1945–47. Leader of Ital. Communist Party.

TORRIGIANI, MARQUIS DOMIZIO, b. 1877; d. 1932. Grand Master of Ital. Freemasons of Grand Orient. Interned when Freemasonry was suppressed, 1925.

UMBERTO, PRINCE OF PIEDMONT, b. 1904. Only son of King Victor Emmanuel III; Crown Prince. G.O.C. North-Western Armies, 1939; as such, in charge of operations against France, June 1940. G.O.C., Central, Southern, and Insular Italy, April 1942. Designated by the King as Lieutenant of the Realm, 12.4.44; assumed office after liberation of Rome, June 1944. After Victor Emmanuel's abdication, King of Italy, styled Umberto II, 9.5.46. Recognized as such by Cabinet, pending the nation's decision. After referendum of 2.6.46 in favour of Republic, Umberto left Italy, 13.6.46, denouncing the Cabinet's procedure as illegal. Lives in Portugal under the title of Count of Sarre.

VACCARI, GENERAL COUNT GIUSEPPE, b. 1866; d. before 1939. Chief of Army Staff, 1921; C.-in-C., Trieste, later Rome Army Corps.

VALLE, GENERAL GIUSEPPE, b. 1886. Chief of Air Staff, 1930; again, 1934–39, Under Sec. for Air, 1933–39. Resigned; became head of industrial undertaking. Placed on retired list, Jan. 1945.

VICTOR EMMANUEL III, KING OF ITALY, b. 1869. Ascended throne when his father was assassinated by anarchist, 1900. For his attitude at time of Fascist Party's bid for power, *see* FACTA. Did not oppose Mussolini's alteration of Constitution. Accepted from Mussolini crowns of Ethiopia and Albania. Dismissed Mussolini, 25.7.43. Fled from Rome, 8.9.43. Announced intention to withdraw from public life, 12.4.44, designating his son as Lieutenant-General of the Realm. Signed decree transferring to him all powers and prerogatives of the Crown, 5.6.44. Lived in seclusion near Naples. Signed Act of Abdication in favour of Umberto, 9.5.46, and embarked for Egypt. Took up residence at Antoniades Palace in Alexandria, under the title of Count of Pollenzo. [Died 28.12.47.]

ZANIBONI, TITO, Major of Alpini Regt. Socialist leader, actively opposed Fascism after Matteotti murder. Imprisoned after attempt to kill Mussolini, 1925. Liberated, autumn 1943. Joint Chairman of first free conference of anti-Fascist parties, Bari, Jan. 1944. Expelled from Socialist Party for accepting post in Badoglio Govt., Feb. 1944. Leader of dissident Socialist group.

WALTHAM FOREST PUBLIC LIBRARIES

INDEX